ELEMENTARY SOCIAL STUDIES AS A LEARNING SYSTEM

ELEMENTARY SOCIAL STUDIES AS A LEARNING SYSTEM

PETER H. MARTORELLA

Temple University

Harper & Row, Publishers

New York   Hagerstown   San Francisco   London

Photographs: Actionmap cover photo, Denoyer Geppert Co., Chicago; Ballard, DPI, 5 top left, 7 bottom; Beckwith Studios, 4 top right, 4 bottom, 5 center; Cade, DPI, 5 top right; Conklin, Monkmeyer, 318, 392 bottom; Denoyer Geppert Co., Chicago, 232; Forsyth, Monkmeyer, 5 bottom, 373; Dorothea Lange, War Relocation Authority, 359; Barbara Pachter, 402, 448; Rogers, Monkmeyer, 4 top left, 6 top, 6 bottom; Rubin, Monkmeyer, 7 center, 392 top; Ruiko, DPI, 7 top; Stoy, DPI, 6 center.

Sponsoring Editor: *George A. Middendorf*
Project Editor: *David Nickol*
Designer: *Frances Torbert Tilley*
Production Supervisor: *Kewal K. Sharma*
Photo Researcher: *Myra Schachne*
Compositor: *American Book–Stratford Press, Inc.*
Printer and binder: *Halliday Lithograph Corporation*
Art Studio: *Vantage Art Inc.*

ELEMENTARY SOCIAL STUDIES AS A LEARNING SYSTEM

Library of Congress Cataloging in Publication Data

Martorella, Peter H
    Elementary social studies as a learning system.

    Includes bibliographies and index.
    1. Social sciences—Study and teaching
(Elementary) I. Title.
LB1584.M34   372.8'3'044   76–18842
ISBN 0–06–044233–6

To the memory of Bill Bingmer—
someone who cared and helped me grow

CONTENTS

MODULE III   Instructional Models and Their Applications: Concluding and Generalizing   141

MODULE IV   Instructional Models and
Their Application: Analytical Tools   195

MODULE V   Instructional Models and Their Applications: Emphasis on Affect   269

MODULE VI   Improving Instruction: Significant Variables in a Learning System   389

CONCLUSION Creating Learning Systems 471

INDEXES 505

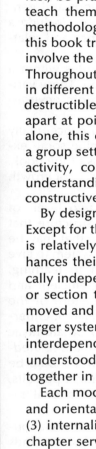

Credibility is a major issue confronting the author of a new methods text. Students are increasingly asking for evidence, if not hard empirical data, that what is "preached" about teaching can, in fact, be practiced. My own students have convinced me that I must teach them as I would have them teach, if they are to take my methodological ideas seriously. Given the limitations of the medium, this book tries to establish credibility in its own way by attempting to involve the reader and to employ the teaching principles it advocates. Throughout the chapters it requires the reader to respond to the book in different ways—indeed to help write it. The book is designed as a destructible learning tool to be physically manipulated, literally torn apart at points, and written upon. While one generally reads a book alone, this one periodically asks readers to carry through an idea in a group setting, usually with peers. The point is not to promote group activity, commendable as that objective may be, but to sharpen understanding and competency in the crucible of mutual sharing and constructive feedback.

By design and definition, a book is linear, but its use need not be. Except for this Preface and the final chapter, the reader of this volume is relatively free to reorganize *components* in whatever fashion enhances their use. The book is organized into modules that are basically independent of one another. *Module* is a term referring to a part or section that helps make up a larger system, but that may be removed and examined or even replaced without dismantling the entire larger system. Within each module are three or more chapters that are interdependent. A module may be separated from the book and understood alone, but all of its three or more chapters must be read together in a sequence in order to be meaningful.

Each module is organized in a three-phase design: (1) introduction and orientation, (2) demonstration and development of models, and (3) internalization and application of ideas. In each module the first chapter serves as an organizer, introducing its dimensions and orienting the reader to what will follow. A following chapter or series of chapters demonstrate and develop related instructional ideas and models and give varied examples of them applied to preschool–grade 8 social studies instruction. The final chapter within a module is always a series of suggested exercises and activities for clarifying, extending, and applying ideas developed within the module. Two final dimensions are a summary of the module and a list of related suggested readings for further growth.

The first module deals with the nature, purpose, and direction of social studies programs and their relationship to the larger environment of the classroom and school. It includes sections that ask the reader to assess some personal competencies, positions, and expectations as he or she begins the book.

Four modules follow that demonstrate and develop a series of instructional models and principles related to concepts, conclusions and generalizations, analytical tools, and dimensions of affect. These include a variety of examples drawing upon many different disciplines and relating to a range of different grade levels, preschool–grade 8.

Module VI deals with some selected instructional variables within a classroom that affect and enter into social studies instruction. These variables center around the areas of assessment of the classroom environment and the managing of instruction.

A final chapter offers the reader some opportunities to conceptually integrate many of the elements within the book, to examine some explicit beliefs of the author, and to evaluate the effectiveness of the book. Among other points, it asks the reader to assess his or her rate of growth since beginning to read the book.

The term *learning system*, as used in this book, has two levels of meaning. At one level it refers to the use of a modular structure that accepts all knowledge as interdependent but with chunks that may be artificially isolated and logically organized into some larger system to give greater meaning to all of the parts. Such an approach to learning, whether it be methodology or social studies, can be an efficient and growth-producing one, *providing the user has a clear picture of the larger whole or system to which the parts belong and are related*. Otherwise, the chunks of modularized knowledge are likely to be atomistic and fragmented without a unifying purpose. The key terms are *relatedness, organization,* and *purpose*. All instructional approaches should be guided by some overall purpose, related to other instructional pursuits, and implemented on the basis of some validated organizational rationale.

At a second level of meaning, *learning system* refers to the relationship of knowledge about social studies instruction to more general kinds of knowledge about instruction. The term *instruction*, rather than *teaching*, is used to indicate the broader range of things that teachers do to facilitate and influence the process of learning, for example, organizing and implementing a learning center. A basic premise of the book is that an analysis of all instruction, including social studies instruction, should be related to the larger instructional system of the classroom and the school. A whole range of factors having nothing directly to do with social studies instruction interact with and profoundly influence it. While many of these factors are discussed in numerous separate and general books, in this text we consider some crucial ones concurrently with ideas about social studies instruction to better understand the total dynamics of the school and classroom.

Knowledge about history, the social sciences, and many other attendant disciplines contributes a great deal to the understanding of the social world each of us creates and participates in. However, no single book, and certainly no *segment* of one book, could distill the essence of such disciplines, let alone reveal their excitement, functional value, and richness. Savoring them sufficiently to reconstruct and employ them usefully in order to enlighten children's understanding of themselves and others takes considerable time, study, and insight. Predigested summaries of such disciplines are a poor substitute for direct contact with the disciplines themselves, and no such summaries are offered in this book. Instead, suggestions for how readers may gain knowledge and an appreciation of the various disciplines are included throughout the book. Also, examples used to illustrate instructional purposes have been designed to offer insights into different disciplines. Wherever a thorough treatment of related significant topics was beyond the scope of this text, a list of suggested readings has been included.

A companion book of readings by this author, *Social Studies Strategies: Theory into Practice*, New York: Harper & Row, 1976, is designed to complement this text. It includes more extensive discussions of various points treated within the present methods text, as well as a broader range of social studies concerns. Moreover, the book of readings provides an array of insights from various authors, rather than one single point of view.

Three groups have been very instrumental in influencing the design of the materials in this book: my university students both undergraduate and graduate, children in the inner-city Philadelphia and Philadelphia suburban area schools, and my own children, Chris, Tim, and Laura. All my students, with varying degrees of competency, dedication, industriousness, good will, and enthusiasm, have relentlessly moved me forward to increasingly more adequate responses to how my instructional goals might be accomplished in the context of the classroom realities they encounter. Over the years I have grown accustomed to the rhetorical query, "Yeah, but will it work with my kids?" It has helped to temper and shape my suggestions.

Working both in field-based programs where graduate and undergraduate courses are taught in schools and in service programs with various school districts has offered a vital contact with the ultimate potential consumers of my ideas—children. Teaching and observing them not only has provided a link with reality and helped me maintain a semblance of credibility as an instructor but has opened new areas of interest and study. When I have been able to be patient and listen carefully to children, they have always been able to teach me.

My own children have contributed immeasurably to this book, so much so that I would advise all authors of similar texts to acquire or borrow for an extended period three children with a developmental span similar to their own. When I began to work on this book, my children were roughly ages 5½, 7, and 8½. As I write now, they are two years older. Always eager to test out an idea, answer questions, listen to tapes, look at materials, talk about their days at school, and comment upon something I had written, they were a vital source of assistance in many chapters. They proved to be a constant contact with the reality the book hopes to help teachers confront.

Peter H. Martorella

MODULE I

MODULE I

Learning Systems: Children, Teachers, and Social Studies

One who learns is to be noted;
one who learns much is to be respected;
one who helps others to learn
is to be welcomed into your home.

SICILIAN PROVERB

CHAPTER 1

Children, Teachers, and Schools

One of the schools and classrooms pictured on the following pages might be yours. In 1974 over 30 million children appeared in schools and classrooms like these, prepared to spend almost ten months doing something called going to school. For some, the ten months was a period of adventure and great intellectual growth; others saw past patterns of frustration and anxiety repeated; still others were swept along on a wave of indifference, neither growing nor seriously floundering. Most remained in that classroom for the school year, but for some it represented just a brief stopping point in a seemingly endless shuffle of moves. (It is not uncommon in some schools to have a 100-percent turnover in the student body within the year; i.e., all first-day students transfer out before the year is over.)

Almost all of these children emerged from a year of study with a label attached to them: "good kid," "chatterbox," "troublemaker," "dummy," "bright," "smart," "immature," "foul-mouthed," "retarded," "eager," "enthusiastic," "considerate," "warm," "slow," "disadvantaged," "fresh," "cute," "snotty," and so on. In some cases these labels will follow the child from grade to grade, to his or her continuous advantage or disadvantage.

As a result of the ten months spent in the school, in most cases with one teacher, each child will emerge with one of three basic attitudes toward education and schools: He or she will like them less, about the same, or even more than before the year started. More than any other single variable, the *teacher* will determine which of these attitudes will emerge and prevail. The responsibility for such attitudes is not one we like to dwell upon for long, but it is always implicit in our job as teachers.

Some of those children arrive at school the first day eager to devour knowledge and open to any even gentle nudge toward mental and emotional growth. They challenge us to keep this spark of intellectual excitement burning, even while they comfort us with their receptiveness to our teaching. Still others come defiant and aggressively uncooperative, full of inner conflicts and hostile toward schools and teachers for engendering and contributing to the sense of frustration that dominates their lives. They challenge us also to prove they are wrong, while we try to convince ourselves with false self-assurance that they are unteachable. The great bulk of children arrive at school somewhere in between those two extremes, seemingly "average" but probably more different than alike. Each child and corresponding parents or parent-surrogates

approach the year with the assumption that something beneficial or positive will happen to that *individual* as a result of the time spent in school.

All these conditions and expectations place a heavy but legitimate burden on the elementary teacher—heavy because it reflects the weight of all previous familial, social, and educational gains and losses that a child has accrued; legitimate because every individual has a right to something of merit in return for a legally required period of attendance. Children do not exist for the schools any more than teachers exist for the administrators. Schools and administrators exist and should remain only insofar as they can show evidence of contributing to significant individual and social goals. Teachers must share a similar responsibility.

A LICENSE TO . . .

Each of you who teaches requires a certificate that looks something like the one in Figure 1.1. Depending upon the circumstances of your teaching and the state in which you live, the certificate is generally issued by the state after it has examined your "morals," health record, and training (read "course" in most cases) or has determined that you have completed the requirements of a program already approved by the state. Normally you will be certified for life in the state indicated, provided you revalidate the certificate by specified dates or complete

Figure 1.1
A teaching license

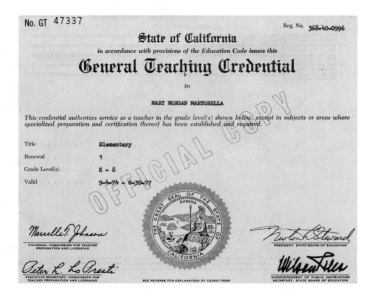

certain additional requirements (usually those involving course work and/or experience). In many cases the certificate will also permit you to teach in states other than in the one issued, through a reciprocity policy agreed upon by some states.

There is little on the license or certificate that spells out what you are empowered to do except to teach between the grades of X and Y. It confers broad authority upon the recipient and correspondingly implies broad competence. As a minimum it certifies that the holder is physically, mentally, and emotionally capable of working with a class of children for a school day or a school year. The presumption of what results from that period of contact remains to be spelled out by the hiring school district, the parents, the community involved and, most critically, by the certificate holder.

No training or certification process can totally prepare an individual teacher to operate with maximum efficiency in any given school at the outset. Like individuals, no two schools are alike, and one must come to understand the dynamics, patterns of helping relationships, potential blockages, operating policies, and cast of characters within the school and school system quickly and accurately *just to be an effective and efficient classroom teacher*. A number of sociological analyses of schools have made this point in a number of ways, but perhaps a classroom teacher perceptively analyzing her own school and school system communicates the issue most clearly:

> Perhaps the most important thing is that you know the individual with whom you are dealing, understand his personality and deal with him accordingly. Each member of our staff, for instance, accepts praise, blame, suggestions, or even gives advice in a somewhat different fashion. One must be cognizant of these differences in the individuals with whom she works if one is to accomplish what she wants and yet remain on good terms with her colleagues. This is true for the kids, too. You can't just treat them all alike. You've got to know as much about them as you can and then work with them while bearing all this knowledge in mind.
>
> It's funny the way each person has his own modus operandi, also. If you want things to run smoothly, you'd better try to stay within the confines of their expectations. The principal, for example, let's you do just about anything within reason; but if you ask him first if it's okay, it builds up his ego as "the boss" and then your project definitely has his blessings.
>
> The secretary will do anything for you as long as you don't seem demanding, do say "please" and do take time to listen to stories about her granddaughter.
>
> The librarian is really helpful, too, but don't ever ask her questions during her lunch time or send kids to the library when she's reading to first or second graders.

The cafeteria help is very defensive, so you really have to weigh your words with them. It's horrible to get on the bad side of them because then they don't give you as big a portion for lunch or add the frills which they're inclined to do if you're in their favor. If you've hurt their feelings, then they're reluctant to loan you kitchen utensils like knives, spoons and bowls which are really necessary for dissecting, carving pumpkins, dyeing Easter eggs, and eating homemade (actually classroom-made) ice cream. The cafeteria people don't mind if you periodically change lunch times with another class, but they get furious if you don't tell them in advance. Actually, I can't see why it makes any difference if you tell them or not because it's still the same number of lunches no matter what order you eat them in but that's the way they like it, so that's the way you do it.

Students are probably the easiest to get along with. You have to be fair and honest with them, trusting and consistent. If you talk things over with them, then things always seem to work out okay. I'd rather work with the kids than with anybody else.

It's tricky to get along with the custodian. He takes an enormous amount of pride in the appearance of the school and in his job, which is great because so many janitors just don't seem to care; but like the cafeteria people, he seems to forget that the school is for the kids, not the adults who oversee the functioning of the school. He's really great about supplying boxes and stuff like that that you want on a minute's notice, but heaven help you if you get anything on that damn rug. The kids all know how to spring into action immediately if something gets on the revered rug—it helps to keep the teacher cool; and besides, they know also that the custodian is their friend, too. After all, who fixes their desks, loans them tools and gets hats and balls off the school roof for them?

The art and music teachers aren't hard to get along with. Just be sure that you send the kids to class on time. The art teacher would probably like me better if I did more art work with my class; but since I don't like it much, I tend to ignore it. I do quite a bit of music with my class, so that puts me in a favorable position with the music teacher.

The guidance counselor is the hardest for me to get along with. He's really got too many kinds to deal with, but I can't stand his wishy-washy manner and his crisis-oriented approach to guidance. To get along with him, though, I just say "um-hummmmm" and "you're right."

The reading specialist is a great person and takes her job very seriously. She has a somewhat defensive personality, however, which isn't helped by her being constantly caught in the middle of quarrels over the program. The director of elementary education and the curriculum coordinator are at diametrically opposite ends on how to run the program, and each tries to dictate to the reading specialist how she should run her program. You have to understand the reading specialist's personality and the silly bickering she's caught in to work with her. What really keeps her happy is if you make sure you tell her well in advance if any of your kids are going to miss her class for some reason. If you take time to listen to her political ideas and her problems with the administration in relation to her federally funded reading program, she'll let you borrow just about any of her reading materials despite the fact the government rules say this is not allowed. She puts her neck on the line for the sake of the kids, and I like that.

The easiest guy to get along with is the superintendent of schools. He is hard-nosed and fair. You can be very frank with him—you never have to beat around the bush. He listens to what you have to say. If he turns down a proposal of yours, it makes you mad; but, at least you know he's given it an unjaundiced appraisal and you respect his opinion.[1]

While it is impossible to anticipate all the patterns and conditions that this observant teacher has noted about her situation after several years of teaching, one *can* learn what to begin analyzing on the first day of teaching. Many teachers do this almost unconsciously, carefully storing away salient observations and then reflecting on them later, as appropriate, to help facilitate instruction. Some of us need to create and refer to lists of key variables or conditions in a school system or school that somehow will impinge upon and interact with our teaching, no matter how remote from it they may seem.

One teacher, using this procedure, developed two such lists shown in Figures 1.2 and 1.3. Figure 1.2 identifies the sources of materials within the school and district and then notes some related procedures, comments, or ideas in the right-hand column. The process is repeated for the category of nonteaching duties in Figure 1.3.

Simple analysis systems such as these can help generate significant questions and quickly process a great deal of information that a teacher might need to know about a school or district. Success in teaching, as in many other professions operating within bureaucratic structures, often depends on how efficiently one can attend to peripheral tasks that are only indirectly related to the job at hand. Learning to cope quickly with such peripheral tasks that are only indirectly related to the job at hand, while not shifting focus from the real job of teaching, requires some attention to management and to an analysis of how things are actually handled within a school and system. Understanding better how the system operates can often help make it function *for* you rather than against you.

TEACHING SOCIAL STUDIES

In this book we will be concerned specifically with what the "teaching of social studies" dimensions of the certification competency should

Figure 1.2
Domain of procuring materials

SOURCES OF MATERIALS	Own Materials	Books	Pictures
		Magazines	Articles
		Charts from educational materials companies	
		Name on everything in case someone borrows it	
		Collected and treasured over the years	
	School Library	Send children to sign out materials	
		Sign out materials yourself	
		Charts	Filmstrips
		Models	Kits
		Stay in good with the librarian so she assists you in gathering these materials	
	School Instructional Materials Center	Audio-visual equipment	
		Film projectors	Records
		Filmstrip projectors	TV
		Tape recorder	Movie screens
		Filmloop projectors	
		Filmstrip previewers	
		Mini-filmstrip projectors	
		Teach children how to sign these out—saves teacher's time	
	District Instructional Materials Center	Pick up or order materials from here	
		Filmstrips	Kits
		Transparencies	Filmloops
		Records	Tape cassettes
		Charts	
		Get as much as you can on your topic before someone else in the district takes it	
		Chat with the secretary about her children or softball team	
	Regional Instructional Materials Center	Films delivered once a week	
		Films ordered once a week	
		Films that arrive never seem to be coordinated with the topic you are teaching	
		Frequently don't get what you order	
	Friends	Magazines and pamphlets of theirs	
		Have them get things for you from their places of employment	
	Other Teachers	Check other teachers' areas to see if they have anything you need	
		Ask a friend who has more pull than you to borrow or order something for you	
	Office	Get in good with secretary and principal	
		Ask nicely as you talk about other things such as their family, illnesses, and vacation plans	
	Janitor	Stay friendly with him at all costs	
		Don't leave your room a big mess	

Source: Joan Ferry, teacher at John Grasse Elementary School, Perkasie School District, Bucks County, Pa.

reflect. We will unavoidably touch upon the broader context of the self-contained classroom in which most preschool–middle-school social studies instruction takes place. Since the term *social studies* is used in most school, curriculum, and layman discussions, we shall continue to use it throughout the book even though *social education* more accurately reflects the broader interpretation of the topic that is inherent in the text. Teachers at the levels preschool–grade 6 are accustomed to being called elementary teachers; those in grades 7–12, on the other hand, are social studies, science, or whatever subject teachers. Teachers in middle schools are still working on the nomenclature of their identities. In reality, elementary teachers wear many subject-matter hats, of course, and we shall focus on the hat of social studies teacher, whenever it may be worn. Thus there will be consistent references to social studies teacher and teacher of social studies. While we unavoidably become preoccupied with this role throughout the book, it should not suggest a lack of interest in or enthusiasm for combining such roles as science, art, reading, and the like with that of social studies teacher. Life and experiences are not parceled out in subject-matter areas, and learning need not be—often it *should* not be. Knowledge is interdependent, and all instruction must take this fact into account. For purposes of analysis, production of knowledge in and efficient mastery of a field, scholars create subject-matter boundaries separating their concerns from those of other scholars. This is reasonable and necessary for knowledge to accumulate and grow, but it also should be recognized that an artificial process with highly arbitrary dividing lines has been imposed upon the production of such knowledge. Neither children nor adults who do not plan to become professional scholars need be bound by such disciplinary constraints in their learning. America's foremost philosopher-turned-educator John Dewey, in commenting on the dual concerns of the individual learner and the organization of subject matter, remarked:

> The educator cannot start with knowledge already organized and proceed to ladle it out in doses.
>
> • • •
>
> When education is based in theory and practice upon experience, it goes without saying that the organized subject-matter of the adult and the specialist cannot provide the starting point. Nevertheless, it represents the goal toward which education should continuously move.[2]

THE SOCIAL STUDIES TEACHER

What makes a good social studies teacher? What qualities do you think a teacher should have? On p. 17 are two sets of characteristics that some have considered to be important qualities for a good social studies teacher. Detach the two sets, separate the series of character-

Figure 1.3
List of nonteaching duties

NONTEACHING DUTIES	Attendance	Write names of absentees in plan book daily
		Mark names of absentees on weekly summary of attendance
		Collect excuses of absentees and attach excuses to summary
		Send summary to office each Monday
	Lunch Count	Mark soup and sandwich, regular lunch, extras, teacher's salad
		Send to cafeteria
	Book Inventory	At beginning and end of year
	Putting Information in Cumulative Folders	Summary of grades
		I.Q. scores
		Comments
		Achievement scores
	Collecting Banking	Collect bankbooks on Tuesday
		Send bankbooks to office in envelope every Tuesday
		Return bankbooks to children on Thursday
	Collecting Money for School Pictures	Write child's name and amount of remittance on envelope
		Collect unwanted pictures
		Send envelope and pictures to office daily
	Collecting Money for Candy Sale	Hand out candy
		Hand out and collect order forms daily
		Collect money daily
	Janitorial-type duties	Keep room clean
		Supervise children's jobs such as dusting, emptying pencil sharpener, scouring sink
		Scrub spots on rug
	Books for Book Club	Distribute order blanks
		Collect money and book orders
		Tabulate orders
		Send in orders
		Distribute books

istics, and organize them into two piles. Examine the twelve given characteristics and eliminate any items you feel are not important qualities from each of the piles. Similarly make up duplicate cards for any characteristics you feel are important but were not included in the original list. These final piles should represent dual sets of all those qualities you consider to be important for a social studies teacher to have.

Take one pile and organize the cards in front of you in a series from the most important quality to that of least importance in the list gener-

(continued)

NONTEACHING DUTIES

After-School Games and Tumbling	Supervise children Wait until all parents come to pick up children
Playground Duty	Settle fights Apply first aid Call some children in for special activities Observe children for unusual forms of social behavior
Serving on Parent-Teachers Organization Executive Committee	Attend meetings every Tuesday night Plan activities for general meetings Plan money-making projects
Serving on Curriculum Committees	Attend meetings after school Formulate philosophies Set goals and objectives Establish learning sequence
Taking Courses for Certification	Time consuming Costly Improves teaching ability
Collecting Money for School Insurance	Send forms home Collect money and forms Send to office Keep list of insured and uninsured children
Completing Student Information Records for Office	Often a duplication of past forms
Giving Out and Keeping Track of Supplies	Books Scissors Pencils Rulers Tablets Compasses Crayons Protractors Erasers

Source: Joan Ferry, teacher at John Grasse Elementary School, Perkasie School District, Bucks County, Pa.

ated. Once you have organized the series, turn over each of the cards face down in place.

Organize the second set of cards similarly directly beneath the first, this time in order of the quality most like *you* (or what you think would be most like you) to that least like *you*. Now turn over the first set of cards and compare the differences in the two sets, if any. The first set represents your idealized social studies teacher, while your second one helps indicate by contrast the direction in which you hope to move.

Jot down your idealized and actual profiles below in order of decreasing importance, and date them for your future reference:

Date: _____

Idealized Teaching Profile   Actual Teaching Profile

_____   Most   _____
_____   Important   _____

_____   _____

_____   _____

_____   _____

_____   _____

_____   _____

_____   _____

_____   _____

_____   Least   _____
                                          Important

THE PURPOSE OF SOCIAL STUDIES TEACHING

Why teach social studies? Why should all children be required to study the subject every year they are in school? It has been an axiom over the years that all curricular planning must include elements of the social studies, but not all educators are in agreement on what the major goals of the social studies should be. Creating "laundry lists" of agreed-upon general purposes is not an especially difficult task for any group of social studies educators, although such lists tend to be contradictory at some point, though well intended (e.g., "encourage open inquiry on all social issues" and "avoid any references that might offend or insult any racial minority or ethnic group"). Individuals tend to differ—often vehemently—on what the list of agreed upon purposes mean as they become translated into specific instructional objectives and on what general goals will be given the highest priority in planning.

All teaching and curriculum planning in social studies requires some overriding purpose that dominates the direction of learning and serves as an overall rationale for the disparate materials and activities that are to be used. Subpurposes exist, but their role is to complement the overall rationale rather than to compete with it for attention. As opposed to such subthemes, an overall purpose should be clearly reflected in the total scope of social studies instruction. A teacher guided by such an orientation does not confuse inconsistency with flexibility in instructional planning. The former term characterizes instruction that is varied

Selects topics for study with a high degree of relevance for students.	Makes subjects exciting.	Shows concern for feelings of others.
Sets high but achievable standards of learning for each child.	Stimulates reflective thought.	Permits controversy.
Treats all points of view as deserving of a hearing.	Is enthusiastic.	Is knowledgeable about subject matter.
Practices what he or she advocates.	Takes stand on major issues.	Is actively involved in social action himself or herself.

Selects topics for study with a high degree of relevance for students.	Makes subjects exciting.	Shows concern for feelings of others.
Sets high but achievable standards of learning for each child.	Stimulates reflective thought.	Permits controversy.
Treats all points of view as deserving of a hearing.	Is enthusiastic.	Is knowledgeable about subject matter.
Practices what he or she advocates.	Takes stand on major issues.	Is actively involved in social action himself or herself.

but to no clear defensible purpose; the latter, in contrast, characterizes specific plans that vary, sometimes dramatically, in order to maintain the overall guiding purpose. Every teacher needs to determine early what overall purpose will guide his or her teaching, be able to articulate and defend it with fellow colleagues and parents, and periodically monitor his or her social studies instruction against this overall goal.

Listed below is a sample of overall purposes that reflect the point of view of various individuals or groups.[3] They indicate the scope of the alternatives but in no way exhaust the possibilities. Examine the list to find one position that most closely approximates what you currently consider to be the *primary* purpose of social studies teaching. If none of the positions exactly expresses your own, revise it so that it does or write your own statement. Write your revision or creation in the space next to the sixth item. Now rank the positions from 1 to 5 (or 6) in order of preference in the spaces provided in the left column.

_____ The main purpose of social studies in the school curriculum is to help evolve a just and humane society. It aims to produce students who act intelligently with respect to social problems and who become active and committed workers for social justice and the alleviation of social ills.

_____ The main purpose of social studies in the school curriculum is to meet the ongoing social needs of children and adolescents. It aims to produce students who develop well-integrated personalities and are relatively free of undue anxiety and personal problems.

_____ The main purpose of social studies in the school curriculum is to keep alive the record of the past insofar as this country is concerned, as well as that of mankind in general. It aims to produce students who will master the best of what has been written and said in the various fields that comprise the social studies.

_____ The main purpose of social studies in the school curriculum is to develop adults who are productive and contributing members of their society. It aims to produce students who become conscientious consumer-producers and law-abiding citizens.

_____ The main purpose of social studies in the school curriculum is the intellectual development of students. It aims to produce students who develop an ability to perceive and investigate human actions in more adequate and complex ways.

_____   _____

    _____

    _____

    _____

    _____

_____ Date

At some point take some time to share your conclusions and rationale, including your decisions for all five or six items, with a group of your peers. Record the date of your decision for future reference and comparison. At the conclusion of this book, you will be asked to reassess your views on the overall purpose of the social studies, as well as to evaluate this author's view.

PERSONAL GOAL SETTING

Much of the value of a book of this sort is the extent to which it can help you move toward goals in teaching including those *you* consider to be important ones. A book reflects certain presumptions on the part of the author as to what is important to know about a topic. If it is to be addressed to an unknown audience, it must allow people with varied backgrounds, needs, and aspirations to gain something of value from it. A first step along this path is to have you establish what you already feel you know about social studies teaching. Let us call this your *area of strength*. Jot down some of the significant things you feel you already have learned on the subject within the box in Figure 1.4. In Figure 1.5, list those things you hope to learn about teaching social studies. This box is designated as your *area for growth*. Note the date of the recording for later reference.

The objective of this text is to help increase your area of strength. As you move through the chapters, receive suggestions from others, and introspect, it is likely that your self-prescribed area for growth may increase also. So much the better, if this reflects your growing aspirations as well as your capacity for objective self-assessment. Unless the book can make a significant contribution to your area of strength, however, it will not have completely fulfilled its purpose.

One reason why a book like this will affect people in different ways is the kind of learning priorities that each reader brings. Put another way, each reader has a different set of urgent expectations in his or her area for growth. Take a moment to transfer some of the items from your area for growth to the list below, in order of their priority for you.

List of learning priorities

1. _____

2. _____

3. _____

4. _____

5. _____

You might take some time to share and discuss your list with others to compare expectations and needs. In the last chapter of the book you

Figure 1.4
Your area of strength. Date _____.

Figure 1.5
Your area for growth. Date _____.

will be asked to reassess your area for growth and area of strength and the extent to which your priorities were responded to. Similarly you will be asked to project a new list of learning priorities.

No static medium, regardless of its merits, can handle all individual concerns or deal adequately with an essentially interactive process of organizing instruction for social studies. As you overview the chapters that follow, you may identify many needs that are not likely to be met by this book. In those cases, the references at the end of the chapters and the suggested readings at the end of the modules may be of greater assistance. Also the various application activities may lead to sought-after answers, while in still other cases an instructor may be the only refuge for ideas. By identifying early what the book seems to be able to do well and not as well for you, you should be more likely to work toward our mutual goals—becoming a better-prepared teacher of social studies.

NOTES

[1] This analysis was provided by Joan Ferry, a graduate student at Temple University.

[2] John Dewey, *Experience and Education* (New York: Macmillan, 1938), pp. 102–103.

[3] This list of purposes is adapted from one provided by H. Michael Hartoonian, Social Studies Specialist, Department of Public Instruction, State of Wisconsin unpublished paper, 1975.

CHAPTER 2

What's a Social Studies?

Think of a little girl entering school on the first day. All around her in the room where she will spend the next ten months is a mixture of strange and familiar sights. Some of the children are familiar to her, but the furniture is strange, as well as the structure of the room. Her eyes light up as she recognizes some of the playthings that she has at home. She thinks she will probably like it here, but she is not sure what kind of person the woman identified as "teacher" will be. She listens with eagerness but with a touch of apprehension to the questions and directions that the lady in the front of the room is stating: "And we also will learn about social studies. . . ." The little girl screws her face into a strange puzzled expression. "What's a social studies?" she wonders.

Reflect a moment on your past experiences with social studies when you were in elementary school. What do you remember about them? Are the memories happy or unhappy ones?

Perhaps a series of dates and capitals and maybe even a few explorers flashed through your mind; certainly a war or two must be mixed in. And don't forget all those community helpers! Were those periods exciting or a seemingly never-ending string of dry, pointless facts? Whatever you conjured up from those long-forgotten moments, chances are they bear little resemblance to what social studies has to offer in the 1970s.

Today you would still recognize many of the old topics; home life, the school, and the community remain, but the activities that children pursue under the labels, the ways they learn, and the materials they use have been radically altered. Scan the activity in Figure 2.1 as a case in point. It is taken from the *Teacher's Guide* of the first-grade component of a forthcoming K–7 social studies program. Contemporary social studies, as we shall see, attempts to help children confront and more adequately cope with typical social realities that they encounter every day. The knowledge it seeks for students is highly functional as well as significant.

WHAT IS SOCIAL STUDIES

Surprising as it may seem, the returns are not yet in on the answer to this question. Prior to the nineteenth century the term *social studies* did not exist. Children studied history and geography. In the early twentieth century the term came into use, taking the name of a committee that was established to expand the curriculum of the schools. In its report, the Committee on Social Studies defined social studies broadly to mean all subject matter dealing with the growth and structure of human society. It went on to posit the cultivation of "good citizenship" as a major goal of social studies, and, in turn, to define good citizenship in terms of noble and lofty social responsibilities.[1]

Over the years "good citizenship" has been translated in many ways ·in the social studies curriculum. In darker times it has represented inculcating children with the dominant socio-civic mores of the controlling culture. A countertrend emerged striking at the ideological weaknesses of this position to argue that knowledge of the *social sciences* of itself could produce the good citizen. This view of social studies sees it as teaching appropriate items selected from the various social science disciplines. While not all scholars agree on what the social sciences are either,[2] a basic nucleus of disciplines on which there is general agreement are anthropology, sociology, political science, economics, geography, history, and psychology.

Much of the 1960s was preoccupied with a search for the underlying structures of the social sciences, which in turn might be used as the bases for social studies curriculum. This move was occasioned partially by Jerome Bruner's influential little book *The Process of Education*, which seemed to many to be a plea for discovering structures, and partially by a reaction against seemingly endless progressions of irrelevant facts in the curriculum. The alternative advanced was to have students learn the basic *concepts* and *generalizations* that made up each of the various disciplines. In so doing, it was argued, the student would learn information that could transcend periods and revisions in data and at the same time would acquire a cognitive structure or framework on which new knowledge could be organized.

While social scientists were never able to agree on definitive structures, a number of alternative possibilities were outlined in various studies, books, and conference reports published during the period.[3] The ramifications for curriculum development were that concepts and generalizations became one of the key organizing structures for the scope and sequence of social studies programs. Programs would frequently list the concepts and generalizations to be taught in their overview, along with a listing of the related social sciences that were incorporated into each grade level. Some of the fruits of this developmental process, the various textbook series of the late 1960s and early 1970s, reflect this pattern in their rationale.[4]

This view of the social studies as being heavily dependent upon the social sciences is reflected in some of the recent curriculum requirements written into law by various states. Witness sections of the Pennsylvania and California codes as examples:

A planned course in the social studies shall be taught in each year of the elementary school. The content of this program shall include

Figure 2.1
Sample lesson from forthcoming basal social studies series

What is a family?

General objectives

To identify the wide range of family types that exist in the United States.

To allow children to identify with family types as a way of clarifying their own family structure.

To identify the basic characteristics of a family.

Materials

The People Book (commercially prepared activity manual).

Commentary

Unfortunately many of the characterizations of families that young children encounter are often stereotypes or, at best, limited. This activity is designed to expose them to a wide range of different family types that can be found in the United States. Families come in different sizes, colors, and groupings, and whichever one the children in our classes belong to should be represented in their discussions. Accordingly, twenty different types of families are presented to the children. At least one, and possibly several, families should be similar to that of every child in your class.

For your summarization of this activity, keep in mind these characteristics of a family: A family is a group of two or more people who (1) live together at least part of the time; (2) satisfy one another's needs in some way; (3) are either related by blood, marriage, adoption, or agreement.

The concept of family is a complex one, and social scientists have defined it in many different ways. While not all would agree with the definition used here, it seems to cover the basic points that you would want to consider.

Suggested procedures/questions

Start the discussion by asking, "How many of you belong to a family?" This question should focus attention on the topic and the fact that every member of the class belongs to a family. Follow with a question such as, "Why do we have families?" Accept whatever responses the students offer that are plausible and gently challenge any that are not.

Be sure that each child has a pencil. Call attention to appropriate pages in *The People Book* by announcing that the class is to hear about many different kinds of families. Point out the numbers beneath each family group and indicate that each of the people in each family live in the same house. This is to explain the meaning of the house outline. Then proceed to tell the class about each family, referring to the numbers as you read. Tell the children to circle the families that seem most like their own.

1. This is the Martinez family. It is made up of Mrs. Martinez and her son.
2. This is the Agronski family. It is made up of Mr. and Mrs. Agronski and their five children.
3. This is the Patterson family. It is made up of Mr. Patterson and his daughter.
4. This is the Cordasco family. It is made up of Mr. and Mrs. Cordasco and their daughters.

(*continued*)

5. This is the Choy family. It is made up of Mr. and Mrs. Choy and Mr. Choy's mother and father.
6. This is the Grier family. It is made up of Mr. and Ms. Grier.
7. This is the Redbird family. It is made up of Mrs. Redbird and her children.
8. This is the Stevens family. It is made up of Mr. and Ms. Stevens and three children whom they adopted. (Check to see if everyone knows what "adopted" means.)
9. This is the Jackson family. It is made up of Mrs. Jackson and her two children.
10. This is the Pagano family. It is made up of Mr. and Mrs. Pagnano and their three children, Mr. Pagnano's mother and father, and Mr. Pagnano's aunt and uncle.

Stop at this point to see if the children are following along, are circling families with which they identify, or have any questions about any of the families described.

11. This is the Wong family. It is made up of Mr. and Mrs. Wong.
12. This is the Juarez family. It is made up of Mr. Juarez and his granddaughter, whose parents have died.
13. This is a commune family. It is made up of Mr. and Mrs. Larson and their children, Mr. Carbo, Mr. and Mrs. Jolson, Mr. and Mrs. Peterson and their children, and Mr. and Mrs. Goldberg.
14. This is the Heller family. It is made up of Mr. and Mrs. Heller and their three children. They belong to a religious group called the Amish, who try to live as people did long ago.
15. This is the Rainwater family. It is made up of Mr. and Mrs. Rainwater and their three children.
16. This is the Thomas family. It is made up of Mr. and Mrs. Thomas and Mr. Thomas' nephew, who has come to live with them.
17. This is the Battaglia family. It is made up of Mrs. Battaglia and her child.
18. This is the Rodriguez family. It is made up of Mr. and Mrs. Rodriguez and their child.
19. This is the Diaz family. It is made up of Ms. Diaz and her child.
20. This is the Chinn family. It is made up of Mr. and Mrs. Chinn and their four children.

At the conclusion, ask if anyone would like to tell which families they circled as most like their own. As the students respond, try to give everyone who volunteers a chance to name at least one family. If a student does not volunteer, do not call upon him or her, but you may want to check the books of the nonrespondents at a later time to note their choices.

In the next phase of the discussion ask, "In what ways were all of these families alike?" and "In what ways were they different?"

Conclude and summarize by stating in some fashion the three basic characteristics of a family cited in the Commentary.

Source: Peter H. Martorella, *McGraw-Hill Elementary Social Studies Series: Grade 1* (New York: McGraw-Hill, 1977).

anthropology, economics, geography, history, political science, and sociology. These may be combined into one general area known as social studies. [Section 20211, based on Section 1511, School Laws of Pennsylvania, 1968.]

The adopted course of study for grades 1 through 6 shall include instruction, beginning in grade 1 and continuing through grade 6, in the following areas of study: Social sciences, drawing upon the disciplines of anthropology, economics, geography, history, political science, psychology, and sociology, designed to fit the maturity of pupils. [Article 2. *Course of Study of Grades 1 through 6;* Areas of Study: 8551, California Code.]

Not all elements of the profession subscribe to the social-studies-as-the-social-sciences position, however. A recent past president of the National Council for the Social Studies leveled the following criticism of the position in his presidential address:

> We, of the profession, have not immediately and clearly grasped this distinction between Social Science and Social Studies. We have devoted our major energies, including our efforts in the "new" Social Studies, to making the Social Sciences alone suffice for the broader needs of citizenship education. In this vein, we have tried to organize the teaching of the Social Sciences in all kinds of orders, sequences, and cycles; we have tried to organize teaching around concepts, generalizations, problems, and values; we have tried fusion, integration, and correlation of the social disciplines; we have tried cases, projects, and contracts as organizing principles; we have prettied up our textbooks, with maps, pictures, diagrams, graphs, charts, and a dozen other paraphernalia; we have thrown in audio-visual aids; we have "Brunerized" the subjects and made inquiry our god. These attempts to fit square pegs into round holes have never been entirely successful. It should be apparent that the social science disciplines, by themselves, do not constitute the whole of citizenship education. The effort to force citizenship education into a strict social science mold either does violence to Social Science, asking more of it than it has to offer, or it neglects the ethical component of citizenship altogether.[5]

The 1970s, then, have ushered in still a different emphasis concerning what the social studies should comprise. These newer thrusts emphasize ecological awareness, activism, affective concerns of beliefs, attitudes, values, and moral development, decision making and generally a broader view of what knowledge is germane to social and individual concerns. What eventual notion of the nature of social studies will ultimately prevail is not clear at this time. Certainly any definition is likely to include an important relationship with the social sciences. For purposes of our discussion, we will identify with this more recent, broader, and more unsettled view of what the social studies curriculum is.

CURRICULAR THRUSTS
OF THE SIXTIES AND SEVENTIES

While a dominant pattern emerges in the design of the curriculum, considerable variation exists in the actual curricular materials that have been developed. The 1960s and early 1970s have been a period of growth for the social studies where both the shape and scope of materials and practices have broadened and diversified. Much of the shift was occasioned by what came to be identified as Project Social Studies. Initiated in 1962 as part of the U.S. Office of Education's earlier attempts to bolster curriculum in the areas of science, mathematics, and foreign language, it was a belated response of our country to the Soviet challenge of Sputnik.

Project Social Studies encouraged experimentation in curriculum development and teaching practices, as well as more effective teacher education programs. Many of the initial projects were based at university centers and were assigned the task of building a total scope and sequence for a series of grades, others took a specific social science focus for a course or courses, and still others took some dimensions of curricular improvement that could cut across grade levels. While the initial funding impetus in most cases came from the federal government, subsequent continued curriculum development was often supported by local, state, university, and foundation grants.

The net effect of this thrust by the U.S. Office of Education was to spur on many other centers of innovation in social studies, funded and nonfunded. Literally hundreds of large and small curriculum innovations of all shapes and sizes sprang up across the United States during the 1960s. Those that were widely disseminated or were taken over by major commercial publishers have come to be considered as national projects, although there exists no formal definition of the term. Perhaps the surprising fact—to those who are familiar with parallel periods of growth in other areas of curriculum development such as science education—is that social studies educators in no way converge on which developments are superior or even desirable for all schools across the United States!

This phenomenon has been a source of both strength and weakness for the social studies curriculum. The "bad news" is that it tends to produce confusion and strikes terror in the hearts of teachers, administrators, and curriculum adoption committees who must make pressured decisions with meager resources at their disposal. "Just tell us what is considered to be the best program!" they cry in desperation. The "good news" is that lack of convergence on any one program or group of projects has promoted diversity in curriculum planning and focused attention where it should always be—on the objectives of each school or district and the indigenous needs of the children it serves. Social studies curriculum development, no matter how exciting and innovative it may be, has not yet reached (and may never reach) the stage of sophistication and comprehensiveness at which a preassembled K–8 program can deal adequately with the social diversity and rapidly changing events in our country, let alone attend to the highly complex social needs of *each* child.

The 1970s might be characterized as years of alerting, consolidating, evaluating, and recharting for social studies educators. Due to the time lag that seems to attend all curriculum development, many teachers are still finding out about the results of the prior decade. Dissemination and diffusion are always a necessary accompaniment of development, and it is a long, time-consuming, and expensive process. Moreover, the actual business of consolidating all of the constructive gains of the period in itself has taken considerable time, since no national information retrieval center for curriculum developments in the social studies existed during this period. Evaluation of the legacy of the 1960s is still ongoing, and with it a recharting of what yet needs to be done (or undone) in the field.

THE DESIGN OF THE K–8 CURRICULUM

While it would be impossible to specify all the variations of social studies curriculum designs that exist across the United States, one could predict with surprising accuracy the general structure of K–6 programs. This interesting phenomenon stems from the widespread impact of the expanding-communities-of-men notion of social studies curriculum design popularized by Paul Hanna. The model, Hanna notes, "starts with the oldest, smallest, and most crucial community—the family placed in the center of the concentric circles—and progresses outward in ever widening bands through the child's neighborhood community; the child's local communities of city, county, and/or metropolis; the state community; the regions-of-states community; and the national community."[6] In spite of the fact that there are many ways to construct a curriculum sequence, each with its own defensible logic, the Hanna pattern dominates, representing virtually a national curriculum design. As R. Murray Thomas and Dale Brubaker state:

> Though all textbook series do not follow precisely the theoretical approach espoused by Hanna, the general concept of expanding communities has been so popular throughout the United States that most textbook series follow some variation of that overall theme. As a result, that approach represents almost a national curriculum design for elementary social studies.[7]

Translated to K–6 grade-level themes, the expanding horizons approach usually has resulted in the following basic pattern:

K–1	Family and School Community
Grade 2	Immediate Community
Grade 3	Towns and Cities
Grade 4	Region of States
Grade 5	American History
Grade 6	World Cultures/Other Countries

The pattern of grades 7 and 8 is less predictable, although it is more likely than not to deal with American history at one year and some form of world cultures in the other. Emergence of the middle-school organizational scheme, usually housing grades 5–8, is likely to have some impact on the structure of the social studies curriculum in those four grades. A fairly secure curriculum generalization is that social studies in the middle-school grades is in a more undefined state than at any other level.

As suggested, the expanding-horizons notion represents just one—albeit a dominant—perspective on curriculum scope and sequence in the social studies. Several variations of and alternatives to this theme are possible. One variation was developed by the Minnesota Social Studies Project in the 1960s. It represents one of the few K–12 articulated programs currently available. The themes for each grade level are as follows:

K	The Earth as the Home of Man
Grades 1 and 2	Families Around the World
Grade 3	Communities Around the World
Grade 4	Communities Around the World: Their Economic System
Grade 5	Regional Studies
Grade 6	United States History: From Community to Society
Grade 7	Man and Society
Grade 8	Our Political System
Grade 9	Our Economic System
Grade 10	American History
Grade 11	Area Studies
Grade 12	Value Conflicts and Policy Decisions

Unlike the other programs, this one does not include student materials but rather is largely a series of teaching and resource units. Each unit specifies teaching strategies and the related objectives they are designed to satisfy, along with a series of materials needed to complete the activities. From four to seven resource units are included in each grade sequence, allowing for considerable flexibility in using the materials.

Accompanying the teacher guides and resource units is a series of background papers explaining much of the theory and rationale of the program. A major trademark of the program is its identification of social science concepts, generalizations, skills, and attitudes in a continuous and sequential K–12 strand. In doing so it achieved a spiraling effect, reintroducing more complex dimensions of the same general structure at each grade level. The K–12 program materials were never published in commercial form, but a duplicated version of them is available from the Green Printing Company, 631 8th Avenue North, Minneapolis, Minnesota 55411.

A program currently under development at Research for Better Schools, Philadelphia, attempts to combine an interdisciplinary focus with Piaget-based developmental concerns. The Social Encounter and Research Curriculum for Humanization (SEARCH) is organized around five psychosocial functions or themes that run through each level of the program. These functions are shown in Figure 2.2, along with topics that might be studied at each stage.

From a different perspective, Bruce Joyce has developed three different ways of constructing a social studies program. Each way reflects a different emphasis or concern that a developer presumably feels should be built into the curriculum. Joyce refers to these approaches as the *social-science-centered curriculum, the citizen-centered curriculum*, and a *person-centered curriculum*. He outlines sample topics for each of the approaches and the various grade levels. The sequence of the first approach emphasizes with increasing complexity the methodology of the social sciences and deals with concepts selected from all of them in a spiraling fashion. The citizen-centered curriculum is designed to increasingly prepare students for effective participation in citizenship and political activity. Of the three, the person-centered curriculum has the greatest flexibility built into it, Joyce notes. "In such a curriculum, many topics cannot be predicted in advance. The important basis for sequence is that the student gradually examine his society and develop personal values."[8]

Still another way to conceive of curriculum organization is to determine what domains of knowledge a K–12 social studies curriculum should represent, that is, what categories of information a student should acquire under the heading of social studies. This framework would provide a guide to selecting different activities but would not necessarily specify which ones should be included. Such an approach allows for an organic curriculum teacher and students may jointly create in concert with their interests, knowledge, and cognitive structures. Similarly movement among the domains could be flexible, with emphases shifting from grade to grade in response to interests and developmental considerations.

Consider the following domains: *self-awareness, social awareness, cultural traditions, aesthetics, analytical tools*, and *questing*.[9] Self-aware-

Figure 2.2
Scope and sequence of search units for grades K, 1, and 2

	Stage I	Stage II	Stage III
Self-realizing Personal Characteristics	1. I have a body. 2. I have an appearance.	3. I have senses. 4. I have feelings.	5. I have an identity. 6. I have a family.
Governing Personal Responsibilities	1. I care for myself. 2. I care for my home.	3. I care for my classroom. 4. I care for my dog.	5. I follow rules. 6. I follow laws and customs.
Producing and Consuming Personal Economy	1. I use my day to do things. 2. I produce and consume.	3. I produce services. 4. I consume other people's goods and services.	5. I pay for things. 6. I shop in a marketplace.
Utilizing Environments Personal Ecology	1. I have surroundings. 2. I travel in my surroundings.	3. I meet people in my surroundings. 4. I map my surroundings.	5. I make maps of my surroundings. 6. I use tools in my surroundings.
Interpreting and Generating Personal Awareness and Achievement	1. I grow and change. 2. I see the seasons change.	3. I know special days. 4. I know special places.	5. I know special times. 6. I know special people.

Source: "SEARCH," *Publishers Alert Service*, U.S. Department of Health, Education and Welfare, National Institute of Education, Copyright Approval Program, December, 1974.

ness and social awareness deal respectively with questions such as "Who am I?" and "What is the world around me like, and how can I become a social actor?" The former focuses on ego needs and self-revelation, while the latter deals with learning more about one's social environment, including how it can be modified. The topic of cultural traditions explores personal, subgroup, national, and international cultural traditions in order of increasing dissimilarity, that is, beginning with the study of one's own cultural traditions and progressing through that of other groups or countries whose traditions are most like yours. Aesthetics deals with the social impact of the arts, how the various arts —music, painting, sculpture, literature, poetry, dancing, and the like— affect the way we feel, see things, react to situations, and generally influence our lives. Analytical tools refer to those skills and general technical capabilities, such as map reading, group organization, effective interpersonal communications, and the like, that we learn not as ends in themselves but as means to another end—getting somewhere or getting a group decision that reflects the best thinking available, for example. The final domain, questing, represents social studies knowledge that the student would like to acquire, apart from whatever curricular choices others have made for him or her. Some children will require teachers solicitations to generate such requests while others can supply them readily.

Figure 2.3 represents the integration of these six domains, with questing and analytical tools cutting across the other four. Since any of the six domains may receive greater emphasis than the others at any grade level, any of the existing quadrants or circles may have its shape and size altered in a specific use. Teachers who apply this approach to curriculum design would (1) determine which domains were to be proportionately emphasized at different grade levels, (2) identify and develop corresponding sets of activities, and (3) determine what they considered to be the most logical orchestration of the various domains.

Most cities and states and many individual school districts publish their own curriculum guidelines for the social studies. A sample section of illustrative guidelines is shown in Figure 2.4.

The National Council for the Social Studies, the professional organiza-

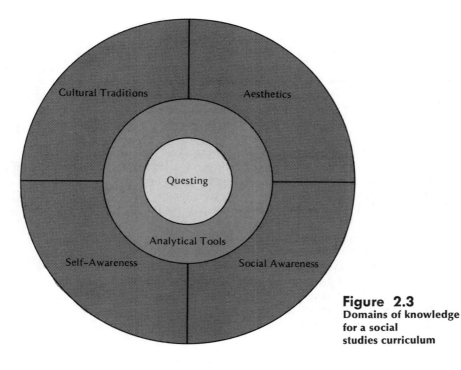

Figure 2.3
**Domains of knowledge
for a social
studies curriculum**

Figure 2.4
Portions of proposed curriculum guidelines

I Introduction

A. Framework

A framework is an official statement of what the State Board of Education desires as the basis for the instructional programs in the social-sciences curriculum for the California Public Schools, kindergarten and grades one through twelve. It states the significance of the subject-matter areas, goals, and suggested pupil-performance outcomes; gives examples of relevant concepts and settings or topics; and recommends sequences of study for the various blocks of grades.

II Social-sciences program

A. The Curriculum

An effective curriculum in social-sciences education for the students of the public schools of California has three major components:

(1) Processes or methods of investigating, and modes or ways of learning in the social sciences.

(2) Concepts and generalizations drawn from the social sciences.

(3) Settings and topics which serve as the selected samples of human experience, both past and present.

III Program design

Themes are assigned for study by blocks of grades as follows:

Grades K–2	Mankind: Man's Distinctive Characteristics
Grades 3–4	Man and Land: Cultural and Geographic Relationships
Grades 5–6	Mankind and Men: Interaction, Diversity, Individuality
Grades 7–9	Man and Systems: Economic and Political: Urban Environments
Grades 10–11	Man: Past and Present (Historical Integration)
Grade 12A	Man as a Decision-maker: Social Policy in the United States
Grade 12B	Man, His Goals and Aspirations: Selected Studies in the Social Sciences

The Program by Blocks of Grades

Within the major theme assigned to each block of grades, the studies are divided into topics. Each topic has as its heading a key analytical question which suggests both the conceptual content of the topic and the processes of inquiry associated with it.

Grades K–2: Mankind: Man's Distinctive Characteristics

Topics

1. What is man?
2. How do men and animals adapt to and change the land they live on?
3. How do men and animals communicate?
4. How do people live together?
5. How are people alike and how are they different?

Grades 3–4: Man and Land: Cultural and Geographic Relationships

Topics

1. What is the relationship between the natural environment and animals on the one hand and man on the other?

(*continued*)

---

2. How have different groups of men developed different ways of living in the same or similar environments?
3. How has urbanization altered man's relation to the natural environment?
4. How are problems of living being met in the modern urban environment?
5. What is human about human beings?

Grades 5–6: Mankind and Men: Interaction, Diversity, Individuality

Topics

1. What happens when different groups of men come in contact?
2. How have ethnic groups and individuals affected American development?
3. How do different groups interact in the contemporary United States?
4. How do human groups interact in different cultures?
5. How is any man like no other man?

Grades 7–9: Man and Systems: Political and Economic: Urban Environments

Topics

1. How do societies decide what is to be done and who is to do it?
2. How do societies decide who gets what?
3. How do market economies develop and function?
4. How do democratic political systems develop and function?
5. How are decisions made in the command political economy?
6. How are decisions made in the mixed political economy of the present-day United States?
7. How can underdeveloped societies cope with the demand for rapid modernization?
8. How did the emergence of cities change the life of man?
9. How have cities varied in their functions and characteristics?
10. How has modern urbanization changed the life of man?
11. How can the quality of urban life be improved?

Grades 10–11: Man: Past and Present (Historical Integration)

Topics

1. How did the United States come to be the way it is, and how is it changing?
   1a. How did the social structure that the colonists brought from Europe change in the course of their life in America?
   1b. How did Americans develop a sense of nationality?
   1c. How did Americans develop a more democratic political system?
   1d. What impact has the introduction of enslaved Africans had on American life?
   1e. How have Americans adjusted to the diversity of peoples and cultures?
   1f. How has the United States responded to industrialization and large-scale business organization?
   1g. How have Americans been affected by their relations with the rest of the world?
   1h. Where is American society headed today?
2. How have national groupings and conflicts affected the life of man?
   2a. What makes a "State" a "State"?
   2b. Why have societies sought to impose their wills on other societies?
   2c. Why do military establishments so universally exist, and how do they affect the societies of which they are a part?

(*continued*)

2d. Can man's technological abilities for destruction be offset by his imagination and the desire to maintain the peace?
3. How has India maintained its cultural unity over such a long period and such a diversity of peoples?
   3a. How did the principal features of traditional Chinese culture take shape and persist?
   3b. How has Hindu India interacted with its invaders?
   3c. How did traditional Indian culture affect the struggle for independence?
   3d. How are traditional and modern elements interacting in present-day India?

Alternate Topic 3. How did China develop mankind's most durable socio-political system, and why has it been replaced?
   3a. How did the principal features of traditional Chinese culture take shape and persist?
   3b. How has Confucian China interacted with its invaders?
   3c. How did the Chinese establish their modern independent nationality?
   3d. How are traditional and modern elements interacting in present-day China?

Alternate Topic 3. Why has Japan become Asia's only technologically advanced society?

Grade 12A: Man as a Decision-Maker: Social Policy in the United States
   Topics
1. How do ordinary citizens influence the decisions that affect them?
2. How are ordinary citizens influenced in making and accepting policy decisions?
3. How are decision-makers influenced by persons with special statuses and by special interest groups?
4. What range of decisions is possible *within* organizations?
5. What is the effect on social policy decisions of relationships *between* organizations?

Grade 12B: Man, His Goals and Aspirations: Selected Studies
   Illustrative Topics
1. Ethnic groups and social policy.
2. The Selective Service System.
3. Immigrant and Black experience in the United States.
4. Islam, Buddhism, and Hinduism in comparative settings.
5. The influence of religion on art and architecture.
6. New African nations and world affairs.

Source: *Proposed Social Sciences Education Framework for California Public Schools: Kindergarten and Grades One Through Twelve—An Abstract* (Revised Draft), Sacramento, Calif.: 1970, pp. 1, 3, 7–8, 9.

tion of teachers of social studies of both the elementary and secondary levels, has begun to assume some responsibility for curriculum evaluation, in addition to its traditional role of dissemination and diffusion. One of its ongoing activities has been the publication and updating of curriculum guidelines. The latest revision is in process as this book goes to press[10]

LEARNING SYSTEMS IN THE SOCIAL STUDIES

Goal setting, organizing, and planning instruction consume a major part of a teacher's day (and night). Years of teaching somewhat reduce the time required for organizing, as one becomes more efficient and knowledgable about available resources. But correspondingly as one learns more about students and effective teaching, the variables to consider in planning and goal setting actually increase. As a new teacher confronts the array of subjects that are to be taught for a year, the goal-setting/organizing/planning task may appear to be a formidable one. What is to be taught? How are the subjects to be orchestrated? What is to be emphasized? How are these emphases to be taught? Or just plain "What shall I do on Monday?"

Faced with these awesome burdens, a teacher frequently falls back on the goal-setting/organizing/planning model implicit in the student-teaching situation, seeks guidance from other teachers in the school, or adopts the suggested guidelines offered by the school district, if available. Occasionally such models may be effectively employed with slight modifications and in all cases offer a starting point for instructional considerations. The reasons why all such formulas, whether abstracted wholesale from realistic classroom settings or from prescriptive textbooks, never seem to be directly applicable to new classroom situations are complex. Every instructional system depends on a variety of variables or conditions either explicitly or implicitly stated, including a teacher's personality and constraints that a school or district may impose.

Ms. Perkins, for example, knows that her metabolism causes her to be a slow starter in the morning and that she reaches her peak of efficiency and enthusiasm right after lunch. Correspondingly for that time she schedules social studies, for which she has the *least* interest, to help counteract her normal inclinations. In another case, Mr. Ferguson faces his instructional task knowing that the only commercial social studies material provided by his district is an inferior textbook series.

Developing an individual goal-setting/organizing/planning system always involves consideration of an assortment of such variables. The more they are consciously considered, the more rational decisions can be. The number of variables that may enter into instructional decision making are myriad, but some have greater significance than others. Translated to questions, some of the more significant variables in social studies instruction become:

> What knowledge is of most worth?
> How much time do I have to spend on it?
> What are my student's capable of doing and what are their limitations?
> What am I capable of doing and what are my limitations?
> How do I think my students learn most effecitvely?
> What do the parents expect the children to learn?
> What does the administration expect the children to learn?

What materials are available to me?
What is the dominant social-emotional climate in the classroom?

All of these questions and others can enter into instructional activities for the social studies. Not all of them are of equal importance, nor are all of them serious considerations in every teaching situation. Take a moment to check off those five questions that you personally feel are the most important ones to consider in goalsetting/organizing/planning. If possible, share your conclusions and reasons with some other teachers, preservice or inservice.

GOAL SETTING AND ORGANIZING INSTRUCTION

Goal setting and organizing instruction require a teacher to simultaneously consider a whole range of variables, similar to those just discussed. *Goal setting, as used here, refers basically to determining what it is that the teacher wants the students to accomplish over the short, intermediate, or long haul.* Many people, including parents and students, may have participated in these goals. They may be as lofty as those stated in presidential inaugural speeches (". . . wipe out poverty in this generation . . .") or as trite as those found on signs in school lunchrooms ("Remember to clean your place before you leave"). In either case they represent something to aspire to or work toward.

The way in which goals are reflected in practice depends on how instruction is organized. If the goals set are commonly agreed upon and seriously entertained as achievable ends, an organizational scheme can move teacher and students toward them. What frequently occurs, however, is that goals are stated in highly idealistic terms that make their achievement totally unrealistic ("All students should treat one another as their brother"), or else they are couched in ambiguous terms that make it impossible to know how to work toward them ("We want to elevate children's spirits"). Somewhere between blind idealism and ambiguous clichés lie social studies goals that can be set to serve as directions for immediate, intermediate, and long-range instructional organization.

> "Students should be able to better understand people who are different from themselves in some way—socially, culturally, economically, physically, and mentally."
> "Students should be able to determine what values are the most important to them, some of the ways that may have caused them to arrive at this state, and the ways in which their choices differ from their peers."

Neither of these sample goals specifies operationally what a teacher should do day by day or what a unit might look like, or even how instructional activities can be sequenced from goal to goal. The goals merely represent some achievable, hopefully understandable aspiration that teacher and students can move toward. *Organizing instruction refers to moving from such goals to designing a pattern of sequenced activities that will help accomplish the goals.* Each activity has as its objective a short-term contribution toward some broader goal. A collection of such activities organized around some theme is commonly designated a *unit*. An organizational scheme for the year in social studies would consist of some sequence of individual activities and units along with related materials needed, directed toward some set of goals. A sample organizational chart for a six-week cycle (the typical report-card period) is shown in Figure 2.5. It reflects a program guided by five goals and indicates a sequence of instruction serving different goals at different times and occasionally several goals simultaneously. Since each activity is not necessarily designed for only a 20–25 or 40–45 minute period of instruction, less than thirty activities (6 weeks x 5 days) are planned.

Each activity, if part of or separate from a unit, must be logically sequenced in some fashion and has a distinct objective and a set of procedures that contribute to the larger goals. The actual structuring of these activities and the way in which the teacher articulates them to others is far less important than how well they are related to the significant goals. Similarly, in articulating specific activities a teacher will have to take into account the variables cited earlier, such as student abilities.

PLANNING

To grossly oversimplify a perennial teacher headache, let us assume that *planning consists primarily of preparing to use available time in the most efficient way possible to achieve set goals and an organizational pattern.* Every teacher in this sense must prepare to use 180± days effectively every year. These days each represent approximately 6 hours of instruction. In cold, calculating terms, then, a school year presents approximately 1,080 hours or 64,800 minutes for direct classroom instruction. Planning, as we have described it, involves using such time constructively to achieve significant goals.

The difficulty with such statistics on time, as every classroom teacher knows, is that they do not realisticallly represent *usable* instructional time, nor do they take into account the fact that all time is *not* of equal value. Much of a typical school day is consumed in noninstructional activities such as collecting milk money, reading announcements, recesses, and so on. Similarly the time immediately before lunch and dismissal is often considered to have less potential for instruction than other periods. To plan effectively for social studies instruction consequently means determining what blocks of usable and desirable time can be identified and sequenced. *If there is great competition from other subject areas, it may mean that time period for subjects should be alternated.* Social studies might occur at 10:00 Monday, Wednesday, and

Figure 2.5
Organizational chart for a 6-week period

		Goal 1	Goal 2	Goal 3	Goal 4	Goal 5
September	9	Activity 1				
	10	A2				
	11	A3	A3			
	12		A4		A4	
	13		A5		A5	
	16			A6	A6	
	17			A7		A7
	18					
	19					A8
	20			A9		
	23					
	24	A10			A10	
	25					
	26			A11	A11	A11
	27					
	30		A12	A12	A12	
October	1					
	2		A13			
	3					
	4				A14	A14
	7					A15
	8					A16
	9		A17	A17	A17	
	10	A18		A18		A18
	11		A19	A19		
	14	A20	A20	A20	A20	A20
	15		A21			
	16		A22	A22	A22	A22
	17			A23		
	18		A24			A24

Friday and at 2:00 on Tuesday and Thursday, alternating with science. Another way to use desirable time equitably among subjects is to integrate them where possible, at least for part of the year. Environmental education is a case in point where science and social studies can naturally come together. Still a third possibility is to have social studies activities only on a few days of the week or during alternate weeks, both for an extended period of time. The main point is that the notion of having every subject at the same time each day represents only one, and not necessarily the most desirable, planning approach.

Let us examine a series of alternative plans for a hypothetical fourth-grade class. Excluding all time estimated as being consumed on noninstructional activities between the students' arrival and departure, the teacher estimates that she has 260 *usable* minutes available for instruction. Of that time approximately 60 minutes are designated as *unde-*sirable time (i.e., before lunch or dismissal). Consequently she has 200 minutes of usable *and* desirable time, although there are 260 usable minutes. She records these figures and projects these possible schedules for social studies instruction:

Schedule 1: Social Studies, Monday–Friday, 9:20–10:00

Schedule 2: Social Studies, Monday, Wednesday, and Friday, 9:20–10:25

Schedule 3: Social Studies, Monday–Friday, 9:20–10:40, every other week

Schedule 4: Social Studies, Monday–Friday, complete at least four activities in the Social Studies Center

The first schedule is designed to accommodate a sequence of instructional activities requiring constant blocks of time such as those found in textbook series. Schedules 2 and 3 allow for more flexibility in organizing instructional activities of varying length and permit other subject-matter areas to share the desirable time periods. The third schedule is particularly appropriate for project-type activities that require large blocks of time over a short period. Schedule 4 is suited to an activity-centered approach and permits a maximum of flexibility and student direction of activities.

Even the best of schedules are made to be broken for good learning reasons, such as when students are deep into the pursuit of an idea. Unfortunately they more frequently have to be ignored for administrative or other noninstructional reasons. Shifts in the schedules of specialty teachers, such as music and art teachers, speech therapists, and gym instructors, require corresponding schedule adjustments. Testing programs and social activities scheduled for the entire school similarly throw off planning. Even so, conscious, deliberate planning for the most effective use of the limited resource of instructional time permits a teacher to better organize instruction in social studies.

The relationship between goalsetting, organizing and planning may be summarized as a series of questions that a teacher asks himself or herself in the sequence noted below.

1. What goals do I have for my instruction? (Goalsetting)
2. What are some possible activities and experiences that I might organize to achieve my goals, and how could I sequence these elements into some pattern? (Organizing)
3. Given the time I have, what specifically will I do on a given day that meets the goals set and fits into the organizational pattern developed? (Planning)

SPECIFYING INSTRUCTIONAL ACTIVITIES

Specifying refers to the way in which your classroom activities are communicated to others, including statements of objectives to be achieved by the activities, the procedures and materials used, and the means of assessing the results of the activities, if any. It concerns largely the *form* of activities. Unfortunately in recent years a great deal of energy has been dissipated by teachers in focusing on articulating and structuring their plans. Formulas for developing lesson plans in what have been described as behavioral terms (i.e., in terms of student behavior expected) have been emphasized, and a number of training materials have been developed to demonstrate how to state objectives behaviorally, the performance expected of students, and the criterion of competence that is acceptable (e.g., "being able to get 75 percent on a related test"). Two sample behaviorally stated objectives are shown below.

Given several pictures of early day farmers and the statement "Man tries to better himself" the child is to point out a minimum of one way for each picture that people have used their growing knowledge to influence a change in farm life. Following this the child is to tell two ways these changes have affected him or her.

After studying farms around the world, the child is to draw pictures of two agricultural products we import and pictures of two agricultural products we export. The child is to give some explanation of why we import or export certain products.

The vigor and breadth of the heated debate that was inspired by the B.O. (behavioral objectives) movement makes for interesting reading but is beyond our focus here.[11] The ultimate legacy of B.O. is still in doubt as teacher opposition appears to be crystallizing in response to some of the more zealous of the B.O. proponents (those with the bumper stickers reading "Help stamp out nonbehavioral objectives"). Obviously teachers through history have been able to specify the nature of their instruction effectively without B.O. Just as obviously, learning to approach some learning tasks through a B.O. frame of reference may help to clarify and organize the job at hand. The key focus for the social studies teacher in organizing and planning instruction is the combination of goals and key variables to be considered. The form by which instruction is specified should *reflect* this focus, not guide it. This point is summed up in the author's maxim: "Never let a behavioral objective interfere with your goal."

In the next few pages (Figures 2.6–2.10) you will see a variety of different ways of specifying activities, mostly from commercially prepared materials. Some reflect a B.O. orientation and some do not. Some of the approaches deal with objectives and procedures that you may not consider to be significant or desirable. In some cases the procedures are sketchy while in others they are detailed. Most of the activities are designed to be read by a teacher, but one is to be used by students in activity centers. As you examine the materials, focus on the alternative

Figure 2.6 Geography Lesson

Lesson Plan—Topic 3a

Topic: Juxtapositional location (first day)

General learning task: The Pupil learns that places can be located relatively.

Specific learning task: The pupil learns that places can be located in terms of juxtaposition to some other phenomena.

Objective: The pupil is able to locate a designated item in his room or on a map when given juxtapositional referents.

Key words:

relative location	right	in front of
juxtaposition	left	behind
border	between	beside

Materials: (1) Map of the classroom for each child with the position of each desk or seat marked with the child's name.

Note: Map should show part of adjacent classrooms or hallway.

(2) Geographical-terms chart.

Pupil text: Pages 7–8.

Procedure: Seat pupils at their desks. Lead them through a brief review of the preceding lesson. Reemphasize the idea that every place has location and a certain character. Location is simply the answer to "where." A place's character simply means what a place is like. You can find out what a place is like by seeing what is at that place.

Begin today's lesson by choosing five pupils to come to the front of class. Arrange them with their backs to the class in the following positions:

<pre>
                        O Sue (in front of)
(beside) Karen O   O Jim (between)   O Bob (beside)
                        O Ken (behind)
</pre>

Explain that today's lesson is about location, and that one way to locate something is in relation to the other things around it. Every thing is located relative to something else. Direct attention to Sue. Ask who can tell where Sue is located in relation to Jim. Confirm, or supply the response. "Sue is in front of Jim." Follow the same procedure for Bob, Ken, and Karen using the positional terms *behind* and *beside*.

Now direct attention to Jim. Ask who can tell where Jim is located in relation to the others. If offered, accept the response, "in the middle" but continue to question until you can confirm or supply the response, "Jim is between Karen and Bob and/or between Sue and Ken."

Have the pupils sit down. Distribute the map of the classroom. Ask if anyone knows what it is. Explain that it is a map of the room and that this is how the room would appear if we looked down through a hole in the ceiling. Have pupils orient the map to correspond to the room. Ask several of the class to tell their location by using the relative terms *in front of, beside, behind,* and *between.* Tell them to refer to other things in the room and not people only.

Review by reemphasizing the idea that things and places can be located in relation to other things and places by using words such as *in front of, beside, behind,* and *between.* Collect and retain the classroom maps for next lesson.

Continue this lesson for a second class period.

Source: William Imperatore, *Place and Environment* (Athens, Ga.: Geography Curriculum Project, University of Georgia, 1969), pp. 29–30. Reprinted with permission of publisher.

Figure 2.7
Learning center activity

Learning Center Activity 5: What Different Types of Maps Tell Us

---

Objective: To be able to identify, explain, and use each of the following types of maps: demographical, road, and topographical.
Materials Supplied: Pretest, posttest, Book List, Exercises Card, Answer Sheet

---

Procedures to Follow

1. Take the pretest in the Center, and check your answers on the Answer Sheet. If you missed fewer than 3 items, see the teacher. Otherwise, continue with the activity.
2. Look up the words *demographical* and *topographical* in the dictionary.
3. Consult any of the books on the Book List and find out how to identify, explain, and use demographical, road, and topographical maps.
4. Select any five exercises from the Exercises Card that you feel will help you better understand how to use the three types of maps. Do each exercise on a separate sheet. Place on the sheet your name, the name of the Learning Center Activity, and the number of the exercise. Completed work should be placed in your folder.
5. Get maps #5, #8, #9, #12, and #13 from the Map File. Then use them to complete the posttest.
6. Turn in to the teacher your answers to the posttest.

Figure 2.8
Grade One Lesson

Lesson 6
Knowledge Objectives: Several members of a family may work. Their job schedules affect the entire family. Working hours may be during the day or at night.
Value Objective: Accepting a variety of family life-styles.
Skills: hypothesizing, comparing
New Words: Perez, post, late, night, hospital, everyday, until, six, o'clock, working, fix, dinner

Introduction
Take a class survey. Ask: "How many have a father who works? How many have a mother who works outside the home? How many have other family members who work?" Have the children who have two working parents, or those who have only one parent who works, tell the class who takes care of them when their parents are at work. Ask: "Do you think it is good for your mother and/or father to work?"

Lesson Development
Page 76: The Perez family
Tell the class that you are going to read about another family and about who works in that family. Read the text. As you read, stop to reinforce the information given with

(continued)

questions such as: "What is the post office? What does it mean to work at night? What is a hospital? What does Mrs. Perez do at the hospital? When does she go to work? When does she come home? How do you think the Perez children feel about having their mother working until six o'clock?"

Page 77: Their family life

Have the children look at each picture and identify what family job is being done by Mrs. Perez and why. Tell the class that most people work five days a week, usually all day or all night. Ask: "Can Mrs. Perez do these things when she is away at work? Why not? Does somebody have to do these things?" Read the text and ask: "Who can figure out who the person is? How do you think the Perez family feels about this? Is the Perez family like your family? How?"

Activities

1. Divide the class to represent family groups similar in size to the pupils' own families. Assign (or let children assign) a mother, father, and children for each group. (Some of the groups may be motherless or fatherless. If any pupils have guardians or baby-sitters, include these in the family groups.) Have each group plan and act out a day in the life of the family, showing where each person goes during the day and how the various jobs at home get done.

2. Have the children suggest all the jobs they can think of which would be connected with a hospital or a post office. List these, and post them under a picture of each place respectively.

Source: *Teacher's Edition, You and Your Family* (New York: Noble & Noble, 1974), pp. 76–77. Reprinted with permission of publisher.

Figure 2.9
Grade Six Lesson

Objectives	Outline of content
A. Is Curious about Social Data.	I. The "Sambo" stereotype of the Negro in the United States resulted from the particular development of the institution of slavery in this country and was not inherent in the African Negro. Many Negroes did not fit the stereotype but the stereotype colored reactions toward the Negro and his position in America.
Sets up hypotheses.	
Draws inferences from a comparison of different map patterns.	
Organizes his information according to some logical pattern which fits his topic.	A. Negroes had developed a number of different cultures in Africa; there were great variations among them, and many were very advanced.

(continued)

Accepts his share of respon-
sibility for the work of a
group; participates actively
without trying to dominate.

1. Negroes had developed various kinds of crafts, different types of agriculture, and other ways of making a living in varied physical environments; the Negroes brought to the United States came from a physical environment which differed greatly from that in the United States.

Teaching procedures   **Materials**

Initiatory Procedures

1. Show the class pictures of pre-Civil War slaves and freedmen in the United States. Ask the students to write a description of what they think the life of these people might have been like in Africa. Discuss the differences in the students' ideas, showing them some of these differences are possibly due to the fact they do not know a great deal about Africa. Then discuss what ideas pre-Civil War Americans might have had concerning the African Negro when he came as a slave, pointing out how little was actually known about Africa and the educational level of many Americans at the time.

Swift, *North Star Shining.*
Hughes and Meltzer, *Pictorial History of the Negro in America.*

2. Show a series of pictures on plantation life in the South and the activities of the slaves. Use them to stimulate a discussion of how similar or different the students feel the life of the slave in America may have been to life of Negroes in Africa.

Illustrated Classroom Pictures set on "The South."
Hughes and Meltzer, *Pictorial History of the Negro in America.*
Cross, *Life in Lincoln's America.*

3. Have pupils examine both a physical map and a vegetation map of Africa. Ask: What occupations might the Africans have followed before they were taken as slaves to America? What difficulties in communication would there have been between groups in different parts of Africa? What differences might these communication difficulties have led to in cultural development and contact with other parts of the world? (Pupils who have come through the Center's second grade course will have studied a modern Hausa village and might be expected to remember something about the kind of climate and vegetation and occupations of the modern Hausa.)

Physical map of Africa.
Vegetation map of Africa.

4. Give pupils an overview of the unit and a list of suggested activities from which they should choose individual and small group projects. You may wish to give them such a list for only the first part of the unit at this time and then give them additional lists as you introduce new sections of the unit (such as on the war itself or on the reconstruction period).

(*continued*)

Many pupils will be presenting small group or individual reports during the rest of the unit. Review suggestions for preparing for and presenting oral reports. Spend more time on discussing types of organization which might fit different kinds of topics. For example, discuss the difference between a narrative organization and an organization to fit exposition of a main idea.

Source: *Grade Six, Resource Unit: Civil War and Reconstruction* (Minneapolis: Project Social Studies, University of Minnesota, 1968), pp. 1–4.

Figure 2.10
Grade Two Lesson

| *Main Idea:* | Community needs are met by groups of people engaged in many related activities. |
| *Organizing Idea:* | Some groups of workers make goods people need; others do work that is needed by other workers or by the people who live in the community. |

Notes to the Teacher	Learning Activities
	Development
If a child seems uncertain about seeking "someone he knows" to let him draw around his hands, suggest that maybe he would like to ask a school worker.	1. Let the children take home sheets of drawing paper to trace around the hands of some adult (parent or others) and find out what work these hands do.
Evaluation of these responses is located following Activity 4.	2. Have each child tell about "his" worker and help him write on the picture what these hands do. For example: • Drive a truck • Type • Sell gas Pin up the "hands of workers" that the children brought from home. Ask: • What do you think would be a good name for our bulletin board? Have the children check to see whether all these workers are on the list (Opener). Add to the list any the children suggest should be there.
	3. Arrange a display of some of the *I Want to Be . . .* books for the children to examine. Ask: • Which of the workers in these books do you think might also be found in our town?

(*continued*)

Children should be encouraged to recognize and admit the tentativeness of their information. When the situation is appropriate, have them label such information and check it later.

The purpose of this activity is to help the children relate workers to their own daily activities and to raise the question of whether all the workers are found in the local community. The children may not be certain at this point just where some services would be located.

Add to the list (Opener) any workers the children think are in their town. If they are uncertain, ask them to suggest a symbol that would mean they are not certain. Have such items checked as the study progresses.

4. Discuss with the children some of the activities that might fill their day and who and what is needed. Ask:
   • What different things might we do in a day?
   • What do we need?
   • What worker is needed?
Chart the children's suggestions on the chalkboard. Use children's terms. The chart might be something like the one shown below:

What do we do?	What do we need?	What worker is needed?
Eat breakfast	Toast	Baker
	Toaster	Store owner
	Electricity	Lineman
	Butter	Farmer (or grocer)
	Knife	Store owner

Some children will indicate that such items as a toaster come from the store; others will say factory. Accept either at this point.

What do we do?	What do we need?	What worker is needed?
Go to school	Books	Librarian
Go to doctor	Car	Service station man
	Shot	Nurse, doctor
Watch TV	TV set	Entertainers
		Salesman

Ask:
   • How many different workers have we shown we need in one day?
   • Which of these do you see in our town?
   • Which of these do you think might be on a farm? In a city?

Source: *The Taba Social Studies Curriculum, Grade Two—Communities Around Us* (San Francisco: San Francisco State College, 1969), pp. 9–11.

ways of articulating and structuring activities *not on the content* with which they deal. (Also consider the form used in Figure 2.1, pp. 26–27.)

In what ways are these approaches similar? In what ways are they different? Which features of them do you like and dislike? How would you alter those features you dislike to create your own form? If you had to pick one, which of these approaches would you prefer to use yourself? If possible, take some time to discuss your rationale with your peers.

Then determine which of these approaches you would prefer to use if you were a substitute borrowing another teacher's organizational scheme? Why? Were there any differences in your choices? If so, why? If none of these approaches appealed to you, construct your own original or composite pattern. Some schools require teachers to adopt a particular procedure for specifying activities as a way of keeping administrators, supervisors, and substitutes abreast of classroom progress. Even in such cases, however, many teachers prefer to "keep two sets of books" and use a parallel format with which they feel most comfortable for their own planning.

PLUGGING IN TO THE FUTURE OF THE SOCIAL STUDIES

"Plugging in" to the future of the social studies requires gaining access to communication networks that intersect with social studies developments. This is a pragmatic need for every teacher of social studies, especially the elementary teacher whose impossible assortment of subject-matter demands consume precious time. Beyond the college/university-course route and workshop sessions, affiliation with a related professional organization and monthly examination of a few key journals will help keep you abreast of social studies ferment. Two organizations specifically focused on the social studies and their addresses are:

National Council for the Social Studies
1201 Sixteenth St. N.W.
Washington, D.C. 20036

National Council for Geographic Education
115 North Marion St.
Oak Park, Ill. 60301

Both councils publish a monthly journal and an annual yearbook focusing on a timely theme, and each holds an annual conference lasting several days, highlighting all the recent developments in the profession. Their respective journals are *Social Education* and *The Journal of Geography*.

An independently published journal, *The Social Studies,* also follows the state of the profession and is issued monthly. A number of other journals publish articles that should be of interest to teachers of social studies in terms of providing either subject-matter background or information on teaching materials and strategies. One of the easiest and quickest ways to identify such related articles is to consult the weekly publication *Current Contents: Behavioral Sciences.* It represents the findings of an information retrieval source that reproduces the table of contents of over 700 periodicals in education and the social sciences and generally will be found in the periodical section of a library. By consulting *Current Contents* for 15 or 20 minutes each week, one quickly gains access to the contents of a large number of periodicals without the usual need for scanning individual journals. If a library does not subscribe to a periodical listed, *Current Contents* will supply a copy of an article for a fee.

The *Current Index to Journals in Education (CIJE)* is usually housed in the reference section of a library and offers a more conventional information retrieval service. A similar number of journals are scanned by *CIJE,* but one locates relevant articles by using an index that is keyed to topics discussed in the article. Both are useful tools, but each does slightly different things.

A third easily consulted source for reference information on new ideas and developments is *Dissertation Abstracts International,* also usually located in the reference section of a library. Listed by topics and according to the year of publication are abstracts of most of the doctoral dissertations in the United States. By reading the short summary listed under each dissertation title, one can discover the essence of a study's findings.

The federal government also has established the Educational Resources Information Center (ERIC) Clearinghouse for Social Studies/ Social Science Education (ChESS), 855 Broadway, Boulder, Colo. 80302. ERIC/ChESS was commissioned to catalog, abstract, and index relevant documents in its subject area. The Clearinghouse transmits findings of ongoing research in social studies as obtained from papers presented at educational conferences and progress reports of researchers. Many of these papers are never published in journals and otherwise might never be made available to a wide audience. In addition, it publishes a newsletter, bulletins, bibliographies, and commissions studies of special-interest topics, such as environmental education. To date the role of ERIC/ChESS largely has been to expedite dissemination, and to some extent diffusion, rather than evaluation.

With respect to listing of curriculum materials, a basic source of information is the *Data Book,* published by the Social Science Education Consortium, 855 Broadway, Boulder, Colo. 80302. It lists many of the newer textbook series, a variety of social studies projects, and assorted materials such as simulation games, along with a brief evaluation statement for each item. A fine source of information on a limited range of materials is the *Social Studies Service Catalog,* still available free on request (as we go to press) from the Service at 10,000 Culver Blvd., Culver City, Calif. 90030. It lists for sale almost 200 pages of filmstrips, transparencies, simulations and games, filmloops, records, maps, and assorted other paraphernalia.

While the social science and the humanities offer a myriad of books including best sellers, for a teacher who wishes to become more knowledgeable in subject matter, several books and series have been written expressly with the idea of communicating succinctly the nature of the disciplines. Among these are the works listed under note 2.

Finally, and perhaps most obviously, to plug in, take an active interest in your society at any level—local, state, national, or international. As you consciously intersect personally and vicariously with the ongoing social drama that surrounds us all daily, you begin to *live* social studies and to enhance your teaching potential. Become an actor or a viewer, but get in on the show!

NOTES

[1] Bureau of Education, "The Social Studies in Secondary Education," Bulletin No. 28 (Washington, D.C., 1916).

[2] See, for example, Raymond H. Muessing and Vincent R. Rogers (eds.), *Social Science Seminar Series,* 6 vols. (Columbus, Ohio: Merrill, 1965); Erling M. Hunt et al., *High School Social Studies Perspectives* (Boston: Houghton Mifflin, 1962); Irving Morrissett and W. Williams Stevens, Jr. (eds.), *Social Science in the Schools: A Search for Rationale* (New York: Holt, Rinehart & Winston, 1971); Irving Morrissett (ed.), *Concepts and Structure in the New Social Science Curricula* (New York: Holt, Rinehart & Winston, 1967); John U. Michaelis and A. Montgomery Johnston (eds.), *The Social Sciences, Foundations of the Social Studies* (Boston; Allyn & Bacon, 1965); William T. Lowe, *Structure and the Social Studies* (Ithaca, N.Y.: Cornell University Press, 1969); G. W. Ford and Lawrence Pugno, *The Structure of Knowledge and the Curriculum* (Chicago: Rand McNally, 1964); Mark M. Krug, *History and the Social Sciences: New Approaches to the Teaching of Social Studies* (Waltham, Mass.: Ginn/Blaisdell, 1967); and Bernard Berelson et al., *The Social Studies and the Social Sciences* (New York: Harcourt Brace Jovanovich, 1962).

[3] For a basic summary of the early part of the period, see Edwin Fenton, *The New Social Studies* (New York: Holt, Rinehart & Winston, 1967).

[4] Many of these series are listed in Chapter 3, p. 61.

[5] Quoted in Shirley H. Engle, "Exploring the Meaning of the Social Studies," *Social Education, 35* (March 1971), 280–288, 344.

[6] Paul R. Hanna, "Revising the Social Studies: What Is Needed?," *Social Education,* 27 (April, 1963), 192.

[7] R. Murray Thomas and Dale L. Brubaker, *Decisions in Teaching Elementary Social Studies* (Belmont, Calif.: Wadsworth, 1971), p. 125.

[8] Bruce R. Joyce, *New Strategies for Social Education* (Chicago: Science Research Associates, 1972), pp. 266–284.

[9] Peter H. Martorella, "Needed Dimensions in a K–12 Social Studies Program," unpublished paper, Temple University, 1973.

[10] *Curriculum Guidelines of the National Council for the Social Studies* (Washington, D.C.: National Council for the Social Studies, in press).

11 For an excellent pro and con discussion of the issue, see W. James Popham et al., *Instructional Objectives* (Chicago: Rand McNally, 1969). For an example of how objectives may be developed in behavioral terms, see Julie S. Vargas, *Writing Worthwhile Behavioral Objectives* (New York: Harper & Row, 1972).

CHAPTER 3

Internalization Set #1

At the end of each module throughout this book there is a chapter called an Internalization Set. As noted in the Preface, each of these chapters contairs a sequence of activities that are designed to help the reader *clarify further, develop,* or *practice through application the ideas and prescriptions contained in previous chapters within the module.* These are meant to be an integral part of the book and are included to help make it a more interactive learning medium.

In some cases where this book is being used in a teacher-education program, the activities may be supplemented or replaced by others that an instructor deems necessary or appropriate. Many of the suggested exercises are to be done alone and require only basic resources that might be found in a library or instructional-materials center. More often than not, however, such individual activities require no additional materials other than the text. For still other exercises, peer groups or elementary/middle-school students may be required. Anticipating these latter types of activities, you may wish to make arrangements in advance for ongoing meetings and contacts, especially where activities within a classroom will be involved.

As the Preface indicated, unlike most books this one encourages you to write in it, tear out pages, and generally to interact with it. Your notations and additions with dates of entry help form a record of how you have changed and grown as you have used the text. Particularly in the Internalization Sets you may wish to insert an informal written record of your reactions and comments in the margins for future reference.

GETTING ACQUAINTED

In using this book within a teacher-education program you will be interacting with various groups of peers from time to time. Getting *to know* people is a far more complex and lengthy process than learning a few facts about them. Getting *acquainted* is a beginning, however, and it can help reveal some common interests, feelings, and concerns that can form the basis of more significant relationships. Two such get-acquainted activities are included here for groups of readers who have not already had a chance to learn some things about one another in some other contexts. *Skip these activities if your group has moved beyond this stage.*

ACTIVITY 1

Indicate your individual answer to each of the following questions in the space after them:

1. What is your favorite dessert? _____
2. What is your favorite television program? _____
3. What is the best film you have seen in the past few years? _____
4. If you could live any where in the world, where would it be? _____
5. Which living person do you admire the most? _____

Share your answers with your peers in groups of five or six. When you are finished, try to summarize the similarities and differences within the group. What are some things you have discovered about the others in your group?

ACTIVITY 2

Either a small group or an entire class can participate in this activity. Get forty-four sheets of paper size 8½" × 11" or larger and separate them into four sets of eleven each. Referring to the four columns of words listed below, print each of the words on the sheets *in the same order as listed*. Place the blank sheet in each pile on top.

A	B	C	D
Tall	Medium	Short	Other
Inner-City	Suburban	Rural	Other
Catholic	Protestant	Jew	Other
Learner	Helper	Teacher	Friend
Republican	Independent	Democrat	Disinterested
Action Oriented	Do Nothing	Go with Majority	Don't Get Involved
Liberal	Moderate	Radical	Conservative
Shy	Friendly	Sophisticated	Cautious
Young	Older	Middle-Aged	Prime-of-Life
Single	Married	"Shopping"	Other

By taping or some other means, place each of the stacks as organized in each of the four corners of the room on the wall or in some other visible place. Remove the blank top sheet from each stack and have the group make their choice for the first set of four items. The stacks all contain terms that we might use to describe ourselves. After looking at the four choices of terms in the first set, select one that best describes you. Move to the corner where the word that you feel best describes yourself is located.

After each selection, take a few minutes to talk about why you selected the term and how you feel about being with that group. When the discussion has run its course, remove the first set of terms and repeat the process, with everyone regrouping for discussion until all sets of terms have been exhausted. If it happens in some set that you cannot identify with any of the four terms, choose the one that is least uncomfortable to you.

THE FIRST YEAR

For many teachers the first year of teaching remains a special one that they will never forget. That initial period of being responsible for the educational growth of a group of children tends to create vivid impressions. For those about to embark on the first year, the waiting period can be mixed with apprehension as well as expectation. In the activity that follows you will read and be asked to respond to some random reactions from a group of first-year teachers commenting on their experiences with students, parents, other teachers, and administrators.

ACTIVITY 3

Examine the comments of the first-year teachers below in a group of five or six of your peers.[1] Identify some issues or concerns in the comments that are of particular interest to you and share your reactions, concerns, and questions with the group.

Teacher 1 The first year the most important thing to me was winning the kids' approval. Now I can look back and say, "OK, I don't need it; I can be a good teacher without everyone liking me."

Teacher 2 I've had to learn how free I could be. That's the hardest thing for a new teacher. At first everybody worked. I thought, man, this is neat—everybody does what they're told. Then I thought, what a bore. It's no fun. And I got a little too free. Now I know they can sense when I start setting my jaw even before I know I'm doing it. They know when to settle down. The hardest thing for me was to learn how to balance teacher control and class freedom.

Teacher 3 The first day I told my class to write two paragraphs, answering in the first "What is the most important thing I can know about you?" and in the second, "What's the most important thing about me you should know?" Most of them wanted to know what teed me off, what would make me explode. They know that every teacher has a boiling point. It's the first day and we're all being friendly. So I said, "I guess it would be a child pushing too far or answering back when I'm trying to be honest." We discussed it. Now they know what to expect and they're happy with that.

Teacher 4 I've considered leaving teaching. I began by saying teaching is marvelous—I've never done anything so fantastic in my life, and I really felt that way. But by the end of the year I was so unhappy with everything I considered maybe I should leave. I feel better, this minute, anyway. Today was just fine. You know, it isn't really just one day, though one bad day can make many days miserable. It's not the kids; I get along very well with kids. It's not the adults, either. But there are days when I really would like someone to come to my room, watch me, and say, "Oh marvelous! I've never seen a better teacher!" You know, maybe once every two weeks someone could do that for me and it would make my two weeks. It's silly, I suppose, but I guess I need approval from other people.

Teacher 5 I'm learning to use the group as a social unit and they're taking the lead. The tough kids don't hassle me and the others follow their lead. But there are times when I'll walk into a class and the kids just won't like me that day. It really has nothing to do with you. There are days when a third of the class is having a bad day and it's contagious. They just don't like you; in fact they hate you. What I've learned to do is laugh it off. I'll say, "You're in good form today! I can see that you really love me." One girl just made faces at me for a week. Finally, I called her up to my desk and said I hated to have faces made at me; it made me feel bad. So either she'd stop or I'd have to transfer her out because it hurt my feelings. She just never did it again. I think she didn't like her faces either, because now I tell her she looks nice and she even smiles.

Teacher 6 I was fighting with my principal every day. When my kids leave here they go to a school where lots of kids are on dope. My sixth-grade boys know what's going on and they come to me after school for information about drugs. I have a friend in the D.A.'s office and I wanted him to come out and talk to the kids about drugs. I could relate it beautifully to the chapter on drugs and alcohol and health. The principal said, "No, absolutely not, not in this school." And I said, "What do I do?" It's like having a pregnant child in the room and saying "I'm sorry, we can't have family life education." I said to him that these kids are coming to me right now for help. What do I think about all summer when they're going into that drug scene and they're asking me life and death questions right now and using the right words? When I know where they can buy it? And they do too.

Teacher 7 Some of them, the staff, are like a history teacher I had in high school. You know, I really admired her because there was never any question about what would happen in her class. You'd walk in, there'd be five questions on the blackboard, you'd read a certain number of pages and write the answers. You'd finish and look up and she'd say, "Are there any questions?" And as she said "questions" the bell would ring. I guess this was her way of controlling the classroom. Her performance and ours were predictable and there was minimal anxiety for her. Now I think that's awful— no exchange of information, no sharing, no real class or teaching.

Teacher 8 It's funny, but two of my best friends on the faculty are straight authoritarian teachers, the kind that say they wish they could hit the kids. I laugh at them because that's so absurd, as if punching kids did anything but make the need for violence even greater. But when I walk into their classroom I see that they're very much in touch with their kids. They're really communicating. They're telling jokes and the kids are having a great time. Those teachers are just as responsive to their kids as they are to me at the lunch table. When they come into my class they're shocked because it's so much more strict. Maybe philosophies have nothing to do with actual practice. When you get into the classroom it's just people.

Teacher 9 There's a teacher in my school who has the most fantastic rapport with some of his most disturbed children because, for some reason, he has this physical thing with them. They come over to him and want to touch him. They're eighth graders but they want this nursery school thing. You know, when you want to touch the teacher you hit the teacher; that's one way to touch the teacher. Now this guy doesn't know a concept from a hole in the blackboard. He teaches the book, chapter by chapter. "Progressive education, what's that?" But I truly admire the rapport he has with those kids. I couldn't be like him and I wouldn't try, but his students have a strong sense of his presence.

Teacher 10 The most agonizing thing that ever happened to me in teaching was with parents. Last summer I learned something about group processes and I thought it would help my class. I know that group process stuff can be dangerous but I only did harmless stuff. We did simple things such as lying on the floor, mentally exploring our bodies. Then we got up and walked around with our eyes closed. Parents started calling up asking that their kids be withdrawn from the class so they wouldn't be exposed to me. And a contingent of parents announced they were going to "take care" of me as soon as they got "their ammunition ready." And a month later a woman called up and said her daughter had had her blouse ripped off and all that guk. All lies, phony. I had permission from my principal. I asked the parents to come and face me with their accusations and they refused. They said I was to go to one of their homes at 7 o'clock in the evening. I refused. I felt it was risky and would put me at a great disadvantage, with all those people ready to tear into me. I felt they could come and see me in my own environment where it concerned them and on my terms. Nothing happened, and nobody ever said anything to me. They just took their kids out of my class. I was terribly upset.

Teacher 11 I usually have the problems of parents coming in and telling me how they really get on the kids—stand over them doing their homework, check their work, make a big fuss over grades, give them flack over everything having to do with school. My response is usually one of, "Well, you know, he's really a good kid; he's fine in my class. Maybe you should ease up."

Teacher 12 The principals are under pressures. Do you realize the number and range of organizations that they have to respond to? Well-organized, very conscientious, vocal. They have to deal with people who want to be involved in the curriculum. There was a call to our school last week: "Hear you're going to have a film on natural childbirth today." She was told she'd heard wrong. The film was about frogs. "I don't hear wrong," she said, and when the film went on, there she was. She got bored to death by the frogs.

Teacher 13 Or the law that says it's illegal for a teacher to live with someone of the opposite sex without marriage. I was warned on that one. I'm getting married to a girl on my faculty and we've been living together for quite a while. People warned me, "Hey, you can get fired." So I said, "OK, for them to find out that we're living together they'll have to invade my private life." Is that legal? And by the way, there are homosexuals on our faculty—who are very good teachers. If they're found out, their jobs are on the line. The circumstances under which the firing's done can be unbelievable. A teacher in another school, not mine, got fired on the basis of a phony story of his soliciting in another city when he could prove he wasn't even there. It took him two years in the courts before he proved it, and it didn't get him his job back.

When your group has completed its discussion of these teacher comments, select five or so of the quotations whose issues particularly interest you and show them to some practicing teachers, first-year or other. Ask them to react to the quotations in terms of their own experiences.

SCHOOL CODES

Many of us teach under a set of educational codes mandated by the states in which we instruct. Not all of them are well known by teachers or even strictly observed in the schools. Often these codes account for the structure of the social studies curriculum in our school district, although the influence of such guidelines varies across states. In addition to state leadership and mandates, many school districts have developed their own specific set of social studies guidelines, usually modeled on some pattern similar to the one discussed in Chapter 2. The two activities in this section give you an opportunity to learn more about the laws in your state concerning social studies courses of study to be used in school districts.

ACTIVITY 4

This activity has two basic parts and an optional third one. Initially you are asked to examine and give your opinions of the two state requirements below from the states of California and Pennsylvania. The first quotation is part of the *legal code* of the state of California; the second is part of the State Board of Education requirements in Pennsylvania. Complete the first phase of the activity with a group of peers.

Each teacher shall endeavor to impress upon the mind of the pupils the principles of morality, truth, justice, patriotism, and a true comprehension of the rights, duties, and dignity of American citizenship, to teach them to avoid idleness, profanity, and falsehood, and to instruct them in manners and morals and the principles of a free government. (*Education Code.* Sacramento, Calif.: State of California, 1963. Vol. 1, p. 356.)

The State Board has ordered that every course in U.S. History and Pennsylvania History taught in the elementary and secondary schools shall include the major contributions made by Negroes and other social and ethnic groups in the development of the United States and the Common-wealth [Pennsylvania]. (Source: Herbert E. Bryan [ed.], *A Handbook of Information on Pennsylvania Law and Legal Opinions Relating to Education.* Harrisburg, Pa.: Pennsylvania School Boards Association, 1973, p. 125.)

Once you have shared your reactions, you can determine what laws relating to the teaching of social studies exist in your state and similarly what guidelines are available. As an optional, additional activity, secure a copy of the American Civil Liberties Union publication *The Rights of Teachers* by David Rubin to determine what rights of teachers have been established in the courts across the United States. The book is organized in a simple question-and-answer format and cites specific judicial decisions and precedents that apply. If the book is not available in your library or bookstore, it may be obtained from the American Civil Liberties Union Inc., 156 Fifth Ave., New York, N.Y. 10010.

ACTIVITY 5

If your college or university library or instructional-materials center has a collection of curriculum guides for various school districts across the United States, including those in your local area, examine some of them to see what program suggestions they make. If such materials are not available, consult a few school districts in your area and ask to borrow or examine a set of their curriculum guidelines dealing with social studies. Not all districts will have them, but many do.

For future reference, make some notes on the titles and sources of the guidelines: what similarities you found in the guidelines, what unique features you encountered, and which set you preferred and why. As you visit schools and examine more materials in the future, be on the lookout for such guides. Some school districts make copies of their materials available to the general public for a nominal fee.

TEXTBOOKS, SERIES, AND CURRICULAR PROGRAMS

There are a variety of basal textbook series available today. Basal series refers to a sequence of texts meant to be the basic social studies program for a level. Many have relatively recent copyright dates and factually correct data. We shall argue later that there is much more to be considered in materials and textbooks than modernity and accurate facts. Suffice it to say that the assortment of texts listed here have various strengths and weaknesses, partly depending on what the reader/teacher/learner is seeking. The listing of the books is not exhaustive and in no way implies endorsement or recommendation; they are merely some series available and in varying degrees of use across the country.

ACTIVITY 6

Because of the static nature of the medium, every book is open to some criticism. The practical issue for every user is always whether the nature and scope of the criticism outweighs the merits of the book. Your task is to examine *three series* from those available to you on the list below. (There may be others you or your instructor may decide to add to the list; space is provided for them.) Working alone or with one other person, pick at least two textbooks and two teacher's guides/manuals from each series. Choose two sets at back-to-back grade levels (e.g., grades 1–2). Thus one collection for evaluation might be as follows: Series A—grades K–1, Series B—grades 3–4, Series C—grades 2–3. Any combination of three series and two sequential levels will do.

There are many ways to evaluate texts for different purposes. We shall use some straightforward questions that should be of general interest to all teachers. Compare the texts and teachers' guides/manuals on at least these criteria:

1. Is the information contained of real worth for children to know?
2. Does the material seem to have real interest potential for students?
3. Is the material developmentally suitable for children (i.e., does it ask them to perform intellectual operations for which they typically are not prepared)?
4. Is the material thought provoking?
5. How well do the two levels go together (i.e., does the transition from grade to grade seem smooth)?
6. What do you assess to be the greatest strengths and weaknesses of the series? (Remember, there always are some of each.)
7. What do you assess to be the greatest strengths and weaknesses of each of the teacher's guides/manuals?
8. Which series would you choose if you could only have one? Why?

After you have completed your evaluations, take some time to share and explain them with your peers. *This final step has been found to be one of the most beneficial parts of the activity.*

Basal Series

Concepts and Inquiry. Boston: Allyn & Bacon.
The Social Sciences: Concepts and Values. New York: Harcourt Brace Jovanovich.
Our Working World. Chicago: Science Research Associates.
Ginn Social Science Series. Boston: Ginn.
Man and His World. New York: Noble & Noble.
Field's Social Studies Program. San Francisco: Field Educational Publications.
The Taba Program in Social Science. Menlo Park, Calif.: Addison-Wesley.
Holt Databank System. New York: Holt, Rinehart & Winston.
McGraw-Hill Elementary Social Studies Series. New York: McGraw-Hill.
Our Family of Man. New York: Harper & Row.
Investigating Man's World. Glenview, Ill.: Scott, Foresman.
Social Studies: Focus on Active Learning. New York: Macmillan.
Social Studies Through Inquiry. Chicago: Rand McNally.

ACTIVITY 7

In addition to basal series and an almost limitless number of supplementary media and books, there are available a number of complete single-grade-level courses of study and programs designed to supplement a basal program. Subsequent chapters will detail many of these programs as appropriate to specific discussions. There are, however, too many of them to be discussed in any length. Many of them are the legacy of Project Social Studies, discussed in Chapter 2, while still others are simply the result of renewed commercial interest in the area of social studies.

This activity repeats the same basic procedures as Activity 6. It is designed to help you evaluate some of the many supplementary social studies programs available. All of the diverse materials listed contain a sequence of organized activities to be used over a period of time to supplement the basal program. They are but a selected sample of the many choices available. Choose any two of the programs that are available to you. In this case you may not need to be concerned about grade levels within a program, since some programs are designed as an integral unit cutting across grade levels. Where no grade levels are specified within the program an asterisk (*) precedes the title.

Using the same general criteria with some necessary modifications, the questions for evaluation are:

1. Is the information contained of real worth for children to know?
2. Does the material seem to have real interest potential for children?
3. Is the material developmentally suitable for children?
4. Is the material thought provoking?
5. What do you assess to be the greatest strengths and weaknesses for each of the programs?
6. What do you assess to be the greatest strengths and weaknesses of each of the teacher's guides/manuals?
7. Which program would you choose if you could only have one? Why?

As in Activity 6, the sharing of results and conclusions is an important final step in the activity.

Supplementary Programs

Social Science Laboratory Units. Chicago: Science Research Associates.
A Teaching Program for Education in Human Behavior and Potential. Cleveland: Educational Research Council.
Man: The Measure. Cleveland: Educational Research Council.
*Decision-Making. Boston: Beacon.
*Match Box Units, Boston: Boston Children's Museum.
*Ethnic Understanding Series. Los Angeles: Asian American Studies Central.
*First Things: Values Series. New York: Guidance Associates.
*First Things: Social Reasoning Series. New York: Guidance Associates.
*Focus on Self-Development. Chicago: Science Research Associates.
Human Development Program. La Mesa, Calif.: Human Development Training Institute.
Dimensions of Personality Series. Dayton, Ohio: Pflaum.
*Developing Understanding of Self and Others (DUSO). Circle Pines, Minn.: American Guidance Associates.
*Toward Affective Development. Circle Pines, Minn.: American Guidance Associates.

ACTIVITY 8

Depending upon the curriculum materials available in your library or instructional-materials center, you may be able to complete this activity only at one level. The first level of the task is to familiarize yourself with the range of single-grade and supplementary programs available that have not been cited in the two previous activities.

Two sources for listings of such materials that are especially useful are the November 1972 issue of *Social Education* (periodical published during most months of the school year by the National Council for the Social Studies; this issue lists many of the major social studies projects) and the *Social Studies Curriculum Materials Data Book*, Social Science Education Consortium, Boulder, Colo. The latter reference source is a relatively complete and periodically updated collection of textbook series, single-grade programs, supplementary programs, and various materials.

At the second level, you are to familiarize yourself with the procedures and materials in one of the programs you have identified from the references. Follow the general analysis procedures spelled out in Activity 8 to complete your evaluation.

ACTIVITY 9

Textbooks have been one of the most criticized elements of school programs; they have been attacked at different times for different reasons by all segments of the community and the academic world. How much say do you think various groups, including parents, should have over the content of social studies textbooks? Before you answer, read the following excerpt from a speech by Terrel Bell, U.S. Commissioner of Education, to the Association of American Publishers:

> As scholars prepare new textbooks and other materials, as you publish them and schools select them I hope everyone involved will keep in mind the idea behind an anecdote I heard the other day.
>
> Following some dispute or other, Johnny pokes his classmate Robert in the nose. Naturally, the teacher chastised Johnny for this action, and Johnny replied: "It's a free country, I know my rights."
>
> "Well, yes," the teacher said, "you have rights, the same rights your classmates have and every American has. But your rights end where Robert's nose begins."
>
> I think this little story says some important things. In writing textbooks and other materials for school use scholars do have the rights, indeed the obligations, to present new knowledge and to comment on social changes in ways that will stimulate and motivate students, excite their curiosity, and make them want to learn.
>
> Teachers have both the right and obligation to use these materials in ways that will enhance the learning program. Indeed, teachers are getting to be very creative in developing supplementary materials to illustrate and expand on textbook themes, and this creativity should be encouraged.
>
> But I feel strongly that the scholar's freedom of choice and the teacher's freedom of choice must have the approval and support of most parents. I do not suggest that we seek to win approval of all parents, for that would not be attainable—but schools without parental support and approval are headed for failure.
>
> Without having books and materials that are so namby-pamby they avoid all controversy, we must seek published materials that do not insult the

values of most parents. Where there is basic conflict, no one really wins, and children suffer. However, parents have the ultimate responsibility for the upbringing of their children, and their desire should take precedence. The school's authority ends where it infringes on their parental rights.

So I think the children's book publishing industry, and the schools, need to chart a middle course between the scholar's legitimate claim to academic freedom in presenting new knowledge and social commentary on the one hand, and the legitimate expectations of parents that schools will respect their moral and ethical values on the other.

What the present controversy comes down to, I believe, is a growing concern on the part of parents that they have lost control over their children's education and therefore over their children's future.[2]

Develop your own thoughts on this subject *before* reading the next section. *Stop.*

After you have reflected on where you stand, read the following analysis of the National Education Association's response to Bell's speech. Then reassess your own view:

The National Education Association followed up Bell's speech with a warning to its state and local units that "a lively, realistic portrayal of contemporary American problems . . . is threatening to those parents who want schools to stress traditional virtues and ignore unpopular or unpleasant ideas."

To beat off attempts to ban controversial curricular materials, the NEA advised its local chapter "to negotiate written policy governing selection of instructional materials and the procedure for handling challenges." This should be a priority bargaining item, the NEA advised. "There should be clear agreement that teachers will remain the primary decision makers, with the school board having the final say," the teachers' organization added.

"In replacing the idealized world of the traditional textbook . . . publishers have satisfied teachers and parents who see the public school as a marketplace of ideas where children can learn to think for themselves," the NEA said.

Thus the new direction in some of today's textbooks generates both praise and alarm. The debate is as old as education. The new twist is the involvement of the USOE. In earlier textbook controversies, the USOE carefully avoided taking a stand.[3]

After you have reassessed your position, consider the action of a local school board in Kanawha County, W.Va., April 1975, in response to a persistent violence-ridden series of protests by community groups over textbooks used in the schools. It adopted a policy that all new texts:

Must recognize the sanctity of the home and emphasize its importance as the basic unit of American society.

Must not contain profanity.

Must encourage loyalty to the United States and emphasize the responsibilities of citizenship and the obligation to redress grievances through the legal process . . . [and must not] teach or imply that an alien form of government is superior.

Shall teach the true history and heritage of the United States. . . . Must not defame our nation's founders or misrepresent the ideals and causes for which they struggled and sacrificed.

Shall teach that traditional rules of grammar are a worthwhile subject for academic pursuit. . . .[4]

How do you react to the policy the school board adopted?

Finally, reflect upon and consider to what extent you agree with the following statement on academic freedom excerpted from Yale University's Woodward Committee report and recommendation on academic freedom. It was developed in response to a campus audience's abridgement of an invited speaker's right to voice genetic views that were perceived by many as "racist":

> The primary function of the university is to discover and disseminate knowledge by means of research and teaching. To fulfill this function a free interchange of ideas is necessary not only within its walls but with the world beyond as well. It follows that the university must do everything possible to ensure within it the fullest degree of intellectual freedom. The history of intellectual growth and discovery clearly demonstrates the need for unfettered freedom, the right to think the unthinkable, discuss the unmentionable, and challenge the unchallengeable. To curtail free expression strikes twice at intellectual freedom, for whoever deprives another of the right to state unpopular views necessarily deprives others of the right to listen to those views.
>
> We take a chance, as the First Amendment takes a chance, when we commit ourselves to the idea that the results of free expression are to the general benefit in the long run however unpleasant they may appear at the time. The validity of such a belief cannot be demonstrated conclusively. It is a belief of recent historical development, even within universities, one embodied in American constitutional doctrine but not widely shared outside the academic world, and denied in theory and in practice by much of the world most of the time. . . .
>
> Without sacrificing its central purpose, [a university] cannot make its primary and dominant value the fostering of friendship, solidarity, harmony, civility, or mutual respect. To be sure, these are important values; other institutions may properly assign them the highest, and not merely a subordinate priority; and a good university will seek and may in some significant measure attain these ends. But it will never let these values, important as they are, override its central purpose. We value freedom of expression precisely because it provides a forum for the new, the provocative, the disturbing, and the unorthodox. Free speech is a barrier to the tyranny of authoritarian or even majority opinion as to the rightness or wrongness of particular doctrines or thoughts. . . .
>
> Shock, hurt, and anger are not consequences to be weighed lightly. No member of the community with a decent respect for others should use, or encourage others to use, slurs and epithets intended to discredit another's race, ethnic group, religion, or sex. . . .
>
> But even when some members of the university community fail to meet their social and ethical responsibilities, the paramount obligation of the university is to protect their right to free expression. This obligation can and should be enforced by appropriate formal sanctions. If the university's overriding commitment to free expression is to be sustained, secondary social and ethical responsibilities must be left to the informal processes of suasion, example, and argument.[5]

COLLECTOR'S ITEMS

Teachers, by nature of their profession, must be great collectors. They collect pictures, articles, artifacts, slides, and many other items that someday may help illuminate their instruction or bring some further enjoyment to a child. It would be helpful and will save many hours of sorting and refiling if early in your career you develop some simple categorization scheme and storage containers for collecting your items. What you store there is almost limitless. Two general all-purpose types of items likely to be of some value for all curricular programs are data on states and data on countries.

ACTIVITY 10

Embassies and consulates and state tourism departments are easily accessible sources of great amounts of material. What they supply will be of varying quality, usually written to impress you with the virtue of the areas they represent, but generally laden with pictures, maps, and a considerable amount of objective background data, too. Moreover, the material is usually free. Develop a simple form letter stating the nature of your request and your reasons for it (i.e., prepare you to teach more knowledgably and better inform students about the country/state) and write to embassies and state departments.

The list of state departments and their addresses is given below:

Alabama Bureau of Publicity and Information, State Highway Building, Room 403, Montgomery, Ala. 36104.

Alaska Division of Tourism, Pouch E, Juneau, Alas. 99801.

Arizona Visitor Section, Department of Economic Planning and Development, 3003 North Central, Suite 1704, Phoenix, Ariz. 85012.

Arkansas Department of Parks and Tourism, 149 State Capitol, Little Rock, Ark. 72201.

California State Office of Tourism, 1400 Tenth St., Sacramento, Calif. 95814.

Colorado Tourism Department, Division of Commerce and Development, 602 State Capitol Annex, Denver, Colo. 80203.

Connecticut Vacation Travel Bureau, Development Commission, State Office Building, P.O. Box 865, Hartford, Ct. 06115.

Delaware Bureau of Travel Development, 45 The Green, Dover, Del. 19901.

Florida Tourist Division, Department of Commerce, Collins Building, 107 W. Gaines, Tallahassee, Fla. 32304.

Georgia Tourist Division, Department of Community Development, P.O. Box 38097, Atlanta, Ga. 30334.

Hawaii Visitors Bureau, 2270 Kalakaua Ave., Suite 801, Honolulu, Hawaii 96815.

Idaho Department of Commerce and Development, Capitol Building, Boise, Id. 83720.

Illinois Tourism Division, Department of Business and Economic Development, 205 W. Wacker Dr., Chicago, Ill. 60604.

Indiana Division of Tourism, State House, Room 336, Indianapolis, Ind. 46204.

Iowa Tourism Department, Development Commission, 250 Jewett Building, Des Moines, Ia. 50309.

Kansas Travel Division, Department of Economic Development, State Office Building, Room 122-S, Topeka, Kan. 66612.

Kentucky Tourist Division, Department of Public Information, Capitol Annex, Frankfort, Ky. 40601.

Louisiana Tourist Commission, P.O. Box 44291, Baton Rouge, La. 70804.

Maine Tourism Division, Department of Commerce and Industry, State Office Building, Augusta, Me. 04330.

Maryland Tourism Division, Department of Economic and Community Development, 2525 Riva Rd., Annapolis, Md. 21401.

Massachusetts Division of Tourism, Department of Commerce and Development, 100 Cambridge St., Boston, Mass. 02202.

Michigan Tourist Council, 300 S. Capitol Ave., Suite 102, Lansing, Mich. 48926.

Minnesota Tourism Division, Department of Economic Development, 51 E. Eighth St., St. Paul, Minn. 44101.

Mississippi Travel and Tourist Department, Agricultural and Industrial Board, 2000 Walter Sillers Office Building, Jackson, Miss. 39205.

Missouri Tourism Commission, 308 E. High St., Jefferson City, Mo. 65101.

Montana Tourist Department, Highway Commission, Helena, Mont. 59601.

Nebraska Tourist Division, Department of Economic Development, State Capitol, P.O. Box 95665, Lincoln, Neb. 62509.

Nevada Travel and Tourist Division, Department of Economic Development, Carson City, Nev. 89701.

New Hampshire Vacation Travel Department, Division of Resources and Economic Development, P.O. Box 856, Concord, N.H. 03301.

New Jersey Tourism Department, Division of Economic Development, P.O. Box 2766, Trenton, N.J. 08625.

New Mexico Tourist Division, Department of Development, 113 Washington Ave., Santa Fe, N.M. 87501.

New York New York State Department of Agriculture, State Campus, Albany, N.Y. 12226. Attn: Vincent Gutsch, Division Affairs.

North Carolina Travel Division, Department of Natural and Economic Resources, P.O. Box 27687, Raleigh, N.C. 27611.

North Dakota Travel Division, Highway Department, Capitol Grounds, Bismarck, N.D. 58501.

Ohio Travel and Tourist Bureau, Department of Economic and Community Development, 65 S. Front St., Columbus, Ohio 43215.

Oklahoma Tourism and Recreation Department, 504 Will Rogers Building, Oklahoma City, Okla. 73105.

Oregon Tourist Department, State Highway Division, 101 Highway Building, Salem, Ore. 91310.

Pennsylvania Tourist Division, Department of Commerce, 402 S. Office Building, Harrisburg, Pa. 17120.

Rhode Island Tourist Division, Development Council, Roger Williams Building, Providence, R.I. 02908.

South Carolina Department of Parks, Recreation and Tourism, 2712 Middleburg Dr., Columbia, S.C. 29202.

South Dakota Travel Section, Department of Highways, Pierre, S.D. 57501.

Tennessee Tourism Division, Department of Economic and Community Development, 1019 Andrew Jackson State Building, Nashville, Tenn. 37219.

Texas Texas Tourist Development Agency, P.O. Box 12008, Capitol Station, Austin, Tex. 78711.

Utah Travel Council, Capitol Hill, Council Hall, Salt Lake City, Utah 84114.

Vermont Travel Division, Agency of Development and Community Affairs, 26 Elm St., Montpelier, Vt. 05602.

Virginia State Travel Service, 911 E. Broad St., Richmond, Va. 23219.

Washington Travel Development Division, Department of Commerce and Economic Development, General Administration Building, Olympia, Wash. 98504.

West Virginia Travel Development, State Capitol Building 6, Charleston, W.Va. 25305.

Wisconsin Vacation and Travel Service, Department of Natural Resources, Box 450, Madison, Wisc. 57303.

Wyoming Travel Commission, 2320 Capitol Ave., Cheyenne, Wyo. 82001.

A similar list for embassies is available in many almanacs, for example *The New York Times Encyclopedia Almanac*. Rather than one person writing to all the agencies, you may wish to divide up sources and plan to share the results at a specified date. In this way you can make a decision on which materials are of most value for a large number of people to request. Keep in mind that state and foreign offices frequently change addresses or temporarily suspend public relation services; so, be prepared for a few disappointments and returned letters.

MAKE LIKE A HISTORIAN/SOCIAL SCIENTIST

Every person is a historian and social scientist. We are all called upon daily to reflect on some elements of our past, use them to inject meaning into our present, and make some estimates about the future. Similarly we make myriad inferences throughout the day. Some are small ones ("It's going to rain," upon seeing black clouds and hearing thunder) and some are giant leaps ("The economy is well on the way to recovery," upon noting that the Dow-Jones average went up 10 points yesterday). We generate hypotheses, we bring past experiences and other relevant data to bear upon them, jump or crawl to some conclusions, and expect to modify them at some point in the future when we get smarter. Most of us also practice the craft of becoming increasingly more knowledgable about some small sphere of our social world, be it the battle of Hellespont or the complex social, economic, political, geographic, psychological, historical, legal, and whatever structure of professional sports in this country. Some of us use more abstract means to collect our data (e.g., books), while others gather them first-hand; some pursue academic sources for their information, while others seek first-hand accounts. ("What's it really like to be in the big leagues, Jock—tell all of our viewers out there.") We are all tied by a common bond, our general processes of arriving at increasingly more accurate information and our focus on social phenomena.

In the five Internalization Sets that follow this one, you will have opportunities to touch base with the various disciplines in further practicing and refining this craft. Several activities are included here at the beginning of the book to remind you at the outset that all would-be teachers of social studies must themselves continue to be social learners in order to encourage others toward similar pursuits.

ACTIVITY 11

One of the basic tools of the cultural anthropologist for coming to understand cultural phenomena is *ethnographic fieldwork*. Fundamentally, *ethnography* is the process of describing in detail some aspect of a culture. As the focus becomes narrower in scope (e.g., a particular drug store, beauty parlor, etc.), the process is referred to as microethnography. A primer on conducting microethnographics is available for beginners: James P. Spradley and David W. McCurdy, *The Cultural Experience: Ethnography in a Complex Society,* Chicago: Science Research Associates, 1972.

For the basic activity that follows, our project and procedures are simple and loose. It is adapted from the chapter entitled "Ethnographic Field Work" in *Involvement in Anthropology Today*.[6]

You are to record as much data about one individual as possible within a 1½–2-hour period. Use a tape recorder for data collection if available and comfortable for the informant (the one who tells you about your subject).

Pick a person who is culturally different from you in some way (e.g., ethnically, racially, or socioeconomically). Be sure that he or she is cooperative, can verbalize ideas and feelings easily, has had varied experiences, and has reflected on his or her life and experiences.

Record the life story of that individual. Include and focus upon earliest recollections; places lived; childhood practices, problems, pleasant memories; relatives who have been a factor in his or her life and in what way; friends who have been a factor in the informant's life and in what way; life crises and transitions from such crises to stability; occupations and the experiences in preparing for them.

Once the data have been gathered, try to form some tentative answers to questions such as these:

1. How much and what did the informant recall, and how much and what was he or she unable to recall?

2. Aside from what you asked, about what did your subject seem most inclined to talk?
3. How has he or she adjusted to the changes in his or her culture and to the changes in the overall culture of which he or she was a part?
4. Have cultural standards and practices changed much over time?
5. What conclusions can you draw about this person's life?

ACTIVITY 12

Read the following excerpt from an ethnographic account of a particular group of people. The account is taken from the article "Body Ritual Among the Nacirema," by Horace Miner:

Nacirema culture is characterized by a highly developed market economy which has evolved in a rich natural habitat. While much of the people's time is devoted to economic pursuits, a large part of the fruits of these labors and a considerable portion of the day are spent in ritual activity. The focus of this activity is the human body, the appearance and health of which loom as a dominant concern in the ethos of the people. While such a concern is certainly not unusual, its ceremonial aspects and associated philosophy are unique.

The fundamental belief underlying the whole system appears to be that the human body is ugly and that its natural tendency is to debility and disease. Incarcerated in such a body, a man's only hope is to avert these characteristics through the use of the powerful influences of ritual and ceremony. Every household has one or more shrines devoted to this purpose. The more powerful individuals in the society have several shrines in their houses, and in fact, the opulence of a house is often referred to in terms of the number of such ritual centers it possesses. Most houses are of wattle and daub construction, but the shrine rooms of the more wealthy are walled with stone. Poorer families imitate the rich by applying pottery plaques to their shrine walls.

While each family has at least one such shrine, the rituals associated with it are not family ceremonies but are private and secret. The rites are normally only discussed with children, and then only during the period when they are being initiated into these mysteries. I was able, however, to establish sufficient rapport with the natives to examine these shrines and to have the rituals described to me.

The focal point of the shrine is a box or chest which is built into the wall. In this chest are kept the many charms and magical potions without which no native believes he could live. These preparations are secured from a variety of specialized practitioners. The most powerful of these are the medicine men whose assistance must be rewarded with substantial gifts. However, the medicine men do not provide the curative potions for their clients, but decide what the ingredients should be and then write them down in an ancient and secret language. This writing is understood only by the medicine men and by the herbalists who, for another gift, provide the required charms.[7]

Based on an admittedly small sample of data, what conclusions can you draw about this group of people? How do you feel toward them? What further questions concerning them would you like to ask?

After you have responded to these questions, locate the journal article in your library (it is a commonly found professional journal) to read the entire article and to find out more about the people and in what part of the world they live. When you complete the article, reflect on what you have learned both about culture and about anthropologists.

ACTIVITY 13

This activity deals with historiography.[8] For the first phase, a group of five or six peers may be helpful to generate hypotheses. It requires you to reflect on the nature of facts and how they are verified.

Tradition has it that on September 1, 1854, a few months after reopening the slavery question by introducing the Kansas-Nebraska Bill, Stephen A Douglas, the "Little Giant," stood before a hostile crowd in Chicago and attempted to justify his action. Booed, jeered, and hissed, Douglas held his ground for over two hours, determined that he would be listened to. Finally, so the story goes, he pulled out his watch, which showed a quarter after twelve, and shouted: "It is now Sunday morning—I'll go to church and you may go to Hell."

How does a historian verify his or her doubts about an interesting catchy story such as this one? What steps might you take to try to verify this story? What clues would you follow up and how would you go about it? Write your responses below:

_____

_____

_____

_____

_____

_____

_____

Once you have decided how you might go about it, examine the actual steps taken by one scholar to validate or refute this legendary story. Consult the article by Granville D. Davis, "Douglas and the Chicago Mob," *American Historical Review, 54* (April 1949), 553–556.

ACTIVITY 14

There are a number of important and useful works on history and the social sciences to consider. No one person could begin to read all of the general books on the topic, let alone the specific ones dealing with individual specialties. A nucleus of four selected suggestions for further advanced reference are included here; the books cited deal with the topic in general.[9] More detailed suggestions and specific bibliographies for individual disciplines may be found in David L. Sills (ed.), *International Encyclopedia of the Social Sciences*, 17 vols., New York: Macmillan, 1968. Examine one or more of them.

Leonard I. Krimerman (ed.), *The Nature and Scope of Social Science: A Critical Anthology*. New York: Appleton, 1969.

Charles A. Beard, *The Nature of the Social Sciences*. New York: Scribner, 1934.

John Michaelis and A. Montgomery Johnston (eds.), *The Social Sciences, Foundations of the Social Studies*. Boston: Allyn & Bacon, 1965.

Bernard Berelson and Gary A. Steiner, *Human Behavior: An Inventory of Scientific Findings*. New York: Harcourt Brace Jovanovich, 1964.

PLUGGING IN TO THE FIELD

"Plugging in" to the field involves minimally reviewing its basic literature. Beyond that point it requires some form of commitment and sense of participation in the larger community of activity. The first activity suggested involves reviewing the periodicals basic to the profession. The second involves an opportunity to participate in the National Council for the Social Studies, the professional base of social studies teachers, by electing to become a member.

ACTIVITY 15

Locate the two periodicals *Social Education* and *The Social Studies* in your library or instructional-materials center. Examine all of the issues for the past two years to get some idea of the sorts of things the periodicals contain and the types of topics and materials discussed. Find at least five articles from five different months for each periodical that particularly interest you.

Read them; jot down their titles, authors, issues, and pages for future reference; and share your results and reactions with a group of your peers. Try to review these periodicals each month as new issues appear.

ACTIVITY 16

An application for membership in the National Council for the Social Studies is a commitment to work with other professionals in learning more about and improving social studies programs, materials, and instruction. By being a member you get the satisfaction of contributing to a goal within a larger community, a yearbook, a periodic newsletter, a subscription to *Social Education*, and a chance to participate in the annual conference of the organization.

If you elect to join, make up a simple facsimilie of the application shown on p. 73 and forward it with the membership fee indicated to the address listed. You may elect to join as a student, if this is your formal status, and receive a reduced rate and some reduced benefits (no yearbook or newsletter).

For office use only

| 11 | | | 12 | | | 13 | | | 14 | | | 15 | | 16 | | 18 | | | | | 19 | | 20 | | 21 | | 30 | |

INDIVIDUAL MEMBERSHIP APPLICATION

MR MS DR	FIRST	INIT		LAST

EXTRA ADDRESS LINE

STREET OR P.O. BOX

CITY	STATE	ZIP CODE

Please provide information requested below. Names of affiliated councils to which you belong are crucial to delegate representation at the Annual Meeting.	NCSS MEMBERSHIP IS: ☐ NEW ☐ RENEWAL

Position:	Grade Level:	Subject:

Local Council:

State Council:

Regional Council:

☐ **REGULAR:** *Social Education* (Oct.-May); Periodic NCSS newsletter; paperbound *Yearbook* (to members as of March 31). **$15.00**

☐ **COMPREHENSIVE:** All publications issued during year of membership (clothbound *Yearbook* to members as of March 31). **$25.00**

☐ **SUBSCRIPTION:** *Social Education* only. **$15.00**

☐ **STUDENT:** *Social Education;* NCSS newsletter **$ 7.50**
(Full-time students only; instructor certification required.)

INSTRUCTOR CERTIFICATION
INSTITUTION

☐ **SSSA:** Social Studies Supervisors Association. **$ 3.00**
(NCSS membership is a prerequisite.)

☐ **CUFA:** College and University Faculty Assembly; **$ 7.50**
Students $1 (NCSS membership is a prerequisite.)

Total Amount Enclosed _____

Send check or money order to:

NATIONAL COUNCIL FOR THE SOCIAL STUDIES
1515 Wilson Blvd., Arlington, Virginia 22209

NOTES

[1] This collection of teacher comments is taken from Eli M. Bower, *Teachers Talk About Their Feelings* (Rockville, Md.: National Institute of Mental Health, 1973), pp. 1–28.

[2] Terrell Bell, quoted in *The Philadelphia Inquirer* (December 13, 1974), 11A.

[3] Quoted in George Neill, "Washington Reports," *Phi Delta Kappan* (February 1975), 435–436.

[4] Quoted in *The Philadelphia Inquirer* (March 2, 1975), 8A.

[5] Quoted in *The New York Times* (January 26, 1975), 16E.

[6] *Involvement in Anthropology Today* (Delmar, Calif.: CRM, 1971), pp. 108–109.

[7] Horace Miner, "Body Ritual Among the Nacirema," *American Anthropologist,* 58, No. 3 (1956), 503–507.

[8] This activity was provided by Michael Wallace, a graduate student at Temple University.

[9] See also the list of books cited in note 2, Chapter 2.

MODULE SUMMARY

Social studies has been and remains many things to many people. While the thematic structure of social studies has remained constant over the years, the content of courses of study and curriculum materials, as well as the teaching strategies, have changed. Much of the shift was occasioned by the flurry of curricular activities in the 1960s, which in turn were spurred on by injection of federal funds and Brunerian ideas. A legacy of that period of excitement and turmoil was the notion that basic concepts and generalizations could provide the structure of the social studies curriculum. This notion was interpreted in many ways, and no single structure was ever agreed upon by the profession. The net result, however, was a closer identification of social studies with the combined disciplines of history, political science, economics, geography, anthropology, sociology, and psychology, with emphasis on the newer social sciences.

At levels K–6, the expanding-communities-of-men notion of curriculum design popularized by Paul Hanna has virtually been institutionalized as a national pattern, although a number of equally defensible schema for curriculum organization exist. Several alternative approaches have been outlined in the preceding chapters, along with a specimen of curriculum guidelines from a major state.

Goal setting, organizing instruction, and planning are the heart of a social studies teacher's task. Goal setting refers to the process of identifying ends that direct immediate, intermediate, and long-range instructional organization. The latter term describes the process of moving from goals to sequenced activities designed to achieve the goals. The ways in which such activities are articulated or specified may take a variety of forms, some behavioral and some nonbehavioral. Goals determine the nature of the specifications and not vice versa. Planning, as described, involves using available time constructively to achieve significant, attainable goals. A number of alternative forms for specifying activities have been provided.

Keeping abreast of new developments in the social studies is a difficult task for the contemporary elementary teacher. The continuing knowledge explosion in the social sciences only aggrevates the problem. A series of resources for "plugging in" to the future were identified, including professional organization, books, reference works, and periodicals.

SUGGESTED READINGS

American Council of Learned Societies and the National Council for the Social Studies. *The Social Studies and the Social Sciences.* New York: Harcourt Brace Jovanovich, 1962.

Curriculum Guidelines of the National Council for the Social Studies. Washington, D.C.: National Council for the Social Studies, in press.

Engle, Shirley. "Exploring the Meaning of the Social Studies," *Social Education*, 25 (March 1971), 280–288, 344.

Fenton, Edwin. *The New Social Studies*. New York: Holt, Rinehart & Winston, 1967.

Fraser, Dorothy McClure (ed.). *Social Studies Curriculum Development: Prospects and Problems*. Thirty-ninth Yearbook. Washington, D.C.: National Council for the Social Studies, 1972.

Goldmark, Bernice. *Social Studies: A Method of Inquiry*. Belmont, Calif.: Wadsworth, 1968.

Joyce, Bruce R. *New Strategies for Social Education*. Chicago: Science Research Associates, 1972.

Performance Education: Social Studies Teacher Competencies. Albany, N.Y.: State Education Department, 1973.

Popham, W. James, et al. *Instructional Objectives*. Chicago: Rand McNally, 1969.

Social Studies Curriculum Materials: Data Book. Boulder, Colo.: Social Science Education Consortium, 1971.

Wehlage, Gary, and Eugene M. Anderson. *Social Studies Curriculum in Perspective: A Conceptual Analysis*. Englewood Cliffs, N.J.: Prentice-Hall, 1972.

MODULE II

Instructional Models and Their Applications: Concepts and Concept Learning

MODULE II

Instructional Models and Their Applications: Concepts and Concept Learning

We sort out the pieces of our life into little drawers.
Everything we have ever done or known is in one of them.

SICILIAN PROVERB

CHAPTER 4

Concepts and the Curriculum

Imagine a pink object larger than a house slowly hopping down the street. It has a large green hand extended from its top that is waving furiously. Strange sounds and flashing lights emerge from the object as it stops at each house along the block.

What would you make of such an object? How would you label it and relate it to your past experiences? And how would you react to it?

In many respects this hypothetical event corresponds to the constant realities of concept learning for children. New objects and events are to varying degrees alike or different from known ones. When they differ radically, they puzzle, disturb, or frighten; we are uncertain of how to respond to them or how we will be affected by them. A child encountering his or her first airplane might feel very much like a person spotting the hypothetical large pink object described above.

THE NATURE OF CONCEPTS

The ways in which we sort out, relate, discriminate, and label new and old objects and events form our conceptual world. As we progress developmentally and grow in our knowledge, experiences, and intellectual capabilities, our conceptual "boxes" are refined, extended, and multiplied. Instead of just one box labeled "planes," we acquire "jets," "props," and "gliders"; we distinguish between "planes," "blimps," "helicopters," "bombers," and "transports" and learn why one object that can go 200 kilometers per hour flies while another does not. A concept represents a set of common characteristics among a group of objects or events, and as we become more aware of similarities and differences and make more subtle observations, we create more and more complex conceptual boxes and linkages. In its simplest sense a *concept* is a category for objects and events that allows us to distinguish them from other phenomena.

Before children can act on and make much sense of their social worlds, they require help in forming appropriate related concepts. This process requires much more than giving them names or symbols for objects and events. It involves informal or formal experiences that lead to the accurate identification of similarities, differences, and relationships among phenomena, along with appropriate labels. Learning the concept of family, for example, requires a child to establish in what ways all families are alike and some ways in which they differ from other familiar social groupings such as gangs, classes, and clubs. Much of this conceptual instruction occurs informally as the child grows up. The concept of grandparent may be learned inferentially as a child discovers bits of information about the people called "Gram" and "Gramps" or through straightforward curiousity: "What are grandparents?" and "What did you say grandparents were?"

Many concepts formed this way are inaccurate, of course; they are *misconceptions*. Each of us carries hundreds, perhaps thousands of these into our daily thinking. For children these misconceptions often present a serious impediment to further learning. (Many other concepts are not developed at all, since they fall outside of a child's commonplace experiences and must be acquired through formal instruction, e.g., colony, treaty, state, nation, and the like.)

We can and do, of course, place the same object or event in many *different* conceptual boxes, as psychologist Roger Brown reminds us:

> Everything in the world is susceptible of multiple categorizations. When something important happens, a parent will often name the persons or objects involved and, thereby, select for a child the particular categorizations believed to be most relevant to the event. Suppose one man punches another while a child looks on. A parent may label the aggressor as an *Irishman* or a *cop* or an *old man* or a *redhead* or something else. All of these can be attributes of the same man.[1]

Try a simple demonstration to see how a concept functions. Examine the following objects and experiences:

Marriage
Traffic lights with green and red lights at street corners
Use of money for purchasing items
Rules for playing baseball
Use of money to buy things
Educating children through schools
Printing sentences in books left to right
Going to church on Sunday or synagogue on Friday
Selecting senators by election

Put each of them into one of five categories and label each of them with one or two words.

There are, of course, many ways to sort out the nine items, with no one way being necessarily correct. The following set of categories merely reflect those that social scientists frequently use to group data concerning societies:

Political Institutions
    Selecting senators by election

Religious Institutions
    Going to church on Sunday or synagogue on Friday

Economic Institutions
   Use of money to buy things
Familial Institutions
   Marriage
Educational Institutions
   Printing sentences in books from left to right
   Educating children in schools
   Rules for playing baseball
   Traffic lights with red and green lights at street corners

A COMPLEX DEFINITION OF A CONCEPT

Actually a concept is much more complex than a mere categorization and discrimination device. David Ausubel reminds us of this when he comments on the use of the simple concept "house":

> When someone, for example, tells us that he sees a "house," he is not really communicating his *actual* experience, but a highly simplified and generalized version of it—an interpretation that reflects the cultural consensus regarding the essential (criterial, identifying) attributes of "house." His *actual* conscious experience of the event is infinitely more particularistic with respect to size, shape, style, hue, brightness, and presumed cost than the message communicated by his generic use of the term "house." If he actually tried to communicate his detailed cognitive experience, it would not only take him half a day, but he would still also be unable completely to express in words many of its more subtle nuances.[2]

Consider Ausubel's statement for a moment, then observe the diagram in Figure 4.1. It summarizes the rich process aspect of a concept, and illustrates how, as one group of authors has stated, "The working definition of a concept is the network of inferences that are or may be set in play by an act of categorization."[3]

Figure 4.1
A Concept of House

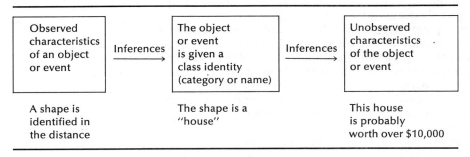

Observed characteristics of an object or event	Inferences →	The object or event is given a class identity (category or name)	Inferences →	Unobserved characteristics of the object or event
A shape is identified in the distance		The shape is a "house"		This house is probably worth over $10,000

Referring to Figure 4.1 again, we may now construct a complex definition of a concept: *A concept is a continuum of inferences by which a set of observed characteristics of an object or event suggest a class identity and then additional inferences about other unobserved characteristics of the object or event.*[4] Thus, we may consider concepts to be simultaneously 1) categories into which our various experiences are organized, and 2) as the larger network of intellectual relationships brought about through categorization. While this complex definition may be cumbersome, it serves to remind us of the fantastic compression of experience within a concept. It also provides us with some instructional considerations when we wish to assist someone in acquiring a new concept.

CONCEPTS AND WORDS

The selective use of words, a student quickly learns, will often pass for "learning" in the conceptual sense in the classroom or in society at large. Both the discussions he or she has with adults and the tests he or she takes frequently emphasize symbol or word transmission and recognition rather than conceptualizing.

Symbols often take on a *situational* meaning apart from their conceptual meaning. Martorella has observed:

> A shrewd student confronted with a question from his teacher such as, "What do you like best about our country?" may discover that he can ease his conceptual burden by replying, "Our democratic process." By doing so, he reflects his grasp of the situational meaning of the terms "democratic process," indicating he recognizes these symbols can be positively related to characteristics of the United States. That the student may attach no conceptual meaning to the term is unimportant here, since chances are he will be rewarded with "That's a good answer, Johnny!" from the teacher. He even may have learned from sad experience that an honest attempt to grapple conceptually with the question in the form of an answer, "Hot dogs, scary movies, and baseball," is frowned upon by the teacher, who categorized this latter response as "silly." Situationally silly, perhaps, but conceptually pregnant with meaning. . . .

> Very small youngsters learn "the symbol game" quickly, as they discover that certain terms, spoken in certain contexts, evoke approval or disapproval from parents in the form of smiles, laughter, frowns, or other reinforcements. From the world around them, youngsters are aware at a very early age that symbols have meaning apart from their conceptual relationship, and so, not surprisingly, when this phenomenon confronts them later in classroom situations, it appears quite natural.

> A cartoon that appeared a few years ago showed an Eskimo parent and child sitting in an igloo reading the nursery rhyme "Little Jack

Horner." The caption on the cartoon read, "What's a corner, Daddy?" The humor of the cartoon derives, in part at least, from the fact that nursery rhymes frequently are regarded as having *situational* rather than *conceptual* import, much like a beer jingle. One need not know what curds and whey are to enjoy Miss Muffett's tale, so the argument goes.

The Eskimo youngster illustrates clearly what occurs when *conceptual* versus *situational* meaning is at issue. Conceptually, he requires an experiential basis, which he now lacks, in order to assimilate his new datum. In effect, he refused to treat the symbolic content as "just part of a nursery rhyme." . . .

In the "nursery rhyme" sense, instruction *can* proceed with little concern for common conceptual referents; "democracy," "justice," and other social science concepts merely become the equivalents of "curds and whey." To the extent that teachers are sensitive to the problem, they, like the Eskimo parent, must answer before they proceed with further instruction.[5]

TYPES OF CONCEPTS

There are many ways to group and classify concepts. Each of them should reveal some new dimensions of concepts that will assist the teacher in designing instruction for concept learning.

SUBJECT MATTER AREAS

A simple way to group concepts is according to the subject matter areas or disciplines they represent. Listed below are a number of concepts drawn from areas of the social sciences: psychology, sociology, anthropology, geography, economics, political science, and history:

Race	Prejudice	Map scale	Group
Agriculture	Ocean	Witness	Custom
City	Institution	Discrimination	Communication
Country	Norms	Transportation	Population
Man	News	Colony	Work
Government	Family	Mountain	Island
Market	Organization	Revolution	War
Nation	Power	Interdependence	Poverty
River	Social change	Culture	Distance
Valley	Resource	Law	Policeman

What is similar about all of these concepts? What is different about them? Can you identify from which of the social science disciplines each is taken? Try to answer each of these questions to your satisfaction before reading further.

While social scientists sometimes claim a particular concept as being unique to their discipline, it is probably a fruitless argument if one's objective is *to teach a concept.* A concept such as "power" is used by sociologists, historians, and political scientists, among others, and it may be illustrated by subject matter drawn from many disciplines. Put in another way, if one's goal is the learning of a concept, the social science disciplines used are a secondary consideration.

In one study, consultation with school district personnel in one state as well as a review of curriculum guides, programs, and social studies textbooks produced a list of over 200 social science concepts for fourth graders.[6] A list of some of the major concepts identified is shown in Table 4.1.

A review of a recently published basal social studies textbook for the first grade revealed that the social science concepts shown in Table 4.2 were mentioned among others.

SIMPLE VS. COMPLEX CONCEPTS

A second way to classify concepts is according to how difficult it is to learn. Several things make learning a concept easy or difficult. One feature is the degree of concreteness or abstractness that a concept has —lake vs. justice, for example. Another way to consider levels of difficulty among concepts is to analyze the characteristics that define them. One classification scheme is broken into three levels of varying difficulty, as illustrated in Figure 4.2.[7]

A *conjunctive* concept is less difficult to learn because it has only one set of characteristics or conditions to be learned. An island, for example, may only be defined as a "body of land surrounded by water

Table 4.1
Some social science concepts identified as appropriate for fourth-grade children

Bay	City	Area
Delta	Country	Continent
Elevation	Democracy	Earth
River	Government	Equator
Topography	Industry	East-West
Lake	Institutions	Globe
Tributary	Market	Map
Peninsula	News	Meridians
Isthmus	Organization	Seasons
Harbor	Society	North-South
Strait	State	Legend (on map)
Ridge	Transportation	Gravity
Mountain	Urban	Boundary
Region	Suburban	Ocean
Prairie	Exchange	Hemispheres

Source: B. Robert Tabachnick et al., *Selection and Analysis of Social Science Concepts for Inclusion in Tests of Concept Attainment.* Working Paper No. 53 (Madison, Wis.: Wisconsin Research and Development Center for Cognitive Learning, 1970), p. 8.

Table 4.2
Social science concepts in a first-grade basal social studies text

Apartment	Future	News
Cities	Globe	Office
Contents	Great-grandmother	Pay
Earth	Home	Plan
Everyone	Hospital	Rules
Everywhere	Ideas	Thought
Family	Love	Villages
Farm	Money	World
		Year

Source: *You and Your Family* (New York: Noble & Noble, 1974).

on all sides." There are many kinds or examples of island, but the easy part of learning the concept is that the basic set of defining characteristics is always the same.

Disjunctive concepts are more difficult to learn because there are two or more *alternative* sets of characteristics or conditions that make up the concept. An illustration of a disjunctive concept is found in baseball. One of the game's more difficult concepts that must be mastered early to participate or understand what is happening at the center of action is a strike. One must learn minimally that a strike is (1) a ball thrown by the pitcher to a batter that passes over a specific area of home plate, or (2) a ball thrown by the pitcher to any area of home plate that is swung at and missed by the batter, or (3) a ball thrown by the pitcher to any area of home plate that is hit by the batter and knocked into the foul zone. In sum, disjunctive concepts may take two or more forms.

Similarly *relational* concepts, the hardest to learn, derive their com-

Figure 4.2
Levels of concept difficulty

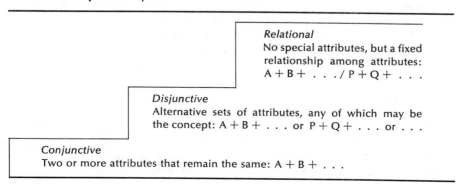

Relational
No special attributes, but a fixed relationship among attributes:
$A + B + \ldots / P + Q + \ldots$

Disjunctive
Alternative sets of attributes, any of which may be the concept: $A + B + \ldots$ or $P + Q + \ldots$ or $\ldots$

Conjunctive
Two or more attributes that remain the same: $A + B + \ldots$

plexity from the fact that they do not have one or even several fixed set of characteristics. Rather they may be defined only as the relationship between objects and events. While an object or event does not change, its relationship to other items may, and hence it becomes a different concept. An empty coffee can, for example, may represent the concept "waste" to the trash collector, while it is seen as an example of a "resource" to the carpenter who uses it to store nails. The coffee can stays the same but its concept status changes as its relationship to new contexts changes. The case is the same with concepts such as "poverty," "wealth," "long," "tall," "near," "far," "big," "little," and the like. Learners of relational concepts must focus on both the characteristics of the object or event being examined and on the other object or event to which it is being related.

Working with preschool children, one investigator has noted they have a tendency to treat relational concepts as conjunctive ones. "When the four-year-old first learns the concept dark, he regards it as descriptive of an absolute class of color—black and related dark hues. The phrase 'dark yellow' makes no sense to him, for dark signifies dark colors, not relative darkness."[8] Similarly, water and oil may be regarded as resources, even when they appear in the form of floods or drippings from a car.

Analyzing whether a concept is conjunctive, disjunctive, or relational allows a teacher to anticipate some of the learning problems that are likely to occur in a classroom and to select an appropriate instructional remedy.

REPRESENTATIONAL FORMS

Yet another way to classify concepts is in terms of how they are represented or acquired by an individual. Each concept experience comes to us through some form or medium. According to Jerome Bruner, objects or events may be classified as being acquired through three representational forms: *enactive, iconic,* or *symbolic*—"knowing something through doing it, through a picture or image of it, and through some such symbolic means as language."[9] Thus one may learn the concept "assembly line" through participating in the process (enactive), through viewing a film of an assembly line in action (iconic), or through reading a book on the subject (symbolic). As children develop, they progress through mastery of each of these three representational forms. (This classification system is discussed in more detail in Chapter 20.)

LEARNING CONCEPTS

Can you remember how you learned what "aunts," "mice," "typewriters," "pain," "automobile," and millions of other concepts mean? It is probably difficult to analyze the process accurately since the initial learning occurred long ago and probably happened in what seemed to be a natural or casual fashion. Our memories may even suggest a single rather than a continuous learning experience.

Evidence indicates that younger children form concepts in different ways than older ones. Young children are more likely to overdiscriminate or make very fine distinctions, as opposed to overgeneralize or include wrong cases in judging whether or not two instances are examples of a concept.[10] Thus the probabilities are that a younger child might be more inclined than an older child to rule out Hawaii as an example of an island than to consider the Mississippi River as an instance of a lake. In effect younger children seem to form concepts on narrower bases, with this tendency decreasing as they grow older. Supporting this finding is evidence that a child's ability to determine differences among concepts develops at an earlier age than the ability to determine similarities. Interestingly, two investigators have discovered that "while the tendency to overdiscriminate drops sharply with increased age, the tendency to overgeneralize tends not to drop.[11]

A developmental model of four different invariant levels of concept learning—the Wisconsin Model—attempts to explain the changes in degrees of mastery of a concept.[12] How do individuals progress from correct recognition of an example of a concept to using it in their thinking and acquiring new concepts? The four levels of the model are shown in the following diagram:

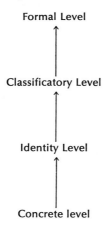

Formal Level

Classificatory Level

Identity Level

Concrete level

At the lowest level, the *concrete* level, an individual is only capable of attending to an object, discriminating it from others, and remembering it. The name of the object may or may not be identified and remembered at the same time.

The *identity* level requires all of the prior level's capabilities plus the ability to generalize that two or more forms of the object are the same thing. (A mountain viewed from an airplane and a nearby hill and its base while appearing different are still the same thing.) Movement to the *classificatory* level requires the additional capability of generalizing that two or more examples are equivalent and belong to the same class of things. At this level, a child viewing shots of the Himalayan, Pocono, Appalachian, and Rocky Mountains is able to generalize that, though different, they are all equivalent and may be labeled "mountain."

At the highest level, the *formal* level, a number of additional capabilities are acquired: (1) discriminating and naming the criterial attributes of the concept, (2) being able to hypothesize what the relevant attributes and/or rules of the concept are, (3) remembering and being able to evaluate such hypotheses, and (4) being able to infer the concept from examples, if necessary.[13] Klausmeier and Hooper state:

> These operations are used by individuals who cognize the information potentially available to them from actual positive and negative instances or from verbally presented descriptions of positive and negative instances. They apparently reason like this: Instance 1 has land surrounded by water. It is a member of the class. Instance 2 has land but it is not surrounded by water. It is not a member of the class. Therefore, lands surrounded by water belong to the class and lands not surrounded by water do not. Being surrounded by water is a defining attribute of the concept. This individual can now properly classify newly encountered instances, based on experiences with only one positive and one negative instance of the concept.[14]

While each level requires that one has mastered the capabilities of the preceding levels, the highest level of attainment may vary among children of the same age. At each level children are capable of increasingly richer and more complex conceptual processes. Though concept naming is not essential for lower-level learning, having the name of the concept and its attributes helps the learning process move to the highest level.

LEARNING A NEW CONCEPT

To appreciate the predicament of a child as he or she is trying to understand what a new concept is, including how to pronounce and remember its name, we need to reexperience how learning occurs. The concepts in the following sets of materials are taken from the work of the Education Development Center. While these materials may be used for many instructional purposes, here we will consider each set of them as teaching a single concept.

Consider the set in Figure 4.3 and try to correctly identify by number the instances of the concept. Then write in, as accurately as possible, what you feel is the correct definition of the concept.

Repeat this procedure for the sets in Figures 4.4 and 4.5, and then compare your conclusions with those of others who have examined the three sets. If your definitions differ, consider whose definition seems the most accurate and in what respects the other definitions are deficient.

Figure 4.3 Gligs

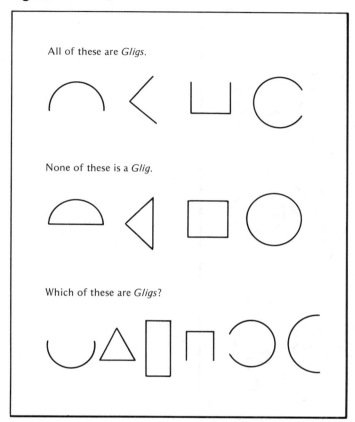

All of these are *Gligs*.

None of these is a *Glig*.

Which of these are *Gligs*?

Source: *Teacher's Guide for Attribute Games and Problems* (New York: McGraw-Hill, 1968), p. 74. Republished without endorsement.

For a final analysis, consider these questions:

1. In what ways are the three sets all alike?
2. What makes some of the concepts easier to learn than others? (In other words, what is one operational definition of "easier" in concept learning?)
3. If anyone was unable to correctly identify or define one or more of the concepts, what were the problems encountered?
4. In what ways is the learning of these nonsense concepts similar to the learning of everyday concepts for a child?
5. How did you feel as you tried to determine what the defining characteristics of the concept were?

Figure 4.4 Gruffles

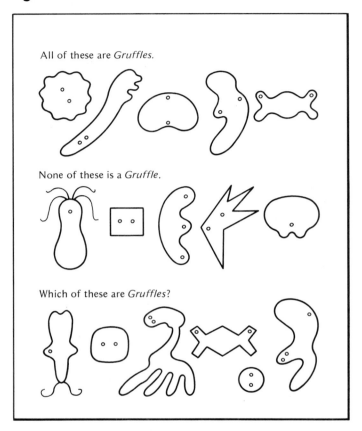

All of these are *Gruffles.*

None of these is a *Gruffle.*

Which of these are *Gruffles?*

Source: Teacher's Guide for Attribute Games and Problems (New York: McGraw-Hill, 1968), p. 75. Republished without endorsement.

These sets should have illustrated some of the problems that a learner experiences in confronting a concept he or she has never encountered before. A final demonstration may suggest yet a few more potential obstacles for learners. You will need sheets of paper, one large enough to cover this page. One sheet is for taking notes and the other two are for covering figures. Follow the instructions carefully, and at the conclusion of the sequence you will be given a short test.

Place one sheet at the top of the page on which Figure 4.6 appears and the second sheet directly following Figure 4.6. Use the third sheet for making any notes that you wish. Once you have finished examining a figure, cover it with the top sheet, and move the bottom sheet until

Figure 4.5 Trugs

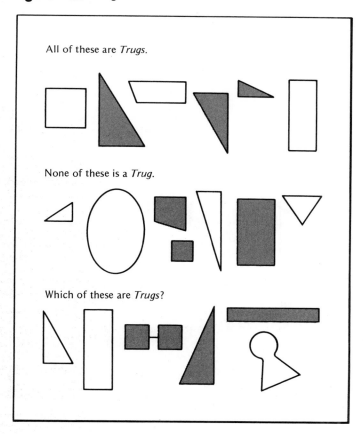

All of these are *Trugs*.

None of these is a *Trug*.

Which of these are *Trugs*?

Source: Teacher's Guide for Attribute Games and Problems (New York: McGraw-Hill, 1968), p. 77. Republished without endorsement.

the next figure has been uncovered and so on. *Do not uncover a figure once it has been examined.*

Figure 4.6 shows an example of the concept you are to learn; the concept name is "slark." Figure 4.7 is also a slark. Figure 4.8, however, is *not* a slark. Figure 4.9 also is *not* a slark. But Figure 4.10 *is* a slark.

Cover the final figure and do not reexamine any of the materials (you will have a chance to do so later). Take the test below, referring to any of the notes you have taken on the third sheet.

Test I. Examine each of the four sets of figures (4.11–4.14) and identify any instances of a slark. (Each set of figures is to be read across from left to right.)

Figure 4.6 This is a Slark

If this test was taken with a group, check to see how many selected Figures 4.11, 4.12, 4.13, or 4.14 as the correct responses. If there are no disagreements, take Test II.

But if you took the test alone or if there were disagreements within the group, use the following procedure before taking Test II. Remove and discard the sheets covering the five figures and reexamine each of them. Compare and contrast similarities and differences in each of the figures. What is your individual or the group's new collective conclusion on which figures in Test I are slarks? If some doubts or dis-

Figure 4.7 This is a Slark

Figure 4.8 This is not a Slark

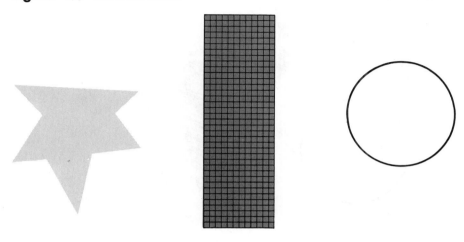

agreements still exist, we will deal with them after you have completed Test II.

Test II. Write below as precisely as possible a definition of a slark:

A slark is _____

_____

Compare your definition with those of others and determine which one appears to be the most accurate.

VARIABLES IN CONCEPT LEARNING[15]

Suppose I were to examine the results of all who participated in the preceding demonstration and discover that 25 percent of the participants did *not* learn from my instruction? That is, what if 25 percent of them did not select numbers 1 and 3 in Test I as examples of a slark and 25 percent did not write a definition essentially similar to this one: *A slark is a circle, triangle, and rectangle arranged in that order* (the correct answer). Which of the following evaluations seems warranted to you?

1. The 25 percent were slow learners.
2. The 25 percent were culturally deprived, that is, they lacked appropriate readiness experiences with slarks.
3. The 25 percent probably had lower IQs than the rest of the participants.
4. Since 75 percent of the group got the correct answers, the 25 percent are the normal number of failure to be expected.

Figure 4.9 This is not a Slark

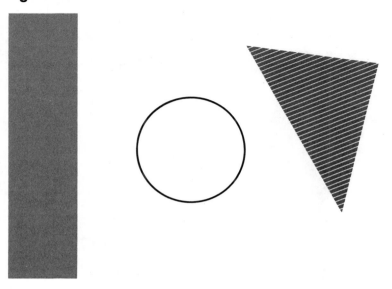

Figure 4.10 This is a Slark

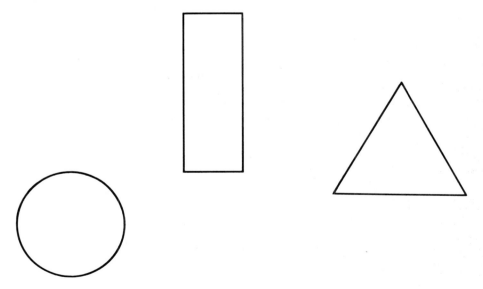

Figure 4.11 Is this a Slark?

If none of these explanations appeals to you, offer one that focuses on the deficiencies of the *instructional sequence,* not of the learner. What in the instruction provided led some learners astray? Talk to those who failed the tests and analyze why they answered as they did.

You are likely to find that those who answered incorrectly have a consistent and logical basis for their answers. For demonstration purposes, there are several pitfalls built into the instruction that invariably mislead some learners. The design follows a sound instructional model. However, it cannot take into account the learning differences of all individuals. Some will focus on size and color or detail in the examples, while others concentrate on the characteristics of just one element in the total array. In trying to learn the concept of slark, these tendencies work to the learner's disadvantage and cause him or her to draw incorrect conclusions. The readers who followed this path paralleled the learning experiences of children who incorrectly infer that the White House is a necessary part of the concept "president" or that dark hair and dark skin are necessarily characteristic of Italians.

Invariably this phenomenon, while deliberately induced in this demonstration, occurs naturally in the learning of academic concepts. On these occasions, unless a teacher is willing to reexamine his instruction rather than fault the learner's capabilities, little progress toward the learning of concepts will occur. An instructor must resist the easy defensive position, "Most of the class got the correct answer when I explained the concept. If you didn't, then I guess you are just not trying hard enough!"

Figure 4.12 Is this a Slark?

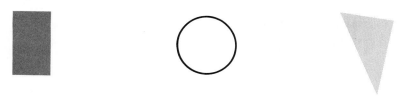

Figure 4.13 Is this a Slark?

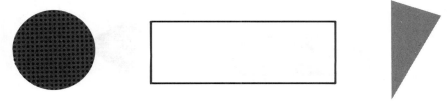

Let us reflect a moment, too, on some of the instructional assistance given to the reader in the learning of the preceding four concepts. Most of the conditions provided for your instruction are seldom operative for children in a typical concept-learning situation.

> *Condition 1:* Relatively little irrelevant material was included with your instruction, that is, material that might divert your attention from the essential characteristics of the concept.
> *Condition 2:* All the cases you needed, the examples and nonexamples, were put before you simultaneously. This fact allowed you to easily recheck conclusions and to compare and contrast cases.
> *Condition 3:* The characteristics of the concepts were relatively simple ones except for the third concept, which had two possible sets of characteristics instead of one. In other words, the first, second, and fourth concepts were *conjunctive*, the least difficult type to learn, while the third concept was *disjunctive* (see Figure 4.2, p. 85).
> *Condition 4:* All four concepts had concise graphic referents that required little or no verbal ability to understand.

Those readers who experienced difficulty with the pronunciation of concept names or who could not now correctly spell some of them should be able to empathize with young children's linguistic burdens. Similarly some readers may have discovered that it is possible to correctly identify *instances* of a concept without being able to accurately explain or define the concept in one's own words. Young children fre-

Figure 4.14 Is this a Slark?

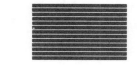

quently exhibit this phenomenon, leading to a misinterpretation of their learning level. All who may be said to have learned a concept should be able to discriminate examples from nonexamples of the concepts. Inferring a correct *definition* of the concept may be considered to be a more advanced level of learning, as the next chapter will show.

CURRICULUM USES OF CONCEPTS

There are many words in our language that have different meanings for different people. "News," "liberal," and "conservative" are common examples. The term *concept* suffers from the same problem. Frequently, it is used synonymously with the words "idea," "theory," "generalization," "theme," or "structure." The end result for social educators has been confusion concerning what is meant by "teaching concepts" or by "concept-oriented" materials.

In social studies curriculum development, the term *concept* has been used in several different ways. Sometimes a concept has been viewed as a broad organizing theme for disparate bodies of subject matter. The work of Hilda Taba and her associates reflects this view.[16] They identified concepts such as culture and interdependence, which they used as broad guidelines for organizing elements of an elementary curriculum.

Shirley Engle and Wilma Longstreet have used a similar approach to construct a social education curriculum organized around six action concepts: conflict, power, valuing, interaction, change, and adjustment. "The six *action concepts*," they write, "would seem to include all conceivable forms of human action on both the personal and the societal levels. They offer the school a logical pedagogical structure for dealing with human behavior. The number of topics that could be chosen for study under these concepts approaches infinity."[17] Engle and Longstreet suggest that the following general questions could be used in relation to the six concepts in any situation to structure curriculum materials:

1. What conflicts exist in this situation?
2. How does power function in this situation?
3. How is valuing involved in this situation?
4. What are the stable interactions present in this situation . . . ?
5. What changes are occurring in this situation?
6. What adjustments are being made in this situation?[18]

Another interpretation of a concept considers it as a "higher-order" type of learning outcome; it is perceived as an enduring element of one's thinking structure and as having wide applicability to many areas of future learning. Usually, in this view, learning a concept is contrasted with learning facts. Still a third usage of the term takes *concept* to mean statements about objects or events. In some cases these are general statements such as "Cities are densely populated geographical areas," which are assumed to have applicability to a wide number of instances.

The net result for the reader or teacher is often confusion. Throughout this text, the term *concept* will be used with a special operational meaning having specific implications for social education instruction. The usage in this text corresponds to that in the psychological literature and will follow the definitions outlined earlier in this chapter (pp. 79–82). Similarly teaching concepts will be differentiated from other intellectual outcomes discussed in following chapters. In short, instruction for concept learning will be seen as requiring a special type of instructional procedure, whereas learning a generalization or other objective will require other types of instructional strategies.

THE VALUE OF CONCEPTS

People create and interact in a conceptual world. They sort things into categories, whether they be experiences or papers in a file drawer. Their concepts make it possible for them to call up and communicate many varied experiences with a relatively small number of words. In short, concepts enable us to simplify, compress, and organize our environment and to transmit our thoughts efficiently.

They also allow us to easily identify components of new situations and hence to understand the situation and anticipate some likely developments. Encountering a strange room, a person notes the chairs, the pattern of their arrangement, a desk, and a blackboard. His concepts allow him to make interpretations about the new situation, to infer some possible events, and to suggest some appropriate responses.

Perhaps most important for our daily activities, concepts once learned reduce the necessity for learning a new fact about every object we encounter. Once we have learned what a tree is, we can categorize all new trees we find without having to be told in each instance what we are seeing. This is an economizing function of concepts that we readily take for granted.

A more subtle value of concepts is that they enable us to distinguish between the real and the apparent. David Elkind reminds us of this point: "On the plane of concrete concepts, for example, our concept of tree enables us to distinguish between a picture of a tree and a real tree. At a more abstract level, our concept of 'democracy' enables us to discriminate between those countries where democracy is real and those where it is only apparent."[19]

For social educators, concept development must be a primary and continuous instructional goal. Concepts are psychologically and figuratively the building blocks of intellectual analysis. As children begin to grapple with urgent social concerns in a social education program, mastery of the concepts implicit in their investigation is an essential prerequisite. Probing the relevant issue of "Why some people in our society are poor" with primary children requires initially that all have a minimal grasp of the concept "poor."

Every academic activity in schools requires the use of concepts, and while the process of concept development may prove to be tedious and time consuming, there is no alternative for meaningful instruction. The boy who reads about the colonies' struggle for independence in his text sacrifices most of his potential involvement in the issue if he only decodes the terms and has no conceptual referents to attach to them.

NOTES

[1] Roger O. Brown, *Words and Things* (New York: Free Press, 1958), pp. 225–226.

[2] David P. Ausubel, *Educational Psychology: A Cognitive View* (New York: Holt, Rinehart & Winston, 1968), p. 505.

[3] Jerome S. Bruner et al., *A Study of Thinking* (New York: Science Editions, 1962), p. 244.

[4] Peter H. Martorella, *Concept Learning: Designs for Instruction* (New York: International Textbook, 1972), p. 5.

[5] Ibid., pp. 10–11.

[6] B. Robert Tabachnick et al., *Selection and Analysis of Social Studies Concepts for Inclusion in Tests of Concept Attainment.* Working Paper No. 53 (Madison, Wis.: Wisconsin Research and Development Center for Cognitive Learning, 1970), pp. 5–13.

[7] Bruner et al., op. cit., p. 41.

[8] Jerome Kagan, "Preschool Enrichment and Learning," *Interchange*, 2 (1971), 17.

[9] Jerome S. Bruner, *Beyond the Information Given: Studies in the Psychology of Knowing* (New York: Norton, 1973), p. 316. See also Chapter 20 in this text, pp. 437–438.

[10] Eli Saltz and Irving E. Sigel, "Concept Overdiscrimination in Children," *Journal of Experimental Psychology*, 73 (January 1967), 1–8.

[11] Ibid., 7.

[12] Herbert J. Klausmeier and Frank H. Hooper, "Conceptual Development and Instruction," in F. N. Kerlinger and J. B. Carroll (eds.), *Review of Research in Education*, 2 (Itasca, Ill.: Peacock, 1974), pp. 3–54.

[13] Ibid., pp. 19–24.

[14] Ibid., pp. 22–23.

[15] This topic is discussed more fully in Martorella, op. cit., pp. 22–51. See also Klausmeier and Hooper, op. cit., pp. 34–41.

[16] Norman E. Wallen et al., *The Taba Curriculum Development Project in Social Studies* (Menlo Park, Calif.: Addison-Wesley, 1969).

[17] Shirley H. Engle and Wilma S. Longstreet, *A Design for Social Education in the Open Curriculum* (New York: Harper & Row, 1972), p. 58.

[18] Ibid., pp. 92–93.

[19] David Elkind, "Conservation and Concept Formation," in D. Elkind and J. H. Flavell (eds.), *Studies in Cognitive Development: Essays in Honor of Jean Piaget* (New York: Oxford University Press, 1969), p. 178.

CHAPTER 5

Teaching and Expanding Concepts

Questions frequently raised in discussing concept learning are, "Doesn't each person have a unique concept?" "Isn't a concept all of the associations that one has with a term?" Hilda Taba and her associates developed a fruitful teaching strategy (discussed later in this chapter) based on this perspective.

PUBLIC AND PERSONAL DIMENSIONS OF CONCEPTS

The position taken in this text is that no two people will have exactly the same concept. Each person's concept, no matter what the object or event, *is* a truly unique combination of all the related associations he or she has had. My concept of "ritual" includes all of the experiences —enactive, iconic, and symbolic—I have had that can be grouped under a common label. While others may have had many similar experiences, they would not have reconstructed or interrelated the associations in the same way. Thus the *personal* dimension of each concept may be distinguished from the *public* aspects that define the concept commonly and that are shared by all.

A diagram may illustrate how the public vs. personal dimensions of a concept may be combined. Using the concept of "island"—a body of land surrounded by water—and by examining Figures 5.1 and 5.2 we can view the schematic representation of a hypothetical conceptual network. A child Billy observes the picture in Figure 5.1 and sets in motion the hypothetical conceptual process shown in Figure 5.2. In this case the primary inferences are land, water, and aroundness that make up the defining characteristics of "island." The secondary inferences that comprise the unique elements of the concept may be explained by finding out the following facts. Land reminded Billy of the astronauts setting down on the moon, which, in turn, suggested space. Aroundness triggered memories of Indians and wagon trains. Water made him think of how dry his throat was, which simultaneously triggered thoughts of the desert he had visited last summer and the lemonade in the refrigerator at home.

INSTRUCTION FOR CONCEPT LEARNING

One important value of concepts is that verbalizing them allows individuals to share experiences efficiently. This fact suggests that common

Figure 5.1
An island

attributes are part of people's concepts. It would seem that it is the critical attributes of concepts that people minimally share in common when they are able to meaningfully discuss subjects. While classroom instruction always contributes to the evolving personal conceptions of students, its primary focus is the public or critical attributes of concepts. What students essentially are assisted in learning in common are the socially accepted, standardized, or academically defined aspects of concepts. Such attributes generally are derived from the mass media, dictionaries, encyclopedias, scholarly works, or authoritative experience.

While the vast majority of concepts are learned by children informally, many are too specialized to be acquired through everyday experiences, or else a child's life sphere may be so limited or different from most other children's that he or she requires formal instruction. For purposes of designing systematic instruction for concept learning, the teacher will require the following information:

1. *Name:* The name or symbol that is used conventionally to define the concept, for example, "island."

Figure 5.2
Billy's conceptual
network

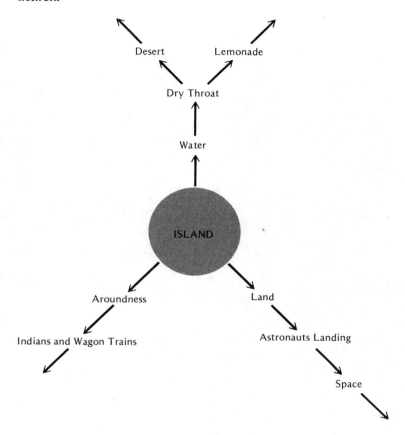

2. *Rule:* A definition or rule that specifies the criteria for identifying the concept and differentiating it from other concepts. The rule should be clear and as succinct as possible, for example, "body of land surrounded by water."
3. *Criterial attributes:* The criterial (critical or relevant) attributes that make up the concept rule, for example, "water," "land," "around-ness."
4. *Noncriterial attributes:* The noncriterial (noncritical or irrelevant) attributes frequently associated with the concept but not essential for defining it, for example, palm trees, oceans.
5. *Examples:* Examples that are clear illustrations of all of the key attributes of the concept, for example, Hawaii, Cuba, islands in a river.

6. *Nonexamples:* Nonexamples that show what the concept is not, for example, isthmus, United States, lake.

The first step merely provides the learner with the conventionally accepted symbol or name for the concept. While not every concept has a name and it is possible to learn a concept without knowing its name, most classroom instruction will involve named concepts and will require their verbalization to evaluate learning.

An explicit operational statement of the concept rule or definition is the most crucial component for designing instruction. If the rule is not immediately known, some sources of information are social science texts, comprehensive dictionaries, the *Dictionary of the Social Sciences,* the *Encyclopedia of the Social Sciences,* the mass media, and even some of the newer elementary social studies texts. Unfortunately for some concepts none of these sources may prove adequate because no commonly agreed-upon operational definition exists! One set of authors warn:

> Some concepts . . . are defined on other bases, including the use of synonyms and antonyms. Further, not all words potentially definable in terms of attributes are so defined, even in unabridged dictionaries. Therefore, the researcher and the developer of curriculum materials alike must ascertain the defining attributes independently, or cooperatively with scholars from the various disciplines.[1]

In effect, where public meanings are not completely clear, the classroom teacher must try to establish a usable or operational definition on the basis of the best evidence available. For purposes of instruction, this contrived definition can serve to create examples and activities. The operational definition, whether borrowed or contrived, should allow a teacher to include all the examples that are considered appropriate to use and exclude all nonexamples that are to be presented.

Once the concept rule is clearly established, the criterial attributes that comprise it can be abstracted and listed individually. Similarly when examples for illustration of the concept have been selected, some noncriterial attributes should be apparent. Examples may be taken from real cases or created with ficticious data. Nonexamples may be considered to be any case in which one or more of the criterial attributes are missing or are organized in a different fashion. A lake, for example, is a nonexemplar of "island" even though it has the attributes of "land," "water," and "aroundness."

One easy way to check the suitability and difficulty of examples and nonexamples is to give a sample to a small group of students along with a definition of the concept. Then calculate the percentage of students who properly classify the cases.

MODELS FOR INSTRUCTION

Once the information discussed in the preceding six steps is obtained, an instructional sequence may be designed. In Chapter 4 you were taught some "new" concepts. Implicit in the instruction you were given was a model or design for how a concept should be taught. To teach other concepts, one should be able to abstract the model and use it.

Reflect a moment on your experiences in learning the concepts. What instructional procedures were used? How were they different from other instructional patterns that you have encountered? In what ways was learning structured, encouraged, and determined? Each of the four instructional models that follow in this chapter provide information concerning how to teach a concept to someone who has never learned it before.

Model #1. This model is abstracted from John DeCecco, *The Psychology of Learning and Instruction.*[2] It employs nine basic structured steps as follows:

1. Describe to the student what you expect him or her to be able to do after he or she has learned the concept.
2. Reduce the number of attributes associated with the concept where possible, and emphasize the key attributes in some fashion.
3. Provide the students with some clear name or label to associate with the concept.
4. Provide a series of examples and nonexamples of the concept.
5. Present the materials as close together as possible or all at once.
6. Present a new case of the concept and see if students can identify it.
7. See if the students have learned the concept.
8. Ask the students to define the concept.
9. Allow students to discuss the concept and indicate when they make correct or incorrect statements concerning it.

DeCecco illustrates how the concept "tourist" might be taught to an elementary group following his model.[3]

1. The teacher begins the lesson by telling the class that they are to learn the concept of tourist. They are told further that when the lesson is over, they should easily be able to identify examples of the concept.
2. The teacher analyzes the concept and decides that it is a conjunctive concept with the criterial attributes "activity," "purpose," and "residence." Related but noncriterial attributes such as "mode of travel" are rejected on the grounds that their introduction would only confuse students.
3. Students make necessary verbal association by responding correctly to the word "tourist" written on the blackboard.
4 and 5. The teacher presents her examples and nonexamples as oral case studies, which also are available on large cards. Each card is then left for examination after the teacher has read from it. Examples include stories such as "Mr. Phog lives in San Francisco

but he is on vacation and he is visiting Rome to see friends and the city." Nonexamples deal with subjects such as Americans who changed their residences to other countries. After presenting each example, the teacher asks a question and indicates whether or not responses are correct.

6. Students are given a new example, "Mr. Angelo is returning to Italy to visit friends and vacation."
7. The teacher presents new examples and nonexamples, varying national origins, regions, and reasons for travel.
8. Students are asked to tell what they think a "tourist" is, and their definitions are compared against the original definition of the concept used by the teacher.
9. The teacher reinforces correct responses and indicates errors. Students now are reminded of the original objectives of the lesson and are given a test dealing with new examples and nonexamples. The results of the test are shared with the students as soon as possible.

In his model DeCecco includes statements of the concept rule as a test, along with correct identification of examples and nonexamples of the concept. As noted earlier, not all children, especially very young ones, will be able to define a concept.

In considering DeCecco's illustration of a hypothetical teacher, one should keep in mind that the subject matter is all imaginary, although it is based on actual cases. It is not material for purposes of concept learning. If the instructional sequence does succeed in teaching the concept of "tourist," the learners should be able to correctly identify an actual case of a tourist.

Model #2. A very similar model is abstracted from the works of Robert Gagné. It is composed of five basic dimensions. Gagné suggests that this model is appropriate for teaching "concrete" concepts or those that have object referents or forms to which one can point—color, tree, cat, shape.[4]

1. Be sure that the students repeat the concept's name to develop a stimulus-response connection between the concept and the name.
2. Have students examine and identify several different examples of the concept by name.
3. Present students with several more examples of the concept and also with some different nonexamples of the concept. Describe the differences between the various concept examples and nonexamples. (Having the students verbalize these differences is optional.)
4. Present more examples of the concept all at once and ask students to identify the name of the concept illustrated.

5. Create a situation in which there is a new example of the concept and ask the students to identify the concept.

Gagné's own illustrations of his model in operation are all drawn from areas outside the social sciences. Let us try to apply his model to the teaching of the concept of "island" discussed earlier with a class of kindergarten children.[5] The concept's attributes have relatively concrete referents: water, land, and aroundness.

1. Ms. Jablonski introduces briefly what the session will be about, asks the group to repeat the word "island" after her, and writes the word on the board.
2. Using pictures, hand-drawn posters, or slides, the teacher introduces several illustrations of different types of islands. All the pictorial representations clearly show a body of land surrounded by water. In each case, the class identifies the concept's name.
3. Some new pictorial examples are introduced, along with some illustrations of what the concept is *not*. Nonexamples include a lake and its surrounding shore, an isthmus, a mass of land, and an ocean segment. A question sequence requiring comparing and contrast is used to bring out similarities and differences among examples and nonexamples (e.g., "In what ways are *these* alike? In what ways do *those* differ?").
4. Some new examples of an island are placed together on a flannelboard and the students are asked what they are called.
5. A new set of numbered pictures are placed on the flannelboard, among them two islands. The students are asked to write down (or circle on a sheet of numbers) the numbers of the pictures that show islands.

Let us alternately consider an older group of students about to learn the concept of nonverbal communication. We might follow a similar format, using pictures and/or role-played episodes as examples and nonexamples. Both scenes from printed advertisements, as well as commercially-made photos and pictures, could be used. Three dimensional models also can be employed effectively as examples and nonexamples. These media have the additional advantage of providing hands on experience with a concept. Simple hand-prepared charts and posters are other media that lend themselves to all concepts.

Both the Gagné and the DeCecco models are skeletal in that they describe only the essential steps in an instructional sequence. Introducing the instruction or focusing attention on the learning task, developing questioning sequences and activities appropriate for calling attention to important attributes of the concept and to noncriterial but frequently found attributes, following up with activities, making alterations in the sequences of the steps to fit particular situations, and selecting interesting, thought-provoking, and varied media for instruction are all additional ingredients for the teacher to consider. With any instructional model, concept learning can often be helped along with some prompting for the learner. This can be accomplished by calling attention to attributes in examples ("Notice there is water all around") and their absence in nonexamples ("Notice there is water only on three sides") or by supplying the concept rule. These aids are especially helpful where the concept rule is complex/or where attributes are obscure.[6]

Model #3. Neither Model #1 nor Model #2 explicitly provides procedures for teaching concepts that are *disjunctive* (have alternative sets of characteristics or conditions that define the concept). Both of the illustrations in the two models dealt with *conjunctive* concepts—tourist and island. These models, however, do suggest a possible third model that may be constructed for teaching a disjunctive concept.[7]

1. Operationally define the concept in as many ways as it is commonly used.
2. Introduce the concept and present different examples of the concept that illustrate the first definition of the concept. Identify each example with the concept name.
3. Present different nonexamples of the concept, emphasizing the ways in which they differ from the examples.
4. Present different examples of the concept that illustrate each of the alternative definitions specified in step 1. Identify each of these examples with the concept's name.
5. Give the students more and varied nonexamples of the concept, emphasizing the ways in which they differ from the examples.
6. Present the examples and nonexamples in close succession or simultaneously. Allow the students to compare and contrast similarities and differences.
7. Test for concept mastery.

To illustrate the use of this model, we will examine a different type of instructional setting, a self-instructional minitext. The concept to be taught is one that has different and often confusing meanings: "witness." Step 1 was completed prior to the design of the minitext; "witness" was identified as a disjunctive concept and defined operationally as (1) someone who has seen or heard an event directly, or (2) someone who has learned about an event from someone who has seen or heard it. Criterial attributes concern personal viewing or hearing, an event to focus on, and a relationship to a viewer or hearer of an event.

Several dimensions of concept mastery, as well as some characteristics of the instructional materials, are measured in the questions at the end of the minitext. Question 1 measures whether, given the name of a concept, the student can select an example of the concept. Question 2 measures whether, given the name of a concept, the student can select a nonexample of the concept. Question 3 measures whether, given an example of a concept, the student can identify its name. Questions 4 and 5 measure whether, given the name of the concept, the student can select the names of relevant attributes of the concept. Question 6 measures whether, given the name of the concept, the student can select the names of irrelevant attributes of the concept. Question 7 measures whether, given the name of the concept, the student can select the correct definition of the concept. Question 8 measures whether, given the name of a concept, the student can select a broader concept to which it is closely related. And questions 9, 10, and 11 measure the student's affective reaction to the instruction he or she has just received.

Piloting of this minitext indicates that students reading at the level for which the material was written respond correctly to at least 70 percent of the first eight questions after completing the instruction.

Model #4. This model deals with relational concepts (those that may be defined only by the relationships between objects or events).[8] None of the preceding three models is completely satisfactory for teaching relational concepts, since they are designed to deal with concepts that have a relatively fixed relationship among the concept's attributes. Consider these relational concepts and try to define them in the same fashion as the concepts used in the first three models: work, play, poverty, wealth, beauty, ugliness, waste, resource. What makes something work or play? To answer, we need to know more than the activity in which one is engaged. Tom Sawyer's fence-painting anecdote makes this point. Painting was work for Tom because of his attitude toward it. By cleverly forming other's attitudes toward his job, however, he made them regard it as play.

Little is known about the most appropriate instructional strategy for developing relational concepts. One general approach with which the author has had some success consists of five steps:

1. Operationally define the concept in a way that will fit all possible cases of the concept, as it is customarily used.
2. Provide diverse examples of the concept, using illustrations with very concrete referents whenever possible.
3. After each example of the concept, provide a nonexample that is very similar to the concept but that differs in one clearly identified respect.
4. Present the examples and nonexamples in close succession or simultaneously allow the students to compare and contrast similarities and differences.
5. Check for concept mastery.

Again, a minitext will be used to illustrate an application of the model. The concept it is designed to develop is "resource," defined as "anything that people can use to satisfy some need." Criterial attributes are people, anything, use, needs, and satisfaction.

Piloting of this minitext, as with the preceding one, indicates a mastery of most items for those students reading at the level of the materials.[9]

In this booklet, you are going to learn some things about a *witness*. Please be sure to read all of the material on all of the pages. This booklet is short and will not take very long to complete. After you have finished reading the material, you will be asked some questions about what you have just learned.

Please do not write in this booklet.

Please turn to the next page.

Witness

When they were smaller, Rose and Richard were watching Robert Kennedy speak on TV. Suddenly a man took out a gun and shot Robert Kennedy. Rose and Richard and millions of other TV watchers *were* witnesses to the shooting.

A lady was called to appear in court. She was in the supermarket when it was held up. She saw the thief take the money, so she *was* a witness to the crime.

When the world was made, there was no person present to see it. There *were not* any witnesses to the making of the world.

Lola and Dwight heard about a car crash in the neighborhood from their mailman. He saw the cars smash into one another. The mailman *was* a witness to the accident. Lola and Dwight also *were* witnesses since the mailman told them about it.

Mrs. Walker was watching TV and saw the spacemen land on the moon. When her husband came home she told him about what she had seen. Mrs. Walker *was* a witness to the moon landing and so *was* her husband. He was a witness because Mrs. Walker told him what she had seen.

You see two boys playing basketball. You tell your friend Steve about it. When Steve goes home, he tells his mom and dad about the two boys. Steve's parents *were not* witnesses. They heard about the boys playing basketball from someone who did *not* actually see the boys.

A man is reading a newspaper. He learns about China from the President's statements. The President gave a talk on what he saw while he was in China. His talk is printed in the newspaper. The man *is* a witness. He is learning about things in China from someone who saw them.

Tom wakes up very early one morning. He looks out the window and sees it is still dark. As he watches the sky, he sees a bright light move very fast and disappear. He has just been a witness to a shooting star.

When Mr. Green gets into his car, he notices that the window is broken. He asks his family and neighbors about it. No one saw who broke it, but two people heard a crash. Someone also saw some kids playing near the car. Mr. Green could *not* find any witnesses. He, his family and friends *were not* witnesses, since they did not see anyone break the window.

Do you think you know now what a *witness is*? If the answer is *yes*, return this booklet to the person who gave it to you. If the answer is *no*, read over the material in the booklet again. Then, return the booklet. When you are ready, you will be asked some questions about what you have just read.

1. Which of these people is a witness?
   a. A woman who heard about a crash from her friend (her friend learned about it from a brother).
   b. A little boy who sees a puppy being born.
   c. A writer who writes a story about the making of the world.
   d. A man taking a nap.
2. Which of these is *not* a witness?
   a. A girl who sees and hears a train pass.
   b. The policeman who hears a burglar shoot at him.
   c. The owner of a house that was robbed while he was at the show.
   d. The fans watching a basketball game.
3. A person who sees a man washing a car
   a. is *not* a witness to the washing of the car.
   b. sees a witness, but is not a witness.
   c. *is* a witness to the washing of the car.
4. What is true about *all* witnesses?
   a. They observe only accidents.
   b. What they learn must be seen or heard.
   c. They must write down what they see or hear.
   d. They cannot tell anyone what they have seen or heard.
5. What is true about *all* witnesses?
   a. The person must have seen or heard something or have learned about it from someone who did.
   b. They are always in a court.
   c. They are always men.
   d. They must actually be at the place or event they are seeing or hearing.
6. Which is *not* true about a witness?
   a. He may have seen something happen.
   b. He may hear about something from someone who has seen or heard it themselves.
   c. He has not seen or heard anything.
   d. He may have heard something happen.
7. A witness is
   a. someone who collects stories about accidents.
   b. someone who has seen or heard an event *or* who has learned about it from someone else who has seen or heard the event.
   c. someone who appears in court.

    d. someone who doesn't like to talk about what he has seen or heard *or* who hasn't seen or heard anything.

8. A witness is a kind of
    a. watcher and listener.
    b. writer.
    c. talker.
    d. teacher.

9. Look at the pictures below. Which face best describes how *you feel* about witnesses? Write the letter of the face on your answer sheet.

A

B

C

10. Which of the answers below tells best how *you feel* about the booklet on witnesses?
    a. I feel very glad.
    b. I feel sort of glad.
    c. It was OK.
    d. I did not like it.
    e. I feel very bad.

11. Would you tell a friend that he ought to read this booklet if he or she asked you about it?
    a. Yes, all of it.
    b. Yes, parts of it.
    c. No.
    d. I am not sure.

Note: If you are done, please return these questions and your answer sheet to the person who gave them to you.

In this booklet, you are going to learn some things about a resource. Please be sure to read all of the material on all of the pages. This booklet is short and will not take very long to complete. After you have finished reading the material, you will be asked some questions about what you have just learned.

Please do not write in this booklet.

Please turn to the next page.

Resource

Some resources are used by everyone on the earth. Water *is* such a resource *when* it is used for drinking. Everyone needs to drink water to live. If children do not get any water to drink, they will die of thirst.

There are other resources that are living things. Animals *are* a resource *when* they are used for something that people need. For example, *when* animals like cows are used as food, they *are* resources. Or *when* the hides of animals are used to make clothing, they *are* resources. Or when they are used in work like camels and horses to carry or pull people or things, they are resources.

Animals *are not* always resources. A cow, for example, may get a disease called hoof-and-mouth disease. Then it *is not* a resource because it *cannot* be used for food or hides. Instead, it must be killed and buried so that its disease does not spread.

Wood *is* a resource *when* it is used to build houses and furniture. Since children like Sarah and William need houses and furniture to live, wood *is* a resource to them.

Some resources *cannot* be replaced once they are used up. Oil *is* a resource *when* it is used to run cars and heat homes. People can use up all the oil on earth. Then there will be no more.

Sometimes oil *is not* a resource. If a ship carrying oil has an accident, the oil spills. Oil on water *is not* a resource. It may wash up on beaches and ruin them for swimmers. Or it may get on the wings of sea birds and keep them from flying. Also, it may kill animals in the water.

People can be resources, too. You *are* a resource *when* you have abilities. Your abilities can be used to do something for yourself or for someone else. You can use your ability to read to make yourself or a younger child have fun.

The light you use to read at night comes from a resource, electricity. *When* it is used for things that people want, like running machines or lighting their homes, electricity *is* a resource.

Often, great storms produce electricity in the sky. This electricity *is not* a resource. It sometimes strikes trees and houses and may set them on fire.

Do you think you know what a *resource* is? If the answer is *yes*, return this booklet to the person who gave it to you. If the answer is *no,* read over the material in the booklet again. Then, return the booklet. When you are ready, you will be asked some questions about what you have just read.

1. Which of these is a resource?
   a. Clothes that do not fit you or that no one wants.
   b. Rats in a house that eat holes in the wall.
   c. Water used for washing.
   d. Trash in the streets.
2. Which of these is *not* a resource?
   a. Old newspapers used to build a fire.
   b. Water flooding a basement.
   c. A horse used for farm work.
   d. Uranium used to make bombs.
3. Being able to read a book is
   a. something that everyone can do.
   b. a special talent that only a few people can have.
   c. something that is not needed.
   d. a resource.
4. Which is true about *all* resources?
   a. They are taken from the ground.
   b. They must be bought.
   c. They are used by people.
   d. Only certain people have them.
5. Which is true about *all* resources?
   a. They are found only in some countries.
   b. They cost a great deal of money.
   c. They must be grown.
   d. They satisfy some need that people have.
6. Which is *not* always true about a resource?
   a. It is used by people.
   b. It is something you can touch.
   c. People need it.
   d. It can be anything.
7. A resource is
   a. anything that is grown.
   b. anything we are given.
   c. anything that is found under the ground.
   d. anything people can use to satisfy some need.
8. A resource is a kind of
   a. mineral.
   b. place where things can be found.

    c. plant growing in the ground.
    d. useful item or ability.

9. Look at the pictures below. Which face best describes how *you feel* about resources? Write the letter of the face on your answer sheet.

   A   B   C

10. Which of the answers below tells best how *you feel* about the booklet on resources?
    a. I feel very glad.
    b. I feel sort of glad.
    c. It was OK.
    d. I feel very bad.

11. Would you tell a friend that he ought to read this booklet if he or she asked you about it?
    a. Yes, all of it.
    b. Yes, parts of it.
    c. No.
    d. I am not sure.

Note: If you are done, please return these questions and your answer sheet to the person who gave them to you.

CONCEPT GAMES

There are many gamelike activities for children that will sensitize them to some of the characteristics of concepts. Categorizing items on the basis of their multiple attributes is one class of exercises. Children can bring used magazines to class and be allowed to cut out pictures they find interesting. If children are required to separate these into five piles on any basis they wish and then to explain the reasons for their grouping, it can be demonstrated that items may be categorized in many different ways. A child himself may be a boy, a son, a third grader, a Cub Scout, and a shy person. Labeling each picture, combining all of them again into one group, and requesting the process be repeated using three piles this time provides further opportunities to discover new attributes. In this way students are encouraged to explore *relative* rather than *absolute* bases for classification. Additionally they are allowed to develop their own categories (and frames of references) rather than starting with imposed ones. Three-dimensional objects and toys (houses, people, items of transportation) may also be used for grouping.

A related grouping activity uses a series of 3″ × 5″ or 5″ × 8″ cards with pictures of various social phenomena, figures, or objects on them (forms of transportation, events, places, different types of people, etc.). The children are given the sets of cards (which they themselves can create) and instructions similar to these: "Put all of the pictures of   (create a category)   in a pile." Repeat the instructions, having the children reassemble the cards each time. After several sessions ask the children which cards appeared in more than one pile and make a list of the multiple categories on the board.

A more complex version of this activity may be used with pictures of people, adults and children. If the teacher wishes, the pictures may be cut out in advance and given to the children. The basic categories to be shared with the class initially are Male and Female. String, knitting yarn, or chalk may be used to fashion two large circles on a table or the floor. After all the pictures are sorted into these categories, a third is introduced, as shown in Figure 5.3.

Children must now find a way to place those items that belong in the new circle *without* moving them from their former categories. Then they may be asked to identify those pictures that are Males and Children and then those that are Female and Children. A fourth category may be added, as in Figure 5.4. Students may then categorize those pictures of Smiling Persons and Males and so on, until three attributes are used for classification.

Another version of the exercise has students first dealing with each category isolated from the others. Then gradually they are combined, either by teacher direction or by allowing a child to do so himself or herself, and the multiple attributes are discussed. Many other variations of the exercises are possible.

For young children, the process of using different attributes simul-

Figure 5.3
Categorization activity

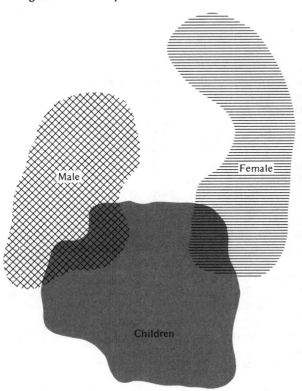

taneously as the basis for classification is a difficult one. The developmental considerations relevant to this issue are discussed in Chapter 20 (pp. 435–441). An important consideration is that activities use concrete graphic materials for classifications rather than purely verbal symbols. Frequent opportunities for children to classify phenomena in various ways and to share their rationale will pave the way for complex concept learning. They will also alert the teacher to developmental differences within a class.

An activity that can take many forms involves students in the construction of *concept folders*. Children can be assisted in constructing or locating a small 8½″ × 11″ folder or box and then assigned a particular concept. After the concept rule and attributes have been explained, the children can be asked to collect pictures over a period of time that are examples of the concept. When the projects are completed, the various concept folders may be exchanged and shared. Where necessary, students can explain the meaning and content of their collections.

A game designed to encourage the discovery of similarities in objects

Figure 5.4
Complex categorization activity

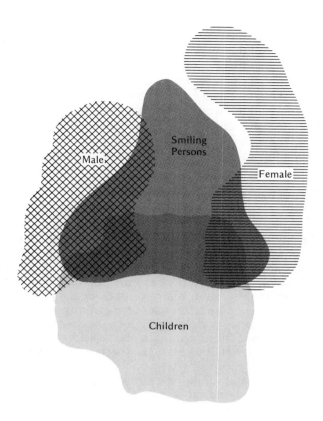

was used by Wallach and Kogan in their studies of thinking in young children. The teacher gives instructions for the game similar to the following basic ones:

"In this game I am going to name two objects, and I will want you to think of all the ways that these two objects are alike. I might name any two objects—like door and chair. But whatever I say, it will be your job to think of all the ways that the two objects are alike. For example, tell me all the ways that an apple and an orange are alike." (The child then responds.) "That's very good. You've already said a lot of the things I was thinking of. I guess you could also say that they are both round, and they are both sweet, they both have seeds, they both are fruits, they both have skins, they both grow on trees—things like that. Yours were fine, too.[10]

Where people or events are to be used, the instructions should be modified accordingly.

Sets of similar items and directions for social studies instructions like the following diverse suggestions might be used:

1. Tell me all the ways in which a city and a state are alike.
2. Tell me all the ways in which a president and a mayor are alike.
3. Tell me all the ways in which a rule and a law are alike.
4. Tell me all the ways in which a map and a globe are alike.
5. Tell me all the ways in which a house and a school are alike.
6. Tell me all the ways in which a train and a truck are alike.
7. Tell me all the ways in which a book and a newspaper are alike.
8. Tell me all the ways in which a mountain and a valley are alike.
9. Tell me all the ways in which a policeman and a soldier are alike.
10. Tell me all the ways in which coins and credit cards are alike.

SELECTING SUBJECT MATTER FOR CONCEPT-LEARNING INSTRUCTION

Suppose Ms. Garcia has selected the concept of "power," which she feels is important for her students to learn. She analyzes the concept and selects an instructional model. What topics should she use or from what subject matter should she draw for her examples? As the preceding chapter suggested, many sources of data may be used to teach a concept. Some criteria for selecting examples are suggested directly by the instructional models used, such as diversity of subjects, clarity, and concreteness. Other criteria to be used in choosing subject matter might be (1) student interests, (2) teacher interests, (3) teacher competencies, (4) relationships to prior or anticipated areas of study, (5) availability of material, (6) maturity level of students, and (7) compatibility with other instructional goals. Any or all of these criteria might serve as the reasons for selecting subject matter. Consider an unlikely hypothetical case where each of the examples of the concept was selected after *all* seven of the foregoing criteria were applied to it.

Ms. Garcia decided that her sixth graders would be very interested in the type of cases she planned to use (see Figure 5.5), especially with the procedures she intended to use—drawing on personal anecdotes, role playing, and using cases currently in the news (criteria 1). She herself found the material exciting (criteria 2) and felt fully conversant with it (criteria 3). These examples would also relate "power" to the nature of institutions, which the class had just been examining (criteria 4). The school had practically no social studies materials apart from the basic text, which had no sections directly relevant to the concept. The sparse library wasn't much help either. By using examples that drew on personal data and the mass media, however, a complete instructional sequence was developed (criteria 5). The students had no problems understanding or identifying with the materials (criteria 6). By using these topics Ms. Garcia was also consistent with her goals of incorporating the various social science disciplines into the curriculum and relating the social studies program to immediate social concerns (criteria 7).

Figure 5.5
Examples identified to illustrate the concept of power

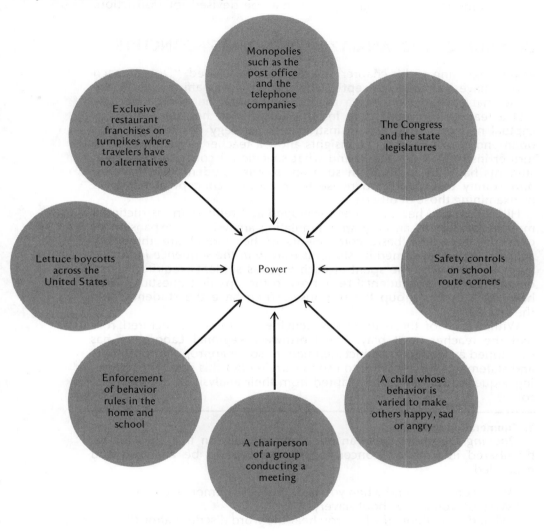

Ms. Garcia's case was unusual in that she was able to satisfy many criteria simultaneously. This will usually not be the case in most classrooms. On the other hand, her case shows how an instructional sequence for concept learning can accommodate flexibility and derive from the immediate concerns of the teacher and the student.

Sketches for examples and nonexamples can be drawn from many sources and can span various areas and time periods.[11] As shown in the DeCecco model, even imaginary cases may be devised for instruction.

EXPANDING AND ANALYZING STUDENTS' CONCEPTS

At the beginning of this chapter, the question was raised, "Doesn't each person have a unique concept?" The response was affirmative in the sense that each person has a unique conceptual network. One way that a teacher can gain some insights into his or her students' conceptual networks is to use an instructional strategy designed to elicit open-ended responses. Such insights allow a teacher to diagnose what further instruction is needed and what specific misconceptions certain students have. In addition, in such an exercise students can have an opportunity to expand and revise their existing conceptual networks by examining those of others.

Hilda Taba and her associates developed and refined an instructional model that permits an easy and stimulating analysis and expansion of concept states. The basic components of her model are three key activities to be performed by students *exactly in the sequence indicated* and with as much time spent at each level as students require.[12] First, enumerate and list students' responses to the opening question. Then have the students group the responses. Then have the students label the groups.

Within each of these three key activities there is a structured role that the teacher must play. The Northwest Regional Laboratory has developed a clear and succinct summary of some appropriate questions and statements for a teacher to use in carrying out this role. The following sequence is drawn and adapted from their analysis of the teachers' role.[13]

---

1. Enumeration and listing

Opening Question. Raise an open-ended question that calls for remembered information concerning the concept to be analyzed and expanded.

"What comes to mind when you hear the word democracy?"
"What do you know about slavery?"
"What do you think of when you hear the word discrimination?"

Refocusing Statement. When the responses indicate that students have begun to stray from the topic, call attention to the opening question.

"Let me repeat the original question."

Clarifying Question. Frequently students use a term that is unclear or that has many meanings. Ask for clarification.

"What sort of modern buildings?"

"Can you give me an example of a weird eating habit?"

"Can you help me out? I'm not sure I understand what you mean by kooky clothing."

Summarizing Question. Frequently a student will respond to your opening question with a paragraph or two. Request that he or she abstract his or her main idea.

"How could we put that on the board?"

"How could we write that in one sentence?"

"Can you help me out? How could we state that to get it in this little space on the board?"

Mapping-the-Field Question. Try to get as much information as possible.

"Are there any areas that we have missed?"

"Can you think of any other things?"

2. Grouping the responses

Grouping Questions. The initial question in the grouping process requests students to group their responses in any fashion they wish.

"Let's look over our list. Can you find any items that could be grouped together?"

"Are there any items on the board that could be grouped together?"

Grouping Rationale Question. A key element in the grouping process is focusing attention on the rationale used to categorize items. When students do not provide it automatically, request a reason.

"Why did you put _____, _____, and _____ together?"

3. Labeling the groups

Labeling Question. The basic question for the labeling process asks the students to analyze a group of items and state a name or label for the grouping.

"Let's look at the first group. What title could we give to this list?"

Unlike the preceding models, Taba's scheme should be followed in exactly the order specified. It is also crucial that the teacher accept all student responses without judging them as correct or incorrect. While, to be sure, students are likely to offer factually incorrect statements or offer apparently illogical groupings and labels, the teacher's role in this model is not to challenge or correct but to accept and list all responses. Keep in mind that the objective is to analyze and expand conceptual associations. In this vein, when students disagree on class-mates' groupings, *they have to be reminded that each individual's conceptual organization is unique, and that the rules of discussion in this case require the freedom of self-expression.*

In a classroom situation the Taba model might be applied as indicated in this hypothetical situation. Mr. Walker wishes to find out what his class of third graders has learned about neighborhoods. So he begins by asking, "What would you expect to find in a neighborhood?"

He accepts all responses without any verbal or nonverbal criticisms and lists all answers on the board. When Suzie volunteered the response "an elephant" and the entire class tittered, Mr. Walker stifled the urge to frown and instructed the class that there were no right or wrong answers since the question asked what each person would expect to find.

While Mr. Walker did not have to make a refocusing statement, it was necessary to raise some clarifying, summarizing, and mapping-the-field questions. When he was satisfied that there were no more questions, he asked the class to look over the list of responses on the board numbered 1 to 35.

Then he asked, "Are there any items on the board that could be grouped together?" His class quickly responded, and they came up with six groups, A, B, C, D, E, and F. After items were grouped together, Mr. Walker placed a letter of the alphabet next to the items to represent each group and asked the person who suggested the grouping to explain why he had done so. Whatever rationale was given was accepted, and whenever a grouping was challenged or an addition suggested the author of the categorizing was allowed to decide whether additions or revisions should be made. Anyone, however, was free to suggest his own grouping.

Finally, the authors of the groupings were asked to provide a name for each cluster. The class were then asked if they thought any of the six categories could be combined. Suggestions were offered and the authors of the categories agreed, so that four final categories remained.

This Taba model may also be used effectively as a general discussion procedure. It serves as a way to open up a group and allow the members to express their views without the fear of threatening cross-examinations or rejections. Used after the class has experienced an event such as a field trip, film viewing, or resource speaker, it allows a teacher to discover some of the *actual* learning outcomes in contrast to the *expected* outcomes. If responses are listed on paper instead of on a board, they may be easily stored and referred to at a later date.

MEASURING CONCEPT LEARNING

When has a concept been learned? Are there different levels of concept learning? In analyzing the various models for concept learning, several types of basic measures were suggested. The minimal test for learning is whether one can correctly identify or select an instance of the concept. This is both a simple and a practical test: Ask a child to locate the map for you and see whether he can spot it. There are obvious limitations to this level of learning, one being that you may be more interested in whether the child has learned about the characteristics or attributes of the map. Being able to verbalize the concept rule provides yet another test of learning that reveals knowledge of the attributes, but it still leaves other questions unanswered.

A scheme that will measure twelve different dimensions of concept learning was developed and tested at the Wisconsin Research and Development Center.[14] The items may be used as multiple-choice or open-ended questions and are arranged in order of increasing complexity. The two minitexts illustrated earlier in this chapter used learning measures taken from the Center's scheme.

For prereaders, simple pictorial tests may be used for certain concepts such as the one in Figure 5.6.

Students can be given instructions to place an X through the picture that shows an island. A standardized pictorial test of the ability to correctly identify basic concepts for prereaders is the *Boehm Test of Basic Concepts*, available through the Psychological Corporation.[15] It provides a basic measure for fifty temporal, spatial, and quantitative concepts such as "under," "beside," and the like.

Commercially made pictures on cardboard backing may also be organized to provide a simple identification test. The study prints in the *Schools, Families, and Neighborhoods* kit serve this function very well.[16] They clearly illustrate a variety of social concepts in different cultural and subcultural settings.

One should keep in mind that measures of concept learning may also be used as a pretest *before* the child has been given any instruction to determine what concepts have already been learned. Children acquire many concepts from direct experience without any formal instruction, and often they have learned ahead of time what the school's program plans to set before them. In other cases a pretest may belie the assumed mastery of a concept that the student's verbalizing suggests. While most kindergarteners can talk knowledgeably about a family, for example, one ought not to misread their level of learning. Like many concepts learned through experience, a youngster's grasp of the concept of "family" is invariably incomplete from a basic social science perspective.

Figure 5.6
Pictorial test: "Which of these pictures shows an island?"

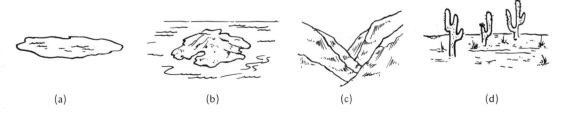

(a)   (b)   (c)   (d)

NOTES

[1] Herbert J. Klausmeier and Frank H. Hooper, "Conceptual Development and Instruction," in F. N. Kerlinger and J. B. Carroll (eds.), *Review of Research in Education, 2* (Itasca, Ill.: Peacock, 1974), p. 19.

[2] John P. DeCecco, *The Psychology of Learning and Instruction* (Englewood Cliffs, N.J.: Prentice-Hall, 1968), pp. 402–416.

[3] Ibid., pp. 416–418.

[4] Robert M. Gagné, *The Conditions of Learning*, 2nd ed. (New York: Holt, Rinehart & Winston, 1970), pp. 172–188.

[5] See Peter H. Martorella and Roger Wood, "Variables Affecting a Geographic Concept-Learning Task for Preschool Children," *Journal of Geography* (December 1971).

[6] Klausmeier and Hooper, op. cit., p. 37.

[7] Peter H. Martorella, "Instructional Products and Designs for Disjunctive and Relational Social Science Concepts," paper presented at the annual meeting of the American Educational Research Association, New Orleans, February 28, 1973.

[8] Ibid.

[9] Ibid.

[10] Michael A. Wallach and Nathan Kogan, *Modes of Thinking in Young Children* (New York: Holt, Rinehart & Winston, 1965), p. 32.

[11] See Peter H. Martorella, *Concept Learning in the Social Studies: Models for Structuring Curriculum* (New York: International Textbook, 1971), pp. 90–107.

[12] Hilda Taba, *Teacher's Handbook for Elementary Social Studies* (Reading, Mass.: Addison-Wesley, 1967), pp. 91–100.

[13] John A. McCollum and Rose Marie Davis, *Trainer's Manual: Development of Higher Level Thinking Abilities*, rev. ed. (Portland, Ore.: Northwest Regional Educational Laboratory, 1969), pp. 160–161.

[14] See Martorella, *Concept Learning: Designs for Instruction* (New York: International Textbook, 1972), pp. 218–232.

[15] Ann E. Boehm, *Boehm Test of Basic Concepts* (New York: The Psychological Corp., 1969). (Address: 304 East 45th St., New York, N.Y. 10017.)

[16] *Schools, Families, and Neighborhoods* (San Francisco: Field Educational Publications).

CHAPTER 6

Internalization Set #2

As with the first Internalization Set, the purpose of this one is to assist you in clarifying, internalizing, and testing the credibility of ideas expressed in the preceding chapters. If any of the exercises presented deal with ideas that are already clear and credible to you, you may wish to skip them. Some of the activities are to be done alone, some require peers, and still others are done with children.

CONCEPT ATTRIBUTES AND RULES

These three exercises are designed to clarify further the nature of concept rules and attributes. A rule, you will recall, is a statement that defines a concept, while its attributes are the essential (criterial) components of the rule. Frequently associated with a concept also are attributes that are really not essential (noncriterial). Many attributes of concepts we all share have never been clearly defined and must be inferred. Let us see how these features of a concept are exemplified in something we all have learned long ago.

ACTIVITY 17

For this exercise you need a regular wooden pencil, new or old, and at least four–five other people to make it interesting. Hold up the pencil for all in the group to see and ask them to imagine a naive little boy who wishes to learn what a pencil is. Try to answer his questions and refer to the pencil as you do. Now you role-play the child and generate the questions, changing the sequence as necessary to make sense.

"What is a pencil?"
"Does it have to be able to write?"
"Does it have to have a point on it?"
"How about lead in it?"
"Must it have wood around it?"
"How about an eraser?"
"Writing on the side?"
"Does its size make any difference?"
"Its shape?"
"What makes this a pencil?"

Now tally up below what your group has decided are the criterial (essential) and the noncriterial (nonessential) attributes of a pencil:

Criterial Attributes   Noncriterial Attributes

_____   _____

_____   _____

_____   _____

_____   _____

_____

Were you able to decide to everyone's satisfaction what the criterial attributes of a pencil are? The noncriterial attributes? The concept rule? Arriving at a definite consensus is less important for this exercise than to acquire a sense of what rules and attributes are, how they may be inferred, and what information concerning a concept is required for more serious instruction.

ACTIVITY 18

Keep the same group that was used in Activity 1, but first perform the task alone; then have each member share his or her results. Refer to Figure 5.2, p. 102, showing a hypothetical conceptual network. Examine it again for a few moments, retracing the continuum of inferences generated. Consider the item below in Figure 6.1 and illustrate *your own* conceptual network, based on a categorization of the item, by filling in Figure 6.2. Take no more than two minutes to complete your network, and respond with your initial inferences without evaluating them.

Compare each individual's results. Examine first the *name* or *label* under which each person categorized Figure 6.1. Then compare the initial inferences and, finally, the secondary and tertiary inferences. In what ways were all of the results similar? In what ways did they differ? At what points in the various sets of results were the criterial attributes of Figure 6.1 illustrated? Which of the inferences dealt with noncriterial attributes? Do the results in Figure 6.2 tell us anything about *your* unique personal conceptual associations with Figure 6.1?

Figure 6.1 An item

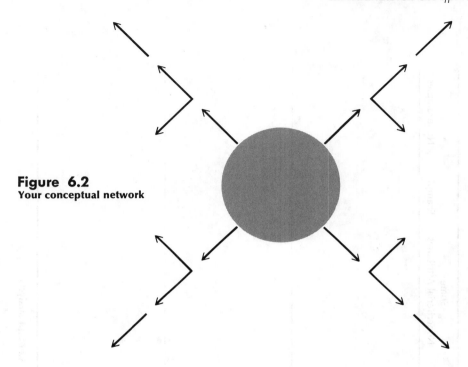

Figure 6.2
Your conceptual network

ACTIVITY 19

Do this exercise alone. When you have completed it, discuss your results with your instructor and/or peers.

Select any three of the social science concepts on pp. 83–85 and test your ability to analyze the properties of a concept in a formal way. For each of the three concepts, provide this information: concept name, concept rule, criterial attributes, some noncriterial attributes, examples of the concept (at least three), and nonexamples of the concept (at least three).

Record your results on the chart found on the next page. Consult any sources for information that you like. If you need help in the search, refer to some of the reference suggestions given in Chapters 4 and 5.

ACTIVITY 20

This activity involves individual game sessions with three children, ages 5–6, 8–9, and 11–12. It is based on one of the Wallach and Kogan games described in *Modes of Thinking in Young Children*.[1] You will need forty to fifty 3″ × 5″ or 5″ × 8″ unlined cards, each with a cut-out, picture, line draw-

Name	Rule	Criterial Attributes	Some Noncriterial Attributes	Examples	Nonexamples
1.					
2.					
3.					

Concept analyses

ing, or sketch of objects or social phenomena similar to these: canoe, tree, book, bridge, auto, television set, arrow, telephone, newspaper, dress, house, and coin. Any similar objects may be used to complete all of the cards, but place a different item on each card. Insofar as possible, keep details in the pictures simple. Use the instructions given by Wallach and Kogan for playing the game:

"Now let's play the picture game. While I spread these pictures out for you I'll name them off so that we will be sure to agree on what each object is. . . . Now your job is to look the picture over and then put all the pictures that seem to belong together into groups. The groups may be large or small, any size you want as long as the pictures in each group belong together for a reason. There aren't any right or wrong answers in this game. Every time I play it with someone the groups turn out differently. So you see, any way you feel like making groups is fine, as long as you have some reason for it. Once you make the groups you can add to them or change them, and if there are any pictures left over at the end that don't seem to fit into any of your groups, you can just leave them separately. Do you see how we play the game?—Good. Now take your time, there's no need to hurry. And remember that your groups can be all different sizes. OK, go ahead."[2]

ANALYZING AND EXPANDING CONCEPTS

The four activities in this section provide experience in tapping and modifying personal concepts and misconceptions. The first three exercises are based upon the Taba model discussed in Chapter 5. While the model appears easy to master at first glance, its proper implementation requires some practice, analysis, and feedback. Once internalized, however, the instructional strategy unfolds smoothly and produces extended discussion and reflection. The last activity is based on a game that the author devised for preschool children but which can be used with any age group, including adults.

ACTIVITY 21

Perhaps your instructor or a class member will volunteer to conduct this exercise with the entire class. If this procedure is not feasible, try it with a group of at least ten people, any age. Refer to the Taba model for concept analysis and expansion outlined in the preceding chapter (pp. 122–123). To internalize this model, it is strongly recommended that you actually experience it in operation as either a leader or a participant. The descriptive summary provided does not convey the dynamics of what actually happens to a group as a discussion leader actually implements the model.

Whoever will conduct the exercise should read through the model description and the suggested questions/statements and have them handy for reference. The topic to be discussed (the concept to be analyzed and expanded) for this demonstration ideally should be something of considerable interest to the group.

After you have finished the exercise, discuss and analyze both the *product* of the session (lists, groups, and labels) and the *process* (discussion patterns, participants' reactions, instructor's behavior). Questions such as the following may be useful to discuss:

1. What percentage of the group participated in the discussions?
2. Were the procedures of the model followed explicitly by the discussion leader? If not, where did he or she deviate, and what happened?
3. Did the leader accept all responses without communicating any verbal or nonverbal judgments of them? If not, how did the judgment make the respondent feel?

When you have finished with the discussion, compare the product of your session with that of one group of undergraduate students in an elementary social studies methods course. The concept examined in that session was "abortion." To open the session the question raised was "What do you think of when you hear the word 'abortion'?"

After approximately 25 minutes of discussion the following responses were generated in the order in which they occurred, exactly as they were given, clarified, and recorded on the board. The discussion could have continued, but it was arbitrarily halted due to time constraints:

1. Destroying human life
2. Unwanted pregnancy
3. Committing a sin
4. Population control
5. Rape
6. Genocide
7. New York
8. Abortion Referral Service on Chestnut Street
9. Future health and happiness to *all* concerned (mother and infant)
10. Psychological hang-up
11. Mental deterioration
12. Complications
13. Quacks
14. Money
15. Self-abortion
16. German measles
17. Thalidomide
18. Why?
19. Why not?
20. Responsibility
21. Misery and depression
22. Women's rights
23. Control of your own body
24. Forced sterilization
25. Doctor
26. A way out
27. Contraception
28. Ignorance (not being careful)
29. Sex (the idea itself)
30. Deformity
31. Methods (vacuum, etc.)

The class then grouped the thirty-one responses in the following way:

E	Destroying human life	F	Self-abortion
DH	Unwanted pregnancy	DG	German measles
E	Committing a sin	DG	Thalidomide
E	Population control	E	Why?
D	Rape	E	Why not?
E	Genocide	E	Responsibility
H	New York	CD	Misery and depression
H	Abortion Referral Service on Chestnut Street	A	Women's rights
		A	Control of your own body
D	Future health and happiness to *all* concerned (mother and infant)	AEF	Forced sterilization
		B	Doctor
		EA	A way out
C	Psychological hang-up	FI	Contraception
C	Mental deterioration	I	Ignorance (not being careful)
CDG	Complications	I	Sex (the idea itself)
B	Quacks	G	Deformity
J	Money	BF	Methods (vacuum, etc.)

In the third step the class assigned the following labels to the groupings:

A = Women's rights
B = Medical
C = Effects on mother
D = Possible reasons for
E = Personal responsibility

F = Methods of prevention
G = Harm to fetus
H = Where to go
I = Ignorance
J = Money

Since the list of groupings was long, we tried to find some that could be combined to form a new group. The ten groupings then were collapsed into three and relabelled as follows:

A, C, D, G = Women's rights
B, H, J = Where to go
E, F, I = Money

ACTIVITY 22

Do this activity alone. Find out how well you have internalized the role that the teacher plays in using the Taba model. You will be involved in a simple role-playing session with some hypothetical students that I have created. You have the role of the teacher, and you have just asked the question, "What do you think of when you hear the word 'democracy'?" Your students have answered as indicated below. After each of their answers in the space provided, note what you would do with their statements or exactly how you would respond to them. *Remember to stay in role and answer just as if you* were actually talking to the student. Be specific in relation to when you would ask for clarification and the like.

Elena: It makes me think about when I was little, and my grandmother and grandfather and aunts and uncles would come over to our house and have a big dinner and then shoot off fireworks every Fourth of July, and stuff like that.

Your response: _____

_____

_____

Chris: The President and the White House and the things that get passed.

Your response: _____

_____

_____

Angelo: Red, white, and blue.

Your response: _____

_____

_____

Trudy: It reminds me of being free, being able to do what I want.

Your response: _____

_____

_____

Tim: My mother and dad never let me do what I want.

Your response: _____

_____

_____

Laura: I think of all kinds of different people doing different things.

Your response: _____

_____

_____

Holly: The Statue of Liberty and Genghis Khan.

Your response: _____

_____

_____

After you have completed your role-play, check with other members of your class to see how they responded. Then refer again to the preceding chapter and compare your response to the specifications of the Taba model. How did you handle the situation?

Finally, consider the following analysis. Elena was verbose and should have been asked to summarize. Chris' comment required clarification, while Angelo's might have been accepted as it stands, or it could have been clarified. Trudy's case is also questionable; probably she should be asked to give an example. Tim's remarks call for a refocusing statement. Laura's statement requires some clarification of terms. And finally, while Holly may have some weird vibrations, they are clear and succinct and apparently are what she thinks of when she hears the word "democracy."

ACTIVITY 23

As a final exercise with the Taba model, try the strategy with a group of elementary youngsters if possible. A minimum of ten students is recommended to provide adequate interaction. Pick any concept you feel is appropriate to examine with the children and provide a 3–5-minute introductory statement to prepare them for the activity.

Try to arrange to have an observer work with you who is conversant with the analysis of the model and who has a copy of the procedure discussed in Chapter 5. This person can then provide you with additional feedback on how well you are actually implementing the model.

ACTIVITY 24

Another type of activity that allows one to easily analyze students' conceptual networks is the game, "Would you like to be?"[3] In playing it with elementary students or your peers, you should have a group of at least fifteen to make the session interesting. The game may be played with any age group. Any type of concepts may be used, and there are no winners or losers.

One person serves as the leader and asks the rest of the group the questions in turn. The rules are as follows:

1. You may not respond to questions with just a "yes" or "no."
2. In responding, your answer must be of the form "(Yes) (No), I (would) (would not) like to be _____."
3. You may not complete your response by using the same word(s) as the ones used in the question.
4. Questions must be of the form "Would you like to be (a) (an) _____?"

   Example "Would you like to be a bear?"
   "No, I would not like to be an animal."

Use any list of concepts you wish, but try to arrange them in the order of concrete to abstract in your questioning. As students have problems in responding, try these aids: Let them reflect, give some clues, return to them later and let them consider it, or finally just substitute a more concrete concept.

After the exercise is completed, analyze what you have learned about the others' concepts. If possible, record the session to provide more accurate information to analyze.

TEACHING A NEW CONCEPT

This series of exercises is designed to provide increasingly challenging experiences in teaching new concepts to children. Completing one or more of them should help in learning how an instructional sequence for children unfolds.

ACTIVITY 25

Begin this section of exercises by discovering just what social science concepts children are confronted with and expected to know/learn in school. Select any basal social studies textbook at any grade level. Take a 5" × 7" card and list your name and that of the text, its grade level, publisher and location, and copyright year. Examine the text and record the first fifty social science concepts you locate.

If a group is completing this activity, try to each take a different series or grade level for comparisons. Compare and contrast your collective results, discussing issues such as the following: Is there overlap among concepts from grade to grade? Are the concepts "easy" or "difficult"? In what other ways might they be classified? What changes do you feel should be made in the texts?

ACTIVITY 26

All that is required here is that you teach one or more of the three concepts that you learned in Figures 4.3, 4.4, and 4.5 (pp. 89–91)—*Glig, Gruffle,* or *Trug*—to some children. (1) Teach the concept(s) to at least three different children who are each a few years apart. Ideally they might be first, third, and fifth grades. (2) Compare and contrast any learning differences and similarities you encounter.

ACTIVITY 27

Select a social science concept from the list on pp. 83–85 or any other one that you wish. (Check with your instructor if you are not sure if your choice qualifies as a social science concept.) Use whatever model you feel is appropriate from Chapter 5 and develop an instructional sequence using strictly *pictorial and oral material* to teach the concept you have selected. Choose your material from any sources you wish and organize it in any media format that suits you (three-dimensional objects, pictures, slides, tapes, posters, drawings, and the like).

This list of procedures may serve as guidelines for developing the activity:

1. Select a concept that you feel is appropriate for instruction.
2. Analyze the concept in terms of the information that is required to use one of the instructional models in Chapter 5.
3. Identify and acquire suitable oral and pictorial material for instruction.
4. Organize the material into an instructional sequence including an introduction and all related questions and comments that may be used in the instruction.
5. Develop oral and pictorial materials to measure in some specified way whether the materials have taught the concept.
6. Identify a population of students for whom your instructional sequence is appropriate; minimally, they must not have learned the concept before.
7. Using only the instructional materials designed, teach the concept to the students you have identified. Then measure the learning.
8. Analyze the results. List the deficiencies in your instruction (if any) and determine how they may be corrected.

ACTIVITY 28

The final exercise in this set is to design a self-instructional minitext to teach a concept similar to the ones illustrated in the preceding chapter. You need not follow the format exactly as shown there. Include whatever additional information and materials, questions, prompts, and the like that you wish. Keep in mind, however, that the minitext should provide all of the information that a student needs.

In addition, the materials to measure whether the students have learned the concept should be an integral part of the text or be available in a separate self-instructional format. Apart from the minitext there should be a brief statement in a preconditions section that answers these questions:

1. What is the concept and what are its characteristics as reflected in the minitext?
2. For what type of person is this minitext designed? (Background, age, abilities.)
3. What else might I want to know about this minitext if I wish to consider using it for instruction?

To evaluate your minitext before giving them to youngsters, you may wish to use a five-point rating system covering its various dimensions. A sample rating system is given below.

Minitext evaluation

Preconditions Component	Rating: 0–5 points
1. Clarity of teacher instructions.	_____
2. Clarity and adequacy of concept definition.	_____

Instructional Component

3. Self-instructional characteristics.	_____
4. Adequacy of number of examples and nonexamples used.	_____
5. Adherence to instructional principles for concept learning.	_____
6. Clarity of instruction in materials used.	_____
7. Appropriateness for students for whom designed.	_____
8. Interest appeal of the minitext.	_____

Evaluation Component

9. Adequacy of measurement items.	_____
10. Appropriateness of items for concept specified.	_____
Maximum Possible Rating: ___50___	Total Rating: _____

NOTES

[1] Michael Wallach and Nathan Kogan, *Modes of Thinking in Young Children* (New York: Holt, Rinehart & Winston, 1965), p. 116.

[2] Ibid.

[3] Taken from Peter H. Martorella, *Concept Learning: Designs for Instruction* (New York: International Textbook, 1972), pp, 237–238.

MODULE SUMMARY

In this text, concepts are basically viewed as categories for objects and events that allow us to discriminate among phenomena. A more complex insight into a concept suggests that it has a dynamic process characteristic. Some observation of reality suggests a category into which the observation is placed, and the placement process in turn promotes the recall of old associations.

While concepts may be acquired from many different realms of experience, different disciplines have identified certain concepts as being central to their area of study. The disciplines of history, political science, economics, sociology, psychology, geography, and anthropology—the social sciences—have identified certain concepts that occur frequently in their literature. Within a social education setting, social science concepts drawn from the various disciplines can serve as the instructional focus. Many conditions make some concepts easier to learn than others. Usually the issue is more complex than whether the concept is concrete or abstract. Often the answer is to be found in the way in which the concept is defined in common usage. Another dimension of difficulty is the extent to which a concept may be classified as conjunctive, disjunctive, or relational. Similarly the representational forms through which a concept is encountered—be they enactive, iconic, or symbolic—affect the ease with which it is learned.

Learning a new concept involves minimally the abstraction of the concept's essential characteristics. This may be accomplished by examining enough examples and nonexamples of the concept, clearly identified as such, and by attending to the essential or relevant features of the concept. A minimal test of learning involves correct identification of illustrations of the concept. A more complex test is the ability to verbalize a correct definition of the concept.

Failure to learn a concept may be caused by conditions outside the learner, contrary to what is frequently assumed in classrooms. The instructional sequence itself, while structurally correct, may inadvertently mislead some potential learners.

Though concepts have been used in several different and sometimes confusing ways in the social studies curriculum, they continue to have a prominent place in instructional considerations. Acquiring concepts summarizes and filters the world for children and generally enriches their intellectual life.

Concepts have personal dimensions that are unique to each individual and public dimensions that represent shared attributes. The latter dimension provides the focus for designing basic instruction. Required are the concept's name, rule, criterial attributes, noncriterial attributes, and some examples and nonexamples of the concept.

Four models were offered for developing basic instructional sequences. An additional model was developed for expanding and analyzing concepts. This model allows for a more unstructured evolution of concepts and provides a teacher with some insights into the unique conceptual networks of students.

Helping students to discover that phenomena may be classified on the basis of multiple attributes is one of the many activities that sensitize them to the properties of concepts. Gamelike activities involving grouping and often including manipulatable items are one way to achieve this end.

One important flexible property of concepts is that they may be derived from many varied areas of subject matter. Thus a teacher is free (within whatever constraints the school imposes upon him or her) to set his or her own criteria for how topics and materials may be selected to illustrate concepts. If a student has learned a concept (in the sense discussed in this chapter) from one set of illustrations, he or she should be able to generalize his or her learning to a new set of examples, whatever their subject-matter designation.

Setting criteria for concept learning and developing some measuring device for determining that it has occurred should be implicit in instruction. Measurement may be a simple identification-discrimination test or an examination of other concept properties. Measurement can be used as a check prior to instruction to determine whether it is necessary or following it to assess its effect.

SUGGESTED READINGS

Brown, Roger. *Words and Things*. New York: Free Press, 1958.

Bruner, Jerome S., et al. *A Study of Thinking*. New York: Wiley, 1956.

Carroll, John B. "Words, Meanings and Concept," *Harvard Educational Review, 24* (Spring 1964), 178–202.

Fancett, Verna, et al. *Social Science Concepts in the Classroom*. Syracuse, N.Y.: Social Studies Curriculum Center, 1968.

Gagné, Robert M. *The Conditions of Learning*, 2nd ed. New York: Holt, Rinehart & Winston, 1970.

Glaser, Robert. "Concept Learning and Concept Teaching," in I. E. Sigel and F. H. Hooper (eds.). *Learning Research and School Subjects*. New York: Holt, Rinehart & Winston, 1963.

Klausmeier, Herbert J., and Frank H. Hooper. "Conceptual Development and Instruction," in F. N. Kerlinger and J. B. Carroll (eds.). *Review of Research in Education, 2.* Itasca, Ill.: Peacock, 1974.

Martorella, Peter H. *Concept Learning: Designs for Instruction*. New York: International Textbook, 1972.

Martorella, Peter H. *Concept Learning in the Social Studies: Models for Structuring Curriculum*. New York: International Textbook, 1971.

Sigel, Irving. *Child Development and Social Science Education. Part IV: A Teaching Strategy Derived from Some Piagetian Concepts*. Boulder, Colo.: Social Science Education Consortium, 1966.

Taba, Hilda. *Teaching Strategies and Cognitive Functioning in Elementary School Children*. Cooperative Research Project No. 2404. Washington, D.C.: U.S. Office of Education, 1966.

Vygotsky, L. S. *Thought and Language*. Ed. and trans. Eugenia Hanfmann and Gertrude Vakar. Cambridge, Mass.: MIT Press, 1962.

West, Edith. "Concepts, Generalizations, and Theories: Background Paper #3." Unpublished paper. Project Social Studies, University of Minnesota.

MODULE III

MODULE III

Instructional Models and Their Applications: Concluding and Generalizing

Reflection is indeed a part of life, but the last part. Its specific value consists in the satisfaction of curiosity, in the smoothing out and explanation of things; but the greatest pleasure which we actually get from reflection is borrowed from the experience on which we reflect.

GEORGE SANTAYANA

CHAPTER 7

Concepts in Action:
Concluding and Generalizing

To what use do we put our concepts? How are concepts combined and used in thought and action? While concepts may be the vital foundation of all intellectual development, they must be learned to some purpose. Applying and relating concepts allows us to acquire a web of knowledge that continually expands and strengthens over time. Having acquired a concept of "role," a child may use it to understand why his or her parents react in different ways in different contexts and, perhaps later, to fathom how roles and social status are interrelated. Viewed from another perspective, he or she will learn that "taxes" and "policeman," seemingly unrelated concepts, are linked together. This process of applying and relating concepts is what is meant by *concepts in action*. Figuratively speaking, when a concept is useful to a child, he or she uses it to "stand on" to get a clearer view of his or her world.

In this chapter the focus will be on the process of using concepts to draw *conclusions* and *generalizations*. Underscoring what was stated in earlier chapters, achieving these instructional goals will require different instructional procedures or models than those used for the teaching of concepts alone.

Figure 7.1
Using a concept to better understand our world

THE NATURE OF CONCLUSIONS AND GENERALIZATIONS

Listed below are a number of statements drawn from different general areas:

1. Pennsylvania is larger in size than Rhode Island.
2. The family exists in every known human society.
3. President Kennedy was shot by more than one assassin.
4. Tom can run faster than Bill.
5. People prejudiced against one ethnic group tend to be prejudiced against others.
6. Cleveland is one of the twenty largest cities in the United States.

After you have examined these statements, sort them into two categories by placing either an A or a B in front of those statements that seem to belong together. Do this before reading on.

What do all of the A statements have in common? The B statements? In what ways are the A and the B statements different?

While the six items may be categorized in many different ways, consider the following: Statements 1, 3, 4, and 6 are *conclusions;* 2 and 5 are *generalizations.* Reexamine the statements and write your definitions of conclusion and generalization based on these cases before reading further.

Definition of conclusion:_____

_____

_____

Definition of generalization:_____

_____

_____

OPERATIONAL DEFINITIONS

In what ways do conclusions and generalizations differ, and how are they distinguished from concepts? Compare your definitions with the discussion that follows. Both conclusions and generalizations state some relationships among concepts and organized data. A conclusion, however, is a much broader category than a generalization. It is any result that follows logically from an investigation, formal or informal, and that is presented in the form of a statement. Conclusions may be based on one or many encounters with data; they may be based on long-term or superficial analyses, and they may be true or false. Studying any topics at any age level may lead to conclusions. A conclusion that on the basis of the best experience available is shown to be true becomes a *fact.*

Generalizations, like facts, are a special class of conclusions. They are more powerful than general conclusions or facts in several respects. Specifically, they summarize and organize more information in a single statement since they apply to a broad range of events, and since they represent widely tested cases, they have an enduring quality. "People prejudiced against one ethnic group tend to be prejudiced against others" represents a predictive statement that tells one what to expect when encountering a prejudiced person, and the power of its prediction derives from the widely tested sociopsychological evidence on which it is based.

A generalization differs from other conclusions, then, in these respects: (1) It is necessarily a true statement (a fact); (2) it has predictive power in the sense that it may be considered an "if . . ., then . . ." statement; (3) it expresses significant relationships among concepts; and (4) it is lawlike in that it applies to all relevant cases without exception.

Over a decade ago political scientist James McGregor Burns noted that scholars generally agreed that in the United States:[1]

1. People between the mid-thirties and the mid-fifties vote more than younger or older potential voters.
2. The turnout of female voters is approximately 10 percent lower than that of male voters.
3. About twice the proportion of whites vote than of blacks.
4. White-collar, professional, and business people vote to a greater extent than semiskilled and unskilled workers.
5. The higher their education level or the higher their income or the more urban their area of residence, the more people, proportionately, show up at the polls.
6. People in the far West have the best voting records; the people in the South have the worst.

Which of these findings do you judge to be conclusions and which to be generalizations, based on what you know today? Why do you feel as you do? Consider the four criteria for a generalization as you respond.

CONCLUSION AND GENERALIZATION LEARNING AS AN INSTRUCTIONAL OBJECTIVE

In a social education program students may be assisted in systematically deriving an infinite number of conclusions but only a limited number of generalizations. As with concepts, it is important for teachers to focus on the process students employ to derive conclusions and generalizations. They may not merely be transmitted to students but must be acquired individually through reflection and analysis. Frequently students will pass from the conclusion to the generalization stage, and often at different rates. Consider the following example.

A sixth-grade class has been involved in a discussion of prejudice. At the end of the session, the question is put to the class, "What can we conclude from our study?" Whatever the responses students actually verbalize, they will likely represent a continuum from more general conclusions to possible generalizations. During the session some students may have moved to the stage of generalization, others may at a later point, while still others may never generalize. Unless the teacher is sensitive to this condition, he or she may press for students' acceptance and verbalization of conclusions and generalizations that he or she considers appropriate. The result in that case is likely to be rote verbalization.

If the instructional goal is to teach for conclusions and generalizations, a teacher has two basic instructional approaches from which to select. One essentially is open-ended, while the other has predetermined ends. Open-ended approaches place less emphasis on all students' arriving at a specific conclusion or generalization that the teacher has determined in advance. Approaches with predetermined goals begin with the intended conclusion or generalization and work backward in designing instructional experiences that will logically guide children along the desired route.

A brief illustration may help. Mr. Washington prepares a series of readings, activities, questions, and media components with the general goal of getting his third-grade class to identify various Indian lifestyles that existed in America prior to the coming of the white man and to examine the impact of colonization upon the Indians. His approach may be categorized as open-ended since he will be satisfied with a wide range of student conclusions. Mrs. Tranowski, the teacher across the hall, learns about the procedures and materials he has developed and asks to borrow them. She uses them to develop a lesson demonstrating that the white settlers in America exploited the Indians. Her goal is highly specific and the conclusion to be drawn is predetermined.

Either approach may incorporate concerns for clear statements of objectives, relevancy of subject matter, free student inquiry, integration of new subject matter with old, careful analysis of data, and developmental considerations. Where the approaches differ is in the degree of structuring of the instructional material and the specificity of conclusions sought from a certain instructional sequence.

Some of the instructional conditions possible with either approach are illustrated in Figure 7.2.

In quadrant A, where the teacher has a predetermined conclusion in mind for a particular lesson, he or she nevertheless provides little structure for students. The effect is to provide considerable ostensible student freedom for inquiry, but there will likely be a corresponding high level of frustration since eventually students will focus less on free inquiry and more on guessing "what teacher is after."

Quadrant B, with low structure and open-ended conclusions, offers maximal student freedom for inquiry. On the other hand it can offer

Figure 7.2
Possible instructional conditions with open-ended and predetermined conclusions

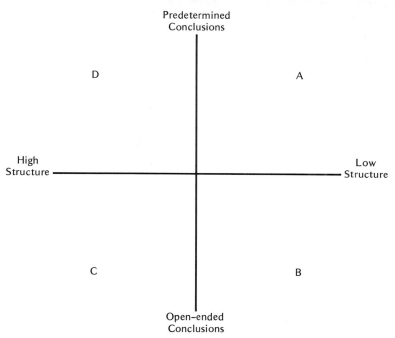

ample opportunities for aimlessness if students are not prepared for the freedom afforded.

In quadrant C the instructional context is more complex. Some degree of freedom for inquiry seems possible, since the teacher has no *explicit* conclusion toward which he or she is working. Given a high degree of structure, however, it is likely that a conclusion is *implicit* in the lesson itself. Quadrant C provides the least amount of freedom possible for student inquiry since it reflects high structure with predetermined conclusions. On the other hand it gives the greatest assurance that specifically what the teacher wishes a class to learn will in fact be learned, all things being equal.

As you examine the four quadrants in Figure 7.3, reflect on how you would categorize your own dominant preferred approach. In which quadrant would you place yourself? Another way to use the figure for self-analysis is to place yourself along the two axes, excluding the center, and then to join the two points as in Figure 7.3. This provides a more accurate self-profile, and if done with a group of peers on a large sheet of paper or a blackboard, the results offer some comparative data for discussion. The larger the triangle you create by the intersection of the

Figure 7.3
Instructional profile of a teacher who believes instruction should have a moderate
degree of structure and the conclusions to be drawn by students should
largely be open-ended

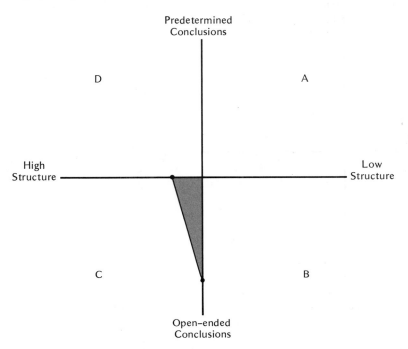

points, the more your position approaches that discussed as representing each of the quadrants. Instructional models that reflect both open-
ended and predetermined approaches will be outlined in the following
chapter.

Aside from the type of instructional approach, other important variables to consider in teaching conclusions and generalizations are prerequisite concepts, generalizations, and analytical tools. These prerequisites may be expressed simply as knowledge that a child must have if he
or she is to understand and efficiently learn new material. If a student
is to move toward generalizing that "cities have more people than any
other single area within a state," he or she minimally must have prior
knowledge of the concepts of "state" and "city." Perhaps his or her
instruction will also require some analytical tools such as reading a map,
interpreting population tables, using a card catalog, and generally how
to identify and solve a problem independently. Particularly as students
are led into instructional settings with low structure and open-ended
conclusions, the teacher must attend to prerequisite knowledge.

Developing instruction to promote conclusions and generalizations without adequate analysis of prerequisite knowledge runs the high risk of encouraging empty verbalizations. Children learn to *say* statements rather than draw conclusions and generalizations. Frequently the problem of attending to prerequisites will require only the restating of a definition or review of a concept. On other occasions it may involve interrupting some planned instruction and injecting an alternative instructional sequence to develop what was erroneously assumed to have been previously learned.

PROBLEM-SOLVING STRATEGIES

Many instructional strategies designated as problem solving are aimed at conclusion and generalization learning. Most of them have their genesis in the educational ideas developed by John Dewey in his book *How We Think,* and in many of his other writings.[2] Among the foremost early proponents of this approach in the teaching of social studies were Henry Johnson, Alan Griffin, Lawrence Metcalf, and their many students.[3] Frequently the terms *reflective thinking* or the *reflective method* were used to designate a problem-solving approach based on Dewey's ideas. While the structure of specific teaching strategies may vary, the common elements of the reflective method are psychological arousal and progressive systematic inquiry on the part of the learner. A *problem,* as we shall see further in the next chapter, occurs when a child is confronted with any datum that "doesn't fit" with what he or she knows, "seems strange," or generally produces some perplexity. Conclusions or generalizations result from interaction with the problem by way of possible explanations of it and sifting of the best evidence available.

Much of the reflective method involves appropriate *climate-setting—* helping students feel and clarify problems, establishing an intellectual and emotional environment in which children can freely explore the problem, while attending to procedural rules for inquiry.[4] Due to the nature of the subject matter under investigation, developmental constraints or other considerations, instruction directed toward a specific conclusion, or generalization predetermined by the teacher may be inappropriate. In any event, instruction for conclusions and generalizations should *move the student from confronting puzzling information, analyzing it with the best intellectual skills available, checking explanations, and relating the result derived to what is already known.* Specific instructional models for implementing this process will be discussed in the next chapter.

CURRICULUM DEVELOPMENT

During the era of Project Social Studies, initiated in the 1960s, many curriculum developers attempted to build social education programs around concepts and generalizations drawn from the social sciences. Often these programs identified what they considered to be important generalizations from each of the social sciences. This pattern is reflected in the *Teacher's Guide* to the second-grade text in the Macmillan basal social studies series. A sample generalization from each of the social sciences as stated in the program is shown below:

> Sociology: A community has need for a great variety of services; some of these are provided by the local government, others are provided by nongovernmental agencies.
> Anthropology: Customs, traditions, values, and beliefs are passed from generation to generation.
> Economics: Families are dependent on many other people to satisfy their wants and needs.
> Political Science: Citizenship is defined in the legal sense: Persons living within the boundaries of a political unit may or may not be legal citizens of that unit.
> Geography: Maps can be used to locate and define certain features about areas of the earth.
> History: Changed expectations in regard to government responsibilities stem from changes in ways of living.[5]

While social scientists may sometimes claim a particular generalization as being unique to their discipline, as with concepts the issue is probably an empty one if the objective is to teach a generalization. A generalization such as "all nations have cities" may be used to represent a variety of disciplines, including economics and geography. In developing his or her own instructional materials, a teacher more prudently might consult his or her own interests and competencies, as well as his or her students, in selecting subject matter to teach generalizations.

THE ROLE OF FACTS

Should we teach facts? This would be a silly question if so many people had not taken it so seriously. *There can be no instruction that does not involve some facts.* To operate without facts in a social studies class would be impossible. The argument "Should we teach facts or concepts and generalizations?" poses a false dilemma if one recognizes that facts are essential for all thinking. While concepts are the essential building blocks of all intellectual activity, facts supply the raw materials.

A more serious issue, however, is the *role* of facts in the instructional process. How are facts to be used by the teacher? Should they be learned as ends in themselves, or should they be acquired in the context of learning concepts, generalizations, and other intellectual phenomena?

This author opts for the latter alternative. Facts in great numbers are crucial to informed social analysis, but in instruction their appropriate function must be kept in perspective. They are to serve as needed in developing concepts, conclusions, and generalizations in systematic ways. Using facts in this fashion, children will be able to see interrelationships of intellectual phenomena and to fit them into a meaningful knowledge pattern.

As a check on the author's position concerning the role of facts in instruction, reflect briefly on the alternative, "Facts should be taught as ends in themselves." Try to develop a strong argument for this position and share your thoughts with peers. Then draw some conclusions concerning what this position suggests for instructional practice. Finally, share your feelings with others about what it would be like to teach in such an instructional program.

NOTES

[1] James McGregor Burns, *The Deadlock of Democracy: Four-Party Politics in America* (Englewood Cliffs, N.J.: Prentice-Hall, 1963), p. 224.

[2] John Dewey, *How We Think* (Boston: Heath, 1933. See also Reginald D. Archambault (ed.), *John Dewey on Education: Selected Writings* (New York: Random House, 1964) and George R. Geiger, *John Dewey in Perspective: A Reassessment* (New York: McGraw-Hill, 1958).

[3] Henry Johnson, *Teaching of History in Elementary and Secondary Schools*, rev. ed. (New York: Macmillan, 1940); Alan F. Griffin, "A Philosophical Approach to the Subject Matter Preparation of Teachers of History," unpublished doctoral dissertation, The Ohio State University, 1942; Maurice P. Hunt and Lawrence E. Metcalf, *Teaching High School Social Studies*, 2nd ed. (New York: Harper & Row, 1968).

[4] See Hunt and Metcalf, op. cit., pp. 186–206, and H. Gordon Hullfish and Philip G. Smith, *Reflective Thinking: The Method of Education* (New York: Dodd, Mead, 1961), pp. 195–229.

[5] Ruth MacDonald, *Teacher's Guide to the World of Communities, One Plus One: Learning About Communities* (New York: Macmillan, 1971), pp. xxii–xxiii.

CHAPTER 8

Strategies for Concluding and Generalizing

Every day of our lives we arrive at conclusions and generalizations about all sorts of social phenomena. It does not matter that we have had no formal instruction along the way nor followed any set of systematic procedures to arrive at our results.

EVERYDAY CONCLUSIONS AND GENERALIZATIONS

"Nixon was a crook."
"People on welfare are shiftless."
"Kennedy was a great President."
"Italians are great lovers but lousy organizers."
"Jews really value education."

Sometimes our conclusions and generalizations are inherited from our parents and acquaintances with little or no direct experience with the data, objects, or people about which or whom we make statements. Other times they are based on extensive but narrow experiences: "I spent three years in Paris and I can tell you the French are cold, aloof, and downright unfriendly!" Frequently, however, our conclusions and generalizations relating to our daily lives are very much on target. They are relatively accurate for our purposes and help to guide our everyday activities with some degree of efficiency: "Bippos stores have the lowest prices on small appliances." "People in this town won't support a symphony orchestra."

For many commonplace purposes, highly systematic, monitored, and verifiable procedures for arriving at conclusions and generalizations would be inefficient and cumbersome, if not impossible. Still other conclusions can be accurately derived only after some empirical tests that generally no one is willing to risk. "Any fool could be elected President" is a potential generalization that only another fool is likely to want to test.

INSTRUCTION FOR CONCLUSIONS AND GENERALIZATIONS

Classroom instruction related to the learning of conclusions and generalizations should focus on those areas that minimally (1) have great potential social significance, (2) have great potential personal significance, (3) help organize large bodies of information, and (4) are tentatively verifiable within practical limits. While these are admittedly nebulous benchmarks, they offer general guidelines for selecting among the wealth of social studies material available to the teacher and students. The processes and tested results that children acquire from instruction so focused should carry over into all areas of their daily lives where applicable, and children can be assisted in making such connections.

If you reflect upon the instructional models for concept learning presented in Chapter 5, you will recall their emphasis upon attributes and exemplars. These concerns, while essential for concept instruction, have little direct relevancy for conclusion-generalization instruction. As indicated in the preceding chapter, instruction for conclusions and generalizations focuses upon applying and relating concepts already learned.

MODELS FOR INSTRUCTION

Several sets of prescriptive procedures or models for leading students systematically to open-ended or specific conclusions and generalizations are outlined in this chapter. Each of the models is abstracted from a broader context of literature to which the reader may wish to refer. As with all models, these are meant to sketch the broad strokes of procedures unless a warning suggests otherwise. After each model has been developed there will be an illustration of how it may be translated to classroom instruction.

Model #1. In his recent writings Robert Gagné uses the term *rule learning* rather than conclusion or generalization.[1] The instructional outcome he describes, however, generally corresponds to what we have identified as a generalization. To prevent confusion, our term has been used in reference to his model. Essentially this set of procedures is designed to move students toward a predetermined generalization:

1. State the general nature of the generalization that you wish students to learn.
2. Develop some instructions to review knowledge of the concepts that make up the generalization.
3. Provide questions or statements that structure the students to verbally organize the generalization. (These may be verbatim statements of the generalization.)
4. Through a series of questions, instruct students to illustrate or apply the generalization.
5. (Optional) Raise questions that require the students to write or say the generalization.

These prescriptions provide only a general pattern, and the application of the model that Gagné supplies is also basic. His illustration uses the generalization "round things roll," one that might be taught to young children. Assuming knowledge of the concepts "round things" and "roll," the instruction initiates with a set of objects including an inclined plane, and a series of question/statements:

"I want you to answer the question, What kinds of things roll? . . . You remember what 'roll' means (*demonstrate with one round object*). . . . Some of these objects are *round*. Can you point them out? . . . (*Student responds*). . . . Do all *round* things roll? (*Student answers 'Yes'*). . . . Show me. . . . (*Student responds by rolling two or three round objects*). . . . Good! . . . What kinds of things roll? (*Student responds 'Round things roll'*). . . . Right!" With the completion of this exercise, it is reasonable to conclude that the rule [generalization] has been learned. However, to test this, a new and different set of blocks may be presented to the student, and he is asked to answer the question, Which of these will roll?[2]

Since Gagné does not offer a social science illustration, let us try to hypothesize one. Suppose the generalization is "the environment influences the type of shelter that people have." This statement satisfies step 1 of the model.

Step 2: The concepts to be reviewed are "shelter," "influence," and "environment." A teacher can check for knowledge of these concepts through several strategies, including question-answer, discussion, and brief information-dissemination sessions.

Step 3: This step is the heart of the instructional sequence, and it requires questions, activities, or materials that cause children to focus the special relationship of the concepts. Some possible questions might be: "What are the parts of your house?" "What are the different types of shelters that people in this area have?" "How are these different shelters constructed?" "What different kind of weather conditions do we have in this area?" "What are some things that all shelters in this area have?"

Possible activities might be as follows: List the parts of the houses of the students and the reasons for their existence on a chart, thus:

Parts	Reasons
Walls	
Floor	
(etc.)	

Then introduce alternative shelters from different environments, emphasizing the differences in parts and the reasons for them. Illustrations might be from Outer Mongolia where yurts (tents) are used, Indonesia where stilt homes over water often are constructed, and Colombia where grass-roof-on-framework houses are used. These examples would reflect climactic environmental elements that influence shelter structure. A chart might be used to summarize these examples, thus:

People	Type of Shelters	Reasons
Outer Mongolians		
Colombians		
Indonesians		

A final activity might be to compare and contrast these shelters and the reasons for their existence with the types and rationale within the United States. Any alternative instruction designed to highlight shelter variations, past or present, that are generated by environmental influences would accomplish the essence of step 3.

Concluding questions designed to summarize this step might take the forms, "What can we say about the type of shelters generally found in areas?" "How are environment and shelter related?" or "What has our discussion indicated about the shelters that are built in different areas?" If the questions fail to elicit a reasonable facsimile of the generalization, the teacher would verbalize it and determine whether the students understood it.

Step 4. Students may illustrate or apply the generalization by analyzing cases that describe either environmental conditions *or* shelter characteristics and then making inferences about appropriate shelter or environmental influences. These may be cases of the variety already presented in the preceding step, but where the linkage between the environment and the shelter is missing and must be supplied by the student.

A more direct expository way to translate step 4 would be to confront students with examples where environmental factors such as economics, religion, climate, defense, material availability, and topography suggested certain shelter characteristics. During or following the examples students could be questioned concerning how each case illustrates the generalization.

Step 5: Some of the ways for further testing the accurate verbalization of the generalization will be discussed later in this chapter within the context of measurement procedures.

Model #2. John Dewey, the New England philosopher whose life spanned both the nineteenth and twentieth centuries, influenced the theory and practice of much of twentieth-century American education, including the teaching of social studies. Most recently his writings concerning reflective thinking, inquiry, and problem solving were rediscovered, given new impetus by the curriculum development concerns of Jerome Bruner, and were reflected in much of the "new social studies."[3]

The instructional model outlined here is abstracted from Dewey's *How We Think* (although it also appears in a number of his other writings).[4] The goal of the model is a carefully tested conclusion resulting from some puzzle, dilemma, discrepancy, irritation, or general problem that a student personally experiences and is led systematically to resolve. Frequently this model has been referred to in the literature as the *problem-solving model* or the *scientific method*. Properly employed it is a powerful strategy for arousing students and aiding them in organizing a large number of facts into a meaningful pattern. Unfortunately many of the model's proponents have overgeneralized its applicability to all types of instructional outcomes and have given too little attention to the necessary preconditions for successful implementation. One educational philosopher has noted:

> Dewey's model of problem solving has won the support of many educators looking for a single, omnicompetent model of thinking. It may be doubted, however, whether this model accurately represents much successful thinking, scientific or practical.
>
> In everyday life we make many decisions on the basis of hunches, intuitions and rapid calculations, because we have neither time nor energy to do anything else. In such indeterminate situations as cutting a class, choosing a tie or dealing with a squabble in the family, it would obviously be impractical to follow the Deweyan method. . . .
>
> • • •
>
> Shorn of excessive claims, Dewey's problem-solving method has real value in the curriculum. Many problems within individual disciplines lend themselves to this kind of thinking. . . .[5]

Some of the prerequisites for successful employment of the model include analytical tools, such as experience in generating and testing hypotheses, ability to logically analyze arguments, and minimal attending behavior.

Basically, the model consists of five steps.[6]

1. Create within the general context of the subject matter to be studied some puzzle, dilemma, discrepancy, irritation, or general problem that students can clearly understand.
2. Once you are certain the students have attended to the problem, have them internalize it. Ask them to verbalize the issue and clarify it where necessary.
3. Solicit from the students some possible solutions or explanations of the problem (hypotheses) that might resolve or account for it. Clarify terminology where necessary and allow sufficient time for students to reflect.
4. Assist students to systematically test (i.e., check the validity of) the hypotheses they offered and to examine any implications of the hypotheses (i.e., project any consequences suggested). Provide corresponding assistance in the use of reference and research tools as necessary.
5. Assist students in arriving at the most plausible conclusion(s) to the problem (i.e., the hypothesis or hypotheses that are most strongly supported by the information available). Emphasize the tentative

nature of conclusions and the possibility of error due to the fact that the analysis in step 3 may be inadequate.

Many of the problems in applying the Dewey model stem from a failure to successfully implement the initial step. In general the type of material that will be perceived as puzzling or problematical by students will be relative to a particular group; that is, a first-grade class in 1A may perceive certain data as problematical while the first-grade class in 1B does not. What is problematical to a majority of a given group may be a coefficient of the background, ability, or developmental stage of the students. Part of the teacher's responsibility in using the model is to diagnose what might be perplexing to students within the context of the issue to be studied. For young children, a vast array of problematical issues are possible since so many events seem peculiar or discrepant. Witness the first-grade child who volunteered the question, "How do people get poor?"

An illustration of the Dewey model applied to classroom instructions is taken from the author's session with a group of ten- and eleven-year-old children. The data under consideration were some statements that Abraham Lincoln had made. The lesson unfolded essentially as described below.[7]

Initially the students were asked to respond to the question, "What comes to mind when you think of Abraham Lincoln?" The function of this question was to settle the class, review their prior associations with Lincoln, and alert them to the problematic episode that was forthcoming. After approximately 10 minutes of free exploration without challenges, the class was told that I wished to share a problem with them.

"Listen to these two statements made by Abraham Lincoln, and then tell me if you can see what my problem is. The first statement, let's call it A, is taken from the works of Abraham Lincoln":

Statement A

Let us discard all this quibbling about this man and the other man, this race, and that race and the other race being inferior, and therefore they must be placed in an inferior position. Let us discard all these things, and unite as one people throughout this land, until we shall once more stand up declaring that all men are created equal.[8]

"Is there anything in this statement that seems odd or out or order?" The students thought not, and we proceeded to the second statement, B. "Listen to this second statement, let's call it B, also taken from the works of Lincoln":

Statement B

I will say, then, that I am not, nor ever have been, in favor of bringing about in any way the social and political equality of the white and black races: that I am not, nor ever have been, in favor of making voters or jurors of negroes, nor of qualifying them to hold office, nor to intermarry with white people. . . .

And inasmuch as they cannot so live, while they do remain together there must be the position of superior and inferior, and I as
much as any other man am in favor of having the superior position
assigned to the white race.[9]

"Do you notice anything wrong now? What is the problem here?" At
this point, students were given some time to reflect upon the statements,
verbalize the discrepancy in various ways, and generally to clarify the
specific problematic issue. After the problem was restated in several
ways, the statements were both repeated to the class.

To implement the third step of the model, the question was raised,
"How do you account for these two statements, both made by Lincoln?"
The students had many immediate hypotheses, which were clarified and
recorded on the board. Four basic hypotheses were suggested as follows:

1. He changed his mind.
2. He was speaking to different groups with each of the statements, and
   he told each group what he thought they wanted to hear.
3. One statement was what he thought to himself (e.g., as in a diary),
   and the other one was the one he told people.
4. He was misunderstood (i.e., his words were taken out of context).

After exhausting the many responses, some of which were simply
variations on the same theme, the point was emphasized that several
possibilities existed concerning our guesses (hypotheses). Only *one*
might be correct, *several* answers might be true, or *none* of our explanations might be correct.

"What kind of information," the students were asked, "would we
need to have in order to check out our guesses and see if they might be
correct?" Responses were clarified and listed on the board under the
label "Initial Facts Needed." They fell into four categories: (1) when the
statements were made, (2) to whom they were made, (3) what the rest
of the statements (context) were like, and (4) where they were made.

At this point several possibilities were open to the author: have the
students themselves initiate a search for relevant facts, either individually or in groups; ask certain students to volunteer or appoint volunteers to research the facts; or provide certain facts for the students to
test the hypotheses. The third option was exercised due to time and
other constraints and to focus attention on the testing rather than on the
data-gathering process. In effect the author acted as a research resource
for the students. Such a role for the teacher is both legitimate and often
efficient, depending on the objectives of a lesson. The amount and sequencing of factual information provided by the teacher, however, are
important variables.

Consider the procedures employed by the author. With respect to the
first fact needed, the students were informed that statement A was made
on July 10, 1858, and that statement B was made on September 18,

1858. These dates were read aloud and then written on the board. The class expressed surprise.

"What do these facts do to any of our guesses?" the class was asked. The students suggested that the facts eliminated the first hypothesis. After soliciting their rationale, the author qualified their conclusion with the observation that "Lincoln *might* have changed his mind on this point in just three months, but it *was* a short period of time for such an important issue."

As to the second fact required, the students were briefly instructed on how the quotes and their sources could be authenticated. "In this case," they were told, "we are placing some faith in the reliability of the historian who gave us the information that it is correct." It was noted that we often have to do this but that sometimes the historian proves to be in error, as later research reveals. In indicating that our best immediate evidence was that the statements were *not* taken out of context, it was also indicated that the statements were parts of speeches.

While I had no information concerning to whom the speeches were made, I could tell the class that statement A was made in Chicago while statement B was given in Charleston. These facts were written on the board alongside the respective dates:

Statement A: July 10, 1858, Chicago.
Statement B: September 18, 1858, Charleston.

These new facts were greeted with "oohs" and "aahs."

Again the question was raised, "What do these facts do to our guesses?" The students suggested that the third and the fourth hypotheses were rejected and the second was strengthened. When pressed for an explanation of how hypothesis 2 was strengthened by the facts, they indicated that the audience for statement A was northern while that for B was southern. When pressed for further clarification of this point, they indicated that the Chicago group, being northern, would be *against* slavery while the Charleston group, being southern, would favor it.

Psychologically speaking the class was ready to stop at this point. It had struggled with a problem and had reached what appeared to be an obvious conclusion supported by facts. Many of the children were smiling with some satisfaction, and all the hands had gone down.

The problem was regenerated quickly, however, with the following sequence of instructions: "By the way, what was Lincoln's purpose in making speeches in 1858?" Some were not sure; most said he was running for President. In a 2–3-minute lecture, the group was briefed concerning Lincoln's remote presidential possibilities in 1858, the conditions that made his nomination actually possible, and how presidents campaigned and were elected in that period. This new information clearly presented some confusion within the class.

Someone then contributed a vague recollection of the Lincoln-Douglas debates and suggested that the statements might have been part of them. No one knew the context of the debates. This information was provided for the class and followed by the question, "In what state did Lincoln's Senate campaign take place?" After some discussion this question was resolved in favor of Illinois.

Then the students were asked, "What would Lincoln be doing campaigning in the *South* for a Senate seat in Illinois?" This question caused considerable consternation and generated a great deal of discussion but was never answered to anyone's satisfaction. I then added two bits of new information to the facts already listed on the board:

Statement A: July 10, 1858. Chicago, *Illinois*.
Statement B: September 18, 1858, Charleston, *Illinois*.

Amid the noisy reactions, I raised in succession the issues of why we had seemed so sure of our earlier conclusion, how the new facts affected our hypothesis, and how Lincoln could make such contradictory public statements in the same state. They acknowledged that their stereotypes of northern and southern behavior colored their interpretation of the earlier facts, that they now required more facts, and that communication systems in 1858 were much different than those we have today.

A wall map of the United States was used to illustrate the next set of facts. Chicago was located and the general characteristics of its population in 1858 noted. Similarly the city of Charleston in the southern part of Illinois was identified on the map. From this discussion it emerged that Illinois in Lincoln's day, much like today, represented sharp divisions in political opinion in the northern and southern sections. The location of Charleston, Illinois suggested the possible kinship with the proslavery stands of the bordering southern states as well as physical separation from Chicago.

The students had renewed confidence in hypothesis 2, after their momentary loss of faith. The final challenge to their tentative conclusion took the form of the question, "How did senators get elected in those days?" No one knew. It was explained that people didn't get to vote for senators until the twentieth century, about the same time that women were given the right to vote. This explanation was followed by the question, "What would Lincoln be doing *campaigning* for the Senate?" A final brief explanation sufficed: Lincoln campaigned for state legislators pledged to vote for him as senator if they were elected to the state legislature.

The entire session lasted 90 minutes with no visible sustained drop-off in interest and attention!

While the discussion related here was lengthy, it omitted many of the nuances and students' reactions during the session. It should suggest, however, that the Dewey model is at best skeletal and should not be followed slavishly in lock-step fashion. As Dewey has indicated, given acts of problem solving frequently juxtapose and recycle through the five steps:

> The five phases . . . of thought that we have noted do not follow one another in a set order. On the contrary, each step in genuine

thinking does something to perfect the formation of a suggestion and promote its change into a leading idea or directive hypothesis. It does something to promote the location and definition of the problem. Each improvement in the idea leads to new observations that yield facts or data and help the mind judge more accurately the relevancy of facts already at hand. The elaboration of the hypothesis does not wait until the problem has been defined and adequate hypothesis has been arrived at; it may come at any intermediate time.[10]

In the session described, the lesson was conducted a few days before Lincoln's birthday, and the general objective was to have the students arrive at some conclusion concerning the political dimensions of Lincoln's career. All of the facts that were intermittently and systematically interspersed during the discussion could have been provided initially for the students in written or oral form. The effectiveness of this lesson, which the author has replicated a number of times, however, derives from knowing how and when to insert facts to optimize and sustain the level of thinking.

What a learner actually does during an act of problem solving is most accurately depicted by the amplified model of problem solving developed by J. P. Guilford and shown in Figure 8.1.

Describing the operations and terminology of the model, Guilford writes:

> The occasion for a problem-solving episode begins with a certain input, mostly through the sense avenues, of course represented at Input I in the model. The E and S stand for environmental and somatic sources of input, respectively. The somatic source may include both motivational and emotional components, from within the brain as well as from internal receptors. A filtering step determines which input goes further and has any appreciable consequences in behavior. Note that the memory storage underlies and potentially affects all steps, beginning with the filtering operation. "Filtering" is a new and more operational name for "attention." Evaluation is another operation that has to be taken into account at all steps along the way, for the organism is perpetually self-checking and self-correcting. Evaluation is not left to the final stage of problem solving, as commonly supposed in traditional models.
>
> Awareness that a problem exists and identification of structuring of the problem are cognitive operations. During these operations there is dependence upon memory storage and there is evaluation of cognized information. In the effort to cognize the problem, there may be a seeking for new input information, as at Input II in the model. Filtering of this input also occurs, as well as evaluation.
>
> With the problem reasonably well structured, there is a search for answers, or for information from which answers can be constructed, in memory storage, with the ubiquitous interplay with evaluation. If a

Figure 8.1
Model for problem solving

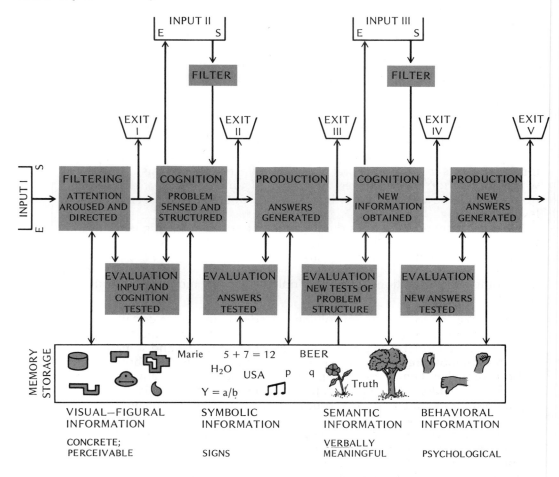

Source: J. P. Guilford, "Intelligence: 1965 Model," *American Psychologist,* 21 (1966), Figure 2.
Copyright 1966 by the American Psychological Association. Reprinted by Permission.

solution is accepted, there is an exit from this problem-solving episode at Exit III. Exit I would be a dodging of the problem. Exit II would
be a giving up or perhaps a result of distraction before the productive
operation got started.

   If no good solutions are found to the problem, and if there are
doubts about its proper interpretation, a new major cycle begins as
shown at the second cognition block. For reinterpretation of the

problem, new input may be sought, with steps similar to those already outlined. A number of these major cycles may go on, in what has often been described as trial-and-error behavior. Within each major cycle there are subsidiary loops in the flow of events, each of which might be followed by a number of similar loops. The looping phenomena follow cybernetic principles, with feedback information involved, and evaluation.[11]

Problematical gestalts or episodes that give rise to reflective thinking and ultimately tested conclusions and generalizations may take many forms.[12] Data may be presented as puzzling pictures, graphs, maps, charts, recordings, or the like, through the medium of films, resource persons, field trips, or personal anecdotes. What the teacher causes students to do with such data determines the extent to which problem solving takes place.

Some varied brief scenarios of activities for problem-solving instruction are offered below.

1. (*Third grade*)   Divide the class into groups and ask each group to list as many national holidays as they can. Compare the lists and make a composite one on the blackboard.

Ask the question, "Are there any special patterns of behavior or customs or practices that usually happen on these holidays?" Discuss each of the holidays and the patterns of behavior associated with them. Follow with the question, "What are the reasons why we have holidays?" (Some examples might be social values—to enrich our lives, economic values—to help stimulate the economy periodically, political—to provide an opportunity for political discussion, educational—to teach us about the cultural heritage of the country, etc.) Students might be asked to arrange the list of holidays according to when they occur during the calendar year and then discuss the economic reasons for their spacing.

Conclude by discussing which groups might be interested in getting a new national holiday accepted and why?

2. (*Eighth grade*)[13]   Read and explain to the class the following quotation about the United States at the turn of the century:

Agriculture, as a calling uniquely productive and uniquely important to society, had a special right to the concern and protection of government. The yeoman who owned a small farm and worked it with the aid of his family was the incarnation of the simple, honest, independent, healthy, happy human being. Because he lived in close communion with nature, his life was believed to have a wholesomeness and integrity impossible for the depraved population of cities.[14]

Place the following figures on the board and ask, "How do you account for the fact that urban population *increased* at the turn of the century, while the ideal of most people was to live in rural areas?"

In pursuing this problem, the students should question (perhaps before defining the problem) whether people from farms were moving to

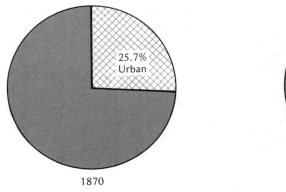 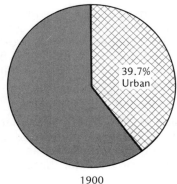

| 1870 | 1900 |

Ratio of Urban Population to Total U.S. Population
(Urban = incorporated areas with 2500 or more people)

the city, whether people from overseas were moving to the cities, or both. Since the object of this lesson is to determine *why* people were attracted to the cities rather than *who* was attracted, this teacher would tell the students that both immigrants and farmers were moving to the city and that these immigrants also had a rural, agricultural background.

Hypotheses that might emerge are as follows:

1. If given a choice, people will choose the excitement and glamour of the city over the monotony and hard work of the country.
2. If immigrants have no money to buy farms, they must settle in the nearest city where there are jobs.
3. If the city offers better pay, people will choose it over the country.
4. If farmers can no longer make an adequate living on the farm, they will move to the city in hope of doing better.

3. *(Fifth grade)* Pass out a map of the United States to each student showing the number of electoral college votes in each state—the total number of senators and representatives (Figure 8.2). Ask them to pretend they are presidential candidates trying to gain the most votes in the electoral college and thereby win the election. They are to try to win by getting the electoral votes of the smallest number of states possible. Raise questions such as the following: How many states are involved? Which are they? Which states' votes are not very significant in the electoral college process? What kind of campaign issues would you raise based on your target states for election? What conclusions or generalizations can you draw about presidential elections based on your analysis of the electoral college operations?

4. *(Sixth grade)* Instruction may sometimes take the form of a structured exercise to be followed up with classroom discussion. The follow-

Figure 8.2
Number of votes in the Electoral College by state. The votes of only eleven states
are required for the election of the president. Which are they?

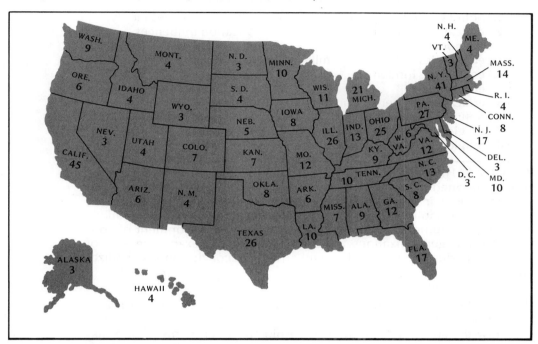

ing activity was used with a class involved in studying the nature of institutions. The handout sheet below was distributed to the class.

Institutions

The exercise below is not intended to be a research project. Use
your background of knowledge and experiences concerning institutions to think out the answers to the questions.

Social scientists state that institutions influence and affect other
institutions. One example is that the political institutions affect the
educational institutions with a compulsory school-age law (school
attendance is required from eight years to sixteen years of age).
Another example is that the religious institutions affect political institutions by forcing changes in certain laws such as the draft (conscientious objectors have helped to cause changes in the draft laws
in that they fulfill their military obligations without bearing arms or
weapons).

Select three pairs of institutions from the list of 13 below; give an example (other than those given above), and explain how one of the institutions in the pair has influenced the other:

1. politics influences education
2. education influences economics
3. economics influences family
4. economics influences education
5. education influences family
6. politics influences economics
7. religion influences politics
8. religion influences family
9. politics influences family
10. education influences religion
11. religion influences education
12. economics influences religion
13. religion influences economics

Model #3. Hilda Taba and her associates developed an instructional model designed to help children work with and to form conclusions and generalizations in a logical fashion. In her model of concept diagnosis, discussed in Chapter 5 (pp. 122–124), students performed the operations of listing, grouping, and labeling. Similarly, in the development of conclusions and generalizations there are three steps: examining sets of data, comparing and contrasting, and arriving at conclusions-generalizations.

Proceed as follows:

1. Have the students identify and examine specific information drawn from sets of facts.
2. Allow the students to draw relationships between items of information through comparison and contrast, and explain these relationships.
3. Assist the students in summarizing their observations and in drawing conclusions-generalizations.

The Northwest Regional Laboratory has provided a clear and comprehensive outline of appropriate procedures to be used with each of the steps in the model.[15]

---

1. Identifying items

Opening Question. Raise an open-ended question that calls for remembering or inferring from the field of information being examined.

"What do you see in the picture?"
"What happened on the field trip?"
"What did we find out about revolutions?"

Supporting Statements. Encourage all students to participate in the discussion and to reflect. Accept all student responses in a nonjudgmental fashion. Control also your nonverbal behavior.

"Take a minute to collect your thoughts."
"State it in your own words."

Mapping-the-Field Question. Attempt to collect as much information as possible from the students.

"Do you see anything else that should be included?"
"Have we left out anything?"
"Are there any points that we have missed?"

Focusing Question. Ask questions that focus upon specific points you wish students to consider but that they have omitted.

"What type of houses do they have in this area?"
"What standard of living do the people have?"

Substantiating Question. Ask the student to give evidence of the basis for his or her responses.

"What did you see in the film that makes you think there are no roads there?"
"When you say the father was angry, what were some of the things he said or did in the story that make you answer this way?"

2. Explaining items of identified information

Interpretive Question. Raise questions that call for the students to draw a relationship between elements in the information being examined.

"What differences do you notice between these two countries?"
"How did Tom and his father feel that was different from how the others felt?"

Substantiating Question. Again, ask the students to provide a rationale for their responses.

"What happened in the story that makes you believe that?"
"How do you explain the differences you mentioned?"

3. Drawing conclusions-generalizations

Capstone Question. Ask a question that calls for a conclusion, summary, and generalization.

"What conclusion could we draw from our discussion?"
"From our reading, what can you say about families?"
"What do you think the point of this story was?"

Substantiating Question. Again, request that students provide a rationale for their responses, particularly in this case to prevent extreme overgeneralizations.

"What did you read that would support what you have said?"
"Do you feel that what you have said would be true under all circumstances?"
"How could you say it another way so that it would fit most situations?"

An illustrative application of this model is found in the grade 1 *Teacher's Guide for People in Neighborhoods,* a text in the Addison-Wesley Taba Program in Social Studies:

Activity 10: Have the children look at the picture on page 64. Ask:

1. What do you see in this picture?
2. Why do you suppose the tracks for this electric train are built above the streets? Read the caption to the children and tell them that the buildings in the Loop are offices, banks, big stores, theaters, and restaurants.
3. What people do you suppose use the trains to go to downtown Chicago?
4. How is this part of Chicago different from Vicki's neighborhood? (If the children do not recall what Vicki's neighborhood looks like, have them look at the pictures on pages 24–26 to note the low buildings, yards, etc.)
5. How is the downtown part of Chicago important to Mrs. Winters? To Vicki? (If necessary, continue questioning until the children relate the downtown area to Mrs. Winters' work and shopping and to the proposed Christmas trip for Vicki.)

Typical responses:
Mr. and Mrs. Winter had to leave their own neighborhoods to work.
Some neighborhoods have more kinds of stores, so people go there to shop.
Different neighborhoods have different kinds of things in them so people go there to get what they need.[16]

Another application of this model involves the use of data retrieval charts, either student- or teacher-created. In this approach students systematically organize information concerning various topics such as countries and groups, construct retrieval charts that summarize their findings, and then draw conclusions based on their analysis of the charts. An illustrative chart is shown below. Students may be given data sheets

Presidential Candidates	Age	Experience	Education	Positions on Major Issues (specify)
Candidate A				
Candidate B				
Candidate C				

with the necessary information or can be asked to research the needed data and then transfer it to large sheets of paper with felt pens. A group of students may be assigned to a candidate, and the categories of data may be expanded or contracted as the teacher feels appropriate. As it collects its data, each group records the necessary items on the chart. With very young children, retrieval charts may be constructed very

Figure 8.3
Pictorial retrieval chart

	Clothing	Houses	Transportation
Now	(Pictures)	(Pictures)	(Pictures)
Then	(Pictures)	(Pictures)	(Pictures)

simply with few categories and one or two words of description. If the children are at the prereading level, a pictorial retrieval chart such as the one in Figure 8.3 may be used.

For certain activities, each student may have an individual assignment to collect data for the chart. For example, in one classroom activity related to the study of rituals, students were each asked to examine their own families' rituals. Specifically they were asked to identify and record family rituals associated with meals, holidays, greetings, and religion. After each student completed his or her assignment, he or she was placed in a group with four other students, and they were asked to complete a chart similar to the one shown in outline form below:

Rituals

Students	Meals	Holidays	Greetings	Religion
1.				
2.				
3.				
4.				
5.				

In using retrieval charts, the following types of questions may be raised upon completion of data recording:

1. As you examine the charts what do you notice about the meal rituals (or whatever the first column item is) of the students in your group (or whatever the row items are)? (Repeat this question for each item in the remaining columns.)
2. In what ways are the members of your group alike?
3. In what ways are the members of your group different?
4. How do you account for these differences?
5. As a result of our discussion, is there anything you can conclude?

A final analysis step may be to have each group exchange its data with another and repeat the questioning sequence. Often groups may be given a written question sequence and then they can conduct their own analysis and discussion.

James Hills, Taba associate, suggests that maps may also be used as a data retrieval chart:

> Maps deserve attention as a special form of data retrieval chart in which the contrasting samples are represented by the symbols of the map key. A population map of the United States makes it possible for students to contrast the density of population in various states or parts of the country. A number of generalizations can be reached from such a single-purpose map.[17]

He suggests that with a population map a question sequence such as the following might be used:

1. What can you tell me from the map legend?
   a. What symbols do you see? . . .
   b. What does each symbol represent? . . .
   c. What meaning is attached to each symbol? . . .
2. Where can you find examples on the maps of . . . (each symbol taken in turn)?
3. Where do the examples of . . . (a specific symbol) tend to concentrate? . . .
4. What patterns of distribution do you observe? . . .
5. What relationships do you observe between these patterns? . . .
6. What is the meaning of these relationships? How can you sum up these relationships in a sentence or two?[18]

USING CASE STUDIES

Case studies provide an excellent vehicle for instructional strategies aimed at building conclusions and potential generalizations. A case study involves examination of a specific event, situation, document, issue, or person in some detail.[19] It is an attempt to analyze in depth a single item on the assumption that conclusions reached will be applicable to a broader class of items. Fred Newmann cites six different types of case materials that may be used.[20] Four are described here:

Stories and vignettes. These are authentic or ficticious narrative dramatized episodes.

Journalistic historical narratives. Included in this category are newspaper accounts, recordings of news events, eyewitness accounts, and the like.

Research data. These refer to the results of studies and statistical analyses.

Documents. A wide range of items can be included in this category: speeches, diaries, laws, records, and generally documentary primary sources.

Teachers may use a wide variety of materials for cases and present them in assorted media formats: hand-outs, transparencies, records, self-made cassettes, film, field trips, and readings. Similarly considerable latitude exists in the choice of topics. Material may be as close as the community newspaper or totally fabricated by the teacher. Three different sample cases using both real and imaginary material are offered below as possible suggestions. As you examine them, consider how you might develop them for use in a classroom. Each offers the raw material for conclusion-generalization learning when built into a complete instructional sequence.

THE EARTH WORLD PEACE ORGANIZATION[21]

By the year 2054 the planet Mars had been colonized by Earth's World Peace Organization. It had been sixty-five years since the war on Earth, and all of the countries were now united under EWPO. The first permanent settlements were on Mars, and the colonists were setting up their own form of government. All of the major decisions for the colonies were made on Earth but a few minor ones were reserved for the colonists to make.

There were six settlements along the Red Canal of Mars, and all of them were flourishing. Prefab units had been set up for housing and work units, and families were demanding the formation of schools. Spaceships had regular landing schedules at three of the colonies, and people traveled back and forth from Mars to Earth in about three weeks' time. There were many things to do on the planet, and it was a very exciting period. It was exactly like being a pioneer.

There was one very important thing that bothered the colonists, however. They could not vote in the EWPO legislature. The EWPO had decided that the distance between Earth and Mars was too great to permit legislators to travel back and forth. The Earth government also felt that the colonists had too much to do on the new planet to be concerned with happenings on Earth. When space travel first began in earnest, it was natural to allow astronauts the right to vote. They were not gone for a very long period of time, and they were based on Earth. When the colonization of Mars started, the situation changed. The colonists were to live on the planet, and·they would return to Earth to visit but not to live.

There was constant interaction between the two planets and supplies arrived regularly by spaceship from Earth. The EWPO wanted to help the new planet prosper. The colonists were the hope of Earth to help overcrowding on the mother planet. In time, it was hoped, Mars would become a satellite planet that would supply Earth with needed minerals and other riches soon to be discovered. EWPO passed all of the laws that would govern the new planet, and for the first twenty years things went smoothly.

As more and more colonists arrived on Mars, the planet became more civilized and developed, and small cities sprang up similar to those on Earth. The new·Martians loved their new planet. It was less crowded than Earth and life was much more exciting. The planet became a true home to the colonists. As things were growing more pleasant on Mars, they were becoming less so on Earth. Even with the new planet being colonized, Earth was still overcrowded. Even with all of the methods of birth control, there were still areas on Earth where billions of people lived. The supply of minerals and food was getting lower and lower. Spaceships brought back as much of the precious matter from the new planet as possible, but travel was difficult and time consuming. The citizens of Mars began to look upon these exportations with a new awareness. It was true that supplies still came from Earth, but as the planet became more settled, it also became more self-supporting. The exports far outweighed the imports, and the people began to resent the demands of Earth. The EWPO found itself needing more and more money to supply the demands of Earth's population. The needs were so pressing that the government began to place duties on the supplies shipped to the new planet. The colonists were forced to pay taxes on prefabricated building units, spaceship supplies, medical supplies, and certain foods.

Most of the colonists were still loyal to Earth. They felt it was their duty to help the mother planet. Their feelings were torn, however, because they felt they had to support the new planet and yet they were now being asked to strongly support the old planet. There were other colonists who were not torn. They were completely loyal to Mars. Many of them had been born on the new planet, and they had little love for the planet Earth. Why should they support the old planet? None of them· had any say as to the governing laws of the planet Earth, so why should they pay for it?

More and more colonists became disenchanted with the ties between the two planets. They became very vocal about their feelings and began to hold meetings to discuss ways in which they could break away from the mother planet. Many colonists were still divided in their allegiance, since they were still loyal to Earth. Many meetings were held in secret to protest Earth's demands. As more and more colonists became dissatisfied with the policies towards Mars, the rebels became more visible. They were just waiting for one more demand before they would actually physically rebel.

It came one day. The colonists on Mars as well as the population on Earth were very fond of a particular vitamin drink. It was delicious, and most of the colonists drank it every day. Spaceships from Earth brought supplies of the drink every three weeks, and they were gone almost as soon as they arrived. The EWPO knew that if they taxed this drink, the revenue would bring a large sum of money back to Earth. They decided to take this action. A tax was placed on the export of Pink Vitade. This act was too much for the colonists. They overtook one of the supply ships and poured all of the drink into the Red Canal.

THE CAPTAIN-JOHN-SMITH-MEETS-POCAHONTAS CASE STUDY

Consider the two following statements, both taken from the writings of John Smith. *They both describe the same episode:*

Account A, published in 1607

> Arriving at Weramocomoco, their Emperour proudly lying upon a Bedstead a foote high, upon tenne or twelve Mattes, richly hung with manie Chaynes of great Pearles about his necke, and covered with a great Covering of Rahaughcums. At heade sat a woman, at his feete another; on each side sitting uppon a Matte upon the ground, were raunged his chiefe men on each side the fire, tenne in a ranke, and behinde them as many yong women, each a great Chaine of white Beades over their shoulders, their heades painted in redde: and with such a grave and Majesticall countenance as drave me into admiration to see such state in a naked Salvage, hee kindly welcomed me with good wordes, and great Platters of sundrie Victuals, assuring mee his friendship, and my libertie within foure days.[22]

Account B, published in 1624

> At last they brought him to Werowocomoco, where was Powhatan, their emperor. Here more than two hundred of those grim courtiers stood wondering at him as [if] he had been a monster, till Powhatan and his train had put themselves in their greatest braveries. Before a fire upon a seat like a bedstead he sat covered with a great robe made of raccoon skins, and all the tails hanging by. On either hand did sit a young wench of sixteen or eighteen years, and along on each side the house two rows of men. And behind them as many women, with all their heads and shoulders painted red, many of their heads bedecked with the white down of birds but everyone with something, and a great chain of white beads about their necks.

At his entrance before the king all the people gave a great shout. The queen of Appomattoc was appointed to bring him water to wash his hands, and another brought him a bunch of feathers instead of a towel to dry them. Having feasted him after their best barbarous manner they could, a long consultation was held. But the conclusion was: two great stones were brought before Powhatan, then as many as could laid hands on him, dragged him to them, and thereon laid his head. And being ready with their clubs to beat out his brains, Pocahontas, the king's dearest daughter, when no entreaty could prevail, got his head in her arms and laid her own upon his to save him from death. Whereat the emperor was contented he should live to make him hatchets and her bells, beads, and copper; for they thought him as well of all occupations as themselves.[23]

SENATE TESTIMONY

The following statement was given to the Senate subcommittee hearing in Washington, D.C. on the effects of TV advertising:

Mr. Chairman:

My name is Dawn Ann Kurth. I am 11 years old and in the fifth grade at Meadowlane Elementary School in Melbourne, Florida. This year I was one of the 36 students chosen by the teachers out of 20,000 5th-through-8th graders, to do a project in the Talented Student Program in Brevard County. We were allowed to choose a project in any field we wanted. It was difficult to decide. There seem to be so many problems in the world today. What could I do?

A small family crisis solved my problem. My sister Martha, who is 7, had asked my mother to buy a box of Post Raisin Bran so that she could get the free record that was on the back of the box. It had been advertised several times on Saturday morning cartoon shows. My mother bought the cereal, and we all (there are four children in our family) helped Martha eat it so she could get the record. It was after the cereal was eaten and she had the record that the crisis occurred. There was no way the record would work.

Martha was very upset and began crying and I was angry too. It just didn't seem right to me that something could be shown on TV that worked fine and people were listening and dancing to the record and when you bought the cereal, instead of laughing and dancing, we were crying and angry. Then I realized that perhaps here was a problem I could do something about or, if I couldn't change things, at least I could make others aware of deceptive advertising practices to children.

To begin my project I decided to keep a record of the number of commercials shown on typical Saturday morning TV shows. There were 25 commercial messages during one hour, from 8 to 9 A.M., not counting ads for shows coming up or public service ads. I found there were only 10 to 12 commercials during shows my parents like to watch. For the first time, I really began to think about what the commercials were saying. I had always listened before and many times asked my mother to buy certain products I had seen advertised, but now I was listening and really thinking about what was being said. Millions of kids are being told:

"Make friends with Kool-aid, Kool-aid makes good friends."

"People who love kids have to buy Fritos."

"Hershey chocolate makes milk taste like a chocolate bar." Why should milk taste like a chocolate bar anyway?

"Cheerios make you feel groovy all day long." I eat them sometimes and I don't feel any different.

"Libby frozen dinners have fun in them." Nothing is said about the food in them.

'Cocoa Krispies taste like a chocolate milk shake only they are crunchy."

"Lucky Charms are magically delicious with sweet surprises inside." Those sweet surprises are marshmallow candy.

I think the commercials I just mentioned are examples of deceptive advertising practices.

Another type of commercial advertises a free bonus gift if you buy a certain product. The whole commercial tells about the bonus gift and says nothing about the product they want you to buy. Many times, as in the case of the record, the bonus gift appears to be worthless junk or isn't in the package. I wrote to the TV networks and found it costs about $4,000 for a 30-second commercial. Many of those ads appeared four times in each hour. I wonder why any company would spend $15,000 or $20,000 an hour to advertise worthless junk.

The ads that I have mentioned I consider deceptive. However, I've found others I feel are dangerous.

Bugs Bunny vitamin ads say their vitamins "taste yummy" and taste good.

Chocolate Zestabs say their product is "delicious" and compare taking it with eating a chocolate cookie.

If my mother were to buy those vitamins, and my little sister got to the bottles, I'm sure she would eat them just as if they were candy.

I do not know a lot about nutrition, but I do know that my mother tries to keep our family from eating so many sweets. She says they are bad for our teeth. Our dentist says so too. If they are bad, why are companies allowed to make children want them by advertising on TV? Almost all of the ads I have seen during children's programs are for candy, or sugar-coated cereal with candy in it.

I know people who make these commercials are not bad. I know the commercials pay for TV shows and I like to watch TV. I just think that it would be as easy to produce a good commercial as a bad one. If there is nothing good that can be said about a product that is the truth, perhaps the product should not be sold to kids on TV in the first place.

I do not know all the ways to write a good commercial, but I think commercials would be good if they taught kids something that was true. They could teach about good health, and also about where food is grown. If my 3-year-old sister can learn to sing, "it takes two hands to handle a whopper 'cause the burgers are better at Burger King," from a commercial, couldn't a commercial also teach her to recognize the letters of the alphabet, numbers, and colors? I am sure that people who write commercials are much smarter than I and they should be able to think of many ways to write a commercial that tells the truth about a product without telling kids they should eat it because it is sweeter or "shaped like fun" (what shape is fun, anyway?) or because Tony Tiger says so.

I also think kids should not be bribed to buy a product by commercials telling of the wonderful free bonus gift inside.

I think kids should not be told to eat a certain product because a well-known hero does. If this is a reason to eat something, then, when a well-known person uses drugs, should kids try drugs for the same reason?

Last of all, I think vitamin companies should never, never be allowed to advertise their product as being delicious, yummy, or in any way make children think they are candy. Perhaps these commercials could teach children the dangers of taking drugs or teach children that, if they do find a bottle of pills, or if the medicine closet is open, they should run and tell a grown-up, and never, never eat the medicine.

I want to thank the Committee for letting me appear. When I leave Washington, the thing that I will remember for the rest of my life is that some people do care what kids think. I know I could have led a protest about commercials through our shopping center and people would have laughed at me or thought I needed a good spanking or wondered what kind of parents I had that would let me run around in the streets protesting. I decided to gather my information and write letters to anyone I thought would listen. Many of them didn't listen, but some did. That is why I am here today. Because some people cared about what I thought. I hope now that I can tell every kid in America that when they see a wrong, they shouldn't just try to forget about it and hope it will go away. They should begin to do what they can to change it.

People will listen. I know, because you're here listening to me.[24]

MEASURING THE LEARNING
OF CONCLUSIONS-GENERALIZATIONS

When have conclusions-generalizations been learned? A variety of schemes exist for measuring different dimensions of learning. Generally they take the form of testing for:

1. Learning of facts related to the conclusions-generalizations.
2. Correct identification of the conclusions-generalizations.
3. Application of the conclusions-generalizations to new situations.
4. Original thinking based on the conclusions-generalizations.

While the extensive mechanics of constructing such measurement items is beyond the scope of this chapter, a few key references and some illustrations may be useful.

SELECTED MEASUREMENT REFERENCES

A clear and brief "how-to-do-it" kit for constructing and analyzing classroom tests by teachers has been developed by the Educational Testing Service, Princeton, N.J. The reference or teacher-materials section of your library is likely to have a copy of Benjamin Bloom et al., *Handbook of Formative and Summative Evaluation of Student Learning*, New York: McGraw-Hill, 1971. It is a comprehensive statement on the application of the taxonomies of educational objectives to evaluation items, including those relating to conclusions and generalizations. Two more recent works offering clear and specific instruction on constructing measurement items are J. Block and L. Anderson, *Mastery Learning in Classroom Instruction*, New York: Macmillan, 1975, and N. Gronlund, *Preparing Criterion-Referenced Tests for Classroom Instruction*, New York: Macmillan, 1973.

An excellent review of available tests for the elementary grades is the *Center for the Study of Evaluation Elementary School Test Evaluations*, Los Angeles: Center for the Study of Evaluation, 1970. It contains a list of tests, keyed to the objectives of elementary subject areas, and, most importantly, an evaluation of each of the tests listed. Criteria used for evaluation are:

Measurement validity—Does the test measure the specific educational objectives?

Examiner appropriateness—How appropriate is the test for the children who are to use it?

Administrative usability—How easy is the test to use, score, interpret, and apply the results?

Normed technical excellence—Does the test always measure the same thing?

Though not a measurement reference, *Human Behavior: An Inventory of Scientific Findings* by Bernard Berelson and Gary A. Steiner, New York: Harcourt Brace Jovanovich, 1964, is an excellent source of social science generalizations derived from research findings.

SAMPLE TEST SPECIMENS

Apart from the mechanics of constructing, administering, and analyzing tests for conclusion-generalization learning, a few samples of actual items may be helpful. One simple procedure, after a series of specific examples of a generalization, is to ask students to summarize the main idea of the instruction. After being shown a series of pictures of different shelters along with a brief statement relating the shelter type to environmental factors, a first-grade class might be asked to summarize what "the pictures seem to tell us about shelters." Without question the responses will not be a verbatim statement of our earlier generalization, "the environment influences the type of shelter people have." They should, however, offer one approximate measure of the success of the earlier lesson described in detail in conjunction with the Gagné model.

The work of the Taba associates produced a number of testing schemes to be used in conjunction with the Taba strategies. A complete collection of these appear in N. E. Wallen et al., *The Taba Curriculum Development Project in Social Studies*, Menlo Park, Calif.: Addison-Wesley, 1969. If your library does not have this report, it can be found in the ERIC microdocument section. A sample of the test items relating to the application of generalizations is reproduced below.[25]

Explanation to students:

This booklet has some stories. After each story there are some sentences about the story. I will read the story out loud to you and you can follow along in your booklet. Then I will read each of the sentences and you are to decide whether the sentence is probably true or probably false.

Many times it may be hard for you to see that either answer is correct, but you need to decide whether it is *probably true* or *probably false*. If you have read a weather forecast for rain tomorrow and I should ask you to score the statement: "It will rain tomorrow," you could answer, "probably true" even though you can't be sure.

Decide on an answer for each sentence that I read to you. Mark your answer with a heavy black mark. If you think the answer is probably true, mark in the space marked A. If you think the answer is probably false, mark in the space marked B.

Example:

Mr. Jones was a farmer in the midwest. When he heard about the discovery of gold in California he left his family and went to California.

1. Mr. Jones went to California with his family.   (B)
2. Mr. Jones was a very rich farmer.   (B)
3. Mr. Jones went to California to look for gold.   (A)

*Note: This document contains: a) an abbreviated statement of the intended generalization appropriate to each item and b) underlining of words which should be clarified by the examiner. In the test form, both of these are, of course, deleted.

In the specimen, correct answers are given in parentheses to the left. To the right of the statements are the generalizations that the students are required to apply in the test. Both the answers and generalizations are omitted in the actual test, of course.

Mr. Jones' grocery store

Mr. Jones owns a grocery store in a wheat farming area. Often in the last few weeks, he has not had enough bread for his customers. It has been an unusually dry season in the area, and the wheat crop has been poor this year.

(PT) 21. The price of bread is higher this year than last year.

21. Decrease in supply increases price in limited economy.

(PT) 22. The wheat farmers are buying fewer things they don't really need this year.

22. Less income leads to less luxury buying.

(PT) 23. The price of chicken in Mr. Jones' store has gone up.

23. When commodity becomes scarce, its price rises and products dependent on it also increase prices.

(PT) 24. The total wages (money) paid by bakeries to their workers have gone down this year.

24. As raw material decreases, labor cuts back—either lay off or reduce wages.

(PT) 25. It is harder than usual to find a job in Mr. Jones' town this year.

25. There is less need for workers when raw material is less available.

(PF) 26. Mr. Smith, who owns the local farm equipment store, says he is going to build a larger store.

26. When a major industry suffers, the broader community feels the impact and constricts.

(PT) 27. The mayor announced that the start of the new high school will have to be postponed.

27. Same as 26.

(PT) 28. Several families who had lived in the town decided they would have to leave.

28. When jobs decrease, people move out of a community.

NOTES

[1] Robert M. Gagné, *The Conditions of Learning,* 2nd ed. (New York: Holt, Rinehart & Winston, 1970), pp. 189–213.

[2] Ibid., p. 196.

[3] See Jerome S. Bruner, *The Process of Education* (Cambridge, Mass.: Harvard University Press, 1960) and Edwin Fenton, *The New Social Studies* (New York: Holt, Rinehart & Winston, 1967).

[4] John Dewey, *How We Think* (Boston: Heath, 1933), *Democracy and Education*

(New York: Macmillan, 1916), and *Logic: The Theory of Inquiry* (New York: Holt, Rinehart & Winston, 1938).

[5] George F. Kneller, *Logic and Language of Education* (New York: Wiley, 1966), pp. 51–52, 55.

[6] Dewey, *How We Think*, op. cit., pp. 106–115.

[7] Peter H. Martorella, *Videotape: Problem-Strategy for Elementary Social Studies*, College of Education, Temple University.

[8] Quoted in Richard Hofstadter, *The American Political Tradition* (New York: Knopf, 1948), p. 116.

[9] Ibid.

[10] Dewey, op. cit., p. 115.

[11] J. P. Guilford, "Intelligence: 1965 Model," in R. A. Weisgerber (ed.), *Perspectives in Individualized Learning* (Itasca, Ill.: Peacock, 1971), p. 75.

[12] Maurice P. Hunt and Lawrence E. Metcalf, *Teaching High School Social Studies*, 2nd ed. (New York: Harper & Row, 1968) and Richard Gross and Raymond Muessig (eds.), *Problem-Centered Social Studies Instruction: Approaches to Reflective Teaching* (Washington, D.C.: National Council for the Social Studies, 1971).

[13] This activity is adapted from material developed by Inez Marrington, now a social studies teacher in the Pennsbury School District, Bucks County, Pa.

[14] Richard Hofstadter, *The Age of Reform* (New York: Knopf, 1955), pp. 24–25.

[15] John A. McCollum and Rose Marie Davis, *Trainer's Manual: Development of Higher Level Thinking Abilities*, rev. ed. (Portland, Ore.: Northwest Regional Educational Laboratory, 1969), pp. 245–247.

[16] Mary C. Durkin, *Teacher's Guide for People in Neighborhoods* (Reading, Mass.: Addison-Wesley, 1972), p. T77.

[17] James L. Hills, "Building and Using Inquiry Models in the Teaching of Geography," in P. Bacon (ed.), *Focus on Geography*. Fortieth Yearbook, National Council for the Social Studies (Washington, D.C.: National Council for the Social Studies, 1970), p. 317.

[18] Ibid., p. 318.

[19] Fred M. Newmann, *Clarifying Public Controversy: An Approach to Teaching Social Studies* (Boston: Little, Brown, 1970).

[20] Ibid., pp. 238–239.

[21] This activity is adapted from material developed by Hinda Goldberg, a graduate student at Temple University.

[22] *Narratives of Early Virginia* (New York: Scribner, 1907), p. 48.

[23] David Freeman Hawke (ed.), *Captain John Smith's History of Virginia: A Selection* (Indianapolis, Ind.: Bobbs-Merrill, 1970), pp. 35–36.

[24] Dawn Ann Kurth, statement delivered in public testimony on May 31, 1972 before the Senate Consumer Subcommittee Hearing on Effects of TV and Advertising on Children, *The New York Times*, July 2, 1972, p. D11.

[25] Norman E. Wallen et al., *The Taba Curriculum Development Project in Social Studies* (Menlo Park, Calif.: Addison-Wesley, 1969), pp. 296, 299.

CHAPTER 9

Internalization Set #3

The two preceding chapters presented some ideas concerning the nature of conclusions and generalizations and how they might be taught efficiently. This brief chapter offers an opportunity to clarify, internalize, and apply some of the points made earlier. Most of the activities can be done alone, but a few involve the use of children or peers.

DISTINGUISHING GENERALIZATIONS AND CONCLUSIONS

You will recall that conclusions were defined as the product of any systematic investigation. Those conclusions that are shown to be true (i.e., clearly supported by the best evidence available) are *facts*. Another special class of conclusions is *generalizations*. A set of criteria for a generalization was given in Chapter 7. Test your understanding of the distinction between a generalization and the broader category, conclusion, by completing these two short exercises.

ACTIVITY 29

For this activity organize a group of five of your fellow students so that you will have other sets of responses to compare with yours. Examine Table 9.1 for several minutes. Being as precise and accurate as possible, state three conclusions and two potential generalizations that seem warranted from the census data.

Compare your results with those of others in the group for similarities and differences. Finally, check the collective group responses against the criteria for generalization stated in Chapter 7.

Probably most of the conclusions you stated were facts; that is, they were true. Thus this activity may also serve to demonstrate how facts can contribute to generalizing. In this case isolated facts were organized toward more meaningful ideas with broader application.

Table 9.1

Fastest-growing U.S. urban areas (population increase based on projected growth, 1965–1975)

Urban Area	Increase (percent)	Urban Area	Increase (percent)
1. Fort Lauderdale-Hollywood, Fla.	51.9	12. Washington, D.C.	25.9
2. Santa Barbara, Calif.	51.6	13. Los Angeles-Long Beach, Calif.	25.6
3. San Jose, Calif.	51.4	14. Lexington, Ky.	25.2
4. Huntsville, Ala.	51.4	15. Tucson, Ariz.	23.8
5. Las Vegas, Nev.	46.6	16. Houston, Tex.	23.4
6. San Bernardino-Riverside-Ontario, Calif.	35.2	17. Lubbock, Tex.	23.2
7. West Palm Beach, Fla.	34.5	18. Dallas, Tex.	23.1
8. Phoenix, Ariz.	34.2	19. Atlanta, Ga.	23.0
9. Sacramento, Calif.	32.4	20. Denver, Colo.	22.5
10. Orlando, Fla.	31.2	21. Madison, Wis.	22.3
11. Tampa-St. Petersburg, Fla.	28.1	22. Albuquerque, N.M.	22.2
		23. Amarillo, Tex.	22.0

Source: U.S. Bureau of the Census.

Conclusions

1. _____

2. _____

3. _____

Potential Generalizations

1. _____

2. _____

ACTIVITY 30

Examine the following list of statements, then place a + in front of those that appear likely to be generalizations and a 0 before those that are not.

_____ 1. As the size of a community changes, the services within the community often change.

_____ 2. Women make the poorest drivers.

_____ 3. Texas increased in population in the period 1960–1970.

_____ 4. Most of the people in the world are basically dishonest.

_____ 5. In all societies, members of a family usually have both responsibilities and privileges.

_____ 6. The Concorde is one of the fastest commercial planes in
existence.

_____ 7. Capitalism has proved to be the most efficient economic system
in the world.

_____ 8. Measures regarded as radical in one generation often are
considered to be moderate in the next.

_____ 9. New York is the largest city in the United States.

_____ 10. The growth of industry within an area normally is mainly
dependent on the availability of raw materials, transportation
networks, and markets.

If you identified numbers 1, 5, 8, and 10 as generalizations, then you have
a firm grasp of the distinctions between general conclusions and the more
specific category, generalizations. Check back to the discussion on pp. 143–
145 in Chapter 7 if you answered any statements incorrectly or if you still are
not certain as to the rule for discriminating statements.

LEARNING CONCLUSIONS AND GENERALIZATIONS

By performing the next three exercises you will be experiencing the
same sensations as the students with whom you will be using the instructional models. For this reason you should make a special point of doing
all three.

ACTIVITY 31

Refer to the historical documents in the John Smith–Pocahontas case in
Chapter 8 (pp. 173–174). Those two excerpts from the writings of Captain
Smith, both describing the same event, offer an excellent discrepancy for
initiating and employing Dewey's problem-solving model. It should provide
you with a sufficiently challenging puzzle to pursue and an opportunity to
test your research tools.

The basic question to be resolved is, "How do you account for these differing accounts of the same event, both by the same man, John Smith?"

Follow these procedures in completing the activity, either individually or
in groups of three to five:

1. Read carefully the two accounts by Smith.
2. In a sentence or two, write out as specifically as possible what you
perceive the problem to be.
3. Brainstorm as many hypotheses as possible, fanciful or otherwise, that
might account for or explain the discrepancies and list these.
4. On a separate list, in three columns, place these headings:

Hypotheses	Facts Needed	Possible Sources
_____	_____	_____
_____	_____	_____
_____	_____	_____
_____	_____	_____
_____	_____	_____
_____	_____	_____
_____	_____	_____
_____	_____	_____
_____	_____	_____

5. Fill out as much of this second list as possible before you initiate your research for the necessary information to test your hypotheses.
6. On a final sheet record the results of your research by listing the most plausible tentative conclusion(s) and the supporting facts.

Tentative Conclusion(s)	Supporting Facts
_____	_____
_____	_____
_____	_____
_____	_____
_____	_____
_____	_____

After completing these procedures, compare the process that you actually employed to resolve the problem with the basic five steps in the Dewey model. Did you retrace any steps? Did you first leap to a conclusion that later evidence supported? Were any of the steps combined into a simple operation?

Two additional extensions of this activity are optional. On the basis of your conclusion(s) about the discrepancy, develop a potential generalization that is to apply to a class of historical figures rather than just to John Smith. Record your potential generalization below in the "if . . . then" format supplied:

If_____

_____

_____ ,

then_____

_____ .

Compare the generalization you postulated with those developed by your peers.

As a final step, locate three elementary textbooks containing the Pocahontas–John Smith incident. Which accounts do they reflect? How do you think they *should* have handled the episode?

ACTIVITY 32

In this exercise you will have an opportunity to use Gagné's model to acquire a new generalization. Consult the Berelson and Steiner text, *Human Behavior: An Inventory of Scientific Findings,* cited in the previous chapter, or any other reference source from which social science generalizations may be abstracted. Basic textbooks in any discipline area or any social science professor on your campus are likely sources.

Select any social science generalization that piques your interest and that you have never considered before. Record the generalization and an alternate one, in the event that information concerning the first one is not readily available:

Generalization: _____

_____

_____

Alternate: _____

_____

_____

Refer to Gagné's model in Chapter 8 (pp. 153–155) and follow the steps he suggests, reviewing relevant social science works and materials. In effect you will be reviewing the concepts embedded in the generalization, examining illustrative cases of the generalization from the literature, and searching for new examples and material that reflect application of the generalization. As a test, try to create a story or vignette (i.e., a fictitious case) that illustrates the generalization. Select any context you wish for the imaginary case.

ACTIVITY 33

In applying the Taba model for conclusions-generalizations, you will receive results that often follow a sustained period of systematic study by individuals or groups and that may be summarized on charts and then analyzed by raising questions about the data. This activity will give you some experience in generating and analyzing such a chart and in functioning as a social scientist.

Organize a group of five peers. As a group, identify any five countries in the world that you suspect may have significant cultural differences and for which information is readily available. Each group member should select a country and accept responsibility for collecting information on the following questions:

1. What is the relative status of women?
2. How is the typical family structure organized?
3. What are some of the important dominant values in the society?
4. What is the relative standard of living?
5. What major problems is the country currently experiencing?

These questions are not meant to be an exhaustive list or to provide a totally balanced perspective on the societies. Rather the questions should generate comparative data with sufficient contrast to offer an interesting discussion. When each member of the group has completed his or her research, summarize the collective report on large sheets of paper with felt-tip pens and hang them on the wall or bulletinboard. An outline for the chart may be constructed as follows:

Countries	Status of Women	Organization of Family	Dominant Values	Standard of Living	Major Problems
1.					
2.					
3.					
4.					
5.					

Allow sufficient space for several items to be entered in each column and row and in large type to be read at a distance. One procedural strategy is to have each member record his or her data on a single sheet and then to splice all five sets of sheets together. Each member should also be prepared to supply factual evidence to support any chart entries made.

Once the chart has been completed, it may be analyzed by responding to the following types of questions:

1. What did we find out about _____, _____, _____, _____, and _____ (countries) in relation to the status of women? (Repeat the same question for each of the other four categories.)
2. How are these five countries alike?
3. How are they different?
4. How do you account for these differences?
5. What conclusions or potential generalizations could we make that might include all of the ideas expressed?

Save the chart for use in Activity 36.

MASTERING THE MECHANICS OF THE MODELS

The question that a teacher uses to initiate a discussion is an extremely important element in any instructional sequence. This question should focus attention on the topic to be discussed, trigger interest, and indicate that all students will have an opportunity to participate in the lesson. An *opening question*—one that allows any student to respond with whatever information he has—accomplishes the three-fold objectives. The opening question allows students to begin organizing their thoughts at a very basic level, so that later more complex evaluative thinking may evolve.

Asking questions that allow a broad rather than a limited range of responses requires both practical experience and attention to how the structural characteristics of a query affect the listener. The first two exercises allowed some practice in grappling with related questioning tactics. The following three activities directly relate to field testing of the three models discussed in Chapter 8.

ACTIVITY 34

There is no single form that may be used to make a question very open-ended. The inflection of a teacher's voice, his or her nonverbal gestures, and the way he or she handles a student's response all enter into whether a question is perceived by students as allowing them to freely participate in a discussion. A beginning step in framing open questions, however, is becoming sensitized to the presence of *inhibiting words and sentence structures*.

Listed below are a series of questions that purport to be "open" but that actually narrow the range of responses possible and consequently limit the number of potential respondents in a class. As you examine each question, follow it with a statement concerning what you perceive to be the shortcoming.

1. What important ideas were in the chapter?

   Shortcoming:_____

   _____

   Alternative:_____

2. What did we learn from the film we just saw?

   Shortcoming:_____

   _____

   Alternative:_____

3. What did you see in the film that was significant?

   Shortcoming:_____

   _____

   Alternative:_____

4. What did you like about the book you just read?

Shortcoming: _____

_____

Alternative: _____

5. What useful suggestions did you get from our recent field trips?

Shortcoming: _____

_____

Alternative: _____

After you have critiqued each of the five questions, try rewriting them in the space marked "Alternative" to make them more open. If you have problems, review the sample forms for open questions given in the preceding chapter (p. 166).

ACTIVITY 35

This related exercise will give you a quick check on another facet of your questioning ability. In the Taba model for developing conclusions-generalizations, a sequence of questions, beginning with an opening question, was outlined. See how well you have internalized it.

Suppose you are working with a sixth-grade class that has just finished viewing a film dealing with the career of John F. Kennedy. Which of the following questioning sequences do you think would be the most appropriate for moving the class systematically to a conclusion or potential generalization?

1. Does Kennedy's career suggest any conclusions about politics? How did he die? In what ways was his career different from Richard Nixon's? What did you see in the film? When was Kennedy President?
2. When was Kennedy President? What did you see in the film? How did he die? Does Kennedy's career suggest any conclusions about politics? In what ways was his career different from Richard Nixon's?
3. What did you see in the film? When was Kennedy President? In what ways was his career different from Richard Nixon's? How did he die? Does Kennedy's career suggest any conclusions about politics?
4. In what ways was Kennedy's career different from Richard Nixon's? Does Kennedy's career suggest any conclusions about politics? When was he President? How did he die? What did you see in the film?
5. What did you see in the film? Does Kennedy's career suggest any conclusions about politics? In what ways was his career different from Richard Nixon's? When was he President? How did he die?

Which sequence did you pick? Why? Which did you reject? Why? If you selected any sequence other than group 3, refer to the discussion of questions and question sequences in the preceding chapter (pp. 166–170).

ACTIVITY 36

You should be ready now to try the Taba model with an uninitiated group. Take the retrieval chart that your group of five constructed earlier in this chapter and use it, along with the question sequence, as the basis for a lesson with a group of students. If available, use an intermediate-level elementary class. Otherwise use a group of peers. Where necessary, revise or explain language but use the same basic question sequence. Compare the responses of your new "class" with that of your group. Use a tape recorder if available and feasible.

ACTIVITY 37

Using the Dewey model as a guide, develop an instructional sequence on any topic for any grade level. Then test it with a group for whom it is designed, if possible. In any event, plan to include the following basic components in your instructional strategy: (1) introductory activity; (2) a clear provocative puzzle, discrepant event, or problem appropriate to the students designated; (3) a questioning sequence to focus attention on and clarify the problem; (4) procedures for inducing hypotheses; (5) a few sample hypotheses; and (6) some likely ways and sources for testing probable hypotheses with students.

ACTIVITY 38

Using Gagné's model as a guide, similarly develop an instructional sequence for any grade level. Select and simplify a generalization derived from one of the several sources suggested earlier or else use one of those listed here:

1. All persons depend on other persons for satisfaction of needs.
2. Geographical settings influence work and transportation.
3. Families differ in the way they live and in what they expect of their members.
4. The basic economy of a society has a major influence on the lifestyle of its people.
5. As societies grow, both their requirements and their problems change.

Illustrative material used for your strategy may be drawn from any context and may take any media form you wish.

DEVELOPING CASE STUDIES

Constructing case studies for instruction gives a teacher considerable flexibility in obtaining curriculum ideally suited to his or her class. The three activities that conclude this Internalization Set give you an opportunity to try your hand at constructing case studies using diverse sources and materials. As indicated earlier, case studies may take many forms and can be drawn from conventional sources such as personal experiences and the mass media, as well as from more academic sources such as texts, diaries, personal papers, and general primary and secondary sources.

ACTIVITY 39

The first activity in this section is to construct a case study of any type suitable for a nonreading population. Specify the level at which you wish to work, K or above, what you hope to accomplish with the case, and which of the four types of cases cited earlier you wish to construct. (Refer to pp. 171–176 for a review of the types.) Since you are aiming for a nonreading group, you will require tapes, slides, pictures, film, oral readings, or some combination. In the event that you intend to use a dramatization, specify all the components involved.

ACTIVITY 40

One of the trademarks of the social scientist is his or her reliance on first-hand or primary accounts of social phenomena to verify social phenomena whenever possible. Often the examination of such primary source material is a painstaking, complex process. A considerable amount of this material is easily available, however, in microfilm or book form.

Select some newspaper or other primary source material dealing with any aspect of U.S. history prior to 1940 and construct from your accounts a case study of any type suitable for use with children. Choose any topics that interest you and seek the help of the reference librarian if you are uncertain as to how to locate or use primary source materials and microdocuments.

ACTIVITY 41

An interesting collection of case studies, document, and primary-source facsimiles, along with questions and related activities, has been distributed by the Grossman Publishing Company, 625 Madison Ave., New York, N.Y. 10022. Materials are organized around themes or topics such as the following and are collected in cardboard packets called *Jackdaws:*

The Mayflower and the Pilgrim Fathers
Columbus and the Discovery of America
The Making of the Constitution
The Slave Trade and Its Abolition
The American Revolution
The Civil War
The Depression

These *Jackdaws* also include instructions for teacher and student use and follow-up activities.

While these materials are available commercially, they are obviously limited in the scope of the topics they cover. They can serve as excellent models for constructing *Jackdaws* on topics of your own choosing. If the commercial materials are available in your instructional-materials center or library, arrange to examine several in detail. Using them as a model, construct your own complete *Jackdaw* for any age and reading level you wish. If the commercial materials are not available, follow the design instructions below:

1. The subject of your *Jackdaw* may be any topic, theme, issue, person, or group.
2. The *Jackdaw* may contain a variety of different types of case studies and materials, but it should be designed to establish a problematical gestalt for students and to assist in resolving the problem (i.e., the kit should promote reflective thinking).
3. Your *Jackdaw* should take into account the interests, intellectual ability, reading level, and so on of the children for whom it is designed.
4. State the characteristics of the population for whom the *Jackdaw* is intended on a separate sheet, along with any other teacher instructions for use of the material.
5. Design your kit to be self-instructional but yet with "leads" to other resources and activities that students could pursue to gain more information concerning the topic.
6. The *Jackdaw* should be evaluated on the basis of the following points; have someone rate each characteristic on a scale of 0–5 (30 possible points):

Interest potential
Originality of materials used
Appropriateness of packet for students designated
Potential for involving students in reflective thinking
Self-instructional characteristics
Adequacy of leads to other resources and activities related to the topic

MODULE SUMMARY

This module deals with instructional processes that apply and relate concepts and result in conclusions and generalizations. *Conclusions* are the logical results of any investigations, formal or informal, brief or lengthy, presented in the form of a statement, which may be true or false. Conclusions verified as true are classified as facts. A special type of conclusion that organizes a broad range of events and represents widely tested data is called a *generalization*. Further characteristics of a generalization are that it is always a fact, has predictive power, expresses only present or future relationships among concepts, and is applied to all relevant cases without exception. While there are a myriad number of conclusions and facts to be discovered in a social education program, only a small number of generalizations exist.

Teaching designed to generate conclusions and generalizations requires instructional models different from those used for concept learning. Similarly instruction must attend to the processes that students employ as well as the verbal outcomes, in order to avoid rote learning.

Conclusions and generalizations may be taught as predetermined products or may be derived in open-ended fashion. Both approaches may have elements in common, and each presents different potential constraints on learning. A final important variable considered in teaching conclusions-generalizations is the extent of prerequisite knowledge.

Three basic instructional models for developing conclusions-generalizations were outlined and illustrated: Gagné's model for developing generalizations, Dewey's problem-solving model for arriving at tested conclusions, and Taba's model for generating conclusions-generalizations. All three models provide specific guidelines but require some flexibility in implementation. Gagné's model is skeletal. Dewey's is highly specific but requires considerable knowledge about the group with whom you are working, as well as subject matter related to the topic. Taba's model requires the internalization of key questions and a specific questioning sequence.

Case studies offer an excellent vehicle for the instructional models discussed. Several types of cases as analyzed by Newmann were sketched, and three examples were provided.

Measuring the learning of conclusions-generalizations may be accomplished through several strategies. Several illustrative measurement references were cited as possible guides for selecting and constructing test items. Two types of sample test items were provided to suggest possible alternative forms.

SUGGESTED READINGS

Bacon, Phillip (ed.). *Focus on Geography, Key Concepts and Teaching Strategies.* Fortieth Yearbook. Washington, D.C.: National Council for the Social Studies, 1968.

Berg, Harry (ed.). *Evaluation in Social Studies.* Thirty-fifth Yearbook. Washington, D.C.: National Council for the Social Studies, 1965.

Berlyne, David F. *Structure and Direction in Thinking.* New York: Wiley, 1965.

Block, James, and L. Anderson. *Mastery Learning in Classroom Instruction.* New York: Macmillan, 1975.

Block, James (ed.). *Mastery Learning: Theory and Practice.* New York: Holt, Rinehart & Winston, 1971.

Bloom, Benjamin S. (ed.). *Taxonomy of Educational Objectives, The Classification of Educational Goals, Handbook I: Cognitive Domain.* New York: McKay, 1956.

Dewey, John. *How We Think.* Boston: Heath, 1933.

Fair, Jean, and Fannie R. Shaftel (eds.). *Effective Thinking in Social Studies.* Thirty-seventh Yearbook. Washington, D.C.: National Council for the Social Studies, 1967.

Gagné, Robert M. *The Conditions of Learning,* 2nd ed. New York: Holt, Rinehart & Winston, 1970.

Gronlund, Norman E. *Constructing Achievement Tests.* Englewood Cliffs, N.J.: Prentice-Hall, 1968.

Gross, Richard E., and Raymond H. Muessig (eds.). *Problem-Centered Social Studies Instruction: Approaches to Reflective Teaching.* Washington, D.C.: National Council for the Social Studies, 1971.

Hullfish, H. Gordon, and Philip G. Smith. *Reflective Thinking: The Method of Education.* New York: Dodd, Mead, 1961.

Hunt, Maurice P., and Lawrence E. Metcalf. *Teaching High School Social Studies,* 2nd ed. New York: Harper & Row, 1968.

Massialas, Byron, and Jack Zevin. *Creative Encounters in the Classroom.* New York: Wiley, 1969.

Taba, Hilda. *Teaching Strategies and Cognitive Functioning in Elementary School Children.* Cooperative Research Project No. 2404. Washington, D.C.: USOE, 1966.

Wallen, Norman E., et al. *The Taba Curriculum Development Project in Social Studies.* Menlo Park, Calif.: Addison-Wesley, 1969.

MODULE A EYEDAY

MODULE IV

Instructional Models and Their Applications: Analytical Tools

Speak your truth quietly and clearly; and listen to others, even the dull and ignorant; they too have their story.

Desiderata, found in Old St. Paul's Church, Baltimore, dated 1692

CHAPTER 10

Analytical Tools for Interpersonal Relationships

Our normal daily activities require many and varied competencies that are usually taken for granted. How do we determine where someone lives? How can we find out what groups of people are thinking? How do we find a reliable and inexpensive auto mechanic to repair our car? How do I let someone know that I like him or her? One who is able to answer these questions easily has already mastered certain competencies either through a trial and error process or through some form of systematic instruction.

For want of a better term, these competencies will be referred to as *analytical tools*—tools, because they help us to accomplish more efficiently something we wish to do, and analytical, because they may be mastered through systematic study or analysis. Analytical tools are instrumental competencies in the sense that they are to be acquired by students generally not as ends in themselves but because they facilitate the achievement of important ends. No instructional model, however efficient, can compensate adequately for a class that lacks appropriate analytical tools. They are significant prerequisites for effective functioning in a social education program, and their development may be considered an urgent and legitimate instructional goal.

Acquisition of such tools is also likely to be reinforced by the larger culture in which the child operates. Americans constantly seem to be on the lookout for new analytical tools. We consume millions of books on the subject, particularly those that describe how to accrue fortunes easily, put our bodies in peak condition, secure lasting inner peace, or quickly win friends and attract mates. We spend countless hours watching "how-to-do-it" programs and attending related lectures, seminars, and courses. In short, we are a nation of tool seekers, even searching for new means of enriching our lives physically and psychologically.

In this chapter and the one that follows, we will examine a range of analytical tools that can help enrich the academic and the everyday worlds of children. These tools (as they will be abbreviated hereafter) are to be taught continuously to children at all ages, as they progress through formal academic training. *Whenever possible, they should be taught in conjunction with other objectives so that students may immediately see their utility*. When this procedure is impossible or unwieldy, application of the tools should be made as soon as possible after their acquisition.

Tools without a clear meaningful function for a child are merely inert abstractions rather than learning facilitators. A teacher must be wary of the trap of trying to get children to "store" tools "for the day they will be needed." Besides the theoretical weakness of this stratagem, it is likely to end in frustration for both the teacher and the students.

In view of the fact that our society stresses the importance of "getting along well with one another," it is surprising that students of all ages acquire so little facility in the process through the formal curriculum of the schools. Granted, considerable moralizing about what students should do, think, or aspire to is done in any elementary school, and most students are eventually socialized into acceptable patterns of interpersonal behavior. What seldom is done, however, is to to train children in how they themselves consciously and systematically may begin to facilitate their own interpersonal growth.

This is one of the most vital types of all tools, since it helps students develop some autonomy in controlling their own social world. As they grow in this respect, their self concept is likely to reflect the image of one who is capable of controlling his or her own destiny. At a very concrete level, students who have acquired such tools should be able to interact successfully with peers and adults if they choose.

There are many types of interpersonal relationship tools that may be taught. Five of the more fundamental ones will be illustrated in this chapter.

LISTENING

As every kindergarten teacher has discovered, listening does not come naturally to children. If the instructor is to realize the goals set for the class, however, the children must learn that listening can work to the benefit of all concerned. In effect they must learn the complex rules to the interactive process of speaking and listening. An early childhood program that emphasizes—among a range of goals—training in listening has been developed by the Human Development Institute. The program's basic strategy for training children to listen is reflected in the specimen below, abstracted from the teacher's guide. It is a set of rules that all the participants must agree to follow in their Magic Circle gatherings (small discussion groups). Further procedures are also given for insuring that all children in the Circle listen carefully to one another.

Rule 1. Everyone must sit still and be quiet.
Rule 2. Only one person can talk at a time. That person will raise his or her hand and first get permission from the teacher. Everyone can have his or her say but we must take turns.
Rule 3. We must listen.[1]

A simple exercise that not only enforces silence while others are sharing thoughts but also encourages careful attention to the *content* of a message is taken from Charlotte Epstein's *Affective Subjects in the Classroom*. Students are placed in a group and are given a topic to discuss about which they are very interested. Following is a description of the technique:[2]

Pretest
Break into groups of not more than eight.
Select an observer.
Discuss the assigned topic for 5 minutes.
(The observer will record his evaluation of the discussion.)
Stage 1
Select a time keeper.
Continue the discussion for 5 minutes, strictly limiting each person's contribution to fifteen seconds.
Stage 2
Continue the discussion for 5 minutes, again limiting each person's contribution to 15 seconds.
However, before a person speaks, he must wait 3 seconds after the previous person has finished speaking.
Stage 3
Continue the discussion for 5 minutes, again limit each person's contribution to 15 seconds and waiting the 3-second interval.
In addition, no person may say what he wants to until he has accurately reflected the contribution of the person immediately preceding him.
Stage 4
Continue the discussion for 5 minutes. Limit each person's contribution to 15 seconds and wait 3 seconds. No one may speak until he has accurately reflected, and no one may speak a second time until everyone in the group has spoken.
Posttest
Continue the discussion for 5 minutes, with no limitations on speaking. Have the same observer as in the pretest record his own evaluation of the discussion.

At the conclusion of the discussion, the observers of each group verbally compare pre- and posttest results. Group members are then asked to draw some conclusions about their listening and speaking behavior in the different stages. Even young children can perform this exercise, Epstein suggests.

The kindergarten child can observe quite well during the pretest if he is coached to observe only one thing, like whether or not the participants interrupt each other. Instead of having one observer, then, two or three children may act as observers, with each one looking for one aspect of interaction. The first-grader can use an egg-timer to keep time or gauge a time interval by how long it takes to put ten blocks into a box.[3]

EFFECTIVE GROUP PARTICIPATION

A related tool is the ability to work in groups effectively or, put another way, to pool talents within a group efficiently to accomplish a goal. Working collectively is of course no guarantee of economy of efforts or productive results. Maximum effectiveness is dependent on members' assuming roles that are appropriate to their talents and on common identification with the goals of the group.

Much of the success of group participation depends on individuals' willingness to exchange competitiveness for cooperativeness in order to achieve a desired goal. A game that measures the degree of cooperative and competitive behavior among elementary children was developed in a study by M. C. Madsen:

> In this task, two children face each other across a table. Each holds a string attached to a wooden marble holder that will move in either direction on a wooden board, depending on which string is pulled. The object of the game is to slide the wooden holder so that the marble will drop into a hole at either end of the board. In order to get the marble into a hole one child has to relax his string while the other child pulls. If both children pull at the same time, the marble holder separates and neither child can then pull the marble to a hole. . . .
>
> Tell the students that they will win two points for each marble they get in their respective holes. The points will be exchanged for prizes after the game is finished. The procedure for getting a marble into one's hole should be described and what happens when both students pull on their strings at the same time should be demonstrated. When both students understand what happens when both pull on their strings and when only one pulls on his or her string, the game begins. Tell the students that they can talk to each other as they play the game. Give the students ten tries at the game, recording the outcome or a sheet of paper. Then inform each student of how many points he or she has earned and give them a prize.
>
> In this game a competitive person will never let his opponent win. A cooperative person will relax his string so that the other player can pull the marble to the other player's hole. The cooperative solution to the game is to have students alternate so that each receives ten points, that is, each pulls the marble into his hole five times. The cooperativeness of the student is indicated by the number of times he lets the other player get the marble.[4]

Getting children to view one another as resources rather than as competitors in achieving common ends can often be a difficult task. Much classroom instruction unconsciously rewards competition and individual success to a degree that obscures how pooled efforts can produce greater results than the sum of individual efforts. Educators and psychologists working in the Austin, Texas, elementary schools in a project to improve relationships between white and nonwhite children devised the *jigsaw puzzle* technique of group activity:

> For example, in the first classroom we studied, the next lesson happened to be on Joseph Pulitzer. We wrote a six-paragraph biography of the man, such that each paragraph contained a major aspect of Pulitzer's life: how his family came to this country, his childhood, his education and first jobs, etc. Next we cut up the biography into sections and gave each child in the learning group one paragraph. Thus, every learning group had within it the entire life story of Joseph Pulitzer, but each child had no more than one sixth of the story and was dependent on all of the others to complete the big picture.[5]

Children learned their "pieces" independently but were responsible for teaching them and for listening to one another. None of them was able to do well without the aid of everyone else in the group.

A different approach to encouraging cooperative behavior in groups was developed by the Mid-Continent Regional Laboratory.[6] It is based on the findings that management, building ideas, evidence, and feedback on processes are important elements of effective group work. Correspondingly each of these four basic functions are assigned to members of four-person groups in the form of a role. Each role has a title and specific behaviors ascribed to it, as shown below:

1. *Technical advisor:* Helps group members build ideas; clarifies meaning of what is discussed; challenges assumptions behind statements; establishes validity and accuracy of information.
2. *Data recorder:* Insures that data, decisions, and evidence are recorded clearly and accurately; checks on work of the Technical Advisor.
3. *Team coordinator:* Manages the decision-making processes; insures that agreements reached are acceptable to all; begins activities and keeps them moving along; insures that all ideas are heard.
4. *Process advisor:* Gathers evidence on the social processes within the group; discusses observed strengths and weaknesses of the group with members; reacts to how well members are filling their roles; represents the group to the teacher.

Students wear signs or badges to identify the roles that they have been assigned. By taking on responsibility for different roles and experimenting with them, students have an opportunity to see that important contributions can be made by all members in group situations, regardless of general capabilities. Also, designation and acceptance of a particular role allow participants to feel the security of knowing they are "doing their job" in the group—even if they do not always contribute verbally.

Related to the act of assuming a role that can contribute to a group goal is the ability to communicate effectively within a group. While "effective" communication is admittedly a subtle and complex process, certain specific facilitative tools can be acquired. One such tool is the ability to diagnose patterns of communication within a group. Who talks within the group? How much? To whom? Does Tommy monopolize the discussion, and does Suzie always get left out? Once a diagnosis is made, an individual or a group collectively can decide to what extent existing communication patterns facilitate or impede achievement of common goals or allow for equitable sharing of ideas.

One basic approach for diagnosing communication patterns is to have an observer simply tally the number of times each person makes a comment during the discussion. Initially a teacher, without informing the class of her objectives, might form groups of six and appoint an observer with secret instructions to tally participant comments. The observer is given a tally sheet similar to the one shown in Figure 10.1. The observer should be instructed to make a tally mark each time a participant speaks. A tally is recorded on the line going from the participant's name to the name of the person to whom the comment

Figure 10.1
Observer's
talley sheet

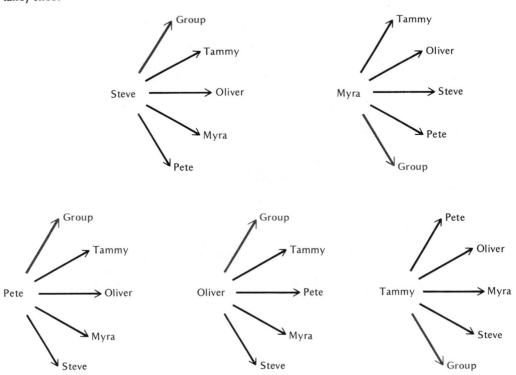

was addressed. If it is not clear to whom a remark is made or if it is made to all, a tally is placed next to "Group."

Then the group is given an interesting problem to solve that all can discuss, and a 10-minute time limit is set. When the dialog is over, the teacher asks the observer to transfer the results to sheets of paper placed on the wall, as shown in Figure 10.2, to indicate each person's communication patterns. Each group is allowed to discuss their findings and diagnose the extent to which communication patterns are effective and may be improved.

The procedure may be repeated with a new problem for the group, and then the two sets of results are compared. This process may be repeated periodically as the group or the teacher feels that communication patterns are not productive.

PARAPHRASING

How many times have you been engaged in a lengthy conversation, only to find at some point that your earlier remarks had been completely misinterpreted? While misinterpretation is not the only source of conflict and misunderstanding, it is frequently a major contributing factor. One way in which all of us can help alleviate communication problems stemming from misinterpretation is to acquire the tool of *paraphrasing*. Put simply, the term means showing another person what his or her idea or remark means to you. In paraphrasing we test our understanding of another person's comment, and we also indicate

Figure 10.2
Hypothetical talley sheet

Group Member Speaking	Person Spoken to					
	Tammy	Myra	Steve	Oliver	Pete	Group
Tammy		III	I	I	I	0
Myra	HHT III		II	I	II	III
Steve	III	0		0	IIII	0
Oliver	I	II	III		0	III
Pete	0	0	HHT I	II		I

that we are concerned enough about what is being said to be sure that we are hearing correctly.

In general, even in complex discussions, we agree or disagree with a speaker on the assumption that what we *think* he or she said is in fact what is *meant*. Paraphrasing is a simple way to avoid possible misunderstandings and to test meanings, but it requires mastery of a few basic points.[7]

1. In paraphrasing, reflect the meaning that you take from a statement; do *not* simply restate it in similar words.

Example   *Sue:* I'm tired of school!
           Sally: You mean you don't like your work?
           Sue: No, it's OK; it's the long day that I don't like.

Not   *Sue:* I'm tired of school!
           Sally: You mean school tires you out?
           Sue: Yeah, I wish I could quit.

In the first case Sally avoided a potential misinterpretation by seeing if her understanding of the statement was what Sue intended. Through paraphrasing Sally got another insight into Sue's problem. The negative example, however, reveals that while Sally reworded Sue's statement, understanding of the comment was *not* tested. All Sally accomplished was the reinforcement of Sue's feeling.

2. Try different ways of revealing what another person's statement means to you.

Example   *Tom:* You really are a fantastic girl!
           Jane: Thank you. It's a relief to find a guy who appreciates a girl's mind.
           Tom: Well, I wasn't really thinking of your mind. . . .

Example   *Wife:* This house is just getting too small for our family.
           Husband: You mean we should sell it and buy a larger place?
           Wife: No, I think what we need to do is reevaluate our lifestyle and lower our expectations.

Example   *Billy:* I think Morris is a rotten kid.
           Wally: Yeah, I know. You think he is mean.
           Billy: No, it's not that. He won't go bicycle riding with me.

3. When you are having an angry discussion or are being criticized, try different ways of showing the other person what his or her idea means to you until he or she agrees with your interpretation.

Example   *Husband:* This house is never clean!
        Wife: Do you mean the floors are dirty?
        Husband: They're fine. It's just that you never clean the cobwebs from the corners.

Example   *Liberal:* The conservatives don't give a damn about poor people.
        Conservative: You mean we don't want to get them jobs?
        Liberal: You want to get them jobs, but you don't care what kind or how low the salaries are.

Besides clarifying arguments, paraphrasing (testing understanding of statements) tends to defuse emotions and keep rhetoric from escalating. With young children, tape recording real or staged conversations for examination is an effective vehicle for practicing paraphrasing. If stopped after each statement, the tape recorder allows children to apply their skills in selecting appropriate responses, and then compare *their* response selection against the one in the conversation.

In argumentative situations, paraphrasing presents one application of Carl Rogers' proposal for dealing with misunderstandings: "Each person can speak up for himself only *after* he has first stated the ideas and feelings of the previous speaker accurately—and to that speaker's satisfaction."

CONFLICT RESOLUTION

Conflict is a normal part of all peoples' lives. In some way all children learn to accept and cope with it. Much of children's conflicts revolve around access to desired objects (e.g., candy, toys), hurt feelings or bodies, or equitable treatment, rather than points of view.

Approaches to conflict should communicate to children that it is a normal everyday occurrence in a complex interdependent society. What differentiates children who are regarded as "bad" from those considered to be "good" are partly the mechanisms they use to deal with their conflict situations. Conflict results when the goals of individuals or groups clash, and its resolution can be destructive, as in the case of a battle, or ameliorative, as in the case of compromise legislation or stronger friendships.

One clear-cut strategy for analyzing conflicts that employs an observational technique is taken from *Man: A Course of Study,* a social studies program for the intermediate grades.[8] At one point in the program youngsters are provided with a sixteen-page booklet in which they are told that they will be observing the behavior of young children: "You will be watching for conflict among young children . . . on how fights start, how they end, and how they are avoided." Sheets in the booklet require children to record data such as "Number of

Boys, Number of Girls," "How Fight Started: Action, Words," "First Thing Said or Done," "Action that Took Place," "Last Thing Said or Done," "How Fight Ended: Action, Words," along with the date and place.[9] Later children are asked to collect all their data sheets, summarize their notes, and draw conclusions and form hypotheses from them concerning "General Topics Children Fight About." Students observe groups of children in classroom and then are asked to list any clues that could tell them when a fight was going to start. Another activity calls for clues that might indicate the end of a fight. The students then turn to observing children in their neighborhood and on the playground, and to recording challenges that do not end in fights. Both the challenge and the behavior specimen that appeared to avoid the fight are recorded.

A different activity calls for students to look for challenges that were accidental, to record the challenge and how it could be interpreted as an accident, and to note the observed consequences. As a culminating activity, students share their kindergarten observations. Based on their cumulative conclusions they then attempt to determine which of the observed fights could be avoided and how, and whether or not it is possible to avoid fighting completely.

Frequently conflict analysis and subsequent resolution may be effected by a rule-dominated discussion, that is, a discussion in which all participants are conscious of and agree to operate by a set of rules. The author developed and used the following procedure effectively with young children to first deescalate fights and shouting matches and then to resolve the conflict generally to everyone's satisfaction. It operates basically as follows, and is called "My Side-Your Side":

1. Everyone has a chance to give "his or her side of the story." The non-speakers must listen quietly without speaking until the speakers are finished.
2. The first speaker tells what happened as he or she saw it. If necessary, the teacher asks for clarification or further details. *No judgments or suggestions are offered, however.*
3. The next speaker(s) repeat(s) the process.
4. After all have spoken in turn, each person is asked to comment on the other's acount.
5. The first speaker is then asked first what he or she thinks that *he* or *she* should do about the problem and then what the others should do.
6. The subsequent speakers are asked to give their opinions of the solution offered. If they disagree, they are asked for alternatives.
7. Comparisons of the alternatives continues until some consensus or compromise is reached (or the issue is put in limbo, if no settlement appears possible).
8. If agreement is reached, each person should be asked to summarize what he or she will do and how he or she feels about the settlement.

In employing this procedure it is important to enforce the listening rule. This is a major ingredient in the promotion of a rational and mutually acceptable settlement of conflicts. Many students who are used to settling arguments by shouting and pushing will require some practice with this technique before they can begin to employ it effectively as a conflict resolution device.

COMMUNICATING FEELINGS

One important way communication can be improved is through more direct statement of one's own feelings. Frequently, however, this is a communication tool that both adults and children learn to avoid. To openly indicate feelings, while improving communications, makes one vulnerable to being hurt by others. Moreover, since it is not common for adults to directly state their true feelings, the act of doing so may be misinterpreted by others. The distinctions between one who has acquired the tool of directly communicating his or her own feelings and one who does so indirectly may be shown in the following examples:[10]

One Who Communicates Feelings Directly	One Who Indirectly Reflects Feelings
"I feel flattered." "I feel embarrassed." "I feel intimidated."	Blushing and saying nothing
"I feel angry." "I feel inadequate." "I feel threatened."	Suddenly becoming silent in a conversation
"I like the way she looks." "I like the way he listens to my problems." "I respect his abilities."	State generalities: "He's a great guy."
"I'm angry with you." "I'm mad at myself." "I feel so bad, I can't stand to hear anyone."	Invective statement: "Shut up!"

One way that children can begin to acquire this tool is through repeated practice in following these two pointers in communicating their own feelings: (1) Use statements that refer to "I", "me", or "my." (2) Use statements that specify some type of personal feeling by name, an action it suggests, or an example it reminds us of. ("It makes me feel good to be with you." "I feel like a wild bull." "I feel like kissing you.") Simple exercises, written or oral, requiring children to rephrase statements can be used to facilitate acquisition of this tool.

This tool may meet with more resistance from older elementary students than from younger children. The reason is simple: As we become more socialized, we are taught to mask our feelings. Relearning to communicate them directly is often an embarrassing and sometimes even painful experience.[11]

WHEN HAVE INTERPERSONAL RELATIONSHIP TOOLS BEEN ACQUIRED?

The acquisition of interpersonal relationship tools should be easy to chart over the course of a school year. Anecdotal records can indicate to what extent an individual in the class gives evidence of growth in listening, effective group participation, paraphrasing, conflict resolution, and communicating feelings. A negative option approach to tool growth assessment is to record only incidents that reflect *absence* of the tools. To simplify and reduce the strain of constant recording, a chart can be used and growth assessed each week. A numerical rating system or a simple checking procedure can be used.[12]

NOTES

[1] Harold Bessell, *Methods in Human Development, Lesson Guide: Level I* (La Mesa: Calif.: Human Development Training Institutes, 1969), p. 4.

[2] Charlotte Epstein, *Affective Subjects in the Classroom: Exploring Race, Sex and Drugs* (New York: International Textbook, 1972), pp. 48–49.

[3] Ibid., pp. 52–53.

[4] Quoted in David W. Johnson and Roger T. Johnson, *Learning Together and Alone: Cooperation, Competition and Individualization* (Englewood Cliffs, N.J.: Prentice-Hall, 1975), pp. 200–201

[5] Elliot Aronson, "Busing and Racial Tension: The Jigsaw Route to Learning and Liking," *Psychology Today*, 8 (February 1975), 47.

[6] Richard M. Bingman, *Handbook on Small Group Methodology in the Development of Inquiry Skills Program* (Kansas City, Mo.: Mid-Continent Regional Educational Laboratory, 1971).

[7] Northwest Regional Educational Laboratory, *Interpersonal Communications* (Tuxedo Park, N.Y.: Xicom, 1969).

[8] Education Development Center, *Man: A Course of Study: Observing Conflict* (Cambridge, Mass.: Education Development Center, 1968).

[9] Ibid., pp. 4–5.

[10] Northwest Regional Educational Laboratory, op. cit., pp. 3–7.

[11] Segregating children by sex, at least initially, may help to reduce anxiety.

[12] For other suggestions and examples, see Robert Fox et al., *Diagnosing Classroom Learning Environments* (Chicago: Science Research Associates, 1966).

CHAPTER 11

Analytical Tools for Research

During their lifetimes all students will need research tools in order to function effectively as members of a complex society. Locating, comparing, and synthesizing material is a basic approach to research, and children become researchers in this sense at a very early age. What systematic training in research techniques does for them is to expand their vistas on what to look for, where to locate it, how to analyze critically what is found, how to organize what is discovered, and how to draw conclusions and generalizations from their data.

Historian-philosopher Carl Becker once wrote an interesting little essay in which he argued that we all are historians.[1] In the essay he introduces us to Mr. Everyman, who uses a series of personal historical documents—namely, records of accounts paid—to establish what bills are still due. Becker has Mr. Everyman using various reference tools, while pointing out that Everyman is functioning as a historian, even though he is unaware of the fact and might even deny it.

EVERYMAN AS RESEARCHER

Similarly a motorist who wishes to avail himself of the best possible price for a new car seeks out one of the many guides now available on newsstands indicating the dealer's price for every item in the car. Another man in Pittsburgh wishes to recommend to a friend a fine restaurant he attended in New Orleans, but he has no record of the place and has even forgotten the name. How can he locate it? Two boys are arguing over whether Ted Williams ever played in the minor leagues. How can they resolve the dispute? Recently a third grader approached the author and, with some agitation, announced that two books gave different accounts of the world's largest snake. He wanted to know what he should say in his report on snakes. He wanted further research assistance to resolve his problem. These situations all call for some basic research tools, and acquiring them helps children to lead more interesting lives and to become more autonomous learners.

Researchers do function effectively without libraries, reference works, card catalogs, and the like. One does not even have to be able to read to be an effective researcher on certain questions. If a child has some structured opportunities to explore carefully selected questions, he or she will be able to pursue research questions that do not exceed his or her related abilities. And as the child becomes more interested in the many questions there are to explore, he or she may have a greater interest in acquiring more related tools; for example, the ability to read, locate reference works, and use a card catalog.

Field trips and resource persons may serve as concrete sources of information on a topic. In this perspective, students are asked to consider visits and visitors, rather than just experiences, as evidence to be analyzed with other data. If a trip or speaker is used by a teacher to generate a problem, suggest a hypothesis for a problem already established, or test a hypothesis that has been raised, it can function as a component of research. Such sources of information have limitations, to be sure, but probably so do most of the books written at the students' level that the teacher is likely to find on the topic. Either way, teacher caution is necessary.

A first-grade class seeking to resolve the question, "How do cities, towns, and communities develop?" will draw some facile generalizations if it restricts its research to the literature on the topic at a first-grade level. Similarly the children will probably overgeneralize if they undertake a study beginning with an examination of patterns of development, followed by discussion with some of the early settlers in the community, and concluded by construction and analysis of a simple map. Both approaches lead only to conclusions that *may be* potential generalizations. The latter experience, however, is probably more in keeping with the developmental needs of first graders and is rooted in more immediate referents. Furthermore, it accepts the fact that only certain components of the question can be answered at a first-grade level. Cities have arisen for complex and occasionally illogical reasons.

REFERENCE TOOLS

Under the heading of reference tools, let us examine two specific tools that children can acquire as soon as they are capable of reading: (1) locating material through the card catalog, and (2) using basic reference works as general research techniques and for validating information.

A common temptation for teachers is to encourage students to acquire these tools as ends in themselves. Often students are even told, "You have to learn these things now, because you will be expected to know them next year (or in junior high, etc.)." Resist the temptation to initiate this pattern and instead reflect on how Mr. or Ms. Everyman calls up such tools in his or her everyday life. When we have a goal in mind that the reference tool helps us achieve, we appreciate its utility. Each of the tools discussed in this section incorporates this latter assumption and suggests potentially meaningful activities for children requiring the use of the tool. In the course of achieving the goal of the activity, each of the tools can be developed.

LOCATING MATERIAL THROUGH THE CARD CATALOG

Consider how odd the cabinet of drawers with lots of little white cards must seem to a young child. Their relationship to the books he or she sees around in the library or instructional-materials center must be even more difficult to comprehend. Yet as the reader knows, the card catalog is one of the most basic useful reference tools in a library.

Perhaps the most direct way to acquaint students with the card catalog is to introduce it in conjunction with a search for books in which a child is interested. Let's say the topic is baseball. A student can discover that one way to locate books is to start hunting on the shelves. This technique actually works fairly well in a very small library with well-segregated titles. The other approach leads to the card catalog, and three basic points about it should suffice for a beginner: (1) It is in alphabetical order; (2) each card represents a book or piece of material, and the subject for which the student is searching will be listed on the card; and (3) each card has a number on it corresponding to the number of the book on the shelf.

From there a child can be taken to the shelves and the location of the number indicated. In most libraries this step will take the most time. Noting such things as why books are missing and how synonyms and related words can be used to expand one's search can come later. As children are increasingly allowed to explore the system on their own, gradually they may be more likely to try to find new applications of the card catalog. Remember that few adults are more interested in any other information in the catalog than what was described above.

USING BASIC REFERENCE WORKS

Every library has its assortment of various basic reference works for children that are used primarily to locate specific items of information —an atlas, for example. A simple assignment such as the following can be used to introduce students to those reference works in the school library that *relate* to countries. Children may be told that Country X is a real country whose identity they are to discover. Whatever relevant reference books the library has may be identified as tools that will help check out the students' guesses.

Country X

Country X lies in two continents and is slightly larger than the state of Texas. Its early history is filled with legends and biblical stories. The country is made up of mountains in the North and South with a high plateau in its center. Its summers are hot and its winters are mild. Agriculture is its chief industry.

Many changes have taken place in Country X in recent years, mostly because of its first President. The style of dress for both men and women has changed, and women are permitted more freedom than they used to have. A new alphabet was also adopted.

As the children examine the brief profile of Country X they will have to locate clues that suggest regions of the world or specific countries. The first sentence provides such a clue, and the class attention may be drawn to it or additional clues added as necessary.[2]

INFORMATION PROCESSING

Accurate information processing requires careful comparisons, analyses, and interpretations of data. Children constantly process information from the time they are babies, and with some fundamental training they can improve steadily in both the efficiency and the accuracy of their processing. Three basic information-processing tools examined in this section are (1) comparing sources of information; (2) interpreting charts, graphs, and tables; and (3) analyzing arguments.

COMPARING SOURCES OF INFORMATION

One starting point for introducing the notion of comparing sources of information can be the study of biographies. Biographies interest many children a great deal, and a considerable number of them exist. Like their adult counterparts, biographies for children often suffer from distortions, idealizations, inaccuracies, and poor scholarship in general. Students cannot possibly be kept from reading all biographies that suffer from these flaws, and often such books are interestingly written. To "shield" students from such works is also unrealistic, since it does not help them to deal with the parallel problems that abound in the mass media and the world of experience in general.

One alternative approach is to have children read several books on the same topic and compare the findings. Unlike adults, children, particularly younger ones, do not seem to find this task repetitive. In fact they may often read the same book several times. A series of questions are suggested below that may be used to guide students analyses with biographies. Their final conclusions can be shared in the form of a written or oral report (perhaps tape recorded). Not all questions will be appropriate for children of all ages.

1. What things were the *same* in the books you read?
2. What things were *different* in the books you read?
3. What did each of the books say about _____ when (he) (she) was small?
4. What did each of the books seem to think was the most important thing that _____ did in (his) (her) life?
5. Whom did each of the books say were the most important people in __'s life?
6. What did you think you learned by reading about __?
7. If a friend asked you to recommend just one book to read about _____, which one would you choose? Why?
8. Why do you think each of the books was written as it was?
9. After you finish answering the other questions, look up _____ in an encyclopedia and see what it says about (him) (her).
10. What kinds of things did the encyclopedia say that were also in the books you read? What kind of things did the encyclopedia *leave out* that were in the books you read? Why do you suppose this is the case?

This type of activity also offers children an excellent opportunity to discover the inevitable shortcomings of otherwise useful reference works such as encyclopedias. Any encyclopedia, for instance, is limited by the amount of space it can allocate to any single subject. No matter how well its topical essay has been researched and written, it must sacrifice myriad details about its subject that might have given the reader broader insights. Without trying to consciously distort a reader's view of a person, group, place, object, or event, reference sources that treat their subjects in very brief essays nevertheless tend to create unbalanced perceptions. Unless these perceptions are qualified by references to fuller accounts or some cautionary remarks from a teacher, children will be misinformed. This issue is a particularly difficult one to raise in a classroom because of its subtlety. In effect, children must learn that what is *not* said may be as important as—or more important than—what *is* related. The truth or accuracy of facts and absence of bias may be necessary but not sufficient tests of effective research.

Test this latter point by completing a short exercise. Pretend that Figure 11.1 is an encyclopedia entry that you are to complete about yourself. Place your name in the space provided in the figure. Then describe yourself (since you are an authority on the subject). Your only restrictions are that (1) the length may not exceed 250 words, (2) everything must be true and objective, (3) it must be written at no higher than a fourth-grade reading level, and (4) it must tell evrything about yourself that you think is important for someone to know *if they had no other information about you.*

Complete the essay to your satisfaction, and then share it with someone else to see how they react to it and what questions they raise. Finish this activity before reading further.

How did you feel about the experience? What did it feel like to sum up the important dimensions of your life in 250 words? What perceptions of you did your account create for others? How many experiences in your life were left out of the account (either because of space limitations or because you just didn't want to share the data)? What questions were raised about your life that were ignored in your essay?

If you feel uncomfortable with the notion of summing up your life in 250 words and having the summary alone represent you to a group, you may be able to appreciate the limitations of even the best of encyclopedias. Entire groups of people or nations have often been characterized in fewer words than you were given to describe your life.

INTERPRETING CHARTS, GRAPHS, AND TABLES

The ability to interpret charts, graphs, and tables accurately and to obtain as much information from them as possible is essential for social education. Yet students are seldom given explicit practice in determining what charts and graphs are actually communicating and what they are omitting. They are usually constructed in order to compress extensive bodies of information efficiently and to permit the drawing of correlations and conclusions. Even young children may be introduced

Figure 11.1
My life in 250 words (or less)

Figure 11.2 Milk consumption chart

Month of January

4	5	6	7	8	11	12	13	14	15	18	19	20	21	22	25	26	27	28	29

227 318 472 485 454   469 480 439 448 372   490 477 445 459 472   481 441 465 470 461

Cartons of Milk Sold Each Day

to simple chart, graph, and table exericses based on their life experiences and then asked to make only fundamental translations and interpolations of the data encountered.

Figure 11.2 is a chart dealing with data taken from typical children's school experiences. The hypothetical data are similar to those that might be obtained through any school cafeteria. Questions similar to the following could be used in interpreting the chart:

1. What do the numbers here mean [pointing]?
2. What does looking at the numbers here [pointing] and the days here [pointing] tell you?
3. On what day were most cartons of milk drunk?
4. On what day were the fewest cartons of milk drunk?
5. Why weren't the same number of cartons drunk each day? Why was that?
6. Why do you suppose there were so few drunk on (date)?

The children may suggest hypotheses such as these: "Maybe a lot of kids were absent on (date)." "I brought my lunch and milk on (day/date) because I didn't like what they were having in the cafeteria. Maybe a lot of kids did that." "I think the sixth graders went to the museum all day." These hypotheses can be checked out easily, and the exercise can be repeated on another day to compare milk-consumption patterns.

A homework exercise can also generate data needed to construct a simple graph that will provide some interesting discussion and interpretation. This activity gives children practice in constructing as well as interpreting graphs and illustrates how putting tabular data in graphic form may reveal more information about the topic.

Determine the days and times that children normally view television and the programs they watch. Choose at least two pupils to view each program to insure some relative validity in the tabulations. Give the following instructions to each of six two-person teams:

1. View an adult or family program during "prime time" for 1 hour.
2. View a children's program on Saturday morning for 1 hour.
3. View an adult program during the weekday afternoon for 1 hour.

4. View a children's program during the weekday afternoon for 1 hour.
5. View a sports event for 1 hour.

In all cases have each student in a team record the type of information shown below for each show. A dittoed sheet may be used.

Information on Commercials

Team Members _____   Show _____

_____   Date Viewed _____

_____   Time Viewed _____

Number of Commercials
(Put a check each time one
    occurs.)

Total Number of Commercials
(Add up checks.)

*What the Commercial Was
    Trying to Sell*
(List.)

*Total Times Each Product
    Mentioned*
(List and put number.)

Students should be given brief instructions on public service commercials, and any necessary adjustments in their tabulations should be made when data are reported. Indicate that parents may help with the éxercise (they, too, may find it instructive) and have each set of teams cross-check their results and discuss any discrepancies in their records. Use a simple compromise formula to settle disputes in observations; for example, divide the difference between the scores in half and add the result to the lowest score.

When you are ready to construct the charts and graphs, you might want to express the data as follows (there are many methods): Once completed, questions may be raised about the number of commercials per hour per each type of program, the types of products advertised, guesses concerning advertisers' assumptions about viewers of the programs, and the like. A culminating activity might be to compare their

Table 11.1
The cost of a loaf of bread (figures are for a 1-pound loaf)

	1972	1974
Flour	.0416	.0741
Other Ingredients	.0211	.0260
Wrapping Materials	.0115	.0108
Manufacturing Wages & Fringes	.0344	.0387
Other Manufacturing Expenses	.0145	.0145
Sales and Advertising Expenses	.1054	.1193
Administrative Expenses	.0123	.0140
Total Expenses	.2408	.2974
Pretax Profit	.0065	.0034

Source: American Bakers Association.

Table 11.2
Executions in the United States

Year	Prisoners Executed				Year	Prisoners Executed			
	Total	White	Negro	Other[1]		Total	White	Negro	Other[1]
All years									
(1930–1969)	3859	1751	2066	42	1950	82	40	42	–
Percent	100.0	45.4	53.5	1.1	1949	119	50	67	2
1969	–	–	–	–	1948	119	35	82	2
1968	–	–	–	–	1947	153	42	111	–
1967	2	1	1	–	1946	131	46	84	1
1966	1	1	–	–	1945	117	41	75	1
1965	7	6	1	–	1944	120	47	70	3
1964	15	8	7	–	1943	131	54	74	3
1963	21	13	8	–	1942	147	67	80	–
1962	47	28	19	–	1941	123	59	63	1
1961	42	20	22	–	1940	124	49	75	–
1960	56	21	35	–	1939	160	80	77	3
1959	49	16	33	–	1938	190	96	92	2
1958	49	20	28	1	1937	147	69	74	4
1957	65	34	31	–	1936	195	92	101	2
1956	65	21	43	1	1935	199	119	77	3
1955	76	44	32	–	1934	168	65	102	1
1954	81	38	42	1	1933	160	77	81	2
1953	62	30	31	1	1932	140	62	75	3
1952	83	36	47	–	1931	153	77	72	4
1951	105	57	47	1	1930	155	90	65	–

[1] American Indians and Orientals.
Source: U.S. Bureau of Prisons.

findings with those reflected in the statement of eleven-year-old Dawn Ann Kurth, who appeared as a witness at a Senate subcommittee hearing on the effects of TV advertising (see pp. 174–176).

Sources of ready-made charts, graphs, and tables abound. Any almanac, newspaper, or handbook of statistical information will provide a wealth of items like those in Tables 11.1–11.4. They can provide an opportunity for practice in interpretation and serve as the basis for the discussion of important social issues as well.

Even young children can begin to see how data may be collected and organized visually in a graph or table. A simple activity that a preschool-primary group might complete involves constructing a birthday graph, shown in Figure 11.3. A marking pen, a jar of paste, a sheet of paper approximately 2' × 4', and twelve sets of different colored paper measuring 1½" × 3", each set with seven pieces, are all the materials needed.

Ask the children to name the months of the year and record them along the bottom of the chart (adding those not named). Let each child

Table 11.3

One out of every four Americans lives in the ten largest urbanized areas; one out of every three in the twenty-five largest

1. New York, N.Y.-Northeastern New Jersey	16,206,841	
2. Los Angeles-Long Beach, Calif.	8,351,266	
3. Chicago, Ill.-Northwestern Indiana	6,714,578	
4. Philadelphia, Pa.-N.J.	4,021,066	
5. Detroit, Mich.	3,970,584	1 in 4
6. San Francisco-Oakland, Calif.	2,987,850	
7. Boston, Mass.	2,652,575	
8. Washington, D.C.-Md.-Va.	2,481,489	
9. Cleveland, Ohio	1,959,880	
10. St. Louis, Mo.-Ill.	1,882,944	
11. Pittsburgh, Pa.	1,846,042	
12. Minneapolis-St. Paul, Minn.	1,704,423	
13. Houston, Tex.	1,677,863	1 in 3
14. Baltimore, Md.	1,579,781	
15. Dallas, Tex.	1,338,684	
16. Milwaukee, Wis.	1,252,457	
17. Seattle-Everett, Wash.	1,238,107	
18. Miami, Fla.	1,219,661	
19. San Diego, Calif.	1,198,323	
20. Atlanta, Ga.	1,172,778	
21. Cincinnati, Ohio-Ky.	1,110,514	
22. Kansas City, Mo.-Kan.	1,101,787	
23. Buffalo, N.Y.	1,086,594	
24. Denver, Colo.	1,047,311	
'25. San Jose, Calif.	1,025,273	

Source: U.S. Department of Commerce, Bureau of the Census. Based on 1970 census.

Table 11.4
Average U.S. retail food prices (in cents)

Year	Flour, white	Rice	White bread	Round steak	Rib roast	Chuck roast	Pork chops	Bacon, sliced	Milk (delivered)	Butter	Cheese	Potatoes	Sugar	Eggs	Coffee
	10 lbs.	lb.	lb.	lb.	lb.	lb.	lb.	lb.	qt.	lb.	lb.	15 lbs.	lb.	doz.	lb.
1913	33	8.7	5.6	22.3	19.8	16.0	21.0	27.0	8.9	38.3	22.1	25.5	5.5	34.5	29.8
1918	67	12.9	9.8	36.9	30.7	26.6	39.0	52.9	13.9	57.7	35.9	48.0	9.7	56.9	30.5
1919	72	15.1	10.0	38.9	32.5	27.0	42.3	55.4	15.5	67.8	42.6	57.0	11.3	62.8	43.3
1920	81	17.4	11.5	39.5	33.2	26.2	42.3	52.3	16.7	70.1	41.6	94.5	19.4	68.1	47.0
1924	49	10.1	8.9	34.8	31.3	21.6	31.0	38.4	13.4	52.2	36.2	42.0	9.0	51.0	42.6
1925	61	11.1	9.3	36.2	32.5	22.8	37.0	47.1	13.9	55.2	37.5	54.0	7.0	55.4	50.4
1927	55	10.7	9.2	38.7	34.1	25.2	37.2	47.8	14.1	56.3	38.6	57.0	7.2	48.7	47.4
1929	51	9.8	8.8	46.0	39.1	31.4	37.5	43.9	14.4	55.5	39.5	48.0	6.4	52.7	47.9
1930	46	9.5	8.6	42.6	36.4	28.6	36.2	42.5	14.1	46.4	36.6	54.0	6.1	44.5	39.5
1931	36	8.2	7.7	35.4	31.0	22.7	29.6	36.6	12.6	35.8	29.7	36.0	5.6	35.0	32.8
1932	32	6.6	7.0	29.7	25.6	18.5	21.5	24.2	10.7	27.8	24.4	25.5	5.0	30.2	29.4
1934	49	8.0	8.3	28.1	23.6	17.5	25.5	29.1	11.2	31.5	25.0	34.5	5.5	32.5	26.9
1935	50.5	8.4	8.3	36.0	30.9	24.0	36.1	41.3	11.7	36.0	27.0	28.6	5.7	37.6	25.7
1937	47.9	8.4	8.6	39.1	32.8	25.7	36.7	41.3	12.5	40.7	29.4	41.9	5.6	36.2	25.5
1939	37.9	7.7	7.9	36.0	29.5	23.4	30.4	31.9	12.2	32.5	25.3	37.1	5.4	32.1	22.4
1941	45.2	8.7	8.1	39.1	31.1	25.5	34.3	34.3	13.6	41.1	30.0	35.2	5.7	39.7	23.6
1942	52.8	12.1	8.7	43.5	34.0	29.3	41.4	39.4	15.0	47.3	34.8	51.3	6.8	48.4	28.3
1944	64.7	12.8	8.8	41.4	33.4	28.8	37.3	41.1	15.6	50.0	36.0	69.8	6.7	54.5	30.1
1946	70.8	14.0	10.4	52.1	43.1	36.6	48.5	53.3	17.6	71.0	50.1	70.2	7.7	58.6	34.4
1948	98.0	20.8	13.9	90.5	73.7	64.4	77.2	76.9	21.8	86.7	65.6	83.8	9.4	72.3	51.4
1950	98.2	16.8	14.3	93.6	74.3	61.6	75.4	63.7	20.6	72.9	51.8	69.2	9.7	60.4	79.4
1954	107.2	19.6	17.2	90.7	70.3	51.4	86.3	81.7	23.0	72.4	57.6	78.9	10.5	58.5	110.8
1956	106.6	17.2	17.9	88.2	70.1	48.4	78.2	57.3	24.2	72.1	57.2	101.6	10.6	60.2	103.4
1958	110.4	18.4	19.3	104.2	81.6	63.3	91.8	79.3	25.3	74.2	58.0	93.9	11.3	60.4	90.7
1960	110.8	18.6	20.3	105.5	81.7	61.6	85.8	65.5	26.0	74.9	68.6	107.7	11.6	57.3	75.3
1961	112.0	18.6	20.9	103.6	80.7	59.4	87.9	71.2	26.2	76.3	72.8	94.4	11.8	57.3	73.6
1962	114.0	19.1	21.2	107.8	84.1	62.3	89.8	70.3	26.1	75.2	72.4	94.8	11.7	54.0	70.8
1963	114.0	19.4	21.6	106.4	83.7	60.3	88.2	68.3	26.0	75.0	72.6	97.7	13.6	55.1	69.4
1964	113.4	18.8	20.7	103.9	82.8	56.8	88.0	66.7	26.4	74.4	73.4	113.6	12.8	53.9	81.6
1965	116.2	19.0	20.9	108.4	89.7	59.5	97.3	81.3	26.3	75.4	75.4	140.6	11.8	52.7	83.3
1966	118.8	19.0	22.2	110.7	93.2	62.2	106.3	95.4	27.8	82.2	84.4	112.4	12.0	59.9	82.3
1967	119.2	18.6	22.2	110.3	94.0	60.7	100.4	83.7	28.7	83.0	87.2	112.1	12.1	49.1	76.9
1968	116.8	18.8	22.4	114.3	98.8	63.5	102.9	81.4	30.3	83.6	88.8	114.5	12.2	52.9	76.4
1969	116.2	18.8	23.0	126.7	109.3	70.4	112.2	87.8	31.5	84.6	94.0	122.4	12.4	62.1	76.5

Source: U.S. Department of Labor.

note the month of his or her birthday and paste a piece of colored paper at the base of the graph above the appropriate month. Use a different set/color for each month, and paste each piece on top of the other.

After all children are finished, count with them the units of papers pasted, listing the numbers at the left of the graph. Have them read the entire graph and ask them what they can tell from it (Figure 11.3).

Figure 11.3 Birthday chart

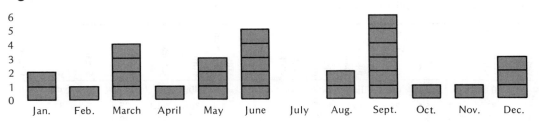

ANALYZING ARGUMENTS

Detecting bias in arguments, beoming sensitive to the use of emotional symbolism, and determining whether a conclusion is valid—these are characteristics that help distinguish the rational person from his or her irrational counterpart. Even little children manage to acquire rudiments of these abilities at an early age if given some prompting and assistance. The youngster who viewed and heard an extravagant claim for a breakfast cereal and remarked, "They're just telling you that to make you buy the cereal," reflects such early training. Systematic continued assistance should strengthen and expand such analytical abilities.

Two books that are clearly written and laced with mild humor are very helpful sources for teachers wishing to develop activities in this area are Darrell Huff's *How to Lie with Statistics* and W. Ward Fearnside and William B. Holther's *Fallacy: The Counterfeit of Argument*.[3] The former work is best described in the author's own words:

> This book is a sort of primer in ways to use statistics to deceive. It may seem altogether too much like a manual for swindlers. Perhaps I can justify it in the manner of the retired burglar whose published reminiscences amounted to a graduate course in how to pick a lock and muffle a football: "The crooks already know these tricks; honest men must learn them in self-defense."[4]

The book is filled with humorous instances of how statistics are deliberately manipulated to sensationalize, inflate, confuse, and oversimplify and, perhaps more importantly, how we misuse statistics ourselves without intending to. When a local pastor bragged from the pulpit at the end of the school year that the elementary students in his suburban parochial school all scored above the national norms on standardized tests, he probably thought he was providing empirical evidence to demonstrate the school's effectiveness. Undoubtedly he would have been affronted and hurt if accused of misusing statistics. Yet he was as misleading as any advertiser who claims something such as, "Four out of five doctors interviewed preferred Blarpies." The suburban parochial sample is compared to national—not suburban—norms and overlooks the fact that suburban parochial students are probably an atypical sample. The commercial claim similarly used a selective, biased sample of doctors in the hope that a listener would generalize from it to all doctors.

The parochial school statistics were also derelict on another important count, one common to many public school claims of effectiveness. Since there were no control data on how *comparable* students did on the test or even any scores of the same group at the beginning of the year, it is not possible to claim the school's program as *the* cause of the test scores. The students actually may have *regressed* as a result of the school's program. Students can be introduced to short statistical anecdotes such as these and the ones Huff provides to sensitize them to how statistics may be manipulated to bias an argument.

An interesting and realistic approach to analyzing arguments is to collect advertisements from magazines and newspapers that use specific or general statistical data, and to deal with each of them as case studies. Also, radio and television commercials may be taped and replayed for analysis. Most commercials will be geared to a basic level of communication and probably will already be familiar to students. They can be encouraged to collect and share their own cases of misuse of statistics.

A few years ago a group called the Campaign to Check the Population Explosion took out a full page ad in *The New York Times*.[5] Half of the page of the ad contained only the following statement in huge type:

A Recent Gallup Poll Shows:
THE AMERICAN PEOPLE OVERWHELMINGLY FAVOR BIRTH CONTROL.

The sponsoring group contained a number of prominent Americans, many well known for their keen logical and analytical minds and integrity. Below the huge caption in much smaller type appeared the following box.

Americans were asked whether or not they felt birth control information should be available to anyone who wants it. Here's what they said.

Gallup Survey

Catholics		Non-Catholics	
Yes	73%	Yes	77%
No	22%	No	18%
No opinion . .	5%	No opinion . .	5%

While a strong vindication of the Bill of Rights, particularly the freedom of speech amendment, the survey results nonetheless reveal nothing about American's position on the act of birth control. You and I might agree to information on genocide being made available to anyone who wants it without favoring it!

Fearnside and Holther describe, illustrate, and explain fifty-one faulty reasoning processes. While not all the processes are appropriate for elementary students, some examples may be used just as they occur in the book. Others may be adapted. Two examples from the book are quoted here:

#1. (Faulty Generalizations). *Example*. Peter is eating Jane's Frozen Peas when he breaks a tooth on a pebble hidden among them. He tells all who will listen never to buy another Jane's product.

Comment. Tired of hearing this complaint, Peter's wife points out that one bad experience with a box of peas does not constitute wide acquaintance with Jane's packaged products. It is not even a fair sample of Jane's Peas.

#33. (Demand for Special Consideration). *Example*. Paul is on trial for a murder committed in California. His lawyer, Peter, points out to the jury that Paul is a veteran with several decorations, that he has a wife and six children, and that he is the sole support of his aged mother.

Comment. Murder is the unlawful killing of a human being with malice aforethought! *Penal Code of California*, section 187.[6]

LOGICAL VALIDITY

Once one has determined that an argument is straightforward, how does he or she know whether it is valid, that is, that the conclusion follows correctly from the argument's premises. Checking the validity of arguments requires some work with logic and may be attempted with older children. A book that may be of help to you on this topic is Robert Ennis' *Logic in Teaching*.[7] Essentially, checking validity involves translating statements into a syllogism and determining whether the rules of the syllogism have been met. Syllogisms are basically a series of statements arranged in the following order:

All men are mortal.
Tom is a man.
Therefore, Tom is mortal.

While most arguments are never presented in the precise form of a syllogism, they can be organized and checked for validation with minor revising and rearranging. Consider this hypothetical conversation between Gertrude and Mergitroid:

Gertrude: How's your love life these days?
Mergitroid: When you come right down to it, all men are beasts.
Gertrude: Yeah, you're right. What about this new guy in the office, Harry?
Mergitroid: He's a man, isn't he?

Organized as a syllogism, the argument appears as follows:

All men are beasts.
Harry, the new guy at the office, is a man.
Harry is a beast.

If one should accept the major premise of this argument, "All men are beasts," it would be valid; that is, its conclusion, "Harry is a beast," *does* logically follow from the initial premise or statement, even though the latter is clearly false. Since Harry is a member of the class "man," which, in turn, is part of the class "beasts," he automatically must also be a beast. Thus a valid argument may result from a false premise.

In more cautious arguments, syllogisms are initiated with *true* premises:

All my cookies are on the table.
This cookie is on the table.
This cookie must be mine.

While the premise *is* true, the argument is invalid since the conclusion does not necessarily follow from the premise. In the class of "(items) on the table" are "all my cookies." But no information states that "this cookie" *must be* in the class of "all my cookies"; it may well be from the class of "all your cookies," which could also exist.

Sometimes in an argument the premise or conclusion is not stated: "Registration of rifles is unnecessary. It is not required by the federal government." This type of argument with a hidden or unstated premise is called an *enthymeme,* and the unstated portion may be added to create a syllogism for analysis:

(What is not required by the federal government is not necessary.)
Registration of rifles is not required by the federal government.
Therefore registration of rifles is not necessary.

One way that students may be helped to visualize the validity or invalidity of arguments is through the use of circle diagrams. Three circles are used to represent each of the three terms in a syllogism.

Example
All teachers are nice.
Ms. Jones is a teacher.
Therefore Miss Jones is nice.

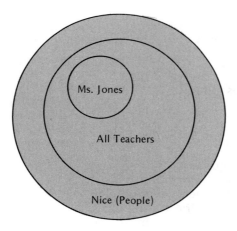

Comment: Since "all teachers" must be placed in the circle "nice people" according to the premise, and since "Ms. Jones" must be placed in the "all teachers" circle by the second statement, the conclusion is valid.

Example
All my marbles are on the desk
This marble is on the desk.
Therefore this marble must be my marble.

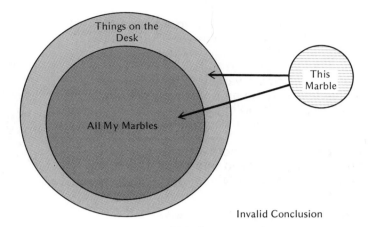

Invalid Conclusion

Comment: As the diagram suggests, "this marble" may be placed anywhere in the circle of "things on the desk." The conclusion need not follow and is therefore invalid.

Fertile sources for logical fallacies are letters to the editor, commercials, and talk shows that have been recorded on a tape recorder. Some of these may even be given as homework assignments or be studied in conjunction with mathematics.

EMPIRICAL DATA COLLECTION

The two strategies for increasing children's facility in empirical data collection are (1) surveys and interviews and (2) systematic observations. While these tools may be less frequently employed by children than adults, they are often essential for obtaining definitive answers to questions that concern us. There are many ways to answer the question, "What's it like to be quarterback for the Miami Dolphins?" But a well-designed interview may be the most fruitful strategy.

SURVEYS AND INTERVIEWS

Taking surveys and conducting interviews are activities students enjoy and that help answer questions such as, "What do the kids in our school think about the cafeteria food?" "How do most people on our block feel about busing to integrate schools?" In the case of many such questions, the only conclusive way to obtain an answer is to conduct surveys or interviews.

A third-grade student recently organized an interview to learn more about the policemen in his community. First Tim considered what he wanted to find out and then wrote out the questions to be used in the interview. In arranging and conducting the interview, the student called the police department, indicated his objective, and set up an appointment for the interview. The actual interview took only 10–15 minutes and was recorded, with the officer's permission, for sharing with the class.

The youngster was acquiring and practicing a variety of tools beyond those of empirical data collection. He was defining objectives, devising a plan of action, organizing a meeting, and handling interpersonal relationships. As he pursued his goals, he sought help from various adults as necessary.

Finally, by replaying and analyzing the tape, both he and the class were able to see where questions might have been improved or where follow-up questions might have been added to obtain more information in the interview. An excerpt is given below:

Tim: My first question is, "Why did you want to be a policeman?"
Police Officer: Why did I want to be a policeman? Well, I wanted to be a policeman because I thought I could help people.
Tim: Why did you decide to live and work in Upper Dublin?
Police Officer: Well, I don't live here. But the reason I decided to work here was I thought it would be a great opportunity for someone who wanted to be a policeman. I think it is a fine township.
Tim: What would you be if you weren't a policeman?
Police Officer: I really have no idea.
Tim: Did you ever have another job?
Police Officer: Oh, yes, I had another job. I was a mailman; before that I was in the army.
Tim: Do you like the job of a policeman?
Police Officer: Do I like the job? Yes, I do like the job.
Tim: What improvements do you think could be made in Upper Dublin?
Police Officer: As far as the Police Department goes, you mean?
Tim: Well, I mean not just about your job, but other things.
Police Officer: Well, I don't know. I think that's up to the taxpayers and the commissioners. I think they're doing a pretty good job, don't you?
Tim: I don't know.
Police Officer: Don't you really?
Tim: Well, I never really studied it.
Police Officer: Well, sure there are improvements that could be made, but I think they're trying their best. I think they're doing the best they can.
Tim: Do you think policemen have good enough equipment?
Police Officer: I think it's going to get better. I think we're trying. I think it's probably not as good as it could be but it's getting better all the time. It's eventually going to get to the point where everything is OK. Yes.
Tim: How many people commit murder a year?
Police Officer: I really don't know. In this township, not too many. In other places, a lot more.
Tim: About how many robberies are there a year?

Police Officer: We have quite a few burglaries, not robberies. We have very few robberies; we have a lot of burglaries.

Tim: What's the difference?

Police Officer: Well, the difference is a robbery is where somebody actually holds you up with a gun. A burglary is where someone, say, breaks into your house or business or something. We have quite a few of those—in the hundreds.

Tim: What do you think Upper Dublin would be like without police?

Police Officer: Well, it would be like any other place without policemen, very bad.

Tim: Are there any things that a policeman does that most people don't know about?

Police Officer: I think there are quite a few things that people don't know about.

Tim: What?

Police Officer: Well, one thing—they work different shifts, which maybe some people know about but they don't really know what the job details; they don't really know what a policeman does.

[At this point the interview is interrupted as the police officer takes and relays to a patrol car a call for assistance.]

Tim: What do policemen do most of the day? What kind of things do they do?

Police Officer: Most of the day, they ride around in the patrol car, observe traffic violations, check suspicious. . . . [Another call interrupts the conversation] They ride around in cars; as I say, they observe things. They try to check various things, in other words, businesses, places of business. They get calls, they answer all calls when people call them on the telephone. In other words, you just heard one here. Right? If someone's in the house, if the person doesn't want them in there, they go and they try their best to get them out of there and possibly to arrest them if they have to. Anything that they're called upon by the general public to do, they try to answer the call.

Tim: OK, thank you.

One social studies program that provides a number of systematic survey and interview activities for students in the upper-elementary grades is the Social Science Laboratory Units, organized flexibly into seven units. Lessons 6 and 7 in Unit 1—"How Do Social Scientists Conduct Interviews?" and "Data Collection Project A"—teach interviewing techniques and provide opportunities for application.[8] Students are introduced to eight dos and don'ts of interviewing through a recording of an exemplary interview between a student and a fourth grader. Following the introduction are three different interviews conducted by other children who have varying degrees of success. A class is asked to rate them according to an observation guide. The next lesson requires the students to apply their interview techniques to a survey of either one another's opinions or those of other classes. The questions concern what school subjects are liked best. After the interviews are completed, the results are rendered quantifiable, tabulated, examined for reliability and validity, and interpreted. A related text for the teacher, *The Teacher's Role in Social Science Investigation*, provides additional information concerning questioning and questionnaire procedures for students to use.[9]

Hilda Taba and Deborah Elkins demonstrated how interviews could be used in conjunction with the study of traditional historical content in the context of a larger unit in a seventh-grade class. Part of their discussion goes as follows:

I opened the study of why people came to America with a discussion of why they themselves had moved, what they had to do to help move, what worries and anxieties they had, and what adjustments they had to make in their new communities. This, I hoped, would motivate them for the study. Also, I wanted to open at the outset an awareness of the emotional problems connected with moving, so that the phrase "hardships and difficulties" would acquire concrete meaning for them. The discussion on moving took at least three full periods because I wanted to give each child who had ever moved a chance to talk. I took very little part in the discussion. I stayed on the sidelines, recording the gist of each child's story. As each child spoke I made entries in four columns on the board telling: why they moved, worries connected with moving, what had to be done to move, and adjustments to the new life.

Children said their families moved because:

We needed more room.
The landlord sold the house, and the new landlord wanted our flat for himself, so he kicked us out.
We came from another city when my father got a job in the aircraft.
My uncle died and left my mother his house so we moved into it.
Our house burned down.
We sold our house and were going to buy another one, but prices got too high.
We were living with my grandmother and when the new project was built we moved in there.
We used to live in a house that they said had to be torn down because it wasn't fit place to live, so we had to move.
We moved down to the first floor because my mother couldn't climb the stairs.

For one child moving day was unclouded by problems or worries. "I thought it was fun," she said. But her classmates recalled troubles aplenty. "When we moved, the other family didn't have their things out of the house yet, and we couldn't move in. Another time we moved, we had trouble with landlords because they didn't want children and we had no place to go, and I remember being very tired after walking and walking. I sat on the suitcases and waited for my mother and father. I was so tired."

. . .

When we finished our listings I gave the children an assignment to interview their parents or grandparents or a neighbor or a relative or a friend who had come to America·from another country. This assignment served two purposes: to list a variety of people—since these children had widely different backgrounds—and to give the children a·chance to relate their own personal experiences in moving to those of people they knew.

In this neighborhood, many people are sensitive about not being accepted because of their foreign background. To put the children and their parents at ease about the assignment I told the story of my own father. When he was only fourteen he escaped being drafted into the Czar's army. Alone in the dead of night, he found his way to the German frontier and later boarded a ship to America. I wanted the children's interviews to cover many points of information, so I covered many points in my own story. I tried to describe vividly the fears and worries of a young boy escaping from his homeland. Then I told them where he settled in America, what he found in·America (such as the opportunity to go to night school), what kind of work he found to do. I had no story to tell about the work he did in Europe, but the children were to try to get this information about the people they interviewed.

The children went home with these points to investigate:

1. Who came and from what country.
2. Why they came.
3. Where they went.
4. What worries they had.
5. What they found here.
6. What kinds of work they found.
7. What adjustments they had to make.

Discussions of these investigations took at least three periods. The reports varied from exciting, detailed stories to lists of bare facts.

We drew up a long list of nationalities represented in our rooms: Italian, Polish, Russian, Irish, English, Scotch, French, French-Canadian, Lithuanian, German, Swedish, Spanish, Portuguese, Finnish, Danish, various combinations of these, and the American Indian.[10]

SYSTEMATIC OBSERVATION

The ability to observe accurately and competently in a given situation seems like such a natural phenomenon once one is conscious of the task that it may appear silly to discuss it. To the contrary, noting perceptions accurately, making maximal inferences from data, and drawing accurate conclusions requires learning, just as does the mastering of other analytical tools.

One author has provided an interesting account of how a young Dakota Indian, Hakada, was taught systematic observational tools over a period of time:

> His uncle asked, "Were there any fish in the lake?" The boy replies, "Yes." How does he know? Well, he has seen them leap up out of the water. His uncle is not satisfied; this is a lazy answer. He then asks, "Is there any other way of knowing? Did you notice those lines on the bottom of the lake? Did you notice those groupings of pebbles on the bottom?" He is teaching the boy not to come to conclusions on only superficial evidence but to look more keenly and to come to conclusions on the basis of more careful observations. The boy has been a little lazy; he has seen all but he has not put his mind on what he has seen. The uncle teaches him to exert his being, to look carefully and to think hard.

> • • •

> Hakada tells, for example, of how his uncle would take him camping at night in enemy territory outside the home ground, unfamiliar to the boy. He was a little boy, perhaps not yet eight. Nameless terrors lurk in the dark, but alas, also definite named ones: wild animals, possibly enemy scouts who, knowing every inch of their territory, are much safer than the intruders. His uncle would say to him, "I want water," and would give the boy a bucket. In the pitch black darkness of the forest, in unknown territory, the boy has to find the presence of water and make his way to it. He has learned how to tell the vicinity of water by the feel of the air he breathes, by the feel of his skin, perhaps its sound or other indirect clues.[11]

Pictures containing a variety of elements are useful for getting children to acquire observational tools. Advertisements from magazines and commercial ready-made pictures are particularly useful. Slides produced by the teacher or students may serve the same purpose. If students are just beginning to read, observational exercises may be built around the pictures in their reading books. If attention is focused on the pictures *before* reading them, the two processes will complement each other. The observation exercise serves as a motivator to read for verification, and the latter activity reinforces the former.

For work on observation and inference, three basic question forms may suffice:

1. "What do you see in the picture?" (To elicit observation.) Or "What does the picture tell you?"
2. "What in the picture makes you think that?" (To verify basis of inference.)
3. "What else do you see?" (To refocus observation.)

An alternative simple approach to observational tactics is to ask children to make a list of everything they see in the picture and then have them compare lists. Some basic anthropological observation techniques also may be employed with children. They can be asked to view brief 3–4-minute film clips involving people in action settings. After the viewing, ask them to review (1) what people were involved (male, female, adult, children), (2) what they did (how and what resources were used), and (3) on what and to what extent time was used. The film clip should be repeated after the three categories have been introduced, and the second set of observations on time, personnel, and resources should be recorded and compared with the first. This same activity, and similar ones, can be repeated on later occasions. The various 8 mm and Super 8 mm film loops that have been marketed commercially, such as the *8 mm Documents Projects Series,* produced by Thorne Films, 1229 University Ave., Boulder, Colo. 80302, are particularly useful for this purpose. They can be viewed and reviewed easily by individual children, and they are silent. These materials are available from the Social Studies School Service (see pp. 51–52).

SPATIAL ORIENTATION

Being able to locate in space and to orient oneself and other items is a valuable if not essential tool in a mobile society. Furthermore this tool can coincide nicely with a child's need for concrete referents in learning. At the same time care must be exercised so that youngsters are not overburdened with abstract spatial tools for which they have little immediate use or clear understanding. The most common way of spatially orienting oneself is through the use of maps and mapping. In its most fundamental sense a map is a representation of part of all the earth. As one author has stated the case, "There can be two fundamental (and very different) kinds of questions that maps can be used to answer: (1) Where is X? (2) What is at X place?"[12]

Based upon her extensive study of maps for children, Barbara Bartz has been highly critical of their design. Her basic charges are directed at the lack of visibility, simplicity, and usefulness of information in maps for children. With an eye to her own findings and to Piaget's and Inhelder's conclusions concerning the child's conception of space, she recommends the following strategies:

> The child's first "map" of the United States should perhaps be a puzzle, many yards wide, with thick pieces so that the child can touch it, walk on it, move it, consider it from different points of view, and break up and reassemble the surface (an operation that he will later need to be able to do intellectually rather than physically). Perhaps children should only rarely look passively at a map hanging in front of them. More often they should have to map things themselves; not just the schoolyard or the classroom or the route home,

but the conversion of observations or numerical data into spatial form. The child could convert rainfall figures into a simple map, or try to think of ways to show different sizes of cities on a population map. Making a simple population map of the U.S. from a real array of data introduces the problems of organizing the data, deciding how many categories to show, worrying about what colors to use to convey the desired impression, etc. Making one map like this is far more valuable than just looking at dozens of population maps in the five or six years of social studies. The ability to make maps nearly guarantees the ability to read them, but too few children are involved in a variety of mapping experiences.[13]

She goes on to suggest further that maps used with children should meet the three basic criteria of simplicity, visibility, and usefulness of content or data.[14] Maps should contain only as much information as needed, should be easily seen and examined, and should deal with information that a child can apply to his or her life experiences.

A number of instructional materials for increasing competency in spatial orientation have been produced for elementary children, though not many would include all of Bartz's specifications. A huge 9' × 12' reinforced-vinyl simplified map of the United States has been produced by Dennoyer-Geppert (Figure 11.4). Entitled the *Action Map*, it is designed to be walked on, crawled on, or written on with special ink pens. The map detail provided is sparse so that features may be added as they are introduced to children, and they can be removed to avoid distractions.

Even very young children can begin to acquire simple spatial orientation tools as they focus on self. One team of investigators found that "A study of toy-play mapping by three-, four-, and five-year-old children

Figure 11.4 Action Map

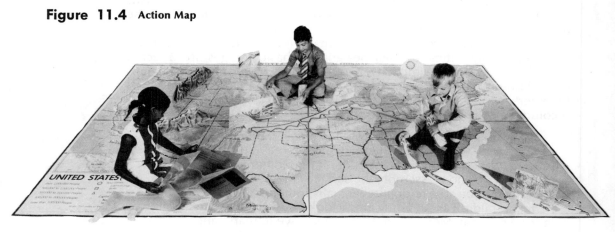

demonstrates that children can clearly represent a cognitive map at the age of three. Mapping, therefore, is developmentally primitive, and formal map-learning can begin at the age of school entrance."[15]

A lesson taken from materials developed by the author for first-grade children is shown below.

How do I look?

General objectives

Observe an outline description of self—one general and basic way to identify personal characteristics. Observe how outlines can provide only a limited description of something; other data are required for a more complete and accurate description. Introduce a basic notion of a map.

Materials

Large sheets of paper for each member of the class or a large roll of paper approximately 4 feet wide.

Commentary

A body map provides a concrete representation of one aspect of self for a child. It is used here to build on the earlier discussion of physical vs. behavioral dimensions of self. The child is led to discover simple mapping and its limitations, namely that it omits many characteristics of an item. He or she experiences the utility of being able to describe something through only an outline map of it, and also the loss of detail when we look no further than the shape of an item.

Suggested procedures/questions

Introduce the activity by a comment such as, "We are going to make body maps today. We are going to discover one way of looking at ourselves." Be sure that a large area on the floor has been cleared or that a large flat section of a wall is available. You may have children lie on the floor or stand against the wall to be traced by you. If you feel that some of the students can do the job capably, let them help you later. In either event, be sure to tape down the corners of the section of paper with which you are working. One suggested strategy is to do four students at a time. If you wish you can have the students hold hands and create a series of linked maps. As you complete a map, write the name of the student in the foot.

Since this sequence of activities will take several days, you may wish to stop at this point. The next steps are to have the children cut out their maps and hang them around the room or on a string clothesline. After the children have done this, have them discuss the following types of questions: "In what ways are all of the maps alike?" "In what ways are the maps different?" "What kinds of things about each of us do the maps show?" "What kinds of things about each of us do the maps leave out?"

At a later point you may wish to have the children add characteristics to their maps through coloring or painting. In concluding this activity, take some time to discuss the point emphasized under the second objective.

The exercise may be supplemented by bringing cut-out shapes to class and arranging them on a bulletinboard. The children may also be encouraged to bring in shapes for others to try and guess.

Two interpreters of Piaget's work, Molly Brearley and Elizabeth Hitchfield, have pointed out the significance of children's mapping their immediate spatial environments:

A full appreciation of the subject of geography includes a sound knowledge of spatial relationships. Recent trends in teaching have been to improve understanding of the subject by encouraging children to make studies of their local environment. In this approach a teacher can assume that the children have a working knowledge of the area they live in, for at least they know places and routes that are important to them, e.g., stations, shops, parks, etc. By expeditions and discussions the children increase their general information and the teacher heightens their awareness of the relationships between places in the vicinity. The children then represent what they know in model or map form. When they have gone through this process of reducing what they know to symbolic form they are in a better position to interpret meaningfully the maps and diagrams of others, which to be understood must be expanded and connected with their previous experience.

Piaget shows that it is not until about nine to ten years of age that the majority of children can get an all-round spatial construction clearly represented in their minds. We must remember that this is an average, a few may reach it earlier and some later.[16]

As they move to later elementary grades students can be introduced to other map activities similar to those developed in *Mapping Games*.[17] These are a set of thirty-nine different activities at varying levels of complexity. Two sample activities, shown in Figures 11.5 and 11.6, illustrate some fundamental approaches teachers may take. A *Teacher's Guide for Mapping, Making Maps,* and *Class Set for Mapping* also are available from the same publisher.

Once children have learned to construct, use, and read maps, they can be trained to make inferences systematically from them. Teacher-constructed maps may be used to initiate problems, such as where the location of a new pizza parlor should be.[18] Similar maps can be developed for problems such as the following: "Where would you pick to live?" "In what ways are these two regions different?" "What effect will it have if an expressway is located in this area?" "Where should the new elementary school be built in this region?" The transparency/spirit master booklet *Making Inferences from Maps* offers some excellent models for creating these types of materials.[19]

The little book *Instructional Implications of Inquiry* by Frank Ryan and Arthur Ellis provides a number of interesting and thought-provoking map activities.[20] One exercise, for example, asks children to use increasing amounts of data to substantiate a hypothesis. Students are first given a basic outline of a country showing only the rivers and then are asked to speculate on where a major city might be located. Three additional maps of the same area are distributed in steps, each one

Figure 11.5
Sample activity

mapping game 10

mapping the room
(1 or 2 people, up to the whole class)

You need
    drawing materials

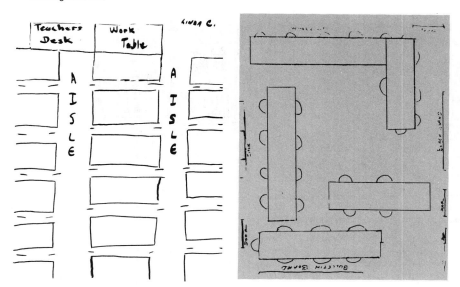

These pictures show some maps that other students have made of their classrooms.

    Can you imagine what these classrooms look like? Are there things you would like to know that you can't find out from the maps?

    Make a map of your classroom. You'll have to decide where things go, how big things should be, where you'll stand when you draw the map, and other things, such as whether or not to show the lights on the ceiling.

    When you've finished, see if you can use your map to help someone else find an object in the room.

Source: Mapping Games (New York: McGraw-Hill, 1971). Republished without endorsement.

Figure 11.6
Sample activity

mapping game 16

drawing different views of the school
(2 people)

You need
    paper
    pencil

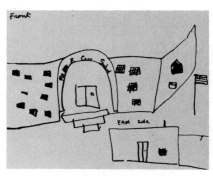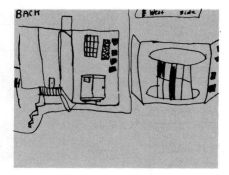

Stand about 100 feet away from the front of your house or school building. Draw a picture of it.

Now, go around to a side or to the back and draw another picture of it.

Stand at one corner of the building. Try to make a drawing of what you see from there.

Imagine that you are in a helicopter hovering over the building. Try to draw what you would see of the building from the air.

Let someone else see your drawings. Have him try to figure where you were standing when you drew each side of the building.

Source: Mapping Games (New York: McGraw-Hill, 1971). Republished without endorsement.

offering new data: landforms, rainfall, and vegetation respectively. With each new piece of spatial data, students reassess their hypotheses and finally test their tentative conclusions through the use of reference sources.

Eventually various types of maps, including aerial photos, may be introduced. Simple outline maps of the United States can be used to show geographical bases of candidate support in presidential elections.[21] Demographic-distribution maps are an especially fertile though little used source of information for important social conclusions, facts, and generalizations. The Superintendent of Documents, Government Printing Office, Washington, D.C., can provide a complete list of a variety of different types of maps published by the federal government and made available at a nominal cost. Available are such inexpensive large wall maps as *Number of American Indians by Counties of the United States, 1970* (GE-50, No. 49, $.50); *Number of Negro Persons by Counties of the United States, 1970* (GE-50, No. 47, $.45); *Percent Change in Population by Counties of the United States: 1960 to 1970* (GE-50, No. 41, $.45); *Population Distribution, Urban and Rural, in the United States: 1970* (GE-50, No. 45, $.50). There are also maps of each of the states ($.20) each) showing all of the counties and many incorporated areas within. Maps for any portion of the United States and its territories are available from the National Cartography Information Center, 12201 Sunrise Valley Drive, Reston, Va. 22092. The Center makes available an index of its holdings upon request. A basic book written for upper-elementary children, Susan Marsh's *All About Maps and Mapmaking*, gives students a comprehensive description of various maps and how they may be constructed.[22] An easy-to-read counterpart volume for teachers is David Greenhood's *Mapping*.[23]

Concrete spatial-orientation referents are exceedingly important for young children, and they may be helped by the use of suitable teacher-made materials such as three-dimensional models of the classroom, neighborhood, or specific regions. Several commercial toy outlets, among them F. A. O. Schwartz and Childcraft, have ready-made sets of three-dimensional materials—houses, stores, cars, and so on—with plastic base sheets showing roads, railroad tracks, and the like.[24] These kits allow children to explore various spatial arrangements on their own, as well as to discuss the social implications of them and to have concrete referents for various spatial items. Inflatable plastic globes, available from Nystrom and various other commerial sources, similarly provide some exploratory engagement with spatial abstractions. Translating the spatial orientation of the world to an elliptical model is a complex cognitive operation; children need as much instructional help with it as a teacher can give.

Specific spatial-orientation tools such as measuring relative distances and learning to use latitude and longitude and determine heights can be acquired in the later elementary years. Geographer William Pattison's little book *How Far?* attempts to teach such tools.[25] The Macmillan

Company also has published a set of programed-instruction materials for elementary students.[26] The first book in the series is entitled *The Earth in Space*. Answers are shown on the left-hand side of the page, and a cardboard slide is used to cover them until each question has been answered.

PROGRAMS TO DEVELOP ANALYTIC TOOLS

While the discussions in this and the preceding chapter have attempted to isolate an assortment of different specific analytical tools, several structured programs have also been developed to help children acquire a sequence of such tools. Perhaps the best known of these is the *Elementary School Training Program in Scientific Inquiry* developed by J. Richard Suchman.[27] It is a program devoted to what is described as "building inquiry skills in young children." It attempts to develop procedures for improving a childs' general ability to inquire productively into causal relationships. Considerable emphasis is placed on children's developing the ability to inquire on their own initiative through the use of searching and data-processing tools. The teacher's role in the school program involves establishing and maintaining procedures of operations, making new information available to the group, and guiding the development of inquiry skills and strategies.

An inquiry session begins with a problem appropriate to the student's level in much the same way as discussed in the Dewey problem-solving model (pp. 156–157). A question then calls for the students to account for the problem. At this point students may seek to explain the problem by asking questions to which the teacher responds, acting as a data source for the class. Certain limitations are placed on the questions, however. They must be structured so as to be answerable in "yes" or "no" fashion. No open-ended questions are permitted. If the question is of the "yes/no" type but cannot correctly be answered with a "yes" or "no," the teacher may qualify his or her responses. Once a child is given an opportunity to raise questions, he or she may continue to ask as many as he or she wishes before passing. A more subtle limitation constrains the teacher from answering "yes" or "no" to any questions calling for approval or rejection of hypotheses to account for the problem (e.g., "Am I doing well?"). In these instances, students' hypotheses are handled with comments indicating that they can be tested by examining the appropriate information. At any point he or she wishes a student may test out a hypothesis. Similarly students may confer with one another at any time by calling a conference.

Periodically students are given guided practice to determine which inquiry strategies have been effective and which have not. One way this may be done, Suchman suggests, is to tape record each inquiry session and then review the merits of each question asked.

Another program by Martin Covington and his associates is called *The Productive Thinking Program*, designed for upper-elementary grades.[28] It consists of fifteen programed lessons built around the adventures of Jim and Lila. In comic-book format, each lesson, like an old-fashioned serial, leaves the reader dangling as to what will happen next. Exercises related to each lesson are provided for the teacher, and each lesson has a corresponding problem-set or workbook activity that reinforces the analytical tool taught in the lesson. The program is designed to assist students in acquiring a series of inter-related analytical tools by providing interesting problems to solve. Claims from field tests with the program are that its users excell in recognizing puzzling facts, asking relevant information-seeking questions, generating quality ideas, seeing problems in new ways, evaluating ideas, and achieving solutions to problems.

Still in the final stages of development is an *Achievement Competence Training Program* produced by Research for Better Schools, Inc.[29] It is a program for grades 5–7 composed of audiotapes, workbooks, games, filmstrips, and a teacher's manual. Basically the objectives of the program are learning to set goals and to work effectively to achieve them. The strategy consists of the following steps:[30]

1. Study self
2. Get goal ideas
3. Set a goal
4. Plan
5. Strive
6. Evaluate

Two lesson specimens from the second unit of the tryout materials are shown in Figures 11.7 and 11.8.

Plans call for the program to be published by McGraw-Hill under the same title by 1976.

WHEN HAVE RESEARCH TOOLS BEEN ACQUIRED?

Generally it should be possible to assess proficiency in reference tools by noting the quality of the results produced by their use, for example, solving of problems requiring the card catalog, locating all the relevant data in reference works, conducting a well-constructed survey or interview, or constructing an accurate map. In other cases it may be possible and appropriate to construct paper-and-pencil test items that are both significant and objective measures of growth. Norman Gronlund's *Constructing Achievement Tests* and *Preparing Criterion-Referenced Tests for Classroom Instruction* and Benjamin S. Bloom's *Taxonomy of Educational Objectives Handbook I: Cognitive Domain* are extremely useful for constructing test items to assess proficiency in analyzing arguments, comparing sources of information, and interpreting charts and graphs.[31] The Thirty-fifth Yearbook of the National Council for the Social Studies' *Evaluation in Social Studies* also contains specific suggestions on constructing test items dealing with research tools and a listing of appropriate standardized tests.[32]

Figure 11.7
Sample activity

⭐ LESSON 1

TIME MACHINE

MY PAST ACHIEVEMENT

Remember a past achievement.
Then answer the questions below.

WHAT WAS YOUR ACHIEVEMENT?_____

_____

WHY WAS IT SPECIAL?_____

_____

_____

_____

WHAT DID YOU DO TO EARN THE GOAL?_____

_____

_____

HOW DID YOU FEEL?_____

UNIT II PART 1   STOP!

Source: Achievement Competence Training Program (Philadelphia: Research for Better Schools, (1974).

Figure 11.8
Sample activity

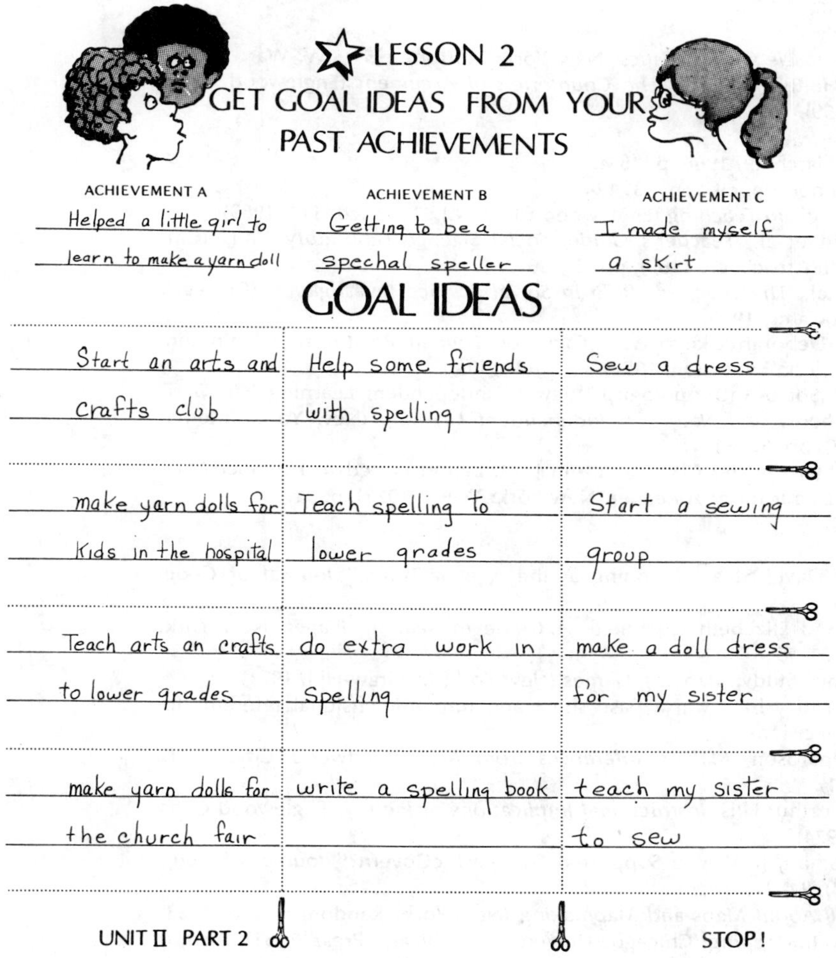

☆ LESSON 2
GET GOAL IDEAS FROM YOUR
PAST ACHIEVEMENTS

ACHIEVEMENT A	ACHIEVEMENT B	ACHIEVEMENT C
Helped a little girl to learn to make a yarn doll	Getting to be a spechal speller	I made myself a skirt

GOAL IDEAS

Start an arts and crafts club	Help some friends with spelling	Sew a dress
make yarn dolls for kids in the hospital	Teach spelling to lower grades	Start a sewing group
Teach arts an crafts to lower grades	do extra work in spelling	make a doll dress for my sister
make yarn dolls for the church fair	write a spelling book	teach my sister to sew

UNIT II PART 2   STOP!

Source: Achievement Competence Training Program (Philadelphia: Research for Better Schools, 1974).

NOTES

[1] Carl L. Becker, "Everyman His Own Historian," *American Historical Review, 37* (January 1932), 221–236.

[2] The country is Turkey.

[3] Darrell Huff, *How to Lie with Statistics* (New York: Norton, 1954); W. Ward Fearnside and William B. Holther, *Fallacy: The Counterfeit of Argument* (Englewood Cliffs, N.J.: Prentice-Hall, 1959).

[4] Huff, op. cit., p. 9.

[5] *New York Times*, March 29, 1968, p. 36M.

[6] Fearnside and Holther, op. cit., pp. 13, 124.

[7] Robert H. Ennis, *Logic in Teaching* (Englewood Cliffs, N.J.: Prentice-Hall, 1969).

[8] See Ronald Lippitt et al., *Teacher's Guide, Social Science Laboratory Units* (Chicago: Science Research Associates, 1969), pp. 28–36.

[9] Ronald Lippitt et al., *The Teacher's Role in Social Science Investigation* (Chicago: Science Research Associates, 1969).

[10] Hilda Taba and Deborah Elkins, *With Focus on Human Relations* (Washington, D.C.: American Council on Education, 1950), pp. 148–150.

[11] Dorothy Lee, "A Socio-Anthropological View of Independent Learning," in G. T. Gleason (ed.), *The Theory and Nature of Independent Learning* (New York: International Textbook, 1967), pp. 60–61.

[12] Barbara Bartz, "Maps in the Classroom," in J. M. Ball et al. (eds.), *The Social Sciences and Geographic Education: A Reader* (New York: Wiley, 1971), p. 91.

[13] Ibid., pp. 99–100.

[14] Ibid., p. 95.

[15] J. M. Blaut and David Stea, "Mapping at the Age of Three," *Journal of Geography* (October 1974), 5.

[16] Molly Brearley and Elizabeth Hitchfield, *A Guide to Reading Piaget* (New York: Schocken, 1966), pp. 71–72.

[17] Elementary Science Study, *Mapping Games* (New York: McGraw-Hill, 1971).

[18] Primary children may be given a base sheet and three-dimensional referents for making their spatial decisions.

[19] Richard D. Shepardson, *Making Inferences from Maps* (Redwood City, Calif.: Visual Materials, 1971).

[20] Frank Ryan and Arthur Ellis, *Instructional Implications of Inquiry* (Englewood Cliffs, N.J.: Prentice-Hall, 1974).

[21] See Everett G. Smith, Jr., "Who Supported George McGovern?" *Journal of Geography* (February 1974), 24–27.

[22] Susan Marsh, *All About Maps and Mapmaking* (New York: Random House, 1963).

[23] David Greenhood, *Mapping* (Chicago: University of Chicago Press, 1951). Also, of broader use, is *The Local Community: A Handbook for Teachers* (New York: Macmillan, 1971).

[24] For catalogs, write: F. A. O. Schwartz, 745 Fifth Avenue, New York, N.Y. 10017 and Childcraft, P.O. Box 94, Bayonne, N.J. 07002.

[25] William Pattison, *How Far?* (Chicago: Rand McNally, 1965).

[26] Cynthia D. Buchanan, *Programmed Geography*, 3 vols. (New York: Macmillan, 1963).

[27] J. Richard Suchman, *Elementary School Training Program in Scientific Inquiry* (Urbana, Ill.: College of Education, University of Illinois, June 1962). A commercial variation of the program also has been published: J. Richard Suchman, *Developing Inquiry* (Chicago: Science Research Associates, 1966).

[28] Martin V. Covington et al., *The Productive Thinking Program: A Course in Learning to Think* (Columbus, Ohio: Merrill, 1972).

[29] Peter Beckinham et al., *ACT, Achievement Competence Training: A Report* (Philadelphia: Research for Better Schools, 1974).

[30] Ibid., p. 2.

[31] Norman E. Grolund, *Constructing Achievement Tests* (Englewood Cliffs, N.J.: Prentice-Hall, 1968); Norman Grolund, *Preparing Criterion-Referenced Tests for Classroom Instruction* (New York: Macmillan, 1973); Benjamin S. Bloom (ed.), *Taxonomy of Educational Objectives Handbook I: Cognitive Domain* (New York: McKay, 1956).

[32] *Evaluation in Social Studies*, Thirty-fifth Yearbook (Washington, D.C.: National Council for the Social Studies, 1965).

CHAPTER 12

Internalization Set #4

You probably already have acquired or are quite familiar with many of the analytical tools discussed in the preceding chapters. Several exercises are suggested in this chapter to assist you in refurbishing whatever tools may have fallen into disuse or to to acquaint you with some new ones. It is recommended that you attempt to complete at least one exercise from each of the six tool categories of interpersonal relationships, research, information processing, analyzing arguments, empirical data collection, and spatial orientation. In selecting exercises that require elementary students to complete, be sure to determine in advance whether the children can handle the tasks involved. Where books or reference materials are needed to complete the activity successfully, check on their availability and the extent to which the children are familiar with them. If elementary students are not available, some measure of practice should be possible through the cooperation of your peers.

INTERPERSONAL RELATIONSHIPS

It seems almost silly to talk about practicing listening and working in groups since we do these things all the time. Nevertheless most of us turn out to be very inefficient listeners and group workers. Being a good listener requires being able to attend carefully to what is being communicated and to interpret the message sent with reasonable accuracy. We demonstrate good listening ability when we are able to act correctly on the basis of something we have just been told. Being an efficient group worker involves many related competencies.

ACTIVITY 42

Try your listening powers right now by completing the Listening Test. You should be able to complete the test within three minutes.

Listening Test
1. Read everything before doing anything.
2. Put your name in the upper-right-hand corner of this page.
3. Circle the word "name" in item 2.
4. Draw five small squares in the upper-left-hand corner of this page.
5. Put an "X" in each square.
6. Put a circle around each square.

7. Sign your name under the title.
8. After the title write "Yes, Yes, Yes."
9. Put a circle around each word in item 7.
10. Put an "X" in the lower-left-hand corner of this page.
11. Draw a triangle around the "X" you just put down.
12. On the reverse side of this page multiply 703 by 8805.
13. Draw a rectangle around the word "paper" in item 4.
14. Call out your first name when you get to this point in the test.
15. If you think you have followed directions up to this point, raise your hand.
16. On the reverse side of this page add 8950 and 9850.
17. Put a circle around your answer. Put a square around the circle.
18. Count out loud in your normal speaking voice backward from ten to one.
19. Now that you have finished reading carefully, do only items one and two.

If you were one of those who unnecessarily completed the tasks in items 3 through 18, you probably could use a little more practice in listening. Review the pattern you followed in completing the test, and reflect upon whether it has been repeated in other tests you have taken or instructions you have read. Have you ever made a mistake on a test or exam because you did not "listen" carefully to the instructions? What makes one attend to or listen carefully to certain statements and not to others?

ACTIVITY 43

Refer to the exercise taken from Charlotte Epstein's *Affective Subjects in the Classroom: Exploring Race, Sex, and Drugs* on pp. 198–199 in Chapter 10. Review the steps she outlines and place a marker in that section of the book. Then read the short article below and complete the exercise as outlined on pp. 198–199.

A team psychiatrist looks at pro football players. By the second or third game of a season, I found *everybody* is hurt. I never saw such injuries, even in my intern years in the emergency rooms of inner-city hospitals. Huge bruises spread over big slabs of the body. Shoulder injuries can make any movement or contact excruciating. Most people with a cracked rib cannot tie their shoes; these men tape the cracks up tight and keep hitting with throbbing aching bodies.

· · ·

On any given Sunday, it is likely that half the players are using stimulant drugs to play, all in defiance of a League rule hastily passed in 1973 against drugs.

· · ·

This game requires a man to wind himself up to a high pitch of rage and aggression every Sunday afternoon at 1:00, and do it with a pain racked body.[1]

How did you feel as you proceeded through the exercise? Did the discussion evolve as you think it would have done normally? How would you feel about always conducting discussions according to Epstein's rules? To the extent that you felt uncomfortable or stifled by the listening/discussion rules, you probably require more experience with studied listening. You might discuss with the members of your group what the implicit or unwritten ground rules are in discussions they usually have with friends. What listening requirements or guidelines do they usually observe?

ACTIVITY 44

Effective group participation can be a highly functional type of tool. Frequently a group is better able to cope with or resolve a problem through the combined efforts of its members than through the effort of any single individual. The following activity will give you a chance to test the efficacy of group vs. individual problem solving with a challenging task. It is alleged to have been used at one time to help train participants in the NASA space program.

Form a group of five members and have each of them individually read the following instructions:

NASA exercise

Instructions: You are a member of a space crew originally scheduled to rendezvous with a mother ship on the lighted surface of the moon. Because of mechanical difficulties, however, your ship was forced to land at a spot some 200 miles from the rendezvous point. During the landing much of the ship and the equipment aboard were damaged, and since survival depends on reaching the mother ship, the most critical items still available must be chosen for the 200-mile trip. Below are listed the fifteen items left intact and undamaged after landing. Your task is to rank them in order of their importance in allowing your crew to reach the rendezvous point. Place the number 1 by the most important item, the number 2 by the second most important, and so on through number 15, the least important.

_____ Box of matches

_____ Food concentrate

_____ 50 feet of nylon rope

_____ Parachute silk

_____ Portable heating unit

_____ Two .45-caliber pistols

_____ One case of dehydrated milk

_____ Two 100-pound tanks of oxygen

_____ Map of the stars as seen from the moon

_____ Life raft

_____ Magnetic compass

_____ 5 gallons of water

———— Signal flares

———— First-aid kit containing injection needles

———— Solar-powered FM receiver-transmitter

Once individual judgments on the rankings have been made, you are ready for the group-consensus judgment: All members of your group must somehow find a way through discussion to arrive at a unanimous agreement on all fifteen rankings. Within the group try to analyze the task logically and support only those solutions that seem reasonable. Try to avoid "giving in" to prevent arguments, "trading off," positions, or reaching decisions through a simple majority vote.

Stop at this point and complete your task. Do not read on until you are finished.

Record Sheet:
Record the group decision, the decisions of each person in the group, and the ranking of importance for each of the fifteen items.

Items	Group Ranking	#1	#2	#3	#4	#5	Correct Answers
Box of matches	————	—	—	—	—	—	————
Food concentrate	————	—	—	—	—	—	————
50 feet of nylon rope	————	—	—	—	—	—	————
Parachute silk	————	—	—	—	—	—	————
Portable heating unit	————	—	—	—	—	—	————
Two .45-caliber pistols	————	—	—	—	—	—	————
One case of dehydrated milk	————	—	—	—	—	—	————
Two 100-pound tanks of oxygen	————	—	—	—	—	—	————
Map of the stars as seen from the moon	————	—	—	—	—	—	————
Life raft	————	—	—	—	—	—	————
Magnetic compass	————	—	—	—	—	—	————
5 gallons of water	————	—	—	—	—	—	————
Signal flares	————	—	—	—	—	—	————
First-aid kit containing injection needles	————	—	—	—	—	—	————
Solar-powered FM receiver-transmitter	————	—	—	—	—	—	————
Differences	————	—	—	—	—	—	————

Solution:
Place the rankings in the following key in the column under *Correct Answers* in the record sheet. Then take the difference between (1) each

individual's ranking on each item and the correct answer, and (2) the group's ranking on each item and the correct answer. Total the differences for each of the fifteen items and place the score in the respective boxes at the bottom of the column on the record sheet.

Correct Answer

15	Box of matches	Little or no use on moon.
4	Food concentrate	Supply daily food required.
6	50 feet of nylon rope	Useful in tying injured together; helpful in climbing.
8	Parachute silk	Shelter against sun's rays.
13	Portable heating unit	Useful only if party landed on dark side of moon.
11	Two .45-caliber pistols	Self-propulsion devices could be made from them.
12	One case of dehydrated milk	Food; mixed with water for drinking.
1	Two 100-pound tanks of oxygen	Fills respiration requirement.
3	Map of the stars as seen from the moon	One of the principal means of finding directions.
9	Life raft	CO_2 bottles for self-propulsion across chasms, etc.
14	Magnetic compass	Probably no magnetized poles— thus useless.
2	5 gallons of water	Replenishes loss by sweating, etc.
10	Signal flares	Distress call when line of sight possible.
7	First-aid kit containing injection needles	Oral pills or injection valuable.
5	Solar-powered FM receiver-transmitter	Distress-signal transmitter; possible communication with mother ship.

Debriefing: The lower the score in the box at the bottom of the column, the greater the degree of agreement with the correct answer. Check how the individuals' decisions compared with the group's decisions. Also discuss how conflicts were resolved and decisions were made within the group. Which activity did each member enjoy the most—the individual one or the group one? Why? Did any one person or did several dominate the decision-making process? How did this occur?

ACTIVITY 45

Related to group-consensus procedures is an activity that provides experience in working cooperatively under some measure of psychological stress. The game was developed by Nylen, Mitchell, and Stout for the National

Training Laboratories Institute for Applied Behavioral Science. This activity requires some advance preparation and a group of five persons who do not know about these instructions:

1. Get some heavy stiff paper; at least five 6" × 6" square pieces will be required.
2. Cut each square exactly as indicated in Figure 12.1 and then mark lightly in pencil the letters shown.
3. Get five envelopes and mark them A through E.
4. Put the pieces from the five squares in each of the envelopes exactly as follows: envelope A, pieces a, b, a; envelope B, pieces c, c, d; envelope C, pieces e, f, f; envelope D, pieces a, h, g; envelope E, pieces a, j,i.
5. After placing the pieces in each envelope, erase the small letters and write the letter of the envelope—A through E—on the pieces so that later they may be easily reassembled.
6. Make five sets of the following instructions for each member of the group. *Instructions:* Each person should have an envelope containing pieces for forming squares. At the signal, the task of the group is to form five squares of equal size. The task is not completed until everyone has before him a perfect square and all the squares are of the same size. These are the rules: No member may speak. No member may ask for a card or in any way signal that he wants one. Members may give cards to other members.
7. Now you are ready to begin. Distribute an envelope and an instruction to each member of the group but ask that they not open the envelopes until signaled. Introduce the exercise by noting that it involves conflict and cooperation.
8. Be sure that all understand the rules and begin.

Figure 12.1
Cooperation squares

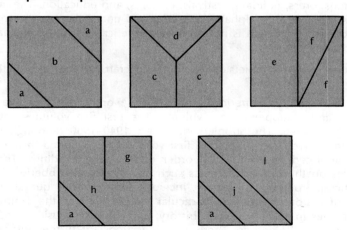

In debriefing, discuss the reactions during various stages of the game. Particularly dwell on the relationship of individual solutions to group solutions and the conflicts that occurred during the game.

SEARCHING

As a teacher of social studies you will have frequent need of a variety of reference works. A myriad number of useful materials exist. A few basic sources are listed in the context of the first activity that follows, while the second asks you to conduct some basic research.

ACTIVITY 46

In this exercise you have an opportunity to get to know how to use some basic reference works. Ten sources are listed with a brief description of the type of information they provide.[2] At the end of the description is a simple representative question for you to answer requiring you to use the reference and learn what it looks like and how it operates. While these ten sources do not exhaust all useful reference possibilities, they are likely to be available in any college or university library. As you locate them you will "bump into" a variety of other related reference tools as well.

1. *The Illustrated Library of the World and Its Peoples.* This work consists of thirty volumes—twenty-nine of facts about individual countries and an index, which is Volume 30. The table of contents lists categories such as the land, the people, history, historical contrasts, fine arts, literature, theater, music, and film. These topics deal with the culture of the country as well as with the geographic facts. There are also lists of maps and reference material such as charts, population tables, principal fishing ports, genealogical tables, and fundamental historical dates. Included also are many illustrations, both black and white and color. There is also information on foods (including recipes), religions, dress, holidays, festivals, customs, and education. The index includes items listed both in alphabetical order and under the country for which they are known; if an item is not found alphabetically, it must be searched under the country's name.

> *Question:* What beliefs concerning witchcraft currently exist in the Malagasy Republic?

2. *Dictionary of American History.* This work consists of five volumes, an index, and a supplementary volume. The first five volumes cover American history to 1940. The supplement covers 1940–1960 (although some articles that may have been slighted in first volumes are included in the supplement). It is arranged in alphabetical order under many headings. There are short articles on the history of topics such as stagecoach robberies, blizzards, and witchcraft from U.S. history. It includes some famous quotations, legislative bills of major importance, particular events such as the Homestead Strike, nicknames in relation to U.S. history, and the arts (music, painting, architecture, etc.) in its entries. There are suggestions for further information at the end of articles and helpful cross-references.

Question: Who was the founder of the Girl Scouts?

3. *Album of American History.* This is the history of the United States in pictures, arranged chronologically. The set contains five volumes. Volumes 1–4 were published with the index; Volume 5 was published later and supplements the set but is not indexed. This reference was prepared to be used as a companion to the *Dictionary of American Biography,* the *Dictionary of American History,* and the *Atlas of American History.* The content of the five volumes is as follows: Volume 1: Colonial period; Volume 2: 1783–1853; Volume 3: 1853–1893; Volume 4: An end of an era, 1893–1917; Volume 5: 1917–1953.

Question: Locate a picture of a hansom cab. What was it and when was it first used?

4. *Encyclopedia of American History.* This reference work presents the essential facts about American history, government, and culture, plus economic, scientific, and technological development from the 1700s to 1964 in fifteen volumes. The index is in Volume 15. It also contains biographical information and color and black and white pictures.

Question: Where was the first American hospital located and what was it like?

5. *Worldmark Encyclopedia of the Nations.* This is a five-volume practical guide to the geographic, historical, political, social, and economic status of all nations, their international relationships, and the United Nations system. The table of contents is arranged alphabetically by the countries of the world. The last part of the book contains an encyclopedia atlas with maps of major countries, religions, language, and so on. Only countries in existence before 1960 can be found in this book.

In addition to much geographic information about the countries, this book gives information on language, ethnic groups, the communication system, armed forces, social welfare, libraries and museums, the press, plus information for tourists and data on famous people of the country. Each country has a bibliography of books for further reference.

Question: How does the per-capita income of Kuwait compare with that of other countries in the Middle East?

6. *United States Government Organization Manual.* This is the official organization handbook of our federal government, published annually. It describes the organization and duties of the executive, legislative, and judicial branches of government. It includes information on the creation of each organization, its purposes, and the activities of various subsidiary organizations operating under it. It also includes the same type of information on independent agencies like the Atomic Energy Commission, the Civil Aeronautics Board, the Commission of Fine Arts, the Federal Communication Commission, the Federal Reserve System, the Federal Trade Commission, the National Aeronautics and Space Administration, the National Labor Relations Board, the National Science Foundation, the Smithsonian Institution, the Tennessee Valley Authority, the U.S. Civil Service Commission, and many others. Also included are some quasi-official agencies like the National Academy of Sciences, the

American National Red Cross, and also some international organizations. A section of charts showing the organization of various agencies is found in the back. Appendix B lists the publications available from the different government agencies and their cost and code numbers, if you should wish to purchase them. There is both a personal names index and a general index.

Question: What are the main functions of the Federal Trade Commission?

7. *Dictionary of American Biography.* This is a biographical dictionary of nonliving persons who made some significant contribution to American life. They can be politicians, artists, scientists, educators, writers, musicians, and so on. The first ten volumes have an alphabetical arrangement. The supplementary Volume 11 is actually two volumes bound together, each volume with its own A–Z arrangement. Biographies vary in length from one column to several pages in length. Bibliographies are found at the end of each article for further reference.

Question: Briefly review Joseph Richardson's biography. What do you consider to be the most significant aspects of his life?

8. *Statesman's Yearbook.* This is a publication providing both statistical and historical information about the countries of the world. It gives information on the constitution and government of each country, area and population, religion, education, social welfare, justice, finance, defense production, commerce, money, weights and measures, and diplomatic representatives. It has four main parts: Part I. International Organizations; Part II: British Commonwealth of Nations; Part III. United States; Part IV. Other Countries of the World. While the book is not in alphabetical arrangement, a good index is provided in the back. There is a small section in the front called Comparative Statistics, which compares major products such as wheat, potatoes, cotton, sugar, and crude oil of the major countries of the world annually.

Question: What are the major industries in the Mongolian Peoples Republic?

9. *Encyclopedia of American Facts and Dates.* This one-volume reference book is a chronological presentation in four columns under these headings: (1) politics and government, war, disasters, vital statistics, and so on; (2) books, painting, drama, architecture, sculpture, and so on; (3) science, industry, economics, education, religion philosophy, and so on; (4) sports, fashions, popular entertainment, folklore, society, games, dress, and so on. There is also a small addenda section in the front presenting last-minute changes in information.

Question: In 1961 President Kennedy met with Premier Khrushchev in Vienna. What major topics were discussed?

10. *School and Library Atlas of the World.* This book contains an exceptionally complete table of contents. It follows contents with an index of maps and a reference text, a master gazeteer, U.S. statistics by state from the beginning up to the 1970 census, the nations of the world and their statistics, possessions, territories, and associated states, principal rivers, mountains,

islands, oceans and seas, and the greatest reservoirs of the world. There are maps and tables of airline routes and distances from selected points to other selected points in the world, and a map showing the members of the United Nations. There is a complete listing of recreational areas in the United States. Each state and country is shown on a large, almost wall-sized map adjacent to its individual index and census figures.

Question: Locate Quakertown in the index for the state of Pennsylvania. What is beside it?

ACTIVITY 47

Imagine an ideal textbook. It would be attractively designed, durable, easy to read, challenging, exciting, not too big, comprehensive, representative of diverse views and the best scholarship available, unbiased, and inexpensive. There are no existing texts for social education that meet all of these criteria, partly because they are contradictory at points, but largely because it is difficult to get agreement among groups on what constitutes meeting the criteria. One of the most extensively researched areas of doctoral study in social education has been textbook analysis. The textbook is a ready target, because unlike a teacher's lesson, it is a finished product that cannot be qualified, revised, or recanted next week. In addition it is expected to represent all of the essentials of the area with which it deals. A textbook rightly or wrongly is often seen as saying to the reader, "Here are the basics of what you need to know about the subject." These expectations are an impossible burden for social education textbooks to carry, and they do not hold up well under it. Generally studies have found them wanting on most counts, and as soon as publishers move to meet one charge, they find they have left themselves open to another. Professional educators have not really helped the publisher much either, since in many cases they have been the very groups writing the books their colleagues are attacking!

Where does this state of affairs leave the social education teacher? Probably with the book that is in his or her classroom. Rather than argue for the perfect book, this author takes the position that all texts can function effectively if appropriately used and that no text, no matter how well designed, is a sufficient tool for social education. It is, in effect, impossible to shield students from all written nonsense, incompetence, racism, sexism, dullness, general bias, injustice, or just plain insensitivity. While some texts may be desirable on some counts, they are likely to be deficient on others, if for no other reason than that they operate under the constraints placed on them because they are books. Like it or not, the chief responsibility for attending to textbook deficiencies will continue to fall upon the teacher.

Try your hand at evaluating a textbook for bias. Detecting slanted or biased arguments may require some practice, since they are often quite subtle. The author of the text is probably even unaware of what the section in question is communicating. Consider some of the following examples of possible sexist bias and alternative approaches:[3]

Sexist Examples	Suggested Alternatives
Arthur Ashe is one of the best tennis players in America today and Billie Jean King is one of the best women players.	Arthur Ashe and Billie Jean King are among the best tennis players in America today.
The candidates were Bryan K. Wilson, president of American Electronics, Inc. and Florence Greenwood, a pert, blonde grandmother of five.	The candidates were Bryan K. Wilson, president of American Electronics, Inc. and Florence Greenwood, credit manager for Bloominghill's Department Store . . . or . . . Bryan K. Wilson, a handsome, silver-haired father of three and Florence Greenwood, a pert blonde grandmother of five.
Write a paragraph about what you expect to do when you are old enough to have Mr. or Mrs. before your name.	Write a paragraph about what you would like to do when you grow up.
Al listened patiently to the ladies chatter.	Al listened patiently while the women talked.
In New England, the typical farm was so small that the owner and his sons could take care of it by themselves.	In New England, the typical farm was so small that the family members could take care of it by themselves.
A slave could not claim his wife or children as his own because the laws did not recognize slave marriages.	Slave men and women tried to maintain family relationships, but the laws did not recognize slave marriages.

The following exercise provides a sensitivity experience in locating instances of bias in the treatment of subject matter:

1. Select a textbook from any area of social education and from any grade level.
2. List the author(s), title, publisher, copyright date, and grade level (estimate if not indicated).
3. Read through the entire text and cite and document (quote passages and indicate page numbers) ten instances of bias or distortion in text passages or the use of pictorial bias. Focus on sexist, racial, or ethnic biases. Do not cite errors or cases of poor scholarship; they are not the concern of this exercise.
4. After each documented instance write a brief explanation of what the author has done that injects bias into the treatment.
5. After the exercise is completed, compare your results with those of others and discuss how you would handle such material if this textbook were being used in your school.
6. Finally, locate two other textbooks on the same topic at the same grade level (or as close as possible). Compare the accounts in these texts with the one you have just evaluated. Is the bias repeated? If not, how did the author avoid it?

INFORMATION PROCESSING

One of the interesting facets of charts, graphs, and tables is that they frequently make it possible to draw conclusions and generalizations from an array of facts. Facts that may lack significance in isolation can take on considerable meaning as part of a series of data.

ACTIVITY 48

The data shown in Table 12.1 offer an excellent example of what statistics organized into a pattern may show.

Table 12.1 Murder data

State	Maximum Penalty for Murder	Murder Rate (1967) per 100,000 pop.	State	Maximum Penalty for Murder	Murder Rate (1967) per 100,000 pop.
Alabama	Electrocution	11.7	Montana	Hanging	2.4
Alaska	Life imprisonment	9.6	Nebraska	Electrocution	2.7
Arizona	Lethal gas	5.6	Nevada	Lethal gas	10.8
Arkansas	Electrocution	8.8	New Hampshire	Hanging	2.0
California	Lethal gas	5.4	New Jersey	Electrocution	3.9
Colorado	Lethal gas	4.1	New Mexico	Life imprisonment[1]	6.4
Connecticut	Electrocution	2.4	New York	Life imprisonment[1]	5.4
Delaware	Hanging	7.8	North Carolina	Lethal gas	9.4
Florida	Electrocution	10.5	North Dakota	Life imprisonment[1]	0.2
Georgia	Electrocution	11.1	Ohio	Electrocution	5.2
Hawaii	Life imprisonment	2.4	Oklahoma	Electrocution	6.7
Idaho	Hanging	4.3	Oregon	Life imprisonment	3.1
Illinois	Electrocution	7.3	Pennsylvania	Electrocution	3.8
Indiana	Electrocution	3.7	Rhode Island	Life imprisonment[1]	2.2
Iowa	Life imprisonment	1.5	South Carolina	Electrocution	11.2
Kansas	Hanging	4.0	South Dakota	Electrocution	3.7
Kentucky	Electrocution	7.2	Tennessee	Electrocution	8.9
Louisiana	Electrocution	9.3	Texas	Electrocution	9.8
Maine	Life imprisonment	0.4	Utah	Shooting or hanging	2.7
Maryland	Lethal gas	8.0	Vermont	Life imprisonment[1]	3.1
Massachusetts	Electrocution	2.8	Virginia	Electrocution	7.3
Michigan	Life imprisonment	6.2	Washington	Hanging	3.1
Minnesota	Life imprisonment	1.6	West Virginia	Life imprisonment	4.6
Mississippi	Lethal gas	8.7	Wisconsin	Life imprisonment	1.9
Missouri	Lethal gas	7.3	Wyoming	Lethal gas	4.8

[1] The death penalty for murder is retained in special cases by the following states: New Mexico—second conviction for murder (lethal gas); New York—killing a peace officer acting in the line of duty and murder committed by a prisoner under sentence of life imprisonment (electrocution); North Dakota—murder in the first degree committed by a prisoner already serving a sentence for murder in the first degree, and for treason (hanging); Rhode Island—murder committed by a prisoner under sentence of life imprisonment (hanging); Vermont—second conviction of murder, provided the two cases are not related, and first-degree murder of a police officer or prison guard who is on duty (electrocution).

Source: Library of Congress and *The New York Times Encyclopedic Almanac 1971* (New York: The New York Times, 1970), p. 277.

Examine the table and answer the following questions:

1. What are the most common types of maximum penalties in those five states with the highest murder rates? List the states and their penalties in descending order below:

   1. _____

   2. _____

   3. _____

   4. _____

   5. _____

2. What are the most common types of maximum penalties in those five states with the lowest murder rates? List the states and their penalties in descending order below:

   1. _____

   2. _____

   3. _____

   4. _____

   5. _____

3. Reflect on the information you have gathered and write out below two potential generalizations that are suggested by the data:

   Generalization 1: _____

   _____

   _____

   Generalization 2: _____

   _____

   _____

4. Compare your potential generalizations with those of your peers. Then reexamine the table, isolating the next series of highest and lowest rates. Discuss whether your prior generalizations should be modified and if so, in what way.
5. What additional kinds of data, besides those contained in the table, would you need to test your generalizations?

ACTIVITY 49

In both general discussions and arguments the use of stereotypes is common. Maintaining and using stereotypes tends to simplify our daily activities and frequently economizes on discussion. To describe someone by saying, "He's a typical Jew" or "She's your standard blonde" allows one to omit a whole series of behavioral descriptions and personality traits. "All of us rely on stereotypes to some extent," Daryl Bem reminds us, "for 'packaging' our conceptual worlds."[4]

It is only when we refuse to accept evidence that does not conform to our stereotypes, or when our stereotypic behavior unjustly harms the innocent, that there is serious cause for alarm. The Japanese accountant who is chosen over equally qualified candidates for a job because the employer feels that "Japs have good business heads" may in fact not mind such stereotypic behavior, while the black accountant who is subtly closed out of a desired suburban neighborhood by those who "know property values drop when blacks move in" rightfully bitterly resents such stereotypic behavior.

Thus stereotypes are two-edged swords and in all cases represent subtly or directly learned feeling patterns upon which we act. One way of beginning to deal with them is to raise them to the level of consciousness in some non-emotional manner. A low-key exercise modified from the Sociological Resources for the Social Studies episode *Images of People* demonstrates how a simple survey may be used to assess subtle stereotypes.[5] A group of at least 15 members will be needed for this exercise. Complete the Adjective Checklist, then tabulate and record class responses on the board by taking a hand count of the number of responses for each item.

Adjective checklist

Male _____	Directions:	For each adjective listed in the left-hand column ask yourself, "Which car owner does this adjective best describe?" Check one—and only one—car owner for each adjective.
Female _____		

	Plymouth Owners	Chevrolet Owners	Mustang Owners	Cadillac Owners
Married				
Modern				
Rough				
Rich				
Brainy				
Active				
Traveled				
Ordinary				
Low-class				
Old-fashioned				

(continued)

	Plymouth Owners	Chevrolet Owners	Mustang Owners	Cadillac Owners
Friendly				
Dangerous				
Plain				
Good				
Particular				
Old				
Busy				
Fat				
Pleasant				
Important				
Popular				

After completing the activity, review the profile of each type of car owner by reading off the four or five adjectives that were most frequently used for that car. Then discuss with the class how this type of strategy could be used with elementary children. How would it be organized if ethnic groups or professions were substituted for automobiles? What limitations does such an exercise have?

ANALYZING ARGUMENTS

The two activities in this section deal with statistical and logical arguments. Both forms of analysis occur frequently in our daily lives.

ACTIVITY 50

In the humorous little book discussed earlier, Darrell Huff's *How to Lie with Statistics,* there are a number of anecdotes cited that may test your understanding (or misunderstanding) of statistics. Each of the following short cases illustrates a misuse of statistics. Examine them and jot down the error(s) in reasoning beneath the quotation.

"Users report 23% fewer cavities with Doakes' tooth paste," the big type says. . . . These results, you find, come from a reassuringly independent laboratory, and the account is certified by a certified public accountant.[6]

Error(s): _____

When Dewey was elected governor in 1942, the minimum teacher's salary in some districts was as low as $900 a year. Today the school teachers in New York state enjoy the highest salaries in the world. Upon Governor Dewey's recommendation, based on the findings of a committee he appointed, the legislature in 1947 appropriated $32,000,000 out of a state surplus to provide an immediate increase in the salaries of school teachers. As a result, the minimum salaries of teachers in New York City range from $2500 to $5325.[7]

Error(s): _____

_____

_____

_____

Plumbers, plasterers, carpenters, painters and others affiliated with the Indianapolis Building Trades Unions were given a 5 percent increase in wages. That gave back to the men one-fourth of the 20 percent cut they took last winter.[8]

Error(s): _____

_____

_____

_____

Compare your results with those of your peers. As you read the evening paper, be on the lookout for similar types of misuses of statistics.

ACTIVITY 51

Since logic is the cornerstone of effective reasoning, one can always use some practice in it. In this activity, which may be done alone or in a small group to compare results, you are asked to assess the validity of several argument sketches. Determine whether one who accepts the premises of the following arguments as true must accept their conclusions:

_____ 1. Countries on our northern border have been guilty of aggression. Clearly China is guilty of aggression, as eyewitness observers have stated. Therefore, China must be on our northern border.

_____ 2. Most racists speak of being lawful and peaceful, but most of them are neither lawful nor peaceful. What it boils down to is that there are some who are neither peaceful nor lawful who speak about being peaceful and lawful.

_____ 3. Every chick in the world hates me! But Laura is not a chick. She doesn't hate me.

_____ 4. Some people want to destroy our country. No one who wants to destroy our country is interested in what made this country great. Therefore some people just are not interested in what made this country great.

————— 5. All beautiful things are inspired by creativity; for example, this statue was inspired by creativity. This statue is truly a beautiful thing.

After you have completed your evaluation of the arguments, construct a circle diagram for each statement to support your conclusion. Refer to the diagrams used in Chapter 11, pp. 224–225.

EMPIRICAL DATA COLLECTION

An interesting popular activity among people is to compare perceptions. Adolescents frequently do this in their discussions of boys and girls. A group of boys sitting responding to the question, "What do you think of Rosalie?" is sharing perceptions. A more complex process is to see how *we* perceive what *someone else's* perceptions are.

ACTIVITY 52

In this activity you have an opportunity to gain some practice in conducting and tabulating surveys and at the same time find out something about yourself in relationship to the other members of the class. There are two parts to the activity; both parts require the participation of all members of the class. To complete the activity you will need to detach the surveys on pp. 261 and 263, or else make duplicate copies for each member of the class.

Each member of the class should first complete the Class Perceptions Survey *anonymously*, then record answers privately for future reference. Save this set of perceptions for later tabulation, and now complete the Self-Perception Survey.

Again record responses on the second survey privately, for future reference. Collect the responses from the class, tabulate both sets of data on a sheet or the board and discuss the results. Discussion might center on the content of the results, the relationships between the two parts of the surveys, which set of results seems the most useful for an instructor to consider, or the design of the surveys themselves as a prototype for related surveys.

Class perceptions survey

Directions: Indicate what you think other members of the class would say about the characteristics of this class; that is, place an "X" under the heading that you feel best describes what the *other* class members would indicate. Do *not* put your name on this sheet, since your responses are to be anonymous.

	Most Would Strongly Agree	Most Would Agree	Most Would Say Sometimes	Most Would Say Not Often	Most Would Say Never
1. There is an adequate level of interaction in our class session.					
2. Class members are putting as much effort into the course as they should.					
3. The class would be a lot better if one or two individuals were not here.					
4. Class sessions are generally enjoyable.					
5. Class members are generally very friendly and pleasant toward one another.					

Self-perception survey

Directions: Indicate how you feel about the characteristics of this class; that is, place an "X" under the heading that you feel best describes the class. Do *not* put your name on this sheet, since your responses will be kept anonymous.

	Strongly Agree	Agree	Sometimes Yes, Sometimes No	Not Often	Never
1. There is an adequate level of interaction in our class session.					
2. Class members are putting as much effort into the course as they should.					
3. The class would be a lot better if one or two individuals were not here.					
4. Class sessions are generally enjoyable.					
5. Class members are generally very friendly and pleasant toward one another.					

SPATIAL ORIENTATION

The last two exercises in this chapter concern spatial-orientation tools. The first one is a simple test of environmental perception, that is, what you perceive to be in the environment around you. The second involves the map as a tool for communication.

ACTIVITY 53

Organize a group of 5–7 peers and give each one a blank sheet of 8½″ × 11″ paper. Do this activity alone first, and then pass around the results to share with others in the group. On your sheet of paper take 8 minutes to draw a map of the floor or level of the building in which you are meeting (e.g., Ritter Hall, 4th floor). You may include anything that you like in your map, but you have only 8 minutes and you are to do it alone. *Stop at this point and complete the map.*

After sharing the results with one another, compare and contrast the similarities and differences in the maps. Who had the greatest detail in their maps? The least? How did these people account for that fact? What items were most frequently included in the maps? Why, do you suppose? Reflect on the larger environment, beyond the floor of your building. What elements of the environment do you regularly focus on or screen out? Think about that fact as you return to your neighborhood today and take a new look at the elements within it.

ACTIVITY 54

While everyone uses maps, perhaps you have never had the occasion to construct a map on which someone else would have to rely to get somewhere. Use the same groups as for the preceding activity and determine quickly where each person considers his or her permanent home residence to be. The rest of the activity will be done out of class meeting.

Again use 8½″ × 11″ blank sheets (for standardization) and construct a map that could be used by any of the members of your group to locate you from his or her home. Two of the 8½″ × 11″ sheets should be taped together to form one 17″ × 11″ sheet and insure good visibility. You may construct the map in any way you wish and add as much detail as you care to or feel is necessary. Feel free to consult any geographic reference tools you need. Remember, however, that your map should be a self-sufficient spatial-orientation tool for all members within your group.

At the next class session, compare and contrast the maps. Questions such as the following may be helpful to keep the discussion rolling: What do the maps include and exclude? What is similar and what is different about the design of the maps? What was absent from some maps that made them difficult to use? After you discuss the characteristics of the maps, some time might be spent discussing the procedures used to construct the maps. How did you begin? What problems did you have? How did you solve them? Where did you go for help?

NOTES

[1] Arnold J.. Mandell, "Pro Football Fumbles the Drug Scandal," *Psychology Today* (June 1975), 40, 43.

[2] These materials were provided by Myrtle Snavely, a librarian in the Bucks County, Pa. schools.

[3] The examples cited all are taken from *Guidelines for Improving the Image of Women in Textbooks* (Glenview, Ill.: Scott, Foresman, 1972), pp. 6–8.

[4] Daryl Bem, *Beliefs, Attitudes and Human Affairs* (Belmont, Calif.: Brooks/Cole, 1970), p. 10.

[5] Sociological Resources for the Social Studies, *Instructor's Guide for Images of People* (Boston: Allyn & Bacon, 1969) (handout sheet).

[6] Darrell Huff, *How to Lie with Statistics* (New York: Norton, 1954), p. 37.

[7] Ibid., p. 85.

[8] Ibid., pp. 110–111.

MODULE SUMMARY

Analytical tools are those competencies that facilitate the achievement of goals considered to be important. Interpersonal-relationship tools are essential for individuals in a complex interdependent world and a highly verbal society. While acquisition of such tools often comes naturally to many individuals through extracurricular socialization processes, many children require systematic training to achieve proficiency. This is the case particularly for specific tools such as listening, effective group participation, paraphrasing, conflict resolution, and communicating feelings. Sample strategies for building competencies in these areas have been outlined.

Analytical tools that might be characterized as research skills have been enumerated. The position developed is that such tools should be taught as functional competencies acquired through the process of meaningful activities. Political scientists, historians, geographers, sociologists, anthropologists, economists, psychologists, and "everyman" are able to function in their goal-oriented pursuits if they have mastered the tools outlined in this module.

Specific activities for helping children acquire and test competencies in the areas of reference, information processing, analyzing arguments, empirical data collection, and spatial-orientation tools were analyzed and illustrated. Three programs were also identified that are designed to teach a cluster of analytical tools: *The Elementary Program for Training in Scientific Inquiry*, the *Productive Thinking Program*, and the *Achievement Competence Training Program*.

SUGGESTED READINGS

Ball, John M., et al. (eds.). *The Social Sciences and Geographic Education: A Reader.* New York: Wiley, 1971.

Brearley, Molly, and Elizabeth Hitchfield. *A Guide to Reading Piaget.* New York: Schocken, 1966.

Ennis, Robert H. *Logic in Teaching.* Englewood Cliffs, N.J.: Prentice-Hall, 1969.

Epstein, Charlotte. *Affective Subjects in the Classroom: Exploring Race, Sex and Drugs.* New York: International Textbook, 1972.

Fearnside, Ward W., and William B. Holther. *Fallacy: The Counterfeit of Argument.* Englewood Cliffs, N.J.: Prentice-Hall, 1959.

Fox, Robert, et al. *Diagnosing Classroom Learning Environments.* Chicago: Science Research Associates, 1966.

Huff, Darrell. *How to Lie with Statistics.* New York: Norton, 1954.

Schmuck, Richard A., and Patricia A. Schmuck. *Group Processes in the Classroom.* Dubuque, Ia.: Brown, 1971.

Taba, Hilda, and Deborah Elkins. *With Focus on Human Relations.* Washington, D.C.: American Council on Education, 1950.

MODULE A

MODULE V

Instructional Models and Their Applications: Emphasis on Affect

Things are interesting because we care about them, and important
because we need them. Had our perceptions no connexion with our pleasures,
we should soon close our eyes on this world; if intelligence were of no
service to our passions, we should come to doubt, in the lazy freedom
of reverie, whether two and two make four.

GEORGE SANTAYANA

CHAPTER 13

The Affective Dimensions of Social Education

"Who am I?"
"What should I do?"
"What are my priorities in life?"
"How can I lead a richer life?"
"What is the best choice?"
"Who is right?"
"How do I feel about this?"
"What and whom do I like and dislike and why?"
"Where am I going?"
"What do I believe?"

A social education program that cannot make a substantial contribution toward resolving some of these vital human questions is sterile and incomplete. Affective growth has been and remains an essential, albeit frequently neglected, objective for social studies teachers. Students want and should receive assistance in identifying, analyzing, and clarifying self concerns.

One of the dominant features of curricular developments in the 1970s has been an emphasis on affect. The emphasis emerges under many labels—humanistic education, sensitivity training, affective education, open education, intergroup education, personalizing education, valuing, value clarification—but there is a common focus regardless of the labels. There is a persistent and underlying concern for the individual and for personal decision making. In one respect the affective movement represents a turning of the social sciences inward to focus on the self—how it is shaped and how it perceives and reacts to the social world it encounters. In some cases affective education emerges as a set of prescriptions flowing from a clearly defined theoretical framework; in others, it is an eclectic amalgam of exercises abstracted from successful teaching experiences.

A major criticism leveled at some elements of the affective movement is that proponents have tampered with problems of self that are more appropriately handled by trained professionals in clinical or semiclinical settings. A lesser but more broadly directed criticism of the movement is that its proponents frequently encourage public displays of self, such as the sharing of feelings about others, without accepting responsibility for dealing with the consequences of such behavior outside of the instructional setting. The net effects of the movement as a whole, and which thrust in affective education will emerge as the most dominant one, remain to be seen.

COGNITIVE-AFFECTIVE DIMENSIONS

Using the frame of reference already established in this book, affective learning refers to those dimensions of learning concepts, conclusions and generalizations, and analytical tools that emphasize the identification, analysis, and clarification of self concerns. While the terms *cognitive* (thinking) and *affective* (feeling) are useful descriptors of teaching objectives, they are false separations when applied to an act of learning: "In all the affective behavior the cognitive element is present and implied."[1] Suppose little Rosa is deeply disturbed by the taunts of her classmates concerning her speech. She shares her problem with her

Figure 13.1
Condensed outline version of the cognitive domain of the taxonomy of educational objectives

1.00 **Knowledge**
    1.10 Knowledge of Specifics
        1.11 Knowledge of Terminology
        1.12 Knowledge of Specific Facts
    1.20 Knowledge of Ways and Means of Dealing with Specifics
        1.21 Knowledge of Conventions
        1.22 Knowledge of Trends and Sequences
        1.23 Knowledge of Classifications and Categories
        1.24 Knowledge of Criteria
        1.25 Knowledge of Methodology
    1.30 Knowledge of the Universals and Abstractions in a Field
        1.31 Knowledge of Principles and Generalizations
        1.32 Knowledge of Theories and Structures

2.00 **Comprehension**
    2.10 Translation
    2.20 Interpretation
    2.30 Extrapolation

3.00 **Application**

4.00 **Analysis**
    4.10 Analysis of Elements
    4.20 Analysis of Relationships
    4.30 Analysis of Organizational Principles

5.00 **Synthesis**
    5.10 Production of a Unique Communication
    5.20 Production of Plan or Proposed Set of Operations
    5.30 Derivation of a Set of Abstract Relations

6.00 **Evaluation**
    6.10 Judgments in Terms of Internal Evidence
    6.20 Judgments in Terms of External Criteria

Source: Adapted from Benjamin Bloom (ed.), *Taxonomy of Educational Objectives, Handbook I: Cognitive Domain* (New York: McKay, 1956).

parents, and together they arrive at some possible ways to deal with the other children. It is difficult in this case to determine whether Rosa's tentative resolution of the problem was initiated by thinking (cognitive) or feeling (affective) processes. It more accurately may be said that thinking and feeling interacted to propel the solution of the problem.

The taxonomies of educational objectives in the cognitive and in the affective domains, written by Bloom and Krathwohl and their associates and outlined in Figures 13.1 and 13.2, were formulated to emphasize the different types of objectives that teachers might consider in developing instruction.[2] The taxonomies are arranged in order of increasing difficulty from the most basic type of objectives to the most complex and are frequently used by teachers in planning and assessing their own instructional objectives. The separation of the two domains by the developers, however, was never meant to suggest that thinking may occur without feeling or vice versa. The authors of the affective domain objective have noted: "The fact should be clear that the two domains are tightly intertwined. Each affective behavior has a cognitive-behavior counterpart of some kind and vice versa. . . . Our split between the affective and cognitive domains is for analytical purposes and is quite arbitrary."[3]

Figure 13.2
Condensed outline version of the affective domain of the taxonomy of educational objectives

1.0 Receiving (Attending)

    1.1 Awareness
    1.2 Willingness to Receive
    1.3 Controlled or Selected Attention

2.0 Responding
    2.1 Acquiescence in Responding
    2.2 Willingness to Respond
    2.3 Satisfaction in Response

3.0 Valuing
    3.1 Acceptance of a Value
    3.2 Preference for a Value
    3.3 Commitment

4.0 Organization
    4.1 Conceptualization of a Value
    4.2 Organization of a Value System

5.0 Characterization by a value or value complex
    5.1 Generalized Set
    5.2 Characterization

Source: Adapted from David R. Krathwohl et al., *Taxonomy of Educational Objectives, Handbook II: Affective Domain* (New York: McKay, 1969).

AFFECTIVE TEACHING

One of the difficulties in affective teaching is the degree to which a teacher may or may not feel comfortable or competent in engaging students in self concerns. Each of us has different feelings about what areas of self concerns are appropriate for classroom analysis and to what extent we are qualified to handle such instructional strategies. Since affective emphases in the classroom touch upon vital and often sensitive student concerns and self-development, it is especially important that a teacher carefully assess his or her understanding and readiness for such instruction.

A relatively simple way to make a self-assessment of one's feeling about affective teaching is to create an Affective Teaching Comfort Zone profile using Figure 13.3. The horizontal axis measures a high or low degree of self concerns, which in this context refer to subject matter that focuses on personal choices and opinions from a student, arising from classroom analysis or clarification. An example of a high degree of self concern would be a teaching exercise dealing with an issue such as, "Should I take up smoking?" An example of a low degree of self concern would be, "When was John F. Kennedy born?" The former illustration focuses heavily on the self while the latter does not at all, or only indirectly.

The vertical axis measures the degree of "ego risk." This term refers to subject matter that a student feels may cause disequilibrium in his or her life if he or she acts upon it. High ego risk is usually associated with student choices such as whether or not to join a gang, while low ego risk is generally attached to questions such as which book should be selected from the library. Obviously, for different individuals any given situation may generate different perceptions of the amount of ego risk involved. Let us observe Walker and Rodriguez in purchasing the same make and model of a car. For Rodriguez the matter involves relatively low ego risk since his selection variables are based on cost/benefit considerations ("What's the most car that I can get for the lowest cost?") and probabilities ("What is the likelihood that this car will perform as expected?"). Walker's case involves much higher ego risk since his selection variables include all those of Rodriguez, plus several more complex ones. Walker feels he must consider how the car will affect his female relationships, his peers' perception of his shrewdness and status as well as his parents' view of how well he is handling the money they give him.

Refer to Figure 13.3 at this point. Assess your own Affective Teaching Comfort Zone by locating yourself as a teacher on both axes; that is, how high a degree of self concerns would you feel comfortable in discussing in the classroom, and, similarly, what is your feeling about engendering ego-risk situations? Mark the farthest points along the axes with which you would feel *comfortable*. Once you have located the two points, draw a straight line connecting them. If you shade in the area within the triangle created by your straight line and the axes, you will

Figure 13.3
Affective teaching comfort zone

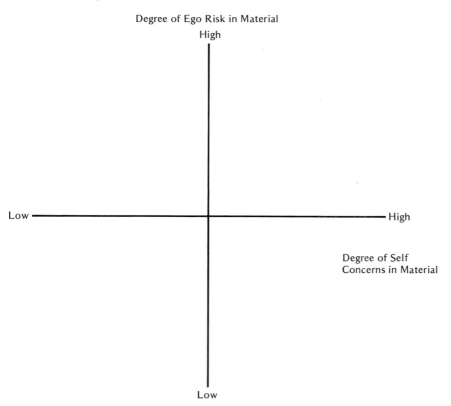

Degree of Ego Risk in Material

High

Low ——————————————— High

Degree of Self
Concerns in Material

Low

have assessed your Comfort Zone. Similarly you can easily compare the degree to which you and your peers vary in your Comfort Zones.

Using Figure 13.4 you can also determine your Affective Teaching Competency Zone by completing a self-profile. This time indicate the degree to which you feel *competent* to handle teaching situations involving the two sets of characteristics—whether you would feel comfortable in doing so or not. Again, connect the two points on the axes and shade the resulting triangle to create your Competency Zone. Note the degree to which the profiles in Figure 13.3 and 13.4 vary. To what extent do the two zones differ, and how do you account for that fact? These zones should provide you with a rough indicator of where you stand with respect to affective teaching and in which direction you may need to move to be the type of teacher you wish to be. To the extent

Figure 13.4
Affective teaching competency zone

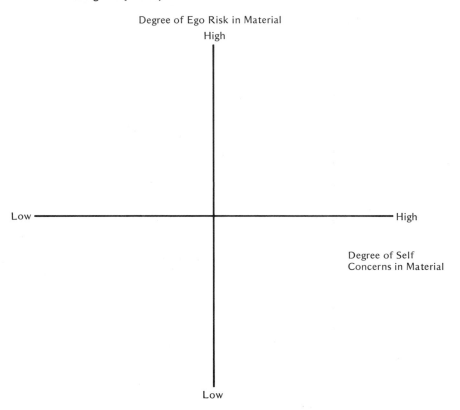

that you wish to become more comfortable and competent with higher degrees of self concern and ego risk in your instruction, you can seek appropriate materials.

A final use of Figures 13.3 and 13.4 is in determining whether a particular teaching strategy or instructional activity might be more generally categorized as affective or cognitive. As shown in Figure 13.5, those strategies or materials whose characteristics cause them to be located in quadrant A might be designated as affective, while those that fall in quadrant C might be labeled cognitive. Strategies or materials falling within quadrants B and D present more problems in labeling. One can create a high degree of self concern simply by telling students that much of their grade in social studies will depend on how well they do in an activity. Similarly a teacher can focus heavily on personal opinions or needs but ask nothing of students in the way of moving to act upon their posi-

Figure 13.5
Dominantly cognitive and dominantly affective approaches

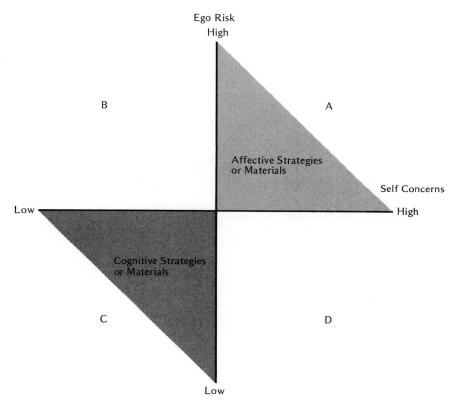

tions. As a rough rule of thumb, consider the zones dichotomized in Figure 13.6 as a possible guide to differentiate cognitive and affective strategies or materials. The shaded area represents an affective orientation, while the remaining areas are cognitive. Any triangle created by the intersection of two points on the axes may be examined to determine whether the majority of the shadings lie within the cognitive or affective zones. Figure 13.7 offers a sample illustration.

After you have completed the readings and the exercises in the next four chapters, you should reassess your Comfort Zone and Competency Zone. Note whether you have advanced in the direction you desired as a result of the experiences provided.

In his book *Learning to Feel—Feeling to Learn* Harold Lyon states this author's view on what the role of the teacher should and should not be in affective education:

Figure 13.6
Approaches that may be designated as affective

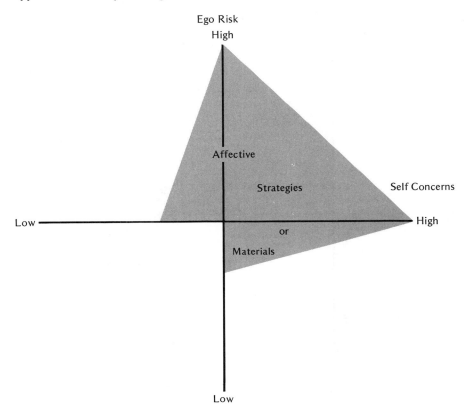

I am not suggesting in this book that teachers should practice therapy in the classroom. Clearly, the classroom is not the place to dig deeply into an individual's past. Educators, however, have been too shy in dealing with "here and now" feeling which invariably foment between students, and between students and teachers. Certainly, most counselors and psychologists have made their message painfully clear that laymen should not be practicing the professional's trade. Some counselors are quite threatened by the advent of the humanistic education movement. It's as though the teacher's dealing with feelings in the classroom will prevent them from having to be dealt with by the counselor outside of the classroom. Of course, if that happened it would be a blessing, but we're far from that utopian stage when children have their concerns so well worked out with their teachers that counselors become obsolete. . . . What I am advocat-

Figure 13.7
Affective strategy: An activity falling predominantly within the affective zone.
(The strategy presents a very high degree of ego risk but only a moderate degree of
self-concerns.)

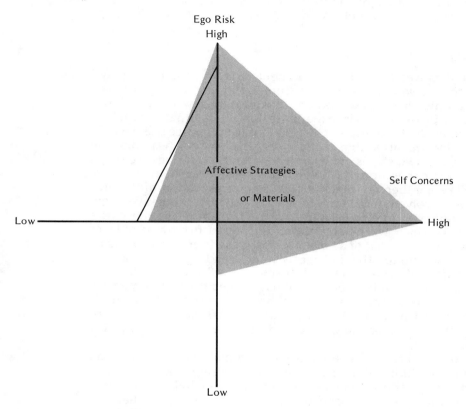

ing is that they have the courage to push forward—and push hard—
against the boundaries that are keeping them confined purely within
the cognitive realm. They must widen their sphere of influence to
include the affective domain as well. Only by stepping out and taking
the inherent risks—risks which are present in all meaningful human
encounters—will progress be made.[4]

SELF CONCERNS

There are a number of ways of categorizing self concerns as they arise
in instructional activities. Partly because of a lack of precision in the

literature dealing with self concerns and largely because many aspects of self defy easy classification, various activities frequently emerge under different labels. Largely as a matter of the author's convenience, self concerns in this and subsequent chapters will be grouped under the headings Self Concept, Values, Beliefs and Attitudes, and Moral Development.

SELF CONCEPT

As the child moves through developmental stages acquiring knowledge, he or she is also forming the self. George H. Mead states: "The self is something which has a development; it is not initially there, at birth, but arises in the process of social experience and activity, that is, develops in the given individual as a result of his relations to that process as a whole and to other individuals within that process."[5] Mead suggests that the self is a product of two stages of development. In the first stage we begin to organize our perceptions of how others react toward us in social situations. "We get then an 'other' which is an organization of the attitudes of those involved in the same process."[6] At a later stage we begin to structure not only individual attitudes but also those of the entire social group to which we belong. One generalizes from a sample of individual responses to that of a collective response from all other members of his social group. This linkage is what Mead designates as the "generalized other." While each child's self is a reflection of this generalized other, it has a unique pattern of its own. As the child organizes the attitudes of others toward him or her, he or she does so through his or her own special perceptual filters, which vary from child to child. Hence the self acquired as the generalized other varies from individual to individual.

Consider one incident in a series where two children are beginning to organize the attitudes of others in their social group toward them. A boy and girl in the second grade are the first ones into their classroom in the morning. They are neatly and brightly dress, and the teacher immediately takes notice. "My, don't you two look pretty today!" Tanya filters this response as, "I am the kind of person who looks pretty and that is good, because I want to be viewed as pretty." Juan processes the same comment as follows: "I am the kind of person who looks like a sissy and that is bad, because I don't want to be seen as a sissy."

The formation of self is also a highly interactive process where each member of a society affects the generalized other in some way. The self is truly social in the sense that it both derives from society and helps shape it in some measure. A class bully not only is forming a notion of self that says, "I am the kind of person who can hurt other people and control them"; he or she also is affecting the self of each peer he or she confronts. The relationships of self to the affective concerns of social studies teaching discussed in this chapter and the two that follow are nicely expressed by Don Hammacheck:

It is through the door of the self that one's personality is expressed. How the self is expressed is a complex phenomena [sic] meaning different things to different people. It is one person's brashness and another person's shyness; it is one person's sympathetic giving and another person's selfish hoarding; it is one person's trusting nature and another person's suspiciousness. An individual's image of himself is constructed from his conception of the "sort of person I am." All of us have beliefs about our relative value and our ultimate worth. We feel superior to some persons but inferior to others. We may or may not feel as worthy or as able as most other individuals, and much of our energy is spent trying to maintain or modify our beliefs about how adequate we are (or would like to be).[7]

The self that each of us acquires and the concept of it that we objectify are intertwined with the social studies activities we will consider. Analyzing and clarifying self concerns is a lifetime process requiring some attention at every level of the social studies curriculum, preschool through adult. The concept of self that each person holds constantly undergoes refinement and testing. By providing children with repeated opportunities to clarify and discover positive aspects of self, teachers help them resolve self concerns. The task is one of eliminating unwarranted negative perceptions of self and maximizing chances for honest positive impressions of self. Hammacheck summarizes the necessary conditions for self growth in this way:

> By sampling new experiences and by testing one's self in as wide a variety of ways as possible, one not only increases the possibility of discovering those things which he does a little better than most, but he also decreases the possibility of being deflated by things he's not particularly good at. Most of us are better than we give ourselves credit for being and taking on new challenges now and then is one good way to find that out.[8]

Helping children develop and focus on honest, positive aspects of self is more of a generalized consideration for all instruction, and hence the shape of specific teaching strategies is not clearly defined. The importance of this dimension of self concern nevertheless merits some specific suggestions for possible lessons, and these will be detailed in the next chapter.

VALUES[9]

Over a quarter-century ago John Dewey wrote: "A skeptically inclined person viewing the present state of the discussion of valuing and values might find reason for concluding that a great ado is being made about very little, possibly about nothing at all."[10] Aimed at the pregnant philosophical and scientific debates of the late 1930s, that remark might be directed equally well at much of the contemporary literature in the social sciences as well as in social studies education. Skepticism notwithstanding, Dewey went on to argue that all deliberate and planned human activities, including science, citizenship, and education, are guided by values; consequently the study of values intersects with all significant concerns.

Value considerations, of course, have always been an important dimension of scientific inquiry. Judgments concerning the relative effectiveness of objectivity determined alternatives to some degree reflect value considerations. Scientists gather and apply data to some purpose, and values may function as the directing mechanism in the process. For the average citizen value-related questions are an especially intriguing and vital part of his or her life. Is a new recreation area needed, and where should it be located? Should the new expressway cut through the northern or the center part of the city? Shall low-cost housing be constructed in our community? Why is so much money spent on defense? Should we build more roads or increase mass transportation? What should we do with our savings? Where should we live? Whom should I marry?

The current state of the dialogue on values in social studies education might best be described as yeasty, if not confusing. The term itself, for example, seems to mean different things to different people. Frequently "value" is used interchangeably with "affect" to connote an emphasis on personal feelings concerning a problem or issue. This meaning covers a particularly wide spectrum of curricular and instructional practices. Sometimes "value" refers to a basic commitment to the fundamental worth of a certain idea—honesty, human dignity, ecological stability. Louis Raths and his colleagues have summarized the definitional problem neatly:

> The meaning of the term "value" is by no means clear in the social sciences or in philosophy. . . . One can find consensus for no definition. About the only agreement that emerges is that a value represents something important in human existence. Perhaps because it is such a pivotal term, each school of thought invests it with its own definition. For the same reason, a particular definition is often not acceptable elsewhere.[11]

A further source of confusion arises from the fact that seldom are distinctions made between a value and other dimensions of affect such as beliefs, attitudes, or just general statements of feelings. Clearly individuals have varying types and degrees of affective responses to experiences, problems, and decisions, but the instructional implications of these differences are seldom stated. Modifying students' behavioral statements concerning cities, for example, is a far different instructional task than getting them to take a stand on the issue of whether urban and suburban school districts should be merged. Similarly, as most tourist bureaus have recognized, positive *attitudes* may be created through certain promotional strategies without any necessary effect on people's more basic *values*.

A third quarrelsome problem stems from the diverse approaches to how value questions should be treated in the classroom. Some educators emphasize the encouragement, fostering, and even inculcation of specific value orientations. Others focus on having students identify, clarify, and analyze their own values, disclaiming responsibility for arriving at any set of "correct" values. Still another group of value educators stresses the discussion and resolution of value priorities, conflicts, and discrepancies and advocates a comparative/analytic approach to values in the classroom.

However conceived, values teaching has always been an important concern of the schools. Historically this concern has often been expressed through an emphasis on "good citizenship" and "desirable socio-civic behavior." While the meanings of these terms were often the subject of considerable debate, the dominant translation emphasized the support and promotion of existing norms of behavior. The implication was that learning to be a good citizen involved being inculcated in the dominant social, economic, and political views of the society.

This perspective on values education created serious problems in those schools where pluralistic value systems were the norm or where a subculture held values at odds with those of the dominant culture, for example, Amish and native American schools. In addition the increasing resistance of minority groups to the norms and mores advocated by majorities, the growing influence of the social sciences on the curriculum, and the rise of the inquiry movement have all contributed to a reaction against efforts to inculcate values in schools. Perhaps the most serious challenge to the validity of the values-inculcation position is the charge that it provides no direction for action in situations involving conflicts between cherished values. Learning loyalty and honesty as desirable absolute values gives no clue as to how to behave in situations where it is impossible to hold both values simultaneously. A presidential assistant, for example, who discovers that his employer has committed some transgression is torn between what his value of honesty may compel him to reveal and what his value of loyalty may compel him to suppress. Both are desirable values, but in the case cited some strategy beyond mere value maintenance is required for decision making.

While there has been considerable interest in the development of values, the schools apparently have had little direct effect on students' values. In the past the prevalent approach in the schools has been to attempt value inculation, supported with intraschool norms where possible and encouraged through role modeling. The results have not been impressive, nor have the methods used been consistent with the dimensions of the task or the demands of a pluralistic society.

For our purposes, values may be regarded as *basic end-states of feelings concerning matters of worth; these undergrid all of our choices and decisions in life.* In effect they function as a first line of filtering that allows us to interpret and organize reality according to its worth and importance to us. Our values not only determine how we shall encounter reality, they predispose us to selectively perceive what is around us. As Hammacheck says:

> We more readily perceive those things, experiences, and people we value, prize, and esteem. For example, have you ever noticed your ability to spot the person you care for in a crowd of people, or your ability to quickly see your name on an entire page of names? Or have you noticed your inclination to buy more food than you really need when exceptionally hungry? The need for something, in this case, food, seems to have the affect of increasing its value potential.[12]

Assessing and analyzing these primary filters of reality—values—is likely to yield the most pregnant information about self concerns. Not surprisingly they are also the most difficult dimension of self concerns to diagnose and observe accurately. At best, in classroom situations a teacher is dealing with verbalizations or paper-and-pencil reflections of values. Neither actions nor statements by an individual, considered separately, may be accurate indicators of what one actually values. This fact should not discourage a teacher from dealing with values but rather caution him or her to avoid easy judgments concerning student values.

BELIEFS AND ATTITUDES

The earth is round.
All Russians are Communists.
Columbus discovered America.
Anyone can be President of the United States.
All people in Africa are black.
The United States is always right.
It is always hot on the equator.
Our wars are good wars.

These all are some beliefs and attitudes that a group of primary children volunteered. Some are based on inaccurate information, and some are probably more strongly held than others. All of them, however, exist as feelings that children will use to assess new experiences they encounter daily.

Besides values, beliefs and attitudes are additional filters of our experiences. Unlike values, they are not basic end-states and are less strongly held by individuals. Beliefs and attitudes, nevertheless, are also an important dimension of self concerns, and children as well as society can benefit from an examination of them. Triandis has observed:

> Many of the important problems of the latter third of the 20th century concern attitudes. Perhaps the biggest problem is that the rich nations are becoming richer while the poor nations are becoming poorer in a world that is progressively getting smaller. We have the

the technological knowledge to change the world, but most of us do not have the attitudes that can bring about that change.[13]

The research efforts of Milton Rokeach and his associates have produced a number of findings concerning beliefs, attitudes, and values. Both the instruments used in their research and their conclusions suggest some significant instructional approaches for social educators. Since beliefs, attitudes, and values are interrelated in Rokeach's scheme, it may be useful to define and differentiate each of the terms. "A belief," Rokeach offers "is any simple proposition, conscious or unconscious, inferred from what a person says or does, capable of being preceded by the phrase 'I believe that. . . .' "[14] All beliefs, according to Rokeach, have thinking, feeling, and potential action components, that is, cognitive, affective, and behavioral components. An attitude is a cluster of interrelated beliefs directed toward a common object that helps control our responses.[15] One may have, for example, a set of related beliefs that form attitudes toward regional planning, population control, the Sierra Club, and so forth.

Rokeach considers a value to be a special class of belief: "I consider a value to be a type of belief, centrally located within one's total belief system, about how one ought or ought not to behave, or about some end-state of existence worth or not worth attaining."[16] Values are few in number, according to Rokeach: "An adult probably has tens or hundreds of beliefs, thousands of attitudes, but only dozens of values."[17] This relatively small collection of values is organized hierarchically for each individual into a value system. A change in the relative status of a single value in the hierarchy will consequently affect the status of other values. Rokeach and his associates also have some evidence that respondents tend to modify their value and attitude systems when they are alerted to inconsistencies in their own value and attitude systems or in those of others:

> The findings suggest that a person may undergo long-term value and behavioral change by merely being exposed to information about value-attitude relationships and inconsistencies as they have been found to exist in others, even if similar information about oneself is not made available. Such information about others can easily be presented in many contexts by lectures to many different types of student and adult audiences by textbook assignments, by face-to-face communication and through the mass media.[18]

MORAL DEVELOPMENT

Moral development is basically the process by which a child grows in ability to decide that a certain course of action is right or wrong. Over the past twenty years Lawrence Kohlberg and his associates have developed, refined, and tested a theory of moral development based on Piaget's notions of hierarchical stages. The Kohlberg findings from research conducted on children in this and other countries reveal six stages of moral reasoning through which all individuals may move:

Stage 1. Orientation to Punishment and Obedience. The physical consequences of an action determine whether it is good or bad.

Stage 2. The Instrumental Relativist Orientation. Right action consists of that which instrumentally satisfies one's own needs and occasionally the needs of others.

Stage 3. Good Boy–Nice Girl Orientation. Seeking approval of others; to gain approval or avoid disapproval. Conforms to stereotype of majority or natural role behavior.

Stage 4. Law and Order Orientation. Adherence to established rules for their own sake. "Doing one's duty" and evidencing respect for authority constitute right behavior.

Stage 5. Contractual Legalistic Orientation. Recognition of an arbitrary element in rules for the sake of agreement. Duty is defined in terms of contract, and respecting the rights of others and the will of the majority. Right tends to be determined in terms of what has been agreed upon by the whole society or more general principles such as "the greatest good for the greatest number."

Stage 6. Conscience or Principle Orientation. Looking to one's own conscience as a directing agent and to mutual respect and trust. Right is defined by the decision of conscience in accord with self-chosen ethical principles that appeal to logic. These are universal principles of *justice,* of the *reciprocity* and *equality* of the *human rights,* and of respect for the dignity of human beings as *individual persons.*[19]

Like Piaget, Kohlberg argues that each stage builds upon the other, the first through the sixth, and that no stage may be skipped. Stage movement for each individual occurs in developmental fashion, but it may be accelerated or retarded. Stage theory has been validated in cross-cultural studies, and with training in the use of coding protocols it is possible to diagnose the dominant stage of an individual's moral reasoning. Kohlberg maintains that most adults become fixated at (never move beyond) stage 3 or 4. While the dominant stage of moral reasoning *may vary for an individual* in a given classroom, the probabilities are that most elementary students will be at stages 1 and 2 with some at stage 3, and most secondary students will be at stages 3 and 4, with some at 2 and a few at 5.

Empirical evidence has also been collected by Kohlberg's associates to support the notion that stage acceleration may be engendered by providing moral reasoning at one stage above that of the child. Individuals tend to be influenced by arguments representing one stage higher than their own; they are unable to understand (though they prefer) arguments representing more than one stage above their own and reject those representing lower stages. By engaging in dialogs with others at stages above your own, Kohlberg assumes, fixation at a lower stage of reasoning will be prevented and upward movement facilitated.

The bases for all of the research of Kohlberg and his associates are a series of moral dilemmas and related probe questions. Respondents are to resolve the dilemmas and share their rationale. Their thinking and discussion are prodded and sustained by the probe questions. In the research studies the cumulative arguments of each respondent over a series of dilemmas are then coded and assessed with respect to stage dominance.

Kohlberg's approach to moral development allows the school to participate in an important area of the child's self growth, while avoiding the pitfalls of moralizing. Children may be aided in growing in their capacity for better moral reasoning without being conditioned to believe in a *particular* moral course of action. In effect Kohlberg's moral development strategies provide a third alternative to the other positions of moral inculcation, or the *laissez-faire* ("do your own thing") orientation.

NOTES

[1] David R. Krathwohl et al., *Taxonomy of Educational Objectives, Handbook II: Affective Domain* (New York: McKay, 1964), p. 53.

[2] Ibid., pp. 3–14.

[3] Ibid., p. 62.

[4] Harold C. Lyon, Jr., *Learning to Feel—Feeling to Learn* (Columbus, Ohio: Merrill, 1971), pp. 80–81.

[5] George H. Mead, *Mind, Self and Society* (Chicago: University of Chicago Press, 1962), p. 135.

[6] Ibid., p. 154.

[7] Don E. Hammacheck, *Encounters with the Self* (New York: Holt, Rinehart & Winston, 1971), p. 8.

[8] Ibid., p. 42.

[9] Part of the discussion in this section is taken from the author's forthcoming chapter, "Valuing as a Teaching Strategy," in G. Manson and M. Ridd (eds.), *On the Matter of Geographic Curriculum and Instruction* (tentative title) (Chicago: National Council for Geographic Education, in press).

[10] John Dewey, *Theory of Valuation* (Chicago: University of Chicago Press, 1966), p. 1.

[11] Louis E. Raths et al., *Values and Teaching: Working with Values in the Classroom* (Columbus, Ohio: Merrill, 1966), pp. 9–10.

[12] Hammacheck, op. cit., p. 37.

[13] Harry C. Triandis, *Attitude and Attitude Change* (New York: Wiley, 1971), p. 1.

[14] Milton Rokeach, *Beliefs, Attitudes and Values* (San Francisco: Jossey-Bass, 1968), p. 113.

[15] Ibid., pp. 112–116.

[16] Ibid., p. 124.

[17] Ibid.

[18] Milton Rokeach and David D. McLellan, "Feedback of Information About the Values and Attitudes of Self and Others as Determinants of Long-Term Cognitive and Behavioral Change," *Journal of Applied Social Psychology*, 2 (1972), 251.

[19] Lawrence Kohlberg, "Stage and Sequence: The Cognitive-Developmental Approach to Socialization," in D. A. Goslin (ed.), *Handbook of Socialization Theory and Change* (Chicago: Rand McNally, 1969), pp. 347–480.

CHAPTER 14

Analyzing and Developing Self Concepts

The feelings each of us has about our self comprise a special class of attitudes that are central to all others. How can a teacher go about helping children deal with and try to resolve the self concerns that they bring with them? Since the emphasis on affective dimensions of instruction is a fairly recent one, the literature and research on the topic has not yielded as much definitive information as a teacher might like. Much of the rapidly growing body of data represents successful classroom experiences in dealing with self concerns. However it does not necessarily reflect either theory and research or any explicit instructional model that can be derived and used to develop other strategies.

Nevertheless some general guidelines are available for treating self concerns relating to self concepts, values, beliefs and attitudes, and moral development. These models will be outlined in this and the following chapter, and their applications to the classroom will be illustrated. As with most of the other models in the previous chapters, the ones sketched here are meant to be skeletal and not restrictive.

THE NATURE OF SELF CONCEPTS

It is evident that children come to school with all sort of ideas about themselves and their abilities. They have formed pictures of their value as human beings and of their ability to cope successfully with their environment. Like an invisible price tag, the child's self image is with him wherever he goes, influencing whatever he does. For some children, the tag reads: "Damaged goods." For others, it may read "A fine value," or "An excellent buy," or even "Top value, one of a kind." Unfortunately, many read "Soiled, marked down" or "Close out, half price." Each of these tags is a social product given to children by the significant people in their lives. Some children enter school with the feeling that they are helpless, unable to cope. Others enter already carefully calibrated, their tag reads "Highly accurate," and they respond carefully to classroom instructions. For still other children the opposite is true, for they have never been encouraged to be careful, accurate, neat, or even honest.[1]

It is conditions such as these described above by William Purkey under which every teacher operates in the classroom. Each child brings a self concept that is the product of myriad factors and interactions, and it will affect in some way everything that occurs in our classes. Much evi-

dence has been amassed over the years to establish what type of impact the concept that one has of himself has on his life. One of the clearest and most revealing facts uncovered is that the self concept one has regarding his or her academic abilities is closely related to the degree of success that he or she will have in school.[2] In other words, those who believe they can do well in school tend to do well. Other linkages between self concepts and other dimensions of our lives similarly may be observed.

Even though a teacher may have little direct control over most of the factors that affect self concepts, he or she must accept some responsibility for helping children develop healthier or more positive self concepts. Combs and his associates underscore this point:

> It is apparent that if the self-concepts a person holds about himself are as important in determining behavior as modern psychology suggests, then teacher-educators must be deeply concerned with the kinds of self-concepts students are developing. This is comparatively new ground for the teacher-education program. Teaching subject matter has always been a recognized task. Even teaching psychology has long been accepted as a responsibility. But few teacher-educators so far have given much thought to incorporating good self-concept development in their programs.[3]

INSTRUCTION FOR SELF-CONCEPT GROWTH

A basic model for treating self concepts in the classroom might consist of four phases:

1. Personal evaluation or introspection on some aspect of our life.
2. Assessment of feelings, characteristics, and perceptions.
3. A self report—either in private or in public.
4. A positive result—a good feeling or a sense of direction for achievable improvement.

In the first phase children are asked to reflect on some segment or span of their lives. They move to assessing or detailing either their feelings concerning the topic or its specific characteristics or noting their perceptions concerning it. Some self report is constructed and possibly made public. It may take a variety of forms, such as written reports, verbal reports, activities, and expressive creations. The net result of the activity should be some positive feeling about self. A child should feel good after completing the activity in the sense that he or she focuses either on something that is nice about him or her or on some way that he or she can become more like what he or she wishes to be.

A series of diverse applications of the model are outlined in this section. The first, Lifelines, is taken and modified from *Man: A Course of Study* (MACOS), a program for the upper-elementary grades designed to teach basically what is human about man.[4] The activity may be used apart from the program for a number of different objectives, including self-concept development. Both children and adults enjoy the activity and invariably learn or recollect a great deal about themselves and others within a group after completing it.

LIFELINES

For this exercise, the following list of materials will be needed for a class:

6' piece of string or yarn for each child
Rolls of transparent tape for each group
Pair of scissors for each child
Pencil or pen for each child
Large box of crayons for each group
Pile of 3" × 5" or 5" × 7" blank cards for each group
Pile of colored construction paper for each group
Several felt-tipped pens for each group (optional)

Organize the children arbitrarily into groups of five in an area where they will have lots of room to spread out with their materials. A floor area is usually the best place. The first two phases of the model are applied through directions such as these: "Will each of you hold up your pieces of string [or yarn] like this?" (Demonstrate by stretching out your arms with one end of the string or yarn in the left hand and the other end in the right.) "This is your lifeline. One end is the beginning and the other is the end of your life. You are to put on your lifeline all the things you can think of that have been or are important in your life. You can draw pictures of the important things, or cut out things that show them" (and write about them on the pieces, if the children are old enough). "After you decide on the important things and make them, put them on your lifelines with tape. Put on the first important thing that happened first" (and so on).*"You may include anything you like and show it in any way you like.* Use and share any of the materials you have in your group."

Where needed, further explanations and demonstrations may be added. You may wish to add also that the first important thing in the children's life was their birth and have them begin their lifeline with its representation. Once each child is started, try to refrain from intervening to avoid structuring their responses and modes of representation. Figure 14.1 shows the lifeline of a child and represents the type of various events that children regard as significant.

In the third phase of the exercise, children are paired off as they complete their lifelines. Ask them to share their lifelines with one another, describing and explaining each event. As each child finishes, create new pairs until every child has finished and has had an opportunity to share with at least two others. Finally, let the children hang their lifelines wherever they like around the room and then move about to examine those they have not yet seen.

For the last phase, let the children respond in open-ended fashion to the activity. Ask what they learned about themselves and how they felt about the activity.

LOOKING GLASSES

This exercise was adapted from a mirror one suggested in Charlotte Epstein's, *Affective Subjects in the Classroom: Exploring Race, Sex and*

Figure 14.1
Lifeline of a child

Drugs.[5] The adapted version appears in a set of early childhood social studies materials developed by this author.

What do I like about me?

General objectives

Emphasize positive aspects of self. Illustrate that each person has qualities that may be prized.

Materials

Set of "looking glasses" (hand mirrors) for each child

Commentary

A child begins to develop his or her self concept at an early age and continues to modify and shape it through life. The feedback he or she receives from others and from self-analysis affect his or her total self-image. In this sense much of the child's social world may be viewed as a looking glass into which he or she peers to see who he or she really is. This activity is designed to help the child see and begin to focus on positive features in his or her psychological looking glass. By starting with a concrete looking glass and concrete personal characteristics, the child can begin to progress toward deeper positive self-insights.

Suggested procedures/questions

Introduce the activity by asking how many have ever heard a story about a looking glass. If no one volunteers any information, briefly relate the relevant part of the Snow White Story ("Mirror, mirror, on the wall . . ."). Inform the children that each one of them is going to have his or her own looking glass during the year. Be sure to distinguish between a fantasy glass in a story and the one they will be using, emphasizing that the latter one does not talk to you. There should be a minor element of fantasy in all looking activities, but children should be prepared for the limitations of the fantasy. They may be told that if they will look into their looking glass in special ways, they will see and learn things about themselves.

Distribute a looking glass to each child and allow a few minutes for random investigations. If someone comments that the looking glass looks just like a mirror, remind him or her that he or she has not yet learned to look in it in a special way. This remark also will help to refocus attention and interest on the next step in the activity.

Ask each child to look into the mirror and be prepared to tell *one* thing that he or she sees that he or she *likes*. Emphasize the positive nature of the observation and give each child a chance to respond. Select a verbal child to begin, and if there is any difficulty in responding, you may start the comments with a self-observation. After everyone has responded, give the class some time to discuss how they felt about the activity and their looking glass.

For the next phase of the activity, pair off boys with boys and girls with girls (generally this will make the observations easier for the children to verbalize). Ask each child to look at the persons next to him or her carefully and then to tell something about him or her that you *like*. Again emphasize the positive nature of the comment.

Allow the class to discuss their feelings about this phase of the activity. Be sure to ask them to verbalize how it felt to have someone say such things about them.

Let the students know that they will be using their looking glass again and will be finding some new ways to look into it. Also indicate that they will have an opportunity to repeat today's activity at a later time. You may wish to repeat the exercise for the class frequently, particularly if you feel there is a general lack of a positive self concept among the class members. An alternative approach is to allow individuals or small groups to repeat the activity as time and interest suggest.

MY FEELINGS BOOK

Examine the *Feelings Book* of Laura, a first grader, shown in Figure 14.2.[6] It represents some events in her life that triggered basic emotional responses. After Laura completed her pictures the teacher wrote the appropriate caption below just as Laura stated it (incorrect tense and all). Note some of the details included and omitted in the pages. On the first page the placenta of the newborn puppies is included, while on p. 4 no situation is cited or represented. Laura could not recall any time that she was ever lonely. On page 6 she recalled a situation but did not feel that she could represent it properly.

After constructing simple books such as this one using construction paper children can share them and discuss their feelings and the reasons for them. In the process they are making legitimate the existence of negative feelings, as well as validating positive ones. A class might also discuss some of the alternative strategies for dealing with negative feelings.

ANIMAL FANTASY

Fantasy and animals are strong motivators for children, and they serve as the vehicle for the following exercise. Animals are used as a device to reflect on self concepts as well as to consider our basic emotions of love and hate. The illustration offered is taken from the author's material in a forthcoming K–7 social studies series. It is drawn from the first-grade level and requires commercially prepared sets of stick-on animals that appear in an activity book. Teacher-made sets of animals, however, may also be used.

How do I feel about myself and others?

General objectives

Provide practice in recognizing and expressing our feelings about self and in expressing strong positive and negative feelings. Provide concrete referents for emotions.

Materials

Activity Book (Contain pictures of various animals)

Commentary

This activity offers a playful, concrete way of expressing feelings about one's self, someone he or she likes very much or loves, and someone he or she dislikes. Animals and their descriptors serve as the vehicle for getting at these emotions. Children and adults typically have the most problems with the negative emotion, since we are socialized at an early age to feel guilty about negative thoughts. A child, however, needs to learn that such thoughts are common to all of us, and the important issue is to distinguish between thought and action.

I am happy when Holly has puppies.

1

I was angry when my brother punched me in the eye.

5

I am sad when I got the chicken pox.

2

I was frustrated when I couldn't get up from the ice.

7

Figure 14.2
Pages from Laura's "Feelings Book"

Negative thoughts are frequently with us, and we need to be aware of them and to try to deal with them in some constructive manner.

Suggested procedures/questions

Direct the students' attention to the exercise in the Activity Book on pp. 7–8. Ask who can identify the animals on the page. Let the children take turns doing this and indicating in some fashion the animals to all the class. All the children should be familiar with all of the animals' names before beginning the activity. Not every child will remember all of the animals, but each child should have an opportunity to recall any old associations with the animals if they exist. You may spend a little time letting the children tell of their experiences, vicarious or direct, with the various animals.

After a number of associations with the animals have been made, it probably will be necessary to arbitrarily halt this discussion, since the children are likely to become very animated. Simply say something like, "Since you all seem to be so interested in animals, let's play an animal game."

Quiet the class and ask them to close their eyes or put their heads down on the desks. Ask them to think of three people: themself, someone they like very much or love, and someone they do not like very much. Students may have some problems with this last choice, and if so, encourage them to think of someone they like less than anyone else as an alternative approach. Ask them to think of the first names of these three people but not to say them out loud.

Once this step has been completed, ask the students to turn all three of these people into one of the animals in their Activity Book. "Pick out an animal that is you. Pick an animal that stands for the person you like very much or love, and pick an animal that stands for someone you do not like very much." Instruct the students to keep their choices secret at this point; sharing will come later. Provide directions on how the animals are to be detached and inserted in the appropriate boxes of the Activity Book. When they have completed their selections, ask them to think of a few words to describe each of the animals, as the instructions at the bottom of the page request.

Results may now be shared in some fashion with other members of the class. Comparisons should begin with each category (i.e., "self" first, "loved one" next, etc.). Choices as well as adjectives for the animals should be shared, and students should be encouraged to express their feelings about the exercise experience and their own personal discoveries.

For older children a teacher may use blank sheets of paper or construction paper and have the children draw, color, or paint the three animals, asking them to print the first names and a few adjectives characteristic of the self, loved one, and disliked one. Sharing can occur by having the class, in turn, name and show the animals and add the descriptions. Three clotheslines can also be set up in the room with each set of animals attached so that the children can compare and contrast easily. One child produced the animals shown in Figure 14.3.

WHO AM I?

This activity is again drawn from the author's materials for the primary grades that focus on self development. It involves a simple procedure requiring only a felt-tipped pen and a large sheet of blank paper.

my Dad
humorous [Loved One]

penguin

Linda
Stubern [Disliked Person]

Donkey

Figure 14.3
A child's set of fantasy animals

MICHELLE
INDEPENDENT [self]

SHARK

Figure 14.4 A self-portrait

I am . . .

General objectives
Provide on opportunity for an individual culminating statement on self.

Materials
Large blank sheet with "I Am . . ." at the top.

Commentary
This brief activity provides each child with an opportunity at the close of this component of the program to make a personal statement of self that he or she wishes to share with others.

Suggested procedures/questions
Put up the chart in advance of the activity. When you are ready to start, gather the children around the chart. Tell them you would like them to think very hard about what they would say if the following situation occurred: A visitor from Mars arrives and he gives you just one short sentence to tell all about yourself. What would you say? Start them out by saying, "I am. . . ." Then ask, "Who is done thinking about how they would finish their sentence?" Record each answer in turn on the sheet until everyone is finished. Call on every child if necessary, but do not force everyone to respond—this should be a personal and voluntary statement. Include your own statement at the conclusions of the session.

Give the children a chance to discuss their feelings about the session. Ask if they felt their task was a difficult one, and if so, why.

A much simpler version of this same activity was used by a sixth-grade teacher in an inner-city school who gave her class the composition assignment, "Who Am I?" The children were asked, "What is it that makes you special or different from every other person in this class, neighborhood, country, or world? What is it that you have that no one else has?"[7] One of her students responded, in part, as follows:

Who Am I? Me the only girl in the world that is the way I am. Me. I'm a child that hopes for love and happiness in the future or someday. I'm a child of 11½ years old. My name is Elisa. Inside of my heart or body I feel lonely and empty. I feel like nothing nobody never pays attention to me. Everybody in my family thinks that I'm stupid. They don't care about me not even my mother. The only ones that I love in my family are my sisters and brothers and they aren't my real brothers and sisters they are only half sisters and half brothers. But still I love them and would give my life for them. They are the only ones in my family that care about me. And my big sister that graduated and works in a bank is the one that buys me and my little sister clothes. She is the one that I love more. And she loves me too. But my mother, my mother is always screaming and yelling at me. And some times I hate her and I wish she were dead and other times I feel sorry for her because she has suffered in this life. But the only problems she has is that she doesn't understand a child. Since she had a hard life she wants me to have a hard and unhappy life like her.[8]

ONE-WAY FEELING GLASSES

This exercise is taken from an account of an activity developed by Gerald Weinstein, reported in Harold Lyon's book, and is described as used by Weinstein with a sixth-grade inner-city class.[9]

A collection of inexpensive sunglasses are required for the activity. Explain to a class that the glasses are "one-way feeling glasses." When worn they make you see things *suspiciously.* Request volunteers to try on the glasses and report what they see in the "suspicious glasses."

After some trials with those glasses try in turn these sets of glasses: "I-know-they-really-care-about-me-no-matter-what-they-say-or-do glasses"; "self-righteous glasses"; "people-are-no-different-from-me glasses"; "strong-points glasses." Beyond these examples cited by Lyon, children may be asked to suggest other glasses to try on. Since much of the activity is open-ended, a number of variations on the self-insight theme are possible.

FEELING FACES

A more basic exercise involving feelings for young children employs a series of facial expressions, sentence-completion sheets, and discussion questions. It is adapted from materials in *The Teaching Program for Education in Human Behavior and Potential.*[10]

Construct a series of facial outlines as shown in Figure 14.5. Let the children identify the emotions portrayed, writing them in below the figures as mentioned. Note that "Sometimes a person's face shows what he or she is feeling. But we don't know why he or she is feeling that way.

Figure 14.5 Faces we wear

Some of the things that have made me feel *angry* are_____

_____..

Some of the things that have made me feel *scared* are_____

_____.

Some of the things that have made me feel *happy* are_____

_____.

Some of the things that have made me feel *sad* are_____

_____.

Some of the things that have made me feel *hurt* are_____

_____.

Some of the things that have made me feel *worried* are_____

_____.

All of us have worn these faces at one time or another. What caused us to feel this way?''

Ask the students to verbalize one thing that caused them to have the emotion shown. After one example for each feeling has been given, distribute the sentence-completion sheets as shown to each child.

When the children have completed the sentences, allow them to share their findings. Request volunteers rather than calling on children. Summarize by asking them to compare the similarities and differences in their experiences. Ask the children to think about which of the faces they might be wearing for the rest of the day and what might cause those faces. Request volunteers to share their thoughts. As a concluding phase to the exercise, have the children identify those faces mentioned that they would *not* like to wear. Let them suggest ways in which it might be possible to avoid the possible causes that might give rise to such emotions. Summarize these and relate them to the specific causes cited earlier by the students.

ADJECTIVE Q-SORT

Q-sort techniques require one to sort a variety of statements or items into piles along some continuum. One or more items may be sorted into each of the piles designated. Applied to self concepts, a Q-Sort may be used to compare self characteristics to those of an idealized self (the person one would like to be) or another, such as a parent or loved one.

A simple illustration of this strategy involves two sets of cards similar to those shown below. Each set of adjective cards is to be sorted into five piles. One pile represents "What you would *most* like to be"; the other piles are arranged in a line, with the fifth being "What you would *least* like to be" and the other piles being points in between. Once sorting into these piles has been completed, the cards are to be turned over. The second set of cards is to be sorted in similar fashion, but this time

Bossy	Mean	Friendly	Smart
Disobedient	Lazy	Happy	Likable
Selfish	Shy	Clever	Strong
Dumb	Bored	Honest	Sense of humor
Weak	Jealous	Feelings easily hurt	Fair
Stubborn	Confused	Careful	Nice
Forgetful	Worried	Good looking	Helpful
Frightened	Uncooperative	Quiet	Tricky

the extreme piles are to be "Most like me" and "Least like me." After this sort, the students are to turn over the first set of piles and compare the similarities and differences in the two piles.

Discrepancies represent the extent to which one is not accepting of his or her self concept. The Q-Sorts generally should be done privately, with students being asked to discuss their reactions and feelings on a voluntary basis. Beyond self-concept analyses. Q-Sorts may be used to register one's feelings or reactions about any topics by changing the labels for the piles and designating different items for the cards.

MY BODY

Children in the elementary grades tend to be preoccupied with their bodies and fascinated with even subtle changes in it, such as the growth of body hair. Their attitudes and concerns about their bodies make up an important part of their self concepts. The "My Body" exercise shown in Figure 14.6 gives children an opportunity to reflect on some things that they like and would like to change about their bodies. The results also provide the teacher with a record of physical self concerns for each child in the class. These data may be used to help counsel and work with children who have many 1s and 2s in their profiles.

Each child should be given a sheet similar to the one in Figure 14.6 and asked to put his or her name on it and complete it privately. At the conclusion he or she should individually assess first what the 3- and 4-rated items are, and then the 1- and 2-rated items. Anyone who wishes to volunteer reactions may share what they have learned before the responses are turned in to the teacher.

COMMERCIALLY MADE MATERIALS

In addition to those commercially prepared materials already mentioned, here are several programs designed to contribute directly to building more positive self concepts at all grade levels. The Lerner Publications Company has published the *In America* series, which features the accomplishments of members of selected racial and ethnic groups in the United States within short picture-filled books.[11] While the books are of uneven quality and one may not always agree with the author's determinations of significant contributors, the books nevertheless offer a significant springboard for letting each member of a multicultural class develop a sense of cultural identity. Through this series a Slovak or a Hungarian child has an opportunity to systematically reflect on how his or her own cultural tradition has been represented in the growth of our country.

The Fitzgerald Publishing Company has published a series of stories about prominent black historical figures in an inexpensive, color-illustrated comic-book format entitled *Golden Legacy*. The publisher notes that "*Golden Legacy* is not a comic magazine, but it is a new approach to the study of history. The intention of our publication is to implant pride

Figure 14.6
Physical self-concept analysis

My body

Look at the items below and next to them put the number of the statement that best describes how you feel.

Statements: 1. I really wish I could change it.
2. I don't like it, but I can live with it.
3. I am satisfied.
4. I consider myself to be really lucky.

_____ Hair		_____ Fingernails
_____ Face color		_____ Shape of body
_____ Appetite		_____ Arms
_____ Hands		_____ Eyes
_____ Amount of hair over my body		_____ Skin
_____ Nose		_____ Lips
_____ Fingers		_____ Legs
_____ Stomach and waist		_____ Teeth
_____ Energy		_____ Feet
_____ Back		_____ Sleep habits
_____ Ears		_____ Health
_____ Chin		_____ Posture
_____ Neck		_____ Weight
_____ Shape of head		_____ Forehead
_____ Height		_____ Face

---

and self esteem in black youth while dispelling myths in others."[12] Some of the current titles in the series are:

Toussaint L'Overture	Robert Smalls
Harriet Tubman	Joseph Cinque & The Amistad Mutiny
Crispus Attucks	White, Wilkins & Marshall
Benjamin Banneker	Black Cowboys
Matthew Henson	Dr. Martin Luther King, Jr.
Alexander Dumas & Family	Alexander Pushkin
Frederick Douglass, Part I	Ancient African Kingdoms
Frederick Douglass, Part II	

Two fine teachers' reference works for beginning the study of ethnic and racial self-identity are the Forty-third Yearbook of the National Council for the Social Studies' *Teaching Ethnic Studies*, edited by James A. Banks, and James A. Banks' *Teaching Strategies for Ethnic Studies*.[13] These works include chapters on teaching about ethnic minority cultures as well as about white ethnic groups. The Lincoln Filene Center for Citizenship and Public Affairs of Tufts University has produced a one-volume set of teaching strategies that, among other objectives, is designed to advance a child's positive self concept. "It seeks to advance student pride in the 'me' and the 'we'."[14] An important adjunct to the volume is an excellent set of photos of inner-city settings developed by Major Morris, a Center staff member.

Two multimedia programs designed for use across several grade levels to help children develop a better awareness and acceptance of self are the Science Research Associates' *Focus on Self-Development* series and the DUSO kits. The former consists of pictures for discussion and role playing, records and filmstrips, and student booklets. Three levels of the program are available, generally keyed to the first three levels of the Taxonomy of Educational Objectives, Affective Domain, outlined on p. 273. The authors describe the program in this fashion: "Its overall objectives are to lead the child toward an understanding of self, an understanding of others, and an understanding of the environment and its effects. Its purpose is to bring out the child's ideas and feelings and to get him to think about them and act on them."[15]

A sample activity from the second level of the program includes a recording of children from various ethnic backgrounds: Efram (Puerto Rican), Leslie (Jewish), Wanda (black American), Heather (suburban white), and John (Mexican-American). The activity operates at several different levels of objectives, including self-identification and self-analysis. One teacher who used the material effectively in a multiracial sixth-grade class described the activity as follows:[16]

I introduced the children on the record to my class by way of a photoboard and explained that these children had gotten together and recorded feelings about their environments. It was important to emphasize that each child was not the spokesman for his group, but was speaking solely for himself. The names of the speakers and their backgrounds were written on the board, so that my class could easily identify them in later discussion.

My students had little difficulty in discussing the impressions and problems of the children on the record. An immediate remark about Efram, the Puerto Rican boy, dealt with his dilemma in overcoming rats. Though most of my class seemed revolted by the thought, some understood the reasons for Efram's problem.

· · ·

One of my students felt that Heather, the white suburban girl, had no problems. "Everything in her life was so nice" was said with a note of sarcasm. Yet, others specified Heather's problems as being stolen stop signs from her neighborhood and wandering dogs. A number of students felt these to be important, for they identified with vandalism and related their own experience with neighbors' dogs.

. . .

Since the children on the record had expressed their feelings about city and suburban living, I asked my students to tell their own ideas about the two. The majority liked the suburbs, because they were cleaner, quieter, and less crowded. Some believed that the city was dangerous. One of my children was deterred by the others in the class, because she related a criminal incident and implied that this could only happen in the city. Her classmates readily pointed out its possibility of occurring anywhere.

In response to my probing their opinions on the buildings and people living in the city, a girl admitted that she ridiculed dilapidated homes, but asserted that she realized that the people who lived in them did not enjoy their condition and were probably forced to live as such. Others, too, demonstrated empathy and reasonable thinking. Another sensed that some people liked the city in that they felt secure in being close to many others. One boy observed that some people did not like to cut grass in the suburbs and instead appreciated the noise and bustle of the city. Another child believed these ideas to be unrealistic. Yet, other children disagreed with her opinion. They had spent part of their childhood in urban areas and commented on their early inability to sleep at night in the suburbs due to the lack of city noises.

Following more discussion, we shared the cultural representations and customs in our backgrounds. Some wanted to investigate more of their customs and report them to the class.

I gathered opinions about the recording itself. Many found it interesting to hear about other ways of life and to receive more information about what they already knew. One Jewish girl enjoyed listening to Leslie since she could compare their feelings about their religion. Open-ended sentences were then distributed as follows:

1. The person on the record I am most like is _____.
2. The person on the record I would like to know more about is

_____.
3. My favorite holiday is _____.
4. Besides being an American, I am _____.
5. Something special about my culture is _____.

The DUSO (Developing Understanding of Self and Others) program comes in kits I and II, roughly corresponding to preschool–primary and intermediate grade levels.[17] Kits contain storybooks, sets of recordings, posters, puppets, related activity cards and props, role-play cards, and other materials for discussion. Both humorous and talking nonhuman figures (e.g., DUSO the Dolphin) are used in the activities. A series of strategies are built around typical children's problem situations.

A program with a strong self emphasis built around a basic student reader/workbook and supplemented with activity charts and ditto-master handouts is called *Dimensions of Personality.*[18] Student materials are essentially a series of work activities preceded by some brief commentary and instructions concerning the tasks. The students produce some behavior specimens related to the unit theme and then analyze them in groups of four. The basic instructional cycle is to read a short passage, respond by supplying some personal data aloud or in writing, and share the results within the groups.

Although its focuses are much broader and its activities diverse, *The Teaching Program for Education in Human Behavior and Potential* contains a number of self-concept development activities.[19] The materials are published for all levels of the preschool–middle grades and contain a *Teacher's Handbook* and student materials. Many of the student materials include role-play scenarios and unfinished stories and case studies..

"To free an environment for the child to develop a healthy self-image (self-respect, self-worth, self-esteem) and an understanding of himself and his self-resources" are stated goals of a series of sequenced 15-minute color films called *Becoming Me*, distributed by the Great Plains National Instructional Television Library.[20] Children in naturalistic settings, as well as fantasy, animation, comedy, and time-lapse photography, are used to present situations with which primary-level children should be able to identify.

People Puzzle, a series of six 20-minute lessons for grade 4 is also distributed by Great Plains. Lesson titles are: The Ways I Am Me, My Actions Tell on Me, Feelings, I Want to Be Wanted, Anger, and Copy Cats. Its primary focus is student self-understanding. "One doesn't have to be like everyone else to be happy—that's the theme of *People Puzzle* programs."

Last but certainly not least, children's literature can be used to help develop positive self concepts as a dimension of a social studies program. This approach to self-concept development is generally described as bibliotherapy. As Eunice Newton puts it:

> For teachers and other educators bibliotherapy is simply the directed reading of books to aid in modifying the attitudes and behavior of children and youth. . . .
>
> While direct personal influence of the child's primary and secondary identifying figures is paramount in the formation of self-concept, it has been long appreciated that models in literature may make a positive contribution. The fact that a literary figure may arouse such close empathy that significant influences upon the reader result is of ancient acceptance.[21]

Two important sources of children's literature that are germane to social studies concerns are: (1) the list of books supplied by the Council on Interracial Books for Children, Inc., 9 East 40th Street, New York, N.Y.

10016; and (2) *Paperback Books for Children,* compiled by the American Association of School Librarians.[22] A more limited but nevertheless quite useful reference specifically for the area of social studies is the collection, "Notable Trade Books in the Field of Social Studies."[23] It is a list of over 100 books selected by a special Book Review Committee of the National Council for the Social Studies–Children's Book Council Joint Liaison Committee.

NOTES

[1] William W. Purkey, *Self Concept and School Achievement* (Englewood Cliffs, N.J.: Prentice-Hall, 1970), p. 37.

[2] Ibid., pp. 14–27. See also Harvey Leviton, "The Implications of the Relationship Between Self-Concept and Academic Achievement," *Child Study Journal,* 5 (1975), 25–35, and Jeffrey M. Schneider and Wilbur B. Brookover, "Academic Environments and Elementary School Achievement," paper presented at the annual meeting of the American Educational Research Association, Chicago, April 1974.

[3] Arthur W. Combs et al., *The Professional Education of Teachers, A Humanistic Approach to Teacher Preparation* (2nd ed.) (Boston: Allyn & Bacon, 1974), p. 25.

[4] Education Development Center, *Man: A Course of Study: Introductory Lessons and Salmon* (Cambridge, Mass.: Education Development Center, 1968), pp. 13–17.

[5] Charlotte Epstein, *Affective Subjects in the Classroom: Exploring Race, Sex and Drugs* (New York: International Textbook, 1972), pp. 58–72.

[6] The idea for this activity came from Susan Mason, a teacher at the Jarretttown Elementary School, Upper Dublin Township, Pa.

[7] Caroline Mirthes, *Can't You Hear Me Talking to You?* (New York: Bantam, 1971), p. x.

[8] Ibid., p. 2.

[9] Harold C. Lyon, Jr., *Learning to Feel—Feeling to Learn* (Columbus, Ohio: Merrill, 1971), pp. 145–147

[10] *Needs and Feelings: Why People Act as They Do* (Cleveland: Educational Research Council of Greater Cleveland, 1967), p. 3.

[11] *In America* (Minneapolis: Lerner Publications, 1966). (Address: 241 First Ave. North, Minneapolis, Minn. 55401.)

[12] *Golden Legacy* (New York: Fitzgerald, 1970). (Address: 527 Madison Ave., New York, N.Y. 10022.)

[13] James A. Banks (ed.), *Teaching Ethnic Studies, Forty-third Yearbook of the National Council for the Social Studies* (Washington, D.C.: National Council for the Social Studies, 1973), and James A. Banks, *Teaching Strategies for Ethnic Studies* (Boston: Allyn & Bacon, 1975).

[14] John S. Gibson, *The Intergroup Relations. Curriculum, A Program for Elementary School Education,* vol. II (Medford, Mass.: Lincoln Filene Center for Citizenship and Public Affairs, Tufts University, 1969), p. 1.

[15] Judith L. Anderson and Melody Henner, *Guide, Focus on Self Development, Stage 3: Involvement* (Chicago: Science Research Associates, 1972), p. 1.

[16] This material is adapted from that provided by Jacquelene Bishop, a graduate student at Temple University.

[17] Don Dinkmeyer, *Developing Understanding of Self and Others,* D-I and D-II (Circle Pines, Minn.: American Guidance Services, 1970, 1974). Materials come in a large metal kit.

[18] *Dimensions of Personality* (Dayton, Ohio: Pflaum/Standard, 1972). The program is available for grades 1–6. For a comparison of this and three other programs that emphasize self-concept development, see Peter H. Martorella, "Selected Early Childhood Affective Learning Programs: An Analysis of Theories, Structure and Consistency," *Young Children, 30* (May 1975), 289–301.

[19] *Teaching Program for Education in Human Behavior and Potential* (Cleveland: Educational Research Council, 1961). (Address: Rockefeller Building, Cleveland, Ohio 44113.)

[20] *ITV Field Report, Special Edition* (April/May, 1974). (Address: Great Plains National Instructional Television Library, Box 8009, Lincoln, Neb. 68501.)

[21] Eunice S. Newton, "Bibliotheraphy in the Development of Minority Group Self-Concept," in E. Ostrovsky (ed.), *Self Discovery and Social Awareness* (New York: Wiley, 1974), p. 200.

[22] American Association of School Librarians, *Paperback Books for Children* (New York: Citation Press, 1972).

[23] "Notable Trade Books in the Field of Social Studies," *Social Education* (March 1975), 172–176.

CHAPTER 15

Analyzing and Developing Beliefs, Attitudes, Values, and Morality

Beliefs, attitudes, values, and morality are closely linked in our daily activities, and they share many structural characteristics in common. Harry Triandis has described the relationship between attitudes and values in this fashion: "We have a structure of attitudes that resembles a tree: the leaves are the millions of concepts that we use to perceive and conceive our world; the branches are different kinds of attitudes, at various levels of abstraction. Finally, the trunk system represents the basic values."[1] Morality represents the process of employing our beliefs, attitudes, and values in deciding that a course of action is proper or improper. As we restructure our beliefs, attitudes, and values, we alter our moral perspective; correspondingly, as we come to or are compelled to certain decisions on what is right or wrong, we change the makeup of our beliefs, attitudes, and values. The soldier who finally finds it necessary to kill another person after painful introspection may find that his unwillingly adopted new morality forces a realignment of his perspectives concerning the importance of human life.

BELIEF AND ATTITUDE ANALYSIS

Milton Rokeach tells us that all beliefs and attitudes have a thinking, feeling, and potential action component attached to them. To "believe" something, then, is to reflect on it in conjunction with feeling and a predisposition to do something in response to it. Each of us carries with him tens of thousands of beliefs, according to Rokeach, which, in turn, means by definition that we have thousands of attitudes (attitudes being a cluster of related beliefs).[2]

Our belief system is formed in concert with our interactions with others and generally the social learning experiences to which we are exposed. It may be altered if some event causes or forces us to reconsider certain beliefs we have, but it usually remains in a state of equilibrium. We tend to maintain our existing belief system, all things being equal. The extent to which our belief system is receptive to entertaining alterations or readjustments is the extent to which it may be said to be "open." Conversely, the tendency of a belief system to avoid or resist possible change leads it to be characterized as "closed." Each of us in this sense has a relatively open or closed belief system. Rokeach maintains that this degree of general open- or closed-mindedness can be measured with a paper-and-pencil test. He and his associates have developed and experimented with a Dogmatism Scale, using a wide variety of subjects from several different countries.[3] The Scale and the results obtained from administering it are detailed in their several books. A short ten-item version of the Scale, shown below, has been developed for administration in situations where time is a factor.

Take a few minutes to complete the Scale before reading further.

Short dogmatism scale[4]

Answer each of the 10 questions by indicating your degree of agreement or disagreement with it as follows:

+1 Agree a little   −1 Disagree a little
+2 Agree on the whole   −2 Disagree on the whole
+3 Agree very much   −3 Disagree very much

Place your + or − rating next to each of the statements.

_____ 1. Fundamentally, the world we live in is a pretty lovely place.

_____ 2. It is often desirable to reserve judgment about what is going on until one has a chance to hear the opinions of those one respects.

_____ 3. A person who thinks primarily of his own happiness is beneath contempt.

_____ 4. In the history of mankind there have been just a handful of really great thinkers.

_____ 5. Most people just don't know what's good for them.

_____ 6. Once I get wound up in a heated discussion I just can't stop.

_____ 7. The worst crime a person can commit is to attack publicly the people who believe in the same thing he does.

_____ 8. In this complicated world of ours the only way we can know what is going on is to rely upon leaders or experts who can be trusted.

_____ 9. In the long run the best way to live is to pick friends and associates whose tastes and beliefs are the same as one's own.

_____ 10. While I don't like to admit this even to myself, I sometimes have the ambition to become a great man like Einstein, or Beethoven, or Shakespeare.

_____ Total Score

When you have completed the Scale, place the following set of numbers in parentheses next to the answers you have given. Then add the ten numbers in parentheses. Place the total in the space next to Total Score.

+1 = (5)   −1 = (3)
+2 = (6)   −2 = (2)
+3 = (7)   −3 = (1)

This figure should be somewhere between ten and seventy. A high score reflects a high degree of closed-mindedness. As with most such instruments, it is important to keep in mind that one *cannot* judge this scale in isolation of the factors that were used to validate it. Individual items may not appear to have much relevance to open- or closed-mindedness, unless one investigates the data upon which they are based.

Just as with values, teachers have a responsibility to reflect on their own belief systems before pursuing related strategies in the classroom. One needs to determine whether his or her primary concern is to have students reflect in an informed and analytical fashion on their own beliefs and attitudes or simply to have them move closer to some desired views. Alan Griffin reminded us almost a quarter of a century ago: *"Unless the public believes that teachers are actually conducting open inquiry, rather than peddling their own preference, either the curriculum or the teacher's freedom as citizen is almost sure to be adversely affected."*[5] He related the following anecdote concerning a teacher he had observed:

> The writer vividly recalls observing a teacher who avowed as her sole aim the development of independent thinking about her pupils. The class had embarked upon the discussion of such current events as happened to be treated in the weekly paper to which they subscribed for this purpose. The lead story was on the then-current coal strike. A boy in the class delivered himself of the idea, "If miners would be sensible with their money, instead of throwing it all away on whiskey, they'd find that their wages were more than they need."
>
> The teacher moved in fast. Under a barrage of well-placed questions, the lad admitted that (1) he had no idea how much a miner was paid; (2) he had no firsthand knowledge of the personal habits of miners; (3) his sole source for the view he had announced was a muttered reaction of his father's at the breakfast table; (4) he doubted if his father had any actual information on either of the relevant points; (5) he recognized that one ought not to make such a drastic or sweeping generalization unless he had facts to back it up. So far, so good.
>
> The next reaction came from a girl who remarked the deep feeling that whenever men strike they lose money, and that this fact so disturbs their wives as to upset their home life very seriously. "So," she concluded, "I think that whenever men strike they must be in the right, or they wouldn't do a thing that's going to be so unpleasant for them." The writer's eyes were on the teacher as he waited for this avowed foe of the facile generalization to swing into action. All that the teacher did, however, was to beam and announce solemnly, "Helen, that's what I call a very nice insight."
>
> Many will say that the major failure in this example was the teacher's refusal to give the class itself chance to do the job of challenging both ideas; and they will be quite right. Sometimes, however, the teacher has to offer the first challenge in order to get an idea considered at all. The writer's sole point is that the teacher who subjects to reflection examinations only those ideas which he regards as "wrong" is engaged in fact (whatever his aim) in cultivating his own attitudes within his students.[6]

Several models exist for aiding children in analyzing and restructuring their beliefs and attitudes in a way that avoids the indoctrination about which Griffin warned. Those discussed in this chapter have been labeled Attitude Scaling, Attitude Triangles, and Challenging Commonly Held Beliefs. Each of the models, as cited below, is based in some respect on psychological theories relating to beliefs and attitudes.

ATTITUDES SCALING

The scaling model described here is based on the principle of the semantic differential developed by C. E. Osgood and his associates.[7] Their instrument allows one to present any attitude object—people, events, conditions, experiences, places, and the like—and to obtain a quantifiable reaction. It employs scales and sets of adjectives representing two polarities. Fifteen sets of adjectives that may be used to assess attitudes have been identified by Osgood and his associates: good-bad, nice-awful, fragrant-foul, beautiful-ugly, sweet-sour, honest-dishonest, fair-unfair, valuable-worthless, kind-cruel, sacred-profane, bitter-sweet, happy-sad, nice-awful, pleasant-unpleasant, tasty-distasteful. Other sets of similar adjectives may be substituted or added to the list.

The semantic differential requires one to rate an item on a number of seven point scales in the following fashion:

My teacher

Fair	___	___	___	___	___	___	___	Unfair
	1	2	3	4	5	6	7	

By checking one of the spaces, an attitude statement is registered. Scores across the sets of adjectives may then be summed.

An example of attitude scaling employing Osgood's adjectives and used to assess an all-Caucasian class' attitudes toward blacks is shown below:

Black people

Happy	___	___	___	___	___	___	___	Sad
	1	2	3	4	5	6	7	
Honest	___	___	___	___	___	___	___	Dishonest
Unfair	___	___	___	___	___	___	___	Fair
	7	6	5	4	3	2	1	
Nice	___	___	___	___	___	___	___	Awful
Ugly	___	___	___	___	___	___	___	Beautiful
Kind	___	___	___	___	___	___	___	Cruel
Pleasant	___	___	___	___	___	___	___	Unpleasant
Good	___	___	___	___	___	___	___	Bad
Valuable	___	___	___	___	___	___	___	Worthless

For certain attitude objects, a teacher-devised set of adjectives sometimes may be more relevant:

People who have no jobs

	1	2	3	4	5	6	7	
Healthy								Unhealthy
Happy								Sad
Alert								Dull

	7	6	5	4	3	2	1	
Full								Hungry
Lazy								Ambitious
Poor								Rich
Shrewd								Dumb
Honest								Dishonest
Lucky								Unlucky

Scores in both examples may range from 9 to 63. The lower the score the more sympathetic is the attitude of the student toward "Black People" and "People Who Have No Jobs." In devising sets of teacher-made adjectives, it is important to assign the polarity adjective considered to represent the most positive attitude response the lowest number.

After individual students have recorded their attitudes, a class average for each set of polarities may be computed. The total value of all students' responses for each item (from 1 to 7) would be summed and divided by the total number of students responding. The class-average profile can be graphed by placing a dot in the middle of the space representing the class average for each set of items and then connecting the dots. A hypothetical class graph is shown below:

People who have no jobs

ATTITUDE TRIANGLES

Suppose that Joe and Anna are engaged to be married and are blissfully in love. In the course of discussing their future attitude relationships, they have learned that they are both in favor of having a small family. Focusing on Joe's behavior, one way to show attitude interrelationships is through a triangle diagram (Figure 15.1).

Figure 15.1 shows that Joe likes Anna, Anna likes small families, and Joe feels likewise. The same discussion uncovers the fact that Anna does not believe in abortions; neither does Joe. Focusing on Anna, we can construct another attitude triangle (Figure 15.2). Figure 15.2 shows that Anna likes Joe and that neither of them cares for abortions.

Both sets of attitude triangles shown may be said to be *balanced*. A balanced triangle results when all three attitude links are positive or when there are two negative ones. Suppose, however, the preceding discussion also reveals that Anna favors premarital sex while Joe does not, and that Joe favors voluntary sterilization while Anna finds it abhorrent. These two attitude triangles are shown in Figures 15.3 and 15.4. Both of them may be said to be *unbalanced,* and when this occurs a relationship is under strain. At this point there will be a tendency to change some of the attitude relationships to restore balance.

According to F. Heider's theory of cognitive consistency, on which these preceding examples are based, balance can be restored if either party can persuade the other to come around to his or her views, or if either learns to dislike the other.[8] Further research has revealed that the theory may be qualified to include alternative responses to an unbalanced attitude triangle, but the basic choices will suffice for our purposes. In applying the model to classroom instruction, the teacher can confront the children with unbalanced attitude triangles in which they are the main focus. The triangle may be used to demonstrate the attitudinal conflict clearly and provide direction for further study of the issue involved.

Viewed another way, an unbalanced attitude triangle provides a springboard for stimulating investigation of an issue. It presents students with a psychological need to find some data to restore balance in the system. To obtain data just for creating unbalanced attitude triangles, a

Figure 15.1 Attitude triangle

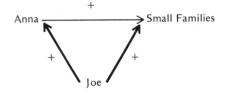

Figure 15.2 Attitude triangle

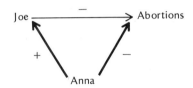

Figure 15.3 Attitude triangle

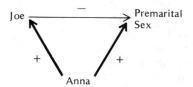

Figure 15.4 Attitude triangle

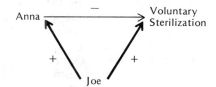

teacher needs to be "on the listen" for typical attitude patterns within the class or else to take brief show-of-hands or paper-and-pencil-check-off surveys. A modified attitude triangle such as the one shown in Figure 15.5 might be used even with primary children to trigger discussion. In this case let us assume the teacher is dealing with a group of Caucasian children who have rather negative attitudes toward blacks. Once each child has completed an attitude triangle, discussion and investigation can begin. Older children may be asked to construct their own triangles and to use plus and minus signs. Also in place of individual triangles, a class triangle may be constructed on the board representing the majority position.

With seventh and eighth graders an attitude triangle similar to the one shown in Figure 15.6 might be constructed on an overhead projector

Figure 15.5
Class attitude triangle

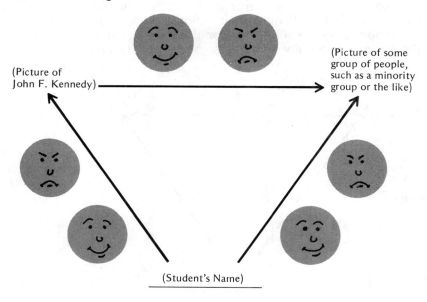

transparency or the blackboard to represent the majority of the class' attitudes. In this example the teacher is attempting to get the students to consider some of the basic principles on which communism is based, and he has extracted a selection from *The Communist Manifesto*. After establishing that the group generally feels negatively toward communism and positively toward economic policies such as the graduated income tax and a minimum wage, the position of the *Manifesto* on these issues is read to the class and recorded. Having created an unbalanced attitude triangle, the teacher now may be able to get the class to consider more objectively and systematically the ways in which competing ideologies are similar and different.

CHALLENGING COMMONLY HELD BELIEFS

One of the ways that beliefs become commonly held is that we grow up with them without ever having them challenged. These beliefs may have been taught overtly, or we may have acquired them almost unconsciously by making certain assumptions about the phenomena around us. Not too many years ago it was possible for a child to grow up in a small town not realizing until much later in life that other races than his or her own existed. The author recalls attending a large university during his freshman year and discovering a student who was surprised to learn that an African baby raised in a conventional U.S. middle-class home would take on the cultural characteristics of his new homeland!

In a classroom guided by a spirit of open inquiry, all provable commonly held beliefs are fair game for analysis. A basic model for belief modification and reconstruction involves bringing these commonly held beliefs to the level of consciousness and then examining them in the light of relevant information that challenges their validity. Since challenging what often may be the "conventional wisdom" not only in your classroom but in the larger community requires some sensitivity and

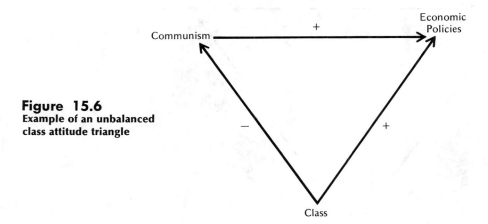

Figure 15.6
Example of an unbalanced class attitude triangle

preparation, some warnings and suggestions for operating are outlined below:

1. The beliefs held should be at least partially inaccurate, otherwise the strategy becomes an exercise in sophistry.
2. The purpose of challenging beliefs is not to substitute "right" for "wrong" ones, but rather to force their examination and necessary modifications in the light of evidence.
3. The beliefs must be testable and verifiable through rational means. Beliefs such as "God does exist" and "Man has a soul" do not qualify.
4. Both you and the students must be able to deal with the topic in a rational manner.
5. In order to ascertain what are some commonly held beliefs in your class, (a) learn as much as possible about the community in which you teach, (b) be alert to comments in class and discussions outside class and use these as the basis for future sessions, (c) develop some inventories for students to check off, and (e) ask your class!
6. Some ways to draw out a belief for purposes of examining it critically are as follows: (a) Locate a case of the belief reflected in some aspect of the mass media—TV commentators, letters to the editor of a magazine or newspaper, talk programs, articles, editorials, films, and so on; (b) attribute the belief to the hypothetical "man on the street"; (c) if a student states a belief, "remove" it from him or her by stating it in a different fashion or writing it on the board, so that the class does not feel like it is attacking or defending a fellow student.
7. Some ways to challenge beliefs are to present examples and facts that refute the belief, for example, case studies, pictures, statistics, eye-witness reports, historical evidence, field trips.

Some typical beliefs that might be current in classrooms, in addition to the sample noted in Chapter 13, are as follows:

Most of the people in the world are like us.
Most of the poor people in our country are nonwhite.
Most people in the United States live in cities.
Anyone can become President of the United States.
Each person's vote for President counts the same.

The first belief listed requires some clarification before it can be tackled. What does "like us" mean? Let us assume that a class identifies some set of these characteristics: race, lifestyle, religion, sex, standard of living, occupations. Part of the challenging can come from the class members themselves who are likely to have picked up information that refutes some aspects of the belief. A whirl of the globe or a trip over a world map accompanied by some statistics and addition will show that the overwhelming majority of the world's people are nonwhite; that, in fact, most of the world's people live in just one continent—Asia. A few case studies of families in different countries will establish the comparative life styles and some inkling of standards of living. Statistics on relative purchasing power and disease and mortality rates will further clarify the latter point. Other statistics will show that Christians are a decided minority in the world—only about one third of it. Pictorial data will help challenge all dimensions of the belief—except perhaps the aspect on the sexes. Even there, while the sex ratio is relatively constant in the world, the roles of male and female are not.

The belief that most poor people in the United States are nonwhite is true only in one respect, namely that the *percentage* of poor people among nonwhites is greater than among whites. Much of this challenge must deal with what it means to be "poor" in the Uniteds States. Income levels that statisticians use obviously do not tell the entire story, and this issue requires some discussion. Study of pictures such as those found in Robert Coles' *Still Hungry in America* not only can dramatize the

relative depths of poverty but can supply evidence of the extent of the large number of poor whites in this country.

While most Americans do live in greater metropolitan areas, the 1970 census figures reveal that we are roughly divided equally among rural, suburban, and urban areas. Challenging the belief of an increasingly urban America can help bring a clearer understanding of how migration patterns and the corresponding living styles in our country are being altered.

The belief concerning presidential qualifications requires more attention. The only ostensible constraints on who may or may not become President are those stated in our Constitution:

> No person except a natural born Citizen, or a Citizen of the United States, at the time of the Adoption of this Constitution, shall be eligible to the Office of President; neither shall any Person be eligible to that Office who shall not have attained to the Age of thirty-five Years, and been fourteen Years a Resident within the United States.

Students might be asked to examine the list of over thirty Presidents and determine how many are female, nonwhite, and non-Protestant. The meager returns from these examinations should establish the point. A similar search could be made for the Presidents-in-waiting—the Vice-Presidents. The memory of John F. Kennedy's campaign is still close enough at hand to serve as a case study with respect to the controversy over his Roman Catholic affiliation. In short, students can be helped to see—in fact, even construct a list of—the many nonwritten, informal barriers to the presidency such as race, sex, party support, religion, appearance, image, financial support, and, frequently, geographical location.

The widely held belief that each person has an equal vote in the presidential election is, of course, invalidated by the operation of the Electoral College. In point of fact, voters actually cast their ballots only for electors pledged to vote for the candidates listed on the ballot. Students may be suprised to learn that the Constitution does *not* even provide for the direct election of a President:

> Each State shall appoint, in such Manner as the Legislature thereof may direct, a Number of Electors, equal to the whole Number of Senators and Representatives to which the State may be entitled in the Congress: but no Senator or Representative or Person holding an Office of Trust or Profit under the United States, shall be appointed an Elector.

Because of the small number of electoral roles in her state, a woman who votes for President in Wyoming has a less significant vote than a woman in California. Viewed from a national perspective, this case reflects the fact that victory in less than one-third of all fifty states is required to win the presidency. Hypothetically a candidate could win one-half plus one of the total votes cast in each of these large electoral-vote states and secure the presidency. Examine the Electoral College map on p. 165 and determine which is the smallest group of states that would be needed to win the presidency. In appraising their election strategy prudent candidates are careful to assess which blocs of electoral votes they have a chance of acquiring, and they allocate their campaign resources and arguments accordingly. To understand how presidential votes are unequal is to better understand how the real vs. the idealized political system in our country. The "real" system gives more power to the heavily populated states.

Beliefs do not always have to be clearly defined and articulated to serve as springboards for class discussions. Often some amorphous impressions that children have acquired are sufficient to provide the grist for a significant challenge. A teacher might inquire of a class what is known about Hitler and his treatment of the German Jews. Followed up with a question concerning whether any such group of people had ever been mistreated in our country, the discussion may move in any one of several directions. Taba and Elkins shared a relevant anecdote concerning the treatment of Japanese-Americans during World War II:

> I read the class a chapter from *The Moved-Outers*. This book tells the story of a Japanese-American family sent to a relocation camp after the bombing of Pearl Harbor. The author describes their feelings at the display of hostility by other Americans. One child asked, "Why did they do that to them?" One boy who had heard many gruesome tales of atrocities insisted it was necessary because of saboteurs; besides, "It was what we should have done anyway. They did worse things to us." The argument became heated, and we decided that we were arguing with few facts at our command.
>
> At this point I passed out to the children our ten copies of *One Nation*. Three children shared each book. I explained what we were trying to do—find facts that would help us understand the points that we had planned to investigate. Information on those topics would help us understand the whole problem. I also told them that I wanted them to learn how to gather information from more than one book, since no one book was likely to tell us all we needed to know. Together we took notes from *One Nation* on Japanese-Americans. We selected only those facts that we needed to answer the questions at hand. Then, since we had no other large set of books, I selected one book and read to them, helping them find what was pertinent. Finally, I distributed a motley collection of books. Two people worked with each book while I went around helping each couple. When everyone had finished, we worked together on how to make a good, well-organized report from our information.
>
> Six children volunteered to meet that night and prepare a report to be presented to the class, "just for practice." We had done some role-playing in literature class, and the group was intrigued with the

idea of acting. Before these six went home that night, they asked whether they could play out the story. I agreed but stipulated that facts must be presented. The next day they performed. The job was surprisingly good. They had a series of family scenes. One showed the family on a boat, talking about why they were coming to America; another showed their difficulty finding a room in Little Tokyo; another showed them looking for a job and portrayed the antagonism toward them; in the fourth scene they finally rented a very small store; in the next scene they were dragged off to a relocation camp; their store was sold; the scene on life at the camp showed how bad they felt at not being considered Americans in spite of all their efforts; the next scene depicted their rejection when they tried to go back to their homes on the Coast when the war was over; the final scene showed their decision to settle in other parts of the country.

We returned to the original argument over putting our West Coast Japanese into relocation camps, the question that had been raised when we discussed *The Moved-Outers*. There were still such arguments as "We couldn't watch all of them." But most of those who took an opposing stand were now able to cite the good record of Japanese soldiers; the fact that the Japanese were invited to come to America originally to do menial tasks that Americans scorned; that we were at war with other countries, too, but did not put into camps people who had originally come from those countries; that "before you put people in jail you're supposed to prove they are guilty"; "that these people are easy to tell apart" so they were "picked on."[9]

VALUE ANALYSIS[10]

A few years ago an article appeared in *The New York Times Magazine* entitled "What Code of Values Can We Teach Our Children Now?" While directed primarily to parents, it raised some significant questions for teachers, such as: "What values are relevant for tomorrow's world? What should we instill in the youngsters who will be adolescents in the late nineteen-seventies and adults in the nineteen-eighties?"[11]

Value questions and concerns are unavoidable in the classroom even if we should be inclined to ignore them. The essence of all decision making, resource allocation, loving, caring, and other consciously derived vital human processes is a value preference or commitment. Scientific progress in the form of aeronautical technology may indicate that an SST can be built and economic analysis can project the desirable stimulator effects of such a project on employment and gross national product figures. A value preference, as reflected in the act of Congress, however, can nullify such a project in favor of safeguarding the environment from potentially significant hazards. The twin sets of scientific achievements and increased economic benefits and environmental protection both were approved social goals. A value choice was necessary on the part of Congress on behalf of the American people.

In this case environmental values won out. On a later date in a different social and political climate, still another complex of values would gain preference over environmental ones in the decision to permit the construction of the Alaskan pipeline.

Value considerations must be an important instructional preoccupation of all social educators, since studies of social phenomena and significant personal choices intersect at some point with value concerns. Social scientists and professional educators have approached the study of values in various ways, and each author tends to perceive and define values in his or her own fashion. This fact has contributed to much of the confusion surrounding the term and what constitutes "values education." All who would be serious about dealing with values in the classroom should address themselves initially to this important definitional issue. Five key questions that might be asked by a teacher concerning any suggested approach to values in the classroom are:

1. Does it set forth explicit criteria for what constitutes a value?
2. Is it supported directly or indirectly by some research of experimentation or evaluation germane to classrooms?
3. Is there a growing body of theory on which it is based?
4. Does the approach violate individual human rights?
5. Can it be used to create instructional strategies with a variety of different topics?

This list is certainly not exhaustive, nor are all of the questions of equal importance. The questions, however, should provide a quick test of the relative merits of different approaches. Each approach in this section provides relatively specific but flexible procedures for constructing value-related strategies. These may serve the reader not only as guidelines but also as stimuli to further perhaps more definitive, models.

THE VALUE-CLARIFICATION MODEL

The broad sweep of the value-clarification approach used by Raths and his associates is most clearly detailed in their book *Values and Teaching*.[12] In essence their position is that values are based on three processes: choosing, prizing, and acting. These three processes are translated into seven criteria that must be present in order for a value to result.

Choosing
1. An item must be freely chosen.
2. Alternative choices must be available.
3. Thoughtful consideration of the consequences of alternatives must precede a choice.

Prizing
4. We must be happy with and cherish our choice.
5. We are willing to publicly affirm our choice.

Acting $\begin{cases} \text{6. We must act on our choice.} \\ \text{7. The choice is repeated in some pattern of our life.} \end{cases}$

"These processes," according to Raths and his colleagues, "collectively define valuing. Results of the valuing process are called values."[13] To employ this strategy a teacher would assist students in moving through the seven steps, by employing devices such as the Value Sheet. A Value Sheet "in its simplest form consists of a provocative statement and a series of questions duplicated on a sheet of paper and distributed to class members."[14] The authors recommend that students first examine and complete these sheets privately and then share their results in discussion with the teacher or other students. Value Sheets may take many forms and incorporate a variety of different questioning sequences, but their basic characteristics are an open-ended episode or case calling for value-related decisions and a series of questions covering the seven steps of the value-clarification process.[15] In turn, Value Sheets are just one of the ways in which value-clarification strategies may be constructed; other value-clarification strategies are also presented in *Values and Teaching*.

Dublinville's School Problem: Where Will the Kids Go?—Figure 15.7 —is a value sheet based on an actual incident.[16] It involves a small number of spatial variables—population distribution, transportation, location, boundaries—and engages students in the process of making a difficult decision. As they grapple with the problem, they will find themselves choosing, prizing, and acting, that is, engaging in the value-clarification process outlined by Raths and his associates.

The following questions should be asked:

1. If you were the School Board President, what would you do to handle the classroom shortage?
2. What do you think will happen if the plan you suggest is put into action?
3. What are the advantages and disadvantages of the position you have taken?
4. Why did you reject the other way of handling the classroom problem?
5. Suppose you were to appear before the School Board to present your solution to the problem. Write out a short statement of exactly what you would tell the Board.
6. Suppose you are a student living in the Jamesville area and a member of one of the "extra" classes. What could you do to get the School Board to accept your suggestion?
7. The classroom-shortage problem may happen again in the school district. What policy or plan do you think the Board should set up to handle any future problems of this type?

Figure 15.7
Value sheet

Dublinville's school problem—where will the kids go?

Dublinville Township has four elementary schools: Farley Glen, Jamesville, Fort Williams, and Sandtown. These are shown in the map. Students who live within the dotted lines shown on the map go to the school that is in their area. This plan for school attendance usually has worked fairly well in the past.

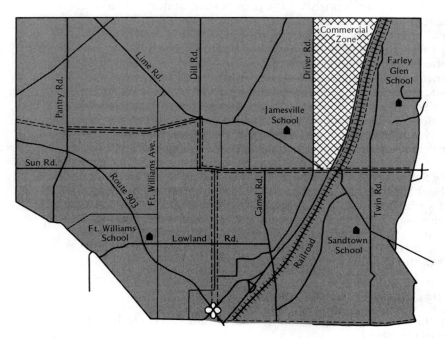

But this year there is a problem in the Jamesville school area. There are now twenty-eight classes of students in the area, but Jamesville has only twenty-six classrooms. There is not time to build new classrooms at Jamesville. Where will the kids go to school?

Fort Williams School does not have any extra space. Sandtown and Farley Glen schools do have extra space and could take the students from Jamesville. But the parents in the Jamesville area do not want their children sent all the way to Farley Glen, the closest school.

It might be possible to increase the number of students in each classroom at Jamesville. Nobody, though, seems to like that idea. It also might be possible to change the size and location (boundary) of each school area. Doing this would mean that students who had gone to one school for several years would now have to go to a new one. Changing school areas is a lot of work, and they might have to be changed again next year if one area gets more children. Some parents and the school board are not in favor of changing the size and location of the school areas.

"I'm just not sure what we are going to do with the two extra classes of students," the School Board President has said.

Figure 15.8

Things I Like to Do							
1.							
2.							
3.							
4.							
5.							
6.							
7.							
8.							
9.							
10.							
11.							
12.							
13.							
14.							
15.							
16.							
17.							
18.							
19.							
20.							

Another type of value-clarification activity suitable for upper-elementary children involves a listing and analysis of things each of us really likes to do. Students are given or are asked to construct a sheet similar to the one in Figure 15.8. Next to the twenty numbers the students are to write down quickly the first things that come to mind that they like to do. These items need not be listed in order of importance. Tell the children to put down those things that they really do like. None will be able to see or learn about their lists unless they want to share later.

When the children have constructed their lists, give them the following directions for filling in the remaining columns:

Symbol	Directions
A/P	Put an "A" next to those activities you do alone and a "P" next to those things you do with other people usually.
$	Put a "$" next to those things that cost money.
Tell	Put a "Tell" next to those things that you would be willing to tell anyone about.
F	Put an "F" next to those things that you think your father would put on his list.
M	Put an "M" next to those things that you think your mother would put on her list.
?	How many times this past year have you done this activity?
Rank	Number the top five things you you like to do in order from 1 to 5.

Have the children look over their lists when they are finished and ask them to think about what they have just learned. If any would like to volunteer, let them share what they have learned.

VALUE SURVEY MODEL

Milton Rokeach, whose work was discussed earlier in the chapter, has devised a Value Survey that assesses an individual's value system. It consists of two sets of eighteen values, designated as instrumental (mode of conduct) values and terminal (end-state) values.[17] Instrumental values are self-controlled, courageous, ambitious, forgiving, cheerful, capable, imaginative, intellectual, logical, loving, obedient, responsible, independent, honest, polite, broadminded, clean, and helpful. Terminal values consist of a comfortable life, an exciting life, a sense of accomplishment, social recognition, national security, freedom, mature love, inner harmony, a world of beauty, happiness, equality, family security, a world at peace, pleasure, salvation, self-respect, true friendship, and wisdom. In Rokeach's Survey respondents are given some explanation for each of the terms and then are asked to rank them in order of perceived importance. Criteria for choice are to be personal, and an individual establishes his own list of priorities. For Rokeach,

> A value is an enduring belief that a specific mode of conduct or end-state of existence is personally or socially preferable to an opposite or converse mode of conduct or end-state of existence. A value system is an enduring organization of beliefs concerning preferable modes of conduct or end-states of existence along a continuum of relative importance.[18]

He further notes that:

> Such a relative conception of values enables us to define change as a reordering of priorities and, at the same time, to see the total value system as relatively stable over time. It is stable enough to reflect the fact of sameness and continuity of a unique personality socialized within a given culture and society, yet unstable enough to permit re-

arrangements of value priorities as a result of changes in culture, society, and personal experience.[19]

Through the raising of one's value system to the level of consciousness, one can generally learn a great deal about his or her own value preferences. Correspondingly, through the sharing of results and rationale for choices with others, reciprocal insights result.

A general use for the results of Rokeach's work and specifically the Value Survey in social education would be to demonstrate to students the value frame of reference they are using to analyze issues. Used in advance of an analysis, the value systems uncovered might alert students to how they are likely to organize their conclusions and to alternative perspectives that they might wish to consider. A recent news report indicated, for example, that a political science professor, partly through an analysis of the value preferences of Supreme Court justices, was able to predict with some accuracy the voting pattern of each justice. As a retrospective exercise, use of the Value Survey can demonstrate the degree to which the conclusions reached do in fact seem to reflect existing value systems.

Another possible application of the Value Survey approach is to try to translate some relevant cluster of values from the survey into an exercise requiring the application of the values to social planning. The product would be a series of statements reflecting the abstract values, to be ranked by students in order of perceived importance and centered about some social issue or problem. Let us consider such a possible translation and application that might be appropriate for very young children, possibly even at the primary level. The cluster of abstract values to be translated into a social context is taken from Rokeach's set of terminal values: freedom, salvation, wisdom, national security, a comfortable life, equality, and family security.

An activity sheet similar to the one Figure 15.9 should be distributed to each member of the class, read aloud, and explained. Each child should complete the task individually. Each of the seven statements is an attempt to reflect, at a child's level, the corresponding values of freedom, salvation, wisdom, national security, a comfortable life, equality, and family security. After each child completes the activity sheet, he or she is asked to share his or her rankings with others and the rationale for such choices. The children should be allowed to offer alternatives and to raise questions about one another's rationale.

One third grader, Tim, who completed the activity sheet, for example, ordered a community that reflected the priorities of family security, wisdom, national security, and equality, as Figure 15.10 illustrates. When this phase of the discussion has been completed, the students' attention can be directed toward the actual planning considerations that would be necessary to construct a community that reflected the value priorities of individuals or of the class. Each student might work from an individual map or a class map might be used based on a class value profile. The latter is obtained by averaging the entire class ranking for each of the

Figure 15.9
Modified Value Survey

Building a new city

A number of new cities are being planned for the United States. Many of our cities just grew without anyone really planning them. In the new cities, most things will be carefully planned: where people will live, where they will shop, work, go to school, and have fun.

One new city being planned will be in Minnesota. It will be called Jonathon. How do you think Jonathon should be planned?

Below are some things that planners will have to think about. Put a 1 in front of the thing that you feel is the most important for the planners to think about. Put a 2 in front of the second most important thing, and so on, until you have numbered everything from 1 to 7.

_____ People should be free to buy a house any place they like.

_____ There should be plenty of churches and temples built.

_____ There should be enough schools and colleges so that everyone can learn.

_____ A police department should be set up.

_____ People should have things to do that they really like.

_____ All people should be treated equally.

_____ There should be jobs for everyone who wants them.

Figure 15.10
Third grader's response to a modified Value Survey

____6____ People should be free to buy a house any place they like.

____5____ There should be plenty of churches and temples built.

____2____ There should be enough schools and colleges so that everyone can learn.

____3____ A police department should be set up.

____7____ People should have things to do that they really like.

____4____ All people should be treated equally.

____1____ There should be jobs for everyone who wants them.

seven statements. As much geographical data as are relevant and appropriate for the class involved can be introduced. If time and interest permit, communities that reflected alternative value systems could be constructed and compared and contrasted.

Having children keep a diary of their daily activities also is a basic and easy way to develop more generally an indirect measure of values as well as beliefs and attitudes. If children are encouraged to record not only their daily activities but also their emotional "highs" and "lows," likes and dislikes, aspirations and expectations *in private,* they can begin to assess what themes appear to dominate and regulate their lives. A diary, honestly and faithfully chronicled, may provide a deep insight into one's value structure. It can reflect where we really place our priorities.

Not all children are able to react effectively to an open-ended invitation to "write about what you do each day." Filling a blank page may prove to be either too formidable to a child who doesn't know where to begin or much too limiting to another child who gets bogged down in recording the minute details of breakfast.

Consequently some structure for diary entries may help a class get started without necessarily limiting their observations. The following characteristics have proved useful to this author in working with children:

Event(s) Description
People Involved
Amount of Time Involved
Place and Time
My Feelings About the Event(s)

Another example of a modified application of the Value Survey occurred in a seventh-grade class using a case study of the Amish, a subculture with a large settlement relatively near to the students' school. The teacher identified in the following way ten values that the Amish appear to espouse.[20]

1. *Love of family:* The family is the dominant force. The family depends on family labor, and parents' roles are protective and supportive.
2. *Ambition:* The goal of all Amish children is to perfect their lives spiritually. Only in school is individual achievement stressed.
3. *Obedience:* Obedience to parents and ultimately to God is a cardinal virtue.
4. *Humility:* The child must be humble in the presence of others, especially older members of society.
5. *Responsibility to others:* Since labor (farm economy) incorporates family labor, this value is most important.
6. *Education:* Education is valued only when it applies directly to the social, spiritual, and economic needs of the family.
7. *Tolerance:* Since humility is an intrinsic value (dress is simple and uniform), class distinction is not in evidence, and there appears to be a high degree of tolerance within the society.
8. *Thrift:* Farming is done on relatively small holdings. Because of this, the Amish have developed an agricultural economy based on thrift.
9. *Independence:* The Amish view themselves as separate from the world. As a group they practice independence from worldly luxuries.

As individuals, conformity is the principle to which the sect members adhere.

10. *Security:* The Amish child is reared and taught that he or she is not self-willed and that his or her dependence on others and responsibility to others will make him or her secure. In the spiritual world, God is security.

Each student in the class then received the handout below. Because of the special relationship of independence and security, these values were combined. Similarly, love of God, an overarching value to the Amish, was included separately.

Directions: On separate sheets of paper which will be given to you, list each of these values:

1. Responsibility to others

2. Tolerance of differences in others

3. Humility

4. Thrift

5. Independence—security

6. Love of family

7. Love of God

8. Obedience

9. Ambition

10. Education

These are not placed in order of importance. Answer this question about each of these values: "What do you do to uphold this value?" If you do not uphold any or all of these values, please state why.

Time was spent explaining each of the values so that the class would have a common frame of reference. An example for each value was also given. In reflecting on each of the values, students were asked to consider questions such as the following:

1. *Responsibility to others:* Would you put the welfare of others ahead of your own welfare?
2. *Tolerance of differences in others:* Do you accept each of your fellow students as individuals? Do you accept the opinions of others even if they differ from yours?
3. *Humility:* Do you consider yourself equal to others in all things? Do you often accept an inferior position in personal situations with your peers? With adults?

4. *Thrift:* Do you hesitate to spend money? Do you check prices in various places before you purchase an item?
5. *Independence:* Do you consider yourself dependent on your family? Are you earning money? If you were left alone tomorrow could you survive?
   Security: Do you feel lost in school when your best friend is absent? Do you feel depressed when your family is arguing?
6. *Love of family:* Do you think of your family first when you are Christmas shopping? Are your favorite trips and happiest memories those spent with your family? Do you spend most of your weekends with a member or members of your family? When someone slanders the name of your family, do you defend it?
7. *Love of God:* Do you enjoy reading the Bible? Do you think about your situation in terms of it's being God's will? Do you do the right thing because you love God? When you do something wrong do you ask God's forgiveness? Do you attend church?
8. *Obedience:* Do you do what you are told to do without questioning it? Do you respect authority?
9. *Ambition:* Do you plan any education after you leave _____ High School? Would you eagerly leave _____? Would you be miserable if you knew you would never advance in life?
10. *Education:* Would you go on to college if you received a scholarship? Would you go on to college if you had to earn every penny to pay your tuition? Do you enjoy _____? Do you look forward to coming to school each day?

After a series of procedures to analyze, discuss, and summarize the results, the data were tabulated and shared, as follows:

	Uphold	Do Not Uphold
Responsibility to others	20	2
Tolerance of differences in others	13	9
Humility	5	17
Thrift	5	17
Independence	22	0
Security	12	10
Love of family	20	2
Love of God	21	1
Obedience	15	7
Ambition	10	12
Education	2	20

Follow-up activities focused on the similarities and differences among the Amish and the seventh graders, as well as the factors that gave rise to such value patterns among the class. The students finally were asked to draw some conclusions and potential generalizations about both the Amish and themselves.

MORAL DEVELOPMENT

Many vital human problems and concerns can be resolved through information, discussion, careful thought, or experience. Some, however, of equal or greater importance, have no easy "right" or "wrong" solution. Decent, informed, and thoughtful people may arrive at opposite conclusions on the same issue, each person equally firm and committed to his or her position. Consider these two positions on legalization of abortion, the first arguing that the act of abortion is morally wrong, the second stating that it is morally right:

Is there anything in this world more innocent, more defenseless, more totally reliant, more worthy of our defense than the unborn baby in the womb of its mother? . . . Such an infant, possessed of life, is in a stage of human development as is a one, two or three year old child.

. . .

Abortion is the willful procuring of premature delivery so as to destroy the offspring, i.e. a human life; murder is the unlawful killing of a human being with malice aforethought, it is also defined as follows: "to kill wickedly, inhumanly, or barbarously."

. . .

Abortion is murder. The legalization of abortion is the legalization of murder.

If some lives are considered not worthy of life by law, all lives are thereby cheapened and blighted. If a month old baby can be murdered by Society through abortion is not a one year old baby or a five year old child thereby susceptible to the State-turned-God?[21]

The question of morality usually centers on whether abortion is equivalent to taking a human life. A fetus is certainly alive—as are the cells destroyed every time you brush your teeth—but it is a *potential* rather than an actual human being. The some thirty thousand eggs present in the ovaries of each human female at birth are also potential human beings one step removed, since they require only sperm—available in abundance—to become embryos. Only a tiny fraction of these eggs are fertilized, however, and society does not mourn the rest. Nor is much thought given to the countless early spontaneous abortions that pass unnoticed in the menstrual discharge. If abortion is "murder," are these "accidental deaths"?[22]

Where do you stand on the matter? What *is* right and what *is* wrong, and why?

Whether we are aware of it or not, we are frequently engaged in moral quests, though their significance for the larger society may not be as great as the one we have just considered. John Dewey counsels us that:

Moral theory begins, in germ, when any one asks "Why should I act thus and not otherwise? Why is this right and that wrong? What right has any one to frown upon this way of acting and impose that other way? Children make at least a start upon the road of theory when they assert that the injunctions of elders are arbitrary, being simply a matter of superior position. Any adult enters the road when, in the presence of moral perplexity, of doubt as to what it is right or best to do, he attempts to find his way out through reflection which will lead him to some principle he regards as dependable.

Moral theory cannot emerge when there is positive belief as to what is right and what is wrong, for then there is no occasion for reflection. It emerges when men are confronted with situations in which different desires promise opposed goods and in which incompatible courses of action seem to be morally justified.[23]

He goes on to observe that *any* act has *potentially* moral significance because its consequences are always part of a larger whole of behavior. Though unintending, we may set in motion a chain of events with moral overtones. Opening a window for some fresh air, Dewey points out, appears to be a neutral, morally indifferent act in itself. If one suddenly recalls that an infirm person sensitive to drafts is present, the act takes on a potential moral dimension. Similarly the act of giving a vagrant alcoholic a quarter can be viewed as morally right, wrong, or neutral, depending on a chain of circumstances surrounding why I gave the money, what consequences I anticipate, and what his or her probable future actions are.

Considerable evidence has been gathered by Piaget and Kohlberg and their respective associates to demonstrate that all children pass through invariant stages of moral development. Piaget contends that children exhibit two basic types of moral decision making; younger children tend to refer to authority figures in moral judgments, whereas older children are more likely to take into account social concerns and cooperativeness.[24] As discussed in Chapter 13, Kohlberg maintains that six developmental stages have been ascertained.

Moral dilemmas of the variety that Piaget and Kohlbreg presented to children offer opportunity for teachers to both involve their students at any age in crucial issues and data and at the same time make a contribution toward moral development. A basic instructional strategy devised and refined by Kohlberg and his associates is to present students with moral dilemmas centering around real or hypothetical issues, with an opportunity to discuss them in groups. Typical dilemmas center around issues such as rights, justice or fairness, and rules. Let us consider the details of the strategy in two steps: the first involves criteria for constructing a dilemma and the second concerns presenting and discussing the dilemma.

Construction of a dilemma requires attention to at least the following basic pointers:

1. The issue presented should offer only two basic choices. (Should A be done or should B?)
2. The issue should be one with which students can readily identify and become involved.
3. There should be no one obvious or culturally approved answer to the issue.
4. The issue must be a question of what is right or wrong, involving conflict over what is a just course of action to take.
5. All the material necessary for consideration of the dilemma should be organized as succinctly as possible, with the moral issue brought into sharp focus.
6. Both choices in the issue should be likely to attract some measure of support in the class.

For the presentation and discussion of a dilemma, the following procedures are suggested:

1. Present the dilemma to students in the form of a hand-out statement, oral reading, role-play incident, maps/statement, or other media format.
2. Allow the students to take a position with respect to the issue raised in the dilemma. Organize them into discussion groups for this purpose.
3. Use a series of probe questions to follow up the dilemma. These should challenge the students to reflect further and look at all sides of the issue. The probe questions also help keep the discussion on track and insure that questions representing the higher-stage arguments are added to the discussion.

Several illustrations of moral dilemmas and their use are offered here. The first case, *Happytown and Sadtown,* is designed for primary-grade children.

Happytown and Sadtown

The people in Happytown really like their town. They have big yards and nice houses. [Refer children to picture of such an area.] There is a fine, large park in Happytown, too. Both children and adults use the park a lot. Everyone has fun there.

Next to Happytown is Sadtown. The people in Sadtown have small yards. Their houses are not very nice. Mostly the children have to play in the streets. [Refer children to picture of such an area.] There is no park. Many people in Sadtown would like to move to Happytown. But there are no more houses to buy in Happytown.

So the people in Sadtown want Happytown to give up its park. People could build houses on the parkland. Then people from Sadtown could move to Happytown. There is no other place besides the park to build new houses in Happytown.

The people in Sadtown want a nice home and a big yard. The people in Happytown do not want to lose their fine park.

In initiating and sustaining the discussion, questions such as the following may be used:

1. Should Happytown give up its park so that Sadtown people can build houses there?
2. Why do you think that is what they should do? (Later, probe questions may be inserted into the discussions.)
3. What if Happytown gives up its park? Will its people have any other place to have fun? If so, where?
4. What will happen to the people in Sadtown if they can't build new houses in Happytown?
5. How would you feel if you lived in Sadtown? Why?
6. Suppose the people in Happytown didn't like those in Sadtown. Then should they give up their park? Why?
7. What would you do if you lived in Happytown? Why?
8. Do the people in Sadtown have a right to ask Happytown to give up its park? Why?

After this phase of the discussion has run its course, the dilemma may be intensified by adding new details to the case, such as the following:

Happytown decides

Happytown has decided to sell its park. Now the people in Sadtown will be able to build homes in Happytown. They will have nice homes and big yards.

Some people in Happytown are not happy about losing their park. They have gone to court. They want the judge to stop Happytown from selling its park. "The park belongs to everyone in Happytown," they say. "Happytown can't sell something that everyone wants and likes."

Ask the following questions:

1. What do you think the judge should do?
2. Should the judge let the park be sold to build houses? Should he let Happytown keep its park? Why?
3. Suppose the judge lives in Sadtown? Would he want the park to be sold?
4. Suppose the judge never uses a park? Will that make any difference about what he decides?

For older students dilemmas may be more complex, that is, contain more variables, and may require some basic research to arrive at decisions.

The second illustration is taken from the materials used by Kohlberg and his associates to study moral development in young children.

Gladys has waited all week to go to the movies. On Saturday, her parents give her some money so she can see a special movie in town that will only be there one day. When Gladys gets to the movie theatre, there is already a long line with many children waiting to buy tickets. Gladys takes a place at the end of the line.

All of a sudden, a big wind blows the money out of Gladys' hand. Gladys leaves the line to pick up her money. When she gets back, there are lots more people in line and a new girl named Mary has taken her place. Gladys tells Mary that she had that place and asks Mary to let her back in line. If Mary does not let Gladys in line, Gladys will have to go to the end of the line and there may not be enough tickets left and she won't get a chance to see the movie.

1. Should Mary let Gladys back into the line?
2. Why do you think that is what Mary should do?

Probe Questions:

3. Does it make a difference if Mary doesn't know why Gladys left the line?
4. How does Mary know whether or not Gladys is telling the truth?
5. Why is telling the truth important?
6. Gladys comes back and tells Mary that she left the line to chase after her ticket money which the wind blew out of her hand. Would you let Gladys in line if you were Mary? Why?
7. If Mary is Gladys' friend, should that make a difference? Why?
8. Suppose that instead of the wind blowing the money out of Gladys' hand, Gladys decided to leave the line to get an ice cream cone. If that is what happened, should Mary let Gladys in line when she comes back?
9. What's the difference between leaving the line to get some ice cream and leaving the line to chase some money?[25]

Guidance Associates has produced a series of filmstrips/records/cassettes kits built around moral dilemmas with which young children can easily identify.[26] Some of the kits use fantasy elements such as a wizard and "Cat Man," while others are developed around everyday contexts that children are likely to recognize.

In employing moral dilemma strategies it is important for a teacher to recognize that it is the quality or structure of an argument rather than its actual content that requires the most attention. One may, for example, resolve the preceding dilemma in favor of Mary's or Gladys' reasoning at any of the six stages. The *type* of reasoning and *not* the position or conclusion determines the stage of moral reasoning. An important distinction between the moral-reasoning strategy and that of value clarification is the assumption that higher-stage reasoning constitutes a more moral response in a discussion. In effect, in moral discussions all opinions may not have equal merit. The *reasoning* in some arguments may be appraised as being superior by the teacher, with the six-stage hierarchy providing the standards.

A teacher-education kit designed to prepare teachers for using moral dilemmas has been developed by Guidance Associates.[27] The following pointers on the teacher's role in translating Kohlberg's theories draws from their materials:[28]

1. *Maintain the focus on the moral dilemma.* It is important to keep the students' attention on the dilemmas to make them grapple with the issue. Frequently they will try to avoid the dilemma by injecting reasonable but spurious solutions. In the case of Happytown presented earlier, students may say, "The Sadtown people could move somewhere else." When children do this, the teacher should "gently" eliminate such compromises that avoid the dilemma by using any feasible strategies (e.g., a simple "There are no other areas for building").
2. *Help keep the arguments balanced.* When it appears there is convergence on one solution, raise questions that will give consideration to the other point of view and generate some conflict in the discussion. If all students feel Sadtown should be allowed to build in the park, the teacher might ask, "How would you feel if you lived in Happytown and had to give up the park in which you played everyday?"
3. *Encourage role-taking.* Whenever feasible, try to get students to identify with characters and feelings implicit in the dilemmas: "What would you do if you lived in Happytown? Why?"
4. *Clarify the dilemma.* As necessary, recast or rephrase a dilemma to insure that the entire class understands it clearly.

MEASURING AFFECTIVE GROWTH

In discussing self concepts, beliefs and attitudes, values, and moral development, a number of ways of measuring changes were identified. Many of the same instruments used to survey a class' feelings or reactions and to offer a basis for diagnosis and discussion also may be used again at a later point to determine change. Anecdotal records on each child, keyed to specific behavioral patterns under investigation, can also be a rich source of evaluative data.

A number of self-concept measures have been developed, and many have been sufficiently tested to have reliability and validity scores. Shown in Figure 15.11 is a list of measures available and the age levels for which they are appropriate, reprinted from the report, *Self-Concept Measures: An Annotated Bibliography.*[29] The report includes annotation for each measure concerning its purpose, structure, administration, and scoring procedures, standardization results, and a source and address for obtaining the measure.

By far the richest general source of information concerning affective measures is the large work *Measures of Social Psychological Attitudes* by Robinson and Shaver.[30] Besides providing lengthy annotations on a variety of different measures including test results and reliability and validity data, the actual measure (or a representative sample) is usually included with the description. Most of the measures described are not

Figure 15.11
Selected list of self-concept measures

	Preschool	Kindergarten	1st	2nd	3rd
Animal Picture Q-Sort	X	X	X	X	
Brown-IDS Self-Concept Referents Test	X	X			
Children's Projective Pictures of Self-Concept	X	X			
Children's Self-Concept Index			X	X	X
Children's Self-Social Constructs Test	X	X	X	X	X
Creelman Self-Conceptions Test			X	X	X
Faces Scale			X	X	X
Global and Specific Self-Concept Scale (Primary)			X	X	X
How I See Myself Scale					X
How Much Like Me?					X
Illinois Index of Self-Derogation—Form 3					X
Inferred Self-Concept Judgment Scale	X	X	X	X	X
Learner Self-Concept Test	X				
Measurement of Self-Concept in Kindergarten Children		X			
Perception Score Sheet		X	X	X	
Pictorial Self-Concept Scale		X	X	X	X
Piers-Harris Children's Self-Concept Scale					X
Preschool Self-Concept Picture Test	X				
Responsive Self-Concept Test		X			
Riley Preschool Developmental Screening Inventory	X				
Self-Concept and Motivation Inventory	X	X	X	X	X
Self-Concept as a Learner Scale—Elementary					X
Self-Concept Instrument—A Learner Scale					X
Self-Concept Interview		X			
Self-Concept Sub-Scale of the Evaluation Scale	X	X			
Thomas Self-Concept Values Test	X	X	X	X	X
When Do I Smile?			X	X	X

Source: *Self-Concept Measures: An Annotated Bibliography,* Head Start Test Collection Report (Princeton, N.J.: ERIC Clearinghouse on Tests, Measurement, and Evaluation, 1971), p. 2.

directly suitable for use with children, but they suggest a number of immediate adaptations. A smaller volume that parallels the Robinson and Shaver work is *Measuring Human Behavior* by Dale Lake and his associates.[31] It differs from Robinson and Shaver's book chiefly in that it does not include actual measures or excerpts. Since it is a more recent work, its listing of measures is more up to date.

An in-depth focus on instruments for use with very young children is Deborah Klein Walker's *Socioemotional Measures for Preschool and Kindergarten Children*.[32] The first part of the book discusses the various ways in which measurement instruments may be classified and related to educational objectives, and why the use of such tools is important for classroom instruction. The second part of the book cites the actual instruments and describes them; provides sample items; indicates time required, scoring procedures, expertise needed, norms available, reliability and validity data; and gives information on the source of the instruments.

The small book *Diagnosing Classroom Learning Environments* by Robert Fox and his associates includes a number of specific examples of easily constructed measures that may be used to diagnose self concepts and general student attitudes.[33] The book is written for the novice classroom teacher and includes a minimum of technical and psychological terminology.

NOTES

[1] Harry C. Triandis, *Attitude and Attitude Change* (New York: Wiley, 1971), p. 66.

[2] Milton Rokeach, *Beliefs, Attitudes and Values* (San Francisco: Jossey-Bass, 1968), p. 162.

[3] Milton Rokeach, *The Open and Closed Mind* (New York: Basic Books, 1960).

[4] John P. Robinson and Phillip R. Shaver, *Measures of Social Psychological Attitudes* (Ann Arbor, Mich.: Institute for Social Research, University of Michigan, 1972).

[5] Alan Griffin, "The Teacher as Citizen," in R. Bell (ed.), *The Sociology of Education* (Homewood, Ill.: Dorsey, 1962), pp. 348–349.

[6] Ibid., pp. 348–349.

[7] Robinson and Shaver, op. cit., pp. 55–56.

[8] Triandis, op. cit., pp. 68–72.

[9] Hilda Taba and Deborah Elkins, *With Focus on Human Relations* (Washington, D.C.: American Council on Education, 1950), pp. 159–161.

[10] Part of the discussion in this section is taken from the author's forthcoming chapter, "Valuing as a Teaching Strategy," in G. Manson and M. Ridd (eds.), *On the Matter of Geographic Curriculum and Instruction* (tentative title) (Chicago: National Council for Geographic Education, in press).

[11] William V. Shannon, "What Code of Values Can We Teach Our Children Now?" *New York Times Magazine* (January 16, 1972), 9.

[12] Louis E. Raths et al., *Values and Teaching: Working with Values in the Classroom* (Columbus, Ohio: Merrill, 1966), pp. 28–30.

[13] Ibid., p. 30.

[14] Ibid., pp. 83–84.

[15] Ibid., p. 106.

16 Actual school names have been changed.

17 Milton Rokeach, *The Nature of Human Values* (New York: Free Press, 1973), pp. 27–31.

18 Ibid., p. 5.

19 Ibid., p. 11.

20 This activity is adapted from materials developed by Rosemary Bieg, a graduate student at Temple University.

21 From a pamphlet distributed at a church.

22 Paul R. Ehrlich and John P. Holdren, "Abortion and Morality," *Saturday Review* (September 4, 1971), 58.

23 John Dewey, *Theory of the Moral Life* (New York: Holt, Rinehart & Winston, 1960), p. 5.

24 Jean Piaget, *The Moral Judgment of the Child,* trans. M. Gabain (New York: Free Press, 1965), chaps. 2 and 3.

25 Lawrence Kohlberg et al., "Moral Judgment Interview," unpublished paper, Harvard University, Cambridge, Mass., n.d.

26 *First Things: Values* (Pleasantville, N.Y.: Guidance Associates, 1972). Current kit titles in the series are *That's No Fair, The Trouble with Truth, What Do You Do About Rules? You Promised!* and *But It Isn't Yours. . . .*

27 *A Strategy for Teaching Values* (Pleasantville, N.Y.: Guidance Associates, 1972).

28 Thomas Lickona, *Discussion Guide: A Strategy for Teaching Values* (Pleasantville, N.Y.: Guidance Associates, 1972), pp. 21–24. See also Clive Beck, *Moral Education in the Schools: Some Practical Suggestions* (Toronto: Ontario Institute for Studies in Education, 1971), pp. 10–22.

29 *Self-Concept Measures: An Annotated Bibliography,* Head Start Test Collection Report (Princeton, N.J.: ERIC Clearinghouse on Test, Measurements, and Evaluation, 1971).

30 Robinson and Shaver, op. cit.

31 Dale G. Lake et al. (eds.), *Measuring Human Behavior* (New York: Teacher's College Press, 1973).

32 Deborah Klein Walker, *Socioemotional Measures for Preschool and Kindergarten Children* (San Francisco: Jossey-Bass, 1973).

33 Robert Fox et al., *Diagnosing Classroom Learning Environments* (Chicago: Science Research Associates, 1966).

CHAPTER 16

Special Tools for Affective Growth

There are a number of special tools at the disposal of the teacher who is concerned about the affective growth of children. These are vehicles for putting potentially sensitive or embarrassing issues "on the table" for discussion in a way that allows children to deal with them systematically without feeling self-conscious, threatened, or guilty. Apart from chastising and disciplining students for oral and physical behavior that offends others or creates disruption within the classroom and school, a teacher can employ such tools to have a class deal analytically with the origins and consequences of such behavior. Once defused and outlined, the issue can then be pursued through careful study. Similarly such special tools can enable a class to stretch the limits of their experiences and emotions and to explore alternative ways of viewing events without fear of reprisals or scorn. Role playing and puppetry, simulation games, and expressive pictures are such vehicles for assisting teachers in these pursuits. Not all affective discussions will require their use, nor will they be appropriate for all issues. Properly implemented, employed, and strategically inserted, however, they should enliven and expedite the consideration of significant self concerns.

ROLE PLAYING AND PUPPETRY

"Mormons are weird!"
"Blacks are just plain lazy!"
"A girl couldn't become President."
"It seems like the Indians just never made much of themselves."
"I don't like Puerto Ricans!"
"I think people should live with their own kind."
"I'd be afraid to go there."
"In the paper yesterday, I read where a black student was let into a law school instead of a better (more qualified) white student. That's not fair!"
"Why don't the Mexicans [Hispano-Americans] fix themselves up?"
"Somebody's gonna think you're retarded."
"What did pioneers' kids do?"
"We reserve the right to refuse service to anyone." [Sign in a restaurant]
"All those hippies never wash and they take drugs."
"I wonder what it's like to be poor."

All of the preceding statements might be either expressed or relayed by children at almost any grade level. The expressions reflect the affective turmoil of the larger society in which the children participate, and the statements may or may not convey sentiments the students themselves actually share. To the extent that such statements seem to occur frequently in the classroom, halls, or play areas and to form a general pattern, they provide the substance of serious social studies activities. In some cases name calling per se may often be merely a temporary lapse of interpersonal amenities among children and, if so, ought not to be treated out of proportion to its significance. Earlier chapters discussed how such common childhood foibles might be handled under the heading of Interpersonal Relationship Tools. As such behavior persists or appears to be a manifestation of more serious underlying problems among class members, the use of role playing may be appropriate to identify concerns. Role playing can also serve to get shy or withdrawn children to participate, or to deepen children's understanding of significant historical events or social issues.

Several excellent sources of information exist on how to organize and conduct role-playing activities, including suggested scenarios and activities. Robert Hawley's *Value Exploration Through Role Playing* offers practical pointers and typical scenarios to use.[1] A compact, highly readable volume, Mark Chesler and Robert Fox's *Role-Playing Methods in the Classroom*, provides a fine introduction to the topic and outlines a number of important procedural considerations.[2] It also has an unusual and helpful index, arranged according to questions teachers usually ask. *Role-Playing for Social Values* by Fannie and George Shaftel is a more comprehensive study.[3] It contains a copious number of stories dealing with typical elementary children's concerns organized around problem themes. The Shaftels also have produced a series of media materials, published by Holt, Rinehart & Winston, to be used along with role-playing techniques: *Words and Action: Role-Playing Photo-Problems for Young Children, People in Action: Role-Playing and Discussion Photographs for Elementary Social Studies*, and *Values in Action: Role-Playing Problem-Situations for the Intermediate Grades.* The *People in Action* series, for example, has four levels of large black and white photographs; each level represents an increasingly older group of children and events and concerns relevant to that age. Activities for the photographs include role-play activities. One group of photographs portrays open-ended problems (i.e., ones that may be resolved in a variety of ways), such as three children standing in front of a library looking apprehensive, with one boy holding a ripped book. In an accompanying *Teacher's Guide*, the Shaftels present a twelve-step strategy for introducing the problem and moving to role playing and follow-up discussions.

In this section we will outline some of the basic procedures for initiating and discussing role-play enactments and offer some examples of role-play scenarios.

THE NATURE AND VALUE OF ROLE PLAYING

What is the difference between role playing and putting on a play? While there are similar elements in both activities, including the taking of parts, there are fundamental differences in both structure and function. A play depends on structure throughout; structure is provided by the cast of characters and the basic plot and settings, but most importantly by its script or complete story line. The ultimate outcome, as well as how each role is to be performed, is scripted in advance. Role playing may be considered to have these basic sequences and characteristics:

1. *Role interpretation:* One accepts a role and invests it with whatever interpretation he or she chooses.
2. *Action interpretation:* The dialog, pantomime, or actions related to the role taken are created, at least in part, by the player.
3. *Interaction:* There are at least two participants interacting in some way in the framework of the role-play episode.
4. *Reality commitment:* Players agree to take their roles seriously and portray them accordingly.

> Basically, role playing calls for a student's stepping outside the accustomed role that he plays in life, relinquishing his usual patterns of behavior in exchange for the role and patterns of another person. This other role may be that of a real person or may be entirely fictitious. . . . The student assumes the role of another person in the present or at a different time and place. He attempts as far as possible to speak like the other person, to behave like the other person, and to feel like the other person; this is the key to successful role-playing.[4]

Role-play enactments may begin with a simple story, problem situation, or scenario and may employ props if desired. Drama (frequently high drama!) is a mainstay of role-playing and accounts for much of its appeal to children, but it should never be allowed to overshadow or supplant the objectives of the activity. Role playing is a *vehicle* not an end in instruction.

Some of the possible values of role playing are as follows. It allows one to:

1. *Test alternative behavior patterns.* By exploring different role behaviors in an enactment, children get an oportunity to test out what might be the alternative consequences.
2. *Prepare to cope with actual or potential problems.* In preparing to deal with a problem situation by acting out possible roles, a student acquires more confidence in his or her ability to handle it.
3. *Empathize with another.* Taking the role of another allows one to "walk a mile in his moccasins," and better understand his or her perspective.
4. *Deal with an issue directly and openly.* The transfer of an issue or common concern that may be sensitive to a public forum permits

class members to take positions without having to defend them as personal ones.

5. *Seek explanations.* Many actions or social events may seem puzzling, particularly to children, if one cannot visualize how a continuous chain of events occurred. The role-play enactment often concretizes abstractions and, through action, injects meaning into otherwise ambiguous causal relationships. An enactment of some of the problems that older people in our society encounter, for example, is probably a strong way to sensitize children to this important social problem.

6. *Demonstrate knowledge in alternative ways.* Students who have difficulty in expressing themselves in either writing or speaking, or those who merely are reluctant to participate in class discussions, often seem to find role playing an acceptable way to share their knowledge.

7. *Test self-expression.* A student who is reluctant to express thoughts and feelings has a nonthreatening forum in which to test them before actually identifying with them personally.

Initiation and Direction. Basically every role-play enactment begins with some problem that the teacher or class members have identified. Consider the introduction and transcript of a role-playing session reported in Taba and Elkins, *With Focus on Human Relations.* The session grew out of a discussion concerning a mother's objection to some young boys walking her daughter home:

> We selected a father, mother, and teen-age daughter—Kurt, Winnie, and Emma respectively. The actors took fictitious names, and we went through the "warming up" process: "How old are you?" "How many children are there in your family?" "What do you do for a living?" "What are you doing right now?" These preliminaries helped the children fall into the spirit of the role they were to play. Winnie was instructed to portray a strict mother, concerned about her daughter. Kurt was to play the kind of father he would like to be when he grows up. The children chose their own setting.
>
> The mother is looking out of the window watching her daughter come up the street; the father is reading the newspaper.

Emma: Hi, Mom. Hi, Dad.
Winnie: What were you doing walking home with all those boys?
Emma: Just walking.
Winnie: What do you mean by that?
Emma: The boys walked all the girls home.
Winnie: Why didn't they walk you home first?
Emma: I live the farthest.
Kurt: What's wrong with the boys walking her home?
Winnie: She's too young.
Winnie: She's only thirteen.

Kurt: That's OK.
Winnie: Did you walk home at thirteen with a gang of girls?
Kurt: This is different.
Winnie: How?
Kurt: This is a modern age.
Winnie: It's not different.
Emma: If I don't let the boys walk me home, the girls will say I'm not
 popular.
Winnie: If the girls walked home with you it would be different.
Emma: What can I say to them, Mother—"My Mother doesn't want
 me to walk home with you fellows"?
Winnie: Why can't you go with the girls who live on this street?
Emma: They're only babies. They don't hang around with our gang.
Winnie: What will the neighbors think?
Kurt: Old gossips!
Winnie: (Turning on him) You weren't allowed to do those things at
 thirteen, and she's not either. She's going to have a good up-bring-
 ing. You didn't have ten girls walk you home. (Turning to Emma)
 You'll not go out again if this happens even once more.
Emma: (Bursts into tears. Speaks between sobs) Suppose you were a
 girl, Mom, and all the girls lived on different streets, and the boys
 walked them home first and then you? How would you like it if I
 had to walk home alone?
Winnie: I wouldn't. I'd go with the girls alone. No more boys!
Emma: Not at all? You know that there are always bound to be less
 boys than girls.
 (Silence)
Emma: We just talk about what happens in school.
Winnie: If you're in school all day it seems to me you should know
 what happens.
Emma: No, it's about the other school.
Winnie: Well, why not hang around with children from your own
 school?
Emma: They're too short—or too big.
Winnie: They'll grow—or you will.
Emma: They're so messy. They never comb their hair. You know the
 girls I go with, Mom. They're nice. You know that. And the boys—
 you know them, and they're nice too.
Winnie: I don't care about them. I'm not their mother. I'm yours.
Emma: Oh, Daddy, can't you make her see?
Kurt: She's your mother!
Emma: I'm tired. We'll talk about it tomorrow.
Winnie: No, that's all!
Emma: Daddy, you talk it over with Mom when I've gone to bed.
Winnie: You going to let her go on as she has been?
Kurt: She's old enough.

> *Winnie:* She's too young. (Time was short, and the children were told
> to bring the scene to a conclusion.)
> *Kurt:* Good night I'm going to bed.[5]

In initiating role playing, the teacher should choose topics of a less
controversial or less sensitive nature until students become facile and
comfortable with the procedures. Once the mechanics have been mastered and the class senses what can be accomplished through role playing, it can move to more urgent concerns.

Before moving to the actual role-play arrangements, as much time as
necessary should be spent in "warming up" or "loosening up" the class
for dramatic activity. Simple pantomime scenes with everyone taking
turns or one-line scenarios will do for warm-ups. A source of clever fantasy games for warm-ups is Richard DeMille's *Put Your Mother on the
Ceiling*.[6] This author frequently uses a simplified version of the game
"Body Talk" marketed by *Psychology Today*. Participants are dealt cards
on which various emotions such as "love" and "anger" are written,
along with pictures that indicate what parts of the body may be used
to express the emotion nonverbally. Each member takes a turn depict-
ing the emotion dealt, and the others try to guess what it is. This procedure involves everyone quickly and in a random-assignment fashion. A
warm-up session may not always be needed, but a class should always
be relaxed before beginning the role-play.

Once the class is ready the actual role-play may begin. It revolves
around five key steps: describing the scenario, assigning roles, enactment, debriefing, and application.

Describing the Scenario. The problem to be discussed should be related
in some way to the children's lives so that they see its importance. The
actual problem episode that is to trigger the role playing may be presented orally, pictorially, or in writing. In some cases everyone, including
the audience, may be let in on all details of the story. In other cases the
audience may be told little or nothing to heighten its interest or to involve it in a special way at a later point. In still other cases different dimensions of the story may be revealed to the various actors and the
audience. A simple story problem may be some variation of this incident: Steve pushes Ken out of line in the cafeteria. Ms. Alvarez sees
Ken and comes rushing up to him.

Assigning Roles. Role assignment needs to be approached cautiously—
to avoid both the appearance of any possible type casting and the inclusion of any really reluctant actors. Using volunteers or drawing by lots
eliminates the suggestion of type casting, but it has the disadvantage of
possibly involving students who cannot function effectively in the roles
to be assigned. Often it may be desirable to select certain students who
are most likely to give the greatest validity to the roles identified and
hence present the problem-solution alternatives most effectively. In
either event, the assignment process requires sensitivity and some trial-
and-error sampling to insure a productive role-play enactment.

Once assigned, each participant (including audience participants) should be briefed on the role they are to play. In most cases this will be an oral briefing. However, role-profile cards such as the one shown here may be supplied and referred to during the role-play if necessary.

Betty Ann: Everyone in this class seems to like you. You are considered to be the smartest one in the class. Most children like to have you on their team when choosing up sides for games. You enjoy school and the work you do there.

Audience participants have equivalent, although temporarily passive, roles. They may be asked to assess whether the roles assigned appear to be enacted genuinely, to think of alternative ways of playing roles, to focus on specific actors and to try to identify vicariously with them, to determine what the issue and roles are (when not shared with them), and to play other roles asigned not in advance but during enactment.

Enactment. A quick briefing with the characters before the role-play begins can establish how they plan to enact their roles. While they may actually revise them or find them inappropriate once the role-play unfolds, reviewing their initial actions will help the children clarify their procedures.

During the enactment, it is important to remind both the actors and the audience to use the names of the characters in the role-play situation. This step focuses attention on behaviors and reinforces the fact that the individual class members themselves are not the objects of analysis. Similarly it may be frequently necessary to remind the actors to stay in role, that is, to deal with situations and events as their characters would. Children have a tendency, in humorous or anxiety-producing situations, to stop the role-play and respond to the events as spectators. Gentle prodding to them and to the audience participants who may become noisy or distracting early in the role-play activity helps establish the ground rules.

As with all activities, attention to time spans is important—particularly with young children. When attention wanders, when actions become repetitive, when the audience gets restless, or when the actors just seem to loose interest (or begin to goof off), the action should be halted even if it hasn't run its course. Part of the subsequent discussion can then focus on the causes of the inattention.

Once a group has had some experience with role playing, you may wish to experiment with three interesting variations that Chesler and Fox describe in detail: soliloquies, role-reversals, and doubles.[7] Soliloquies occurs when the action is interrupted, and the actor tells the audience and the other actors what his character is thinking or feeling at that point in time. When the action is halted and players are asked to switch or reverse their roles, they have an opportunity to experience what it is like to have to deal with the results of the behavior they have created in their former roles. Such role-reversals may be used several times during the role-play. A "shadow" may be appointed from the audience for each character to concentrate on the player's role. When the enactment is stopped, the shadow is asked to state what he feels the character's private thoughts or reactions are. To increase audience participation and attention this author has also used an "action-freeze" technique, where the role players are asked to freeze in their places briefly (2–3 minutes maximum). The audience is then asked to speculate on what they believe each of the characters will do next. After the brief discussion, the actors are "unfrozen" and allowed to proceeed. Discrepancies between the hypothesized and actual reactions can be discussed in the debriefing session.

Debriefing. The debriefing period should follow immediately after the enactment. Each of the characters should be allowed to share any feelings they had during the role-play and possibly to ask and answer questions from the audience. At some point an exploration of alternative ways of handling the characters' roles should occur. If participants are willing, they can be asked to reenact the role-play in different ways. The subsequent discussion can focus on which approaches seemed the most effective and why.

The debriefing session may take many different forms depending on the issue, the age of the group, and its experience with role playing. This phase is a critical and integral part of role playing and requires the greatest degree of attention and guidance on the teacher's part to insure productive results.

Application. The basic test of the value of any social studies activity is the extent to which it brings additional meaning to the life of the student. Children's views on the usefulness of the enactment in helping them better understand or cope with self concerns may be assessed in a variety of ways. Open discussions, paper-and-pencil responses, short compositions, and the like offer several avenues. Demonstrated application may be unobtrusively measured through anecdotal records on children's behavior relating to the role-play issues or through assignments requiring the use of insights gained through role playing.

PUPPETRY

Not all puppetry involves role playing as described in the preceding sections. Some puppetry follows a relatively structured or teacher-improvised script with a story line designed to present some problem or issue for discussion and resolution. In the course of the discussion the puppets may even be employed to demonstrate the issue or alternative ways of resolving the problem. The following exercise, taken from primary-grade materials developed by the author, is an example of this particular type of puppetry application.

What can females be? What can males be?

General objectives

Break down sex stereotyping in the selection of potential occupational roles.

Materials

Adult and children puppets.

Commentary

All the female children in your class may not decide to become telephone linemen or doctors, and all the male children may not want to become nurses and secretaries, but they should not have these occupational alternatives closed off through sex stereotyping. Put simply, sex stereotyping is the assigning of roles (in this case occupational ones) solely on the basis of one's sex. In many ways it is similar to racial and ethnic stereotyping.

The purpose of this activity is to demonstrate to children that no occupational role should be shut off to someone just because he is male or she is female. Occupations should be chosen and filled primarily on the basis of one's interest and qualifications.

Suggested procedures/questions

Initiate the discussion of sex stereotyping with a puppet enactment. Have the two children puppets argue over whether a girl can be a fireman, truck driver, doctor, and so on, and whether a boy can become a nurse, secretary, telephone operator, and so on. After the enactment let the class discuss their reactions and feelings on the issue. Ask the children why they think only males or females should select certain occupations.

Return to the puppets and enact a sketch where the parents enter the earlier scene and begin to point out to the children instances of where sex stereotyping is breaking down and where the results seem to be satisfactory (female linemen, male telephone operators, male hairdressers, female doctors, female lawyers, male nurses, female soldiers, female prison guards, female police officers, etc.). Again, after the enactment let the class discuss their feelings and reactions concerning the issue.

Conclude the discussion by focusing on the fairness issue of certain jobs being only for men and only certain jobs being for women. Ask the children whether they feel this is fair and why. At some point in this discussion direct the children's attention to the pictures of occupations that were identified in an earlier activity—"What Would I Like to Be?"—and ask them which jobs they think could not be done by a woman or man and why. (If necessary, present the condition, "If a woman were not married" to open up the possibilities.)

Similarly puppets can be used to reenact and dramatize historical events and social issues and to demonstrate social phenomena, such as customs, rules, and mores. This use of puppets is mainly to present a story issue in an interesting, arresting manner, and it is an easy way to begin to introduce even very young children to role playing. Puppets are perceived as toys, and often they can be used to encourage shy or verbally reticent children to participate in role playing. For other children puppetry may serve to further concretize and embellish role playing. The use of puppetry in role playing is demonstrated below. This activity is also taken from the author's primary-grade materials.

Puppet role-play situations

General objectives

Act out typical children's problem situations using puppets. Experiment with various problem-resolution strategies by trying out different roles. Evaluate the effectiveness of various problem-resolution strategies.

Materials

Adult and children puppets.

Commentary

In addition to the suggestions for using puppets found in the activity "Expressing Feelings Through Puppetry," a number of pointers are outlined here for the role playing of problem situations. A series of specific problem situations are outlined for a series of activities that are to extend over several days. The general rule of thumb is that only one problem situation should be handled in each session and that the sessions should be interspersed with other types of activities rather than handled in continuous success.

Suggested procedures/questions

Working with the role playing of problem situations is often much easier for children if they are able to use the protection of puppets. Working behind a puppet, a child may be able to more freely and honestly represent his or her feelings and thoughts.

In conducting the role playing it is particularly useful to replay the same activity several times, allowing children to change roles and gain further insight into the feelings of others. In the problem situations outlined for role playing, there are no specific scripts. Rather a brief outline of the problem is sketched and the "script" or dialog is to be created by the players spontaneously as the puppet activity develops. Each child is to play the role he or she takes as he or she believes the person represented would. To begin these unscripted puppet activities it is often helpful to select highly extroverted and verbal children. As the others observe the initial role playing, they are likely to lose much of their reluctance to participate.

As you begin the problem enactments, consider the following series of possible steps:

1. Select the puppeteers from volunteers. Do not force any children to participate. Remember that the nonparticipants are still learning and function as a reacting audience.

2. Describe the scene to be enacted briefly before turning it over to the students. Be certain that the players understand their role and offer clarifications that seem necessary.

   Example "Rita is going to play the part of Tina who has just heard that she can't watch her favorite TV program. How does Tina feel, Rita? What is she going to do now? How will she act? . . ."

3. Let the students role-play the scene until it seems to be boring the audience or until the players run out of things to do or say.

4. Discuss the role-play enactment with the players and the audience once it is finished. *This is a very important step and should always be included to maximize learning.* Questions such as the following might be used in this discussion:

   "Why was _____ sad?" (or whatever emotion was expressed)
   "How did _____ feel when that happened? Why do you think that was the case?"

"Do you think the solution to the problem was fair to _____? Why do you think so? Do you think it was fair to _____? Why do you think so?"

"Do you think the solution to the problem that was shown was the best one? Why?"

"What would you have done? Why?"

"Has anything like this ever happened to you?"

"Do you remember what you did? How did your solution work out?"

Remember that the purpose of a role-play puppet activity is *not* to reach the consensus or discover *the* best solution (since usually there is none). The children have an opportunity to test out alternate conflict-resolution strategies that seem consistent with the attitudes and values their parents have taught them and wish them to hold.

5. Replay the puppet activity again, allowing players to change their roles or letting new volunteers try new approaches and solutions. Again follow these reenactments with another discussion session involving the entire class.

The problem sketches for enactment by the class are:

1. Connie and Jay's father has just lost his job and he can't find another one. They have no money left, and the family is not sure what they are going to do. The scene starts as the father tells the family what has just happened.

2. Suzanne and Bruce both always want to sit in the chair closest to the television set. So do their mother and father, but they never get to. The scene starts with Bruce and Suzanne fighting over who is going to get to sit in the chair.

3. Timmy has just turned 7 years old and he thinks he should get an allowance to spend as he pleases. His father thinks that he is too young to have an allowance and that if he gets one, he will just spend it on lots of silly things like bubble gum cards. His mother thinks an allowance is OK but that it should be saved for when Timmy goes to college. Timmy doesn't agree with either his father or mother. The scene begins with Timmy's parents telling him how they feel.

A variety of commercially produced puppets are available. The Instructo Company, Paoli, Pa., produces sets of black and Caucasian families (Figures 16.1 and 16.2) in hand puppets and also a relatively inexpensive series of face-puppet families. Face puppets are relatively easy to construct either by a teacher or by older children, and the Instructo sets may serve as models. Glove-and-paperbag puppets are also easy to construct and are inexpensive. An excellent reference on how to make and use all sorts of puppets is Gertrude Pels' *Easy Puppets*.[8]

SIMULATION GAMES

For our purposes simulation games refer to any gamelike activity designed to provide participants with lifelike problem-solving experiences. Its elements represent a more-or-less accurate representation of some real phenomena. These characteristics distinguish it from a simple game,

Figure 16.1
Black Family Face Puppets
Source: Instructo Corporation, Paoli, Pennsylvania.

FUN WITH FACES: FAMILY FACE PUPPETS (BLACK). Same as above. Often used in conjunction with White Family Face Puppets to broaden social under—standings.
No. 1186 . . . . $5.95

FACE PUPPETS

Use a dramatic play prop to free children's language; provide a means to express feelings. Face Puppets appeal, are easy to hold, store conveniently. Durable hardboard with wipe-off surface. 12" high.

FUN WITH FACES: FAMILY FACE PUPPETS (WHITE). Learn about the family. Children play-act perceptions of roles based on everyday experiences. Assess children's concepts, enhance language development. Includes Mother, Father, Sister, Brother, Grandmother, and Grandfather.
No. 1185 . . . . $5.95

Figure 16.2
Caucasian Family Face Puppets
Source: Instructo Corporation, Paoli, Pennsylvania.

which characterizes any situation in which there are some players, rules, and some end-goal—baseball, for example. Just as with games in general, well-designed simulation games attract children's interest and, once initiated, may operate largely without teacher intervention or control. Often, too, a simulation game enables students to relate easily to a problem they might otherwise not be interested in considering or examining extensively. Furthermore it enables them to assume major control over the direction of their learning and to be less dependent on the authority of the teacher. Relevant to our concerns here, too, is the fact that simulations allow a child to encounter a simplified environment with only those variables prominently featured that are appropriate to his or her concerns. This facet of simulations requires some careful supervision, since it provides equally well for an opportunity to distort seriously the reality it attempts to simulate.

COMMERCIALLY DEVELOPED SIMULATION GAMES

Simulation games have been developed commercially covering a wide range of historical events and dealing with a variety of social decision-making processes. Probably the most comprehensive source of information concerning the simulation games available is *The Guide to Simulation Games for Education and Training* by David W. Zuckerman and Robert E. Horn.[9] It contains information for each game such as: age level, objective, number of players, playing time required, roles, components, costs, and producer and address. Just a small sampling of the simulation games listed and available are as follows: *Population: A Game of Man and Society, Extinction, Pink Pebbles—A Game About How Money Began, Market, Where Do We Live?, Down with the King, Discovery,* and *Crisis.*

Not all games listed in the *Guide* are of equal quality, nor are they appropriate for all grade levels. Very few simulation games are designed for primary children, largely because of the difficulties in simplifying social variables sufficiently to make rules and issues clear but without so distorting the actual event represented as to make the activity meaningless. Three representative simulation games this author has found to work effectively with children and that are relatively inexpensive or easy to explain are *Powderhorn,*[10] *The Road Game,*[11] and *Explorers I and II.*[12] *Powderhorn* deals with the distribution and manipulation of power as reflected in the setting of a frontier society. *The Road Game,* through the vehicle of having teams compete to construct roads through areas, allows students to examine behavior in situations where power and status are at issue. *Explorers I and II* give students an experience in simulating the early explorers of North and South America in encountering uncharted lands.

CONSTRUCTING AND USING SIMULATION GAMES

As with role playing, there are several excellent books that describe the mechanics of constructing and using simulation games. The Zuckerman and Horn source already cited contains a clear, succinct, and brief section at the back of the book on constructing simulation games, as well as a short simulation game for the novice teacher or user to play. Alice Kaplan Gordon's *Games for Growth* not only explains the mechanics well but includes actual games for classroom use.[13] *Simulation Games: An Introduction for the Social Studies Teacher* by Samuel A. Livingston and Clarice Stasz Stoll covers similar ground in a more concise fashion.[14] It also includes a chapter discussion of research on simulation games. An interesting simulation game on inner-city housing demonstrates how a finished product should look and provides the reader with an easy opportunity to have a simulation-game experience.

Most of the discussions on the development of simulation games emphasize a series of steps similar to these:

1. Define the problem or issue to be considered.
2. State the objectives of the simulation as clearly and narrowly as possible.
3. Specify the actors or parts that are to be played.
4. Delineate the roles that the actors are to play or the objectives they have.
5. Indicate the resources and constraints that exist for the actors.
6. Specify the rules and decision-making mechanisms.
7. Develop a trial version of the simulation game.
8. Field-test it and "de-bug" it (that is, remove the problems).

The basic structure of a homemade simulation game involving the fictitious community of Pleasantville and dealing with environmental pollution is shown below. It was field-tested and then used with fifth- and sixth-grade children.

Pollution case study[15]

Pleasantville can be described as a rather average small city with a population of just over 50,000. A glance at the map of the city (Figure 16.3) shows that Pleasantville has some general characteristics in com-

Figure 16.3
Map of Pleasantville

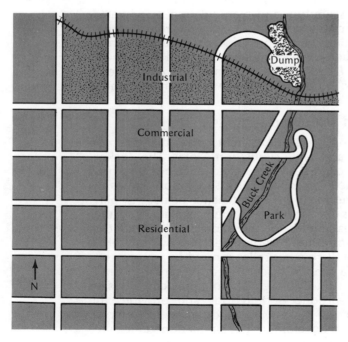

mon with most other cities of its size in that we find homes, businesses, and some industries located in the city. Pleasantville has other characteristics common to most cities, which do not show on the map, such as schools, social organizations, and a city government.

Another characteristic Pleasantville has in common with many other cities is that it has a problem about which its citizens are concerned. The problem is that of how to dispose of all the trash, garbage, and junk produced by the people, businesses, and industries in the city. In the past the residents neither knew nor cared what happened to their refuse once the garbage truck picked it up. The residents of Pleasantville have become more aware of the problem of solid waste disposal, however, as they have begun to notice rubbish and junk accumulating in vacant lots, on the stream banks, and along the roadsides at the edge of the city.

The problem of environmental pollution has arisen partly because Pleasantville has grown in size over the past few years and there is more and more refuse to dispose of. This has resulted in more work for the Department of Sanitation. Another result has been that more trash is being hauled to the city dump, which at present is nearly filled to capacity.

Many residents of Pleasantville have noticed that the major contributor to the unsightly trash piles in vacant lots and to the filling of the dump has been the "immortal" container, that is, the pop-top aluminum can and the nonreturnable, nonreusable glass bottle. Cans and bottles can be found nearly everywhere—along the railroad tracks, in the park, and along the stream banks. They may even be found in front yards after someone has carelessly tossed a can or bottle from a car window.

Hoping to help solve the problem, the local Conservation Club has organized a "Clean Environment" campaign. Through the urging of Conservation Club members and other concerned residents, local ordinances have been posted threatening fines and possible arrest for the illegal dumping of "immortal" containers and other junk. The cans and bottles keep sprouting, however, and parts of the local environment have become disgraceful eyesores.

This pollution of the environment has become a daily and often heated topic of discussion in Pleasantville. One of the most controversial issues arising as a result of the "Clean Environment" campaign concerns a locally owned industry—the Kool-Kola Bottling Company. Kool-Kola is bottled in pop-top aluminum cans and nonreturnable glass bottles. Many of these containers end up along the roadsides and in vacant lots. Members of the Conservation Club have asked representatives of the Kool-Kola Company to help solve this problem by marketing Kool-Kola in either returnable or easily disposed-of containers. The Kool-Kola Company hesitantly agreed to try the first alternative for a limited time period. However, when the local grocers stated that they were not willing to sell soft drinks in returnable containers because of the extra handling costs involved, the Kool-Kola Company withdrew its offer. Presently the Conservation Club is attempting to arouse public support for a boycott of Kool-Kola if the company continues to market it in non-returnable containers.

As a result of the gradual filling of the dump and the unsightly buildup of trash along the streets, stream, and tracks, several local groups have decided that they should consider more drastic actions toward the solution of the problem. The question they hope to answer is: "What steps do we take to rid ourselves of the cans and bottles that are cluttering up Pleasantville's environment?"

Procedures for Simulation. The simulation experience is to provide for the resolution of a specific aspect of the solid-waste problems in Pleasantville, that of dealing with nonreturnable soft-drink containers. Interest groups that will have a voice in the decision-making process leading to the resolution of the problems are (1) the Pleasantville Conservation Club, (2) local grocers, (3) the Kool-Kola Bottling Company, (4) the Department of Sanitation, (5) the City Council, and (6) the local electorate. The teacher should provide for the selection of individuals to play specified roles. The authors recommend that three pupils represent each of the first four groups, seven pupils represent the City Council members, and the rest of the class represent the local electorate.

Phase I

The authors suggest the following sequence for the simulation:
1. Present the class with the Pleasantville case study.
2. Identify the various actors and select people to fill the roles, explaining that they are to receive the problem in the best way possible by acting out the roles assigned to them.
3. Explain that the representatives of the Conservation Club, grocers, Kool-Kola Company, and Department of Sanitations are to arrive at one or two alternative solutions to the solid-waste problem in Pleasantville that reflect basic concerns of their particular group (note the list of concerns following no. 4 below).
4. Allow time for the interest groups to caucus.

A. *Concerns of the Conservation Club*
   1. General cleanliness of the environment.
   2. Elimination of nonreturnable, immortal containers.
   3. Elimination of pollution caused by the present city dump.
   4. Elimination of the pest problem.

B. *Concerns of the Local Grocers*
   1. Satisfaction of consumer demand.
   2. Maximize profits.
   3. Minimize handling costs.

C. *Concerns of the Kool-Kola Company*
   1. Satisfaction of consumer demand.
   2. Satisfaction of dealer demand.
   3. Maximize profits.
   4. Minimize costs.

D. *Concerns of the Department of Sanitation*
   1. Satisfaction of the maximum number of constituents.
   2. Avoid the conversion of solid-waste pollution to other forms of pollution.
   3. Speed of disposal.
   4. Cost of disposal.
   5. Aesthetic considerations.

Phase II
   1. Once the groups have arrived at their alternative solutions to the problem, the solutions may be presented to a public meeting of the City Council. After the presentations by the concerned groups and discussion by the council members, the meeting should be opened for discussion of the issues by the electorate.
   2. Following the discussion the City Council should select, modify, or formulate three solutions that will be submitted to the electorate in a referendum.

Phase III
   1. Before the actual voting takes place, individual members of the electorate may wish to try to persuade others to accept a particular point of view.
   2. The final decision is made when the voting takes place.

Evaluation
   After the pupils have simulated the resolution of the environmental problem, the teacher should not hesitate to encourage student evaluation. This evaluation may take two forms. First, the final solution to the problem might be considered. Questions such as the following may be asked:

1. Was the solution relevant to the problem?
2. What will be the consequences of the solution?
3. Will the solution create new problems?

Second, the simulation experience itself may be evaluated:

1. Was the simulation experience realistic and accurate?
2. In what ways can the simulation be changed or improved?
3. Did the simulation provide for meaningful interaction of all participants?
4. Can simulation experiences provide for the interaction of other actors in the resolution of related environmental problems?

In a real sense, what happens after the simulation game is completed is potentially the most important part of the activity. Livingston and Stoll observe:

Possibly the greatest advantage of simulation games as a technique for teaching social studies is the degree to which they stimulate discussion among students. A large part of the learning that results from simulation games probably occurs during the discussions that follow the playing of the game. The discussions give the students a chance to compare strategies and thus benefit from each other's experience. Often a game moves so quickly that the players have no chance to think about the relationships operating in the game. The post-game discussion gives them this chance; it allows the students who have "caught on" to the game to point out to the other students the relationships they have observed. Class discussion is also the primary means of integrating a game into the course of study, by making the students aware of the connection between the game and their other classroom work.[16]

Class discussions may focus on the strategies students used in playing the game, their reactions to their roles during and after the process, what they feel they have learned, and what analogs—if any—to reality they see. For older children some attention may be drawn to the issue of how the variables in the game simplify or distort reality. An effective and productive period requires some time and a blend between open and structured questions.

EXPRESSIVE PICTURES

Pictures of all types have long been a mainstay of teachers' resource files. It would be impossible to cite all the many types of pictures available and that might profitably be used in social studies activities within a book of this type. The intent, instead, is to highlight those special types of pictures that tend to encourage evocative responses from children. Such expressive pictures offer the basis for the analysis of self concerns. An expressive picture is one that portrays human moods, events, problems, or aspirations in ways that are subject to varying interpretations. Their specific characteristics are not always defined. The basic quality is people who are experiencing feelings and with whom the viewer is somehow able to easily identify. Pictures like these—whether they be of tortured souls in Auschwitz or babies crying—seem to call forth emotional responses from their viewers and in the process reveal a bit of ourselves.

What feelings does the picture in Figure 16.4 evoke? How did you feel earlier as you examined the picture on p. 318?

The children shown here and the 110,000 interned Japanese-Americans that they represented may evoke shame or rationalization, but in either event they help us to confront our historical beliefs and attitudes. Pictures such as these are an extremely important asset for the social studies teacher, and one that you may begin to develop immediately as you read daily. In addition several commercial firms offer these types of pictures. The list here is meant to be suggestive, not exhaustive. The Shaftel and Shaftel problem-episode photographs were cited earlier in

Figure 16.4
Young interned Japanese-Americans

the chapter. A similar series for kindergarten and first-grade children, *Problem-Focus Pictures*, is a component in the *McGraw-Hill Elementary Social Studies* series.[17] A series of black-and-white photos entitled *Pictures in Need of Titles* is distributed by the Social Studies School Services.[18] The Service also markets an outstanding collection of documentary photos representing historical events and eras. The David E. Cook Company has developed an excellent inexpensive series of color photos featuring a multiracial collection of youngsters in different moods.[19] Expressive pictures may also be posters with strong affective themes, as illustrated in Figure 16.5.

The photoboards in the Lincoln Filene Intergroup Relations Curriculum discussed in Chapter 14 contains some excellent expressive pictures representing mostly adults in inner-city settings.[20] An ever-present rich source of expressive pictures, of course, is children's literature.

Figure 16.5
Order for internment of Japanese-Americans in San Francisco

WESTERN DEFENSE COMMAND AND FOURTH ARMY
WARTIME CIVIL CONTROL ADMINISTRATION
Presidio of San Francisco, California
May 3, 1942

INSTRUCTIONS
TO ALL PERSONS OF
JAPANESE
ANCESTRY
Living in the Following Area:

All of that portion of the County of Alameda, State of California, within the boundary beginning at the point where the southerly limits of the City of Oakland meet San Francisco Bay; thence easterly and following the southerly limits of said city to U. S. Highway No. 50; thence southerly and easterly on said Highway No. 50 to its intersection with California State Highway No. 21; thence southerly on said Highway No. 21 to its intersection, at or near Warm Springs, with California State Highway No. 17; thence southerly on said Highway No. 17 to the Alameda-Santa Clara County line; thence westerly and following said county line to San Francisco Bay; thence northerly, and following the shoreline of San Francisco Bay to the point of beginning.

Pursuant to the provisions of Civilian Exclusion Order No. 34, this Headquarters, dated May 3, 1942, all persons of Japanese ancestry, both alien and non-alien, will be evacuated from the above area by 12 o'clock noon, P. W. T., Saturday, May 9, 1942.

No Japanese person living in the above area will be permitted to change residence after 12 o'clock noon, P. W. T., Sunday, May 3, 1942, without obtaining special permission from the representative of the Commanding General, Northern California Sector, at the Civil Control Station located at:

920 - "C" Street,
Hayward, California.

Pictures that children themselves color, draw, or paint are also rich sources of materials for discussion. A child's picture can reflect thoughts and feelings and serve as a basis for his subsequent self-expression. A child may be asked to draw a picture showing when he or she is happy or sad and then later to "Tell me about your picture." Sticking to a simple open-ended question formula such as the preceding one increases the possibility of gaining a richer response. Care must be exercised in interpreting or reading pictures or in jumping to conclusions about the thinking of children without follow-up discussion.

Consider the picture in Figure 16.6, drawn with crayons by a second-grade boy to represent a story he has just heard. The picture itself appears fairly sterile and not especially enlightening. When asked, "Tell me about your picture," however, the boy proceeded to explain that the picture was about "The Three Billy-Goats Gruff." To the left (outside the picture) were the advancing billy-goats and under the bridge completely hidden from view was the troll!

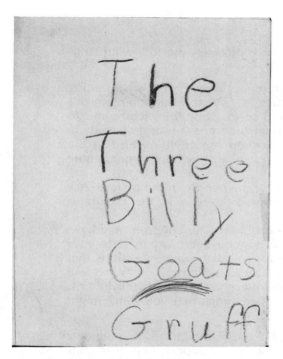

Figure 16.6
Chris's picture with an untold story

In handling the discussion of expressive pictures, the following steps are suggested:

1. Encourage the children to make inferences about what is happening in the picture through a question such as, "What is happening in this picture?" Allow the children some time to study the picture and to think about it. Encourage expansion on short answers and diversity in responses by questions such as, "Do you see anything else in the picture?" and "Can anyone else tell me what they think is happening in this picture?"
2. Focus on the feelings and intentions of the people in the picture. Ask students questions concerning how each person in the picture is feeling or thinking.
3. Elicit alternative resolutions of the problem. The children may have some difficulty with this stage, so it may be necessary to state your questions several ways. Basically your role is to raise questions that seek a solution such as "What will _____ do now?" or "What will happen now?" If the children do not offer many alternative solutions, try to prod them: "Are there any other things that you think might happen?"

Collages represent a special form of expressive pictures. In essence a collage is a cluster of pictures, words, scraps of papers, and other bits of material organized into some whole to tell a story. Usually they are highly personal creations that often are most meaningful to the creator. Though they are an art form, no artistic talent is required to construct them.

Large sheets of paper, posters, or sections of cardboard can form the basis of a collage. Colored paper, newspaper and magazine clippings, colored tissues, aluminum foil, assorted realia, paste, and scissors are the basic ingredients for construction. Given these materials, each student is free to construct an expression of some theme agreed on by him or her and the teacher. In effect the collage is the child's representation or story of the theme as conveyed by a limited range of elements. There is no right or wrong way to tell the story, although some rules for construction may be set down by the teacher.

Themes for collages are limitless: just a few examples are: Me, Poverty, Happiness, Friends, Peace, Security, Love, The Future, The Past, Brotherhood, Caring, and Hope.

ALERTING PARENTS

Since affective components represent a relatively new thrust in social studies programs, it is important to communicate with parents concerning the nature of activities. All of us, including parents, have an image of what social studies is, often based on our own past experiences with the subject. When events do not meet with our image, we are puzzled and, occasionally, irritated.

Alerting parents in simple but clear and complete ways about the introduction of affective materials and programs forestalls misunderstanding and may enlist some help at home in achieving your goals and objectives. This process may be especially important if you anticipate instructional activities that will require children to collect some data at home. A simple mimeographed letter under your and perhaps the principal's name, along with an open invitation to sit in on activities or examine materials, may be sufficient to communicate the nature and aims of your program.

The Jarrettown Elementary School in Maple Glen, Pennsylvania, introduced its fifth-grade program by sending the following letter to all parents involved:

Dear Parents:

Two years ago a new textbook series, entitled *Dimensions of Personality* was introduced to some of our students. Its contents all relate to the dimensions of one's personality; growth—both physical and mental, awareness, feelings, behavior, and so on. (We're enclosing more complete information about the topics and objectives of the book your child will be using. We ask you to read it at your leisure.)

The new program is designed primarily to help your child accept himself with all his strengths and weaknesses. It is intended to help him live a happy, useful life.

The first assignment your child will receive when he begins using *Dimensions of Personality* will be to bring his book home so that you can read it too. In fact, the book contains a special note for parents. We hope you'll take the time to read it.

As the course progresses, we feel the children will talk to you a lot about themselves. If you care to share some of your reactions with us, know that we will welcome the opportunity to talk with you.

Sincerely yours,

_____

Principal

_____

Teacher

Whatever the medium used, parents need to be informed to their satisfaction concerning your plans for dealing with affective concerns. For many parents this is a new role for the schools to undertake, and they may exhibit some natural apprehensions about the process.

NOTES

[1] Robert Hawley, *Value Exploration Through Role Playing* (New York: Hart, 1975).

[2] Mark Chester and Robert Fox, *Role-Playing Methods in the Classroom* (Chicago: Science Research Associates, 1966).

[3] Fannie Shaftel and George Shaftel, *Role-Playing for Social Values* (Englewood Cliffs, N.J.: Prentice-Hall, 1967).

[4] Chesler and Fox, op. cit., p. 3.

[5] Hilda Taba and Deborah Elkins, *With Focus on Human Relations* (Washington, D.C.: American Council on Education, 1952), pp. 50–51.

[6] Richard DeMille, *Put Your Mother on the Ceiling* (New York: Viking, 1967).

[7] Chesler and Fox, op. cit., p. 40.

[8] Gertrude Pels, *Easy Puppets* (New York: T. Y. Crowell, 1951).

[9] David W. Zuckerman and Robert E. Horn, *The Guide to Simulation Games for Education and Training* (Lexington, Mass.: Information Resources, 1973). (Address: P.O. Box 417, Lexington, Mass. 02173)

[10] R. Gary Shirts, *Powderhorn* (La Jolla, Calif.: Simile II, 1971). (Address: P.O. Box 1023, 1150 Silverado, La Jolla, Calif. 92037)

[11] Thomas E. Linehan and Barbara Ellis Long, *The Road Game* (New York: Herder & Herder, 1970). (Address: 1221 Avenue of the Americas, New York, N.Y. 10020)

[12] Jay Reese, *Explorers I and II* (La Jolla, Calif.: Simile II, 1972).

[13] Alice Kaplan Gordon, *Games for Growth* (Chicago: Science Research Associates, 1970).

[14] Samuel A. Livingston and Clarice Stasz Stoll, *Simulation Games: An Introduction for the Social Studies Teacher* (New York: Free Press, 1973).

[15] This material is adapted from James B. Kracht and Peter H. Martorella, "Simulation and Inquiry Models Applied to the Study of Environmental Problems," *Journal of Geography* (May 1970), 273–278.

[16] Livingston and Stoll, op. cit., p. 15.

[17] Peter H. Martorella, *Kindergarten and First-Grade Social Education Action Kits* (tentative title) in *McGraw-Hill Elementary Social Studies Series* (New York: McGraw-Hill, in press).

[18] Address: Social Studies School Services, 10,000 Culver Blvd., Culver City, Calif. 90230.

[19] Address: David E. Cook Company, Elgin, Ill. 60120.

[20] Available from the Lincoln Filene Center, for Citizenship and Public Affairs, Tufts University, Medford, Mass. 01730. See also Betty Atwell Wright, *Urban Education Studies* (New York: Day, 1965), a series of large 18″ × 18″ black-and-white albums of various city scenes.

CHAPTER 17

Internalization Set #5

Self concerns are universal and common to all age groups. Teachers as much as students are concerned with personal affective growth; self-insights are an important—if not an overriding—goal of all humans in all places. As those who would help others better come to deal with and analyze self concerns, we must introspect first on our own affective postures and our emotional capabilities for facilitating growth in others. We are what we will let ourselves become, and our teaching will reflect the latitudes we allow ourselves. Recognizing the parameters we create on self-evolution, as well as the various shades that we paint our world, should help us to better understand not only ourselves but also how we are likely to affect others.

The activities and exercises in this chapter are intended as a blend of self-assessments along several dimensions and competency-building opportunities. They may, in some respects, duplicate similar activities in other settings or may strike you as inappropriate, for whatever reasons, to your own personal situation or course setting. For this reason, none of the eighteen suggestions are specifically urged to be used by the reader. They have all been used in some way by the author with preservice and inservice teachers and found to be extremely useful in preparing them to deal with children's self concerns.

SELF CONCEPT IMAGES

"Self-conscious" has come to refer to a condition in which one is actually aware that he or she is under examination. It does not usually refer to a pleasant sensation; adults in our society are not usually pleased when they are put in situations where they become conscious of self. Not surprisingly, then, adults tend to greet such exercises as the ones that follow—initially, at least—with resistance. The three described below are all nonthreatening, usually quite pleasant and interesting to do, and generally quite informative for participants.

ACTIVITY 55

Constructing a Lifeline is an enjoyable and instructive experience and an excellent way to become better acquainted with members of a group, such as classmates, with whom you will be working for a period of time. Over a period of five years this author has periodically constructed and shared with his classes his and their Lifelines. Each time the experience has proven to be revealing and an easy way to learn more about members of the group.

Refer to the list of materials and procedures regarding the construction and sharing of Lifelines on pp. 291–292, and go ahead!

ACTIVITY 56

An Admiration Ladder is an easy device for assessing what you idealize and how you size up to your ideal aspirations.[1] Refer to the ladder shown below and indicate a range of people you admire, from the most to the least. Next to the top and bottom choices, indicate what causes you to rank them as you

What I Admire Most
About This Person

_____

_____

_____

One Most Admired

What I Especially Dislike
About This Person

_____

_____

_____

One Least Admired

do. Then locate yourself at some point along the ladder. Why did you place yourself at that point? Jot down your reason here: _____

_____

_____

In what specific ways would you have to change your behavior, conditions, or goals to reach the level you aspire to?

1. _____

_____

2. _____

_____

3. _____

_____

If you have already reached the level you aspire to, what circumstances have prompted that situation? _____

_____

ACTIVITY 57

This activity calls for the anonymous completion of an open-ended positive self statement. An effective way to conduct the activity is to involve a large group, such as a class, and to distribute some uniform size cards such as 3″ × 5″ ones. Each member of the group, including the leader, is to complete

I like myself because . . .

I like to do things for other people, and when they feel good, I feel good as well.

I like myself because . . .

I am a girl, student, and wife.

I like myself because . . .

I know I am capable in certain fields and because I am able to relate to people in a way that pleases me.

I like myself because . . .

I'm me, and because I'm trying to be the type of person I want and not what. others want me to be.

the sentence, "I like myself because . . ." Some sample "I like myself because . . ." cards completed by preservice teachers are shown on pp. 367–368. The cards are completed anonymously, turned face down, collected, shuffled, and read aloud. Those who wish to may react to the statements in any way they care to. Subsequent discussion should focus on how individuals felt as they completed the statements and on similarities and differences among the statements. (If this activity is also done with children, anonymity is less important, since they are less self-conscious. Anonymity may even be undesirable, since it robs the teacher of important self data on individuals.)

BELIEFS AND ATTITUDES

Our beliefs and attitudes are constantly undergoing scrutiny—either by ourselves or by others—and modification. Teachers are especially "on stage," since students, parents, administrators, and the community at large are curious about their beliefs dealing with a range of topics. Because teachers' stock in trade is knowledge, and because they operate in a democratic society, they have a special dual obligation: to respect the rights of all students to hold their own beliefs and attitudes, and to challenge those that lack supporting data or promote undemocratic practices. The responsibility is often a taxing one, calling for a balance between acceptance and argumentation.

Examining our own beliefs and attitudes is an important step toward a recognition of how well prepared we are to help others in the same area. Two exercises in this section ask you to undergo such an examination, while the third provides a teaching activity to try with a group of children.

ACTIVITY 58

Organize a group of five to seven peers without any advance preparation. Each of you should list below five things you believe are stated in the U.S. Constitution, without any consultation with one another. *List the items in sentence form,* since it will make checking your beliefs much easier later. Write out the items as specifically as you are able:

1. _____

_____

2. _____

_____

3. _____

_____

4. _____

_____

5. _____

_____

When each member has finished, pass around your answers and discuss the lists. Make any modifications that seem warranted in the light of your discussions and seek out a copy of the Constitution to check your beliefs. Discuss your findings within the group, at some point focusing on where and why members were at error on this most fundamental basis of our democracy. What potential generalizations concerning other fundamentalist beliefs (if any) does this experience suggest to you?

ACTIVITY 59

You are asked to register your attitudes toward a single issue that preoccupies considerable social attention in every generation. Public mores concerning the topic shift periodically, often dramatically, and the subject seems to be under constant discussion. The topic is the degree to which it is socially acceptable to show the human body to others—in short, nudity. Clearly part of the human body must always be potentially exposed to others, but people everywhere for centuries have argued and even raged on which members of society, under what conditions, and to what degree may expose the body to others. The Moroccan female, almost totally enshrouded to males other than her husband, appears bizarre, perhaps amusing, or even shocking to western eyes. However her cultural enactment is only a dramatic degree of the constraints on nudity that each of us also has established. Let us see where we stand.

This activity may be done privately but is more interesting to discuss when done in a group of five. Cut out all of the characteristics cards on p. 371. Clear a 6-foot stretch on a table on the floor for each person. Imagine a continuum with the poles "Totally Unacceptable" to the left and "Very Acceptable" to the right. Arrange your cards along the continuum in terms of how you feel about each of the items mentioned on the cards. (You are not indicating whether *you* would do the action *personally*, just whether you feel it is acceptable for it to occur.)

After all the cards have been distributed along the continuum, take some time to reflect on the positions. If done in a group, discuss the rationale behind your attitudes. You also might raise other issues related to nudity that were not listed and ask each member of the group to indicate their position in relation to the continuum. Attitudes toward other issues or the actions of individuals may be explored in similar fashion.

Finally, discuss your reaction to the excerpt below that purportedly appeared in an article in the *Richmond News Leader:*

> The name of Ruby Laverne Code remains relatively unknown outside the boundaries of Seattle, Wash., but Miss Code may have initiated a whole new school of "communication."
>
> Not long ago, Miss Code was arrested at the Lucky Lady Tavern for her topless performance; she was charged with indecent exposure, and her boss, Frank L. Hinkley, was arrested for sanctioning her performance. After both were convicted, they appealed to the Superior Court.
>
> The court has overturned their convictions, on the grounds that Miss Code's dancing is a form of communication covered by the First Amendment.
>
> "Miss Code is a go-go dancer with five years of experience," the Superior court said, "and therefore I believe that she can be classified as a professional dancer. Topless go-go dancing is communication, although the court and other people may not like the message. Miss Code has the right to communicate through her dancing."

Public baths—sexually segregated	Photos of nude males and females **together**	Nude sunbathing in one's own yard
Frontal nude photos of males in magazines	Topless waitresses	Nudity in films
Rear nude photos of males and females in magazines	Bottomless waitresses	Nude hat-check girls
Pictures of nude children	Topless waiters	"Going nude" in one's own home
Photos of scantily clad males	Bottomless waiters	Photos of attractive nude males
Nudist camps	Topless female dancers	Photos of unattractive nude males
Private beaches for nude bathing	Bottomless female dancers	Photos of unattractive nude females
Nude restricted areas on public beaches	Bottomless male dancers	Photos of attractive nude females
Nudity in plays	Verbal or written descriptions of nudity	Children appearing nude in public
Nude bathing in regular public swimming area	Pornographic nude photos	Erotic but not pornographic nude photos
Parents (of both sexes) undressing in front of their children (of both sexes)	Appearing nude when everyone else is clothed	Female appearing nude above the waist at a social gathering
"Streaking" at a public event	Nude art modeling	Sleeping in the nude

ACTIVITY 60

For this teaching activity you will need a group or class of children, prefer-ably primary level, and a photograph similar to the one shown in Figure 17.1. The picture is not absolutely necessary, but it helps provide a continuous reference point for the group. The objective for you is to gain some experience in helping children raise to the level of consciousness and examine their beliefs and attitudes concerning other ethnic groups and races and those in general who are different than they. Be sure the children can all see the picture and then read the following story taken from Alice Miel's *The Short-changed Children of Suburbia:*

> The Jones family like their home very much. They have worked hard to make it a nice, comfortable place to live. Then some new people moved next door to them. This disturbed the Joneses so much that they want to sell their home and move away from the neighborhood.[2]

Figure 17.1
The "Jones" family

For the discussion phase, prepare a series of questions appropriate to the racial and ethnic composition of the group and designed to uncover beliefs and attitudes about other groups. Open-ended sentences such as "The people who moved in probably were . . ." for the group to complete will help to get the ball rolling. Get as many prejudices, stereotypes, and garbled facts "on the table" (or blackboard) as possible without challenging them before you introduce new data. Finally, deal with a consideration of the feelings of those who are the object of the negative beliefs and attitudes.

VALUES

Values are trickier than beliefs and attitudes to pin down. While they govern our daily activities, undergird the social fabric of our country, and permeate the establishment and regulation of our laws, it is not always easy to determine what values are operative in a situation. Then again, what appears to be a value or a primary indicator of what we truly espouse often turns out to be really an ephemeral indicator. In classrooms we generally address ourselves at best to indirect expressions of values or values as seen through what we do or say. The exercises that follow attempt to help you look further inward to analyze what your basic end-states or values are. Activity 61 is modified slightly and taken from the activity described in *Values Clarification*.[3]

ACTIVITY 61

Organize a group of three to five peers. Complete the following task individually, then share the results and rationales with one another. Identify ten issues on the local, state, or national level and write a short identifying title for each of them in the spaces provided on p. 375. Next to the issue, summarize your own position in a few words.

Refer back to the seven steps in the Raths et al. value-clarification model described on p. 322. Proceed through each of the steps, treating each of them as a question addressed to your position on each of the ten issues, for example, "Are you proud of . . . ?"

ACTIVITY 62

In a very popular film of several years ago, *The Reivers* starring Steven McQueen, an emotional series of scenes occur roughly midway through the film. Briefly, in the scenes the main characters are a reformed warm and lovable

Issue	Position	Step 1	Step 2	Step 3	Step 4	Step 5	Step 6	Step 7

prostitute, her boyfriend-soon-to-be-husband, and a hideous sheriff. The setting is roughly the first third of the twentieth century. Through a series of events too complicated to describe here, the prostitute, the boyfriend, and an assorted group of their friends run afoul of the law in the course of performing a good deed. They end up in a small-town jail presided over by a sheriff who is the quintessence of every stereotyped red-neck lawman. Justice is out of the question. The sheriff, however, is willing to short-cut the legal niceties and let the group go if the reformed prostitute, to whom he has taken a fancy, will spend the night with him. He leaves her and the group to decide what to do.

She reasons that her action would only involve a temporary, albeit painful, relapse into her old profession, and it would extricate the whole group from what appears to be a most desperate situation. Her boyfriend is indignant at her even considering the idea. He commands her not to submit, reminding her that she promised to "swear off" when they fell in love. After painful introspection, she decides to agree to the sheriff's proposition. Her boyfriend is furious, and after the group is released, he beats her up and rejects her in heartbroken rage. He cannot understand how she could have agreed to the sheriff's demands, no matter what the consequences!

With your group or class of peers, reflect on this story and examine the continuum shown below. Consider the characters—the prostitute (P), the boyfriend-soon-to-be-husband (B), and the sheriff (S)—and indicate your rating of their characters by placing them on the continuum. After each member of your group has done this individually, have each person record his or her results on a master continuum drawn on the board..As each person indicates his or her ratings, have him place his or her initials in parentheses beneath the characters.

Rating Continuum

```
|----------------------------|----------------------------|
Despicable                                           Admirable
```

At the conclusion let individuals discuss the reasons for their ratings. Then analyze what, if anything, you have learned about your values and the extent to which the value orientations expressed in this exercise are reflected in other areas of your life.

ACTIVITY 63

The world is constantly faced with an immense variety of problems, many of them vastly overshadowing the ones we encounter in the United States. The problems we perceive and feel strongly about reflect the values we hold, as well as our general world view. Organize a group of five to seven peers and think about the world's problems for a few moments. Then ask each member of the group individually to list what they consider to be the top ten problems facing the world. Do this privately without consultation.

Personal list

1. _____
2. _____
3. _____
4. _____
5. _____

6. _____

7. _____

8. _____

9. _____

10. _____

After everyone has completed the list, discuss the choices and the reasons for them and develop a group-*consensus* list.

Group-consensus list

1. _____

2. _____

3. _____

4. _____

5. _____

6. _____

7. _____

8. _____

9. _____

10. _____

Several years ago, a Gallup poll surveyed 265 world leaders from 75 countries. Included were statesmen and diplomats, elected and appointed public officials, educators, scientists, corporate executives, economists, bankers, physicians, attorneys, and media executives. The Soviet Union and mainland China were not included. Each leader was given a list of fifteen problems and asked, "Which of these problems do you regard as the five most urgent problems facing your nation?" The top ten domestic problems, listed in order of frequency of mention, are shown on p. 385. Compare the list with those that you and your group constructed.

MORAL DEVELOPMENT

Moral development in children is a gradual process. Dramatic shifts do not occur overnight, although developmental differences over a period of time are noticeable. Actual moral decision making in natural settings is difficult to assess in children and is normally done only through carefully constructed and unobtrusive experiments or chance observations. The activities in this set relating to assessment deal with indirect verbal moral decision making and are based on Piaget's and Kohlberg's work with moral reasoning. The first activity gives you an opportunity to take a stand on a typical moral dilemma and to explain your reasoning. The dilemma is one that Kohlberg and his associates frequently use in their work with all age groups.

ACTIVITY 64

Organize a group of seven to ten peers and read the story below. When everyone has finished, each member should take a stand and present his or her rationale. Then consider the other questions listed following the dilemma.

> In Europe a woman was near death from cancer. One drug might save her, a form of radium that a druggist in the same town had recently discovered. The druggist was charging $2,000, ten times what the drug cost him to make.
> The sick woman's husband, Heinz, went to everyone he knew to borrow the money, but he could only get together about half of the necessary sum. He told the druggist that his wife was dying and asked him to sell the drug cheaper or let him pay later, but the druggist said, "No, I invented the drug and I can do what I want with it."
> The man was desperate and broke into the store and stole the drug for his wife.[4]

Consider the following questions: (1) Should Heinz have stolen the drug? Why? (2) Is it a husband's duty to steal the drug for his wife? Why? (3) What if Heinz did not like his wife, should he steal the drug? Why?

Following your session refer back to the discussions concerning moral development on pp. 285–287, if necessary, to gain some perspective on the type of moral reasoning that appeared to dominate arguments.

ACTIVITY 65

Each member of your class, if possible, should complete the following exercise to provide a sizable sample of responses. Listed below are several simple stories concerning a basic moral issue, either taken from or based on similar ones used by Piaget.

Below each story are three different age levels. Your task is to identify one or more children in each of the three age groups and to present them with the stories and record their responses.

At the conclusion tally the entire class' results and analyze them. What developmental differences did you record? What characteristics did the answer of each age group have?

> Once, long ago, and in a place very far away from here, there was a father who had two sons. One was very good and obedient. The other was a good sort, but he often did silly things. One day the father goes off on a journey and says to the first son: "You must watch carefully to see what your brother does, and when I come back you shall tell me." The father goes away and the brother goes and does something silly. When the father comes back he asks the first boy to tell him everything. What ought the boy to do? Why?[5]

Answer of 4–5-year-old: _____

_____

_____

Reason: _____ _____

_____

_____

Answer of 7–8-year-old: _____

_____

_____

Reason: _____

_____

_____

Answer of 10–11-year-old: _____

_____

_____

Reason: _____

_____

_____

Once there were two children who were stealing apples in an orchard. Suddenly a policeman comes along and the two children run away. One of them is caught. The other one, going home by a roundabout way, crosses a river on a rotten bridge and falls into the water. Now what do you think? If he had not stolen the apples and had crossed the river on that rotten bridge all the same, would he also have fallen into the water? Why?[6]

Answer of 4–5-year-old: _____

_____

_____

Reason: _____

_____

_____

Answer of 7–8-year-old: _____

_____

_____

Reason:_____

_____

_____

Answer of 10–11-year-old:_____

_____

_____

Reason:_____

_____

_____

Here are two stories about some little girls. One little girl named Ellen wanted to surprise her mother while her mother was away. She decided to wash and dry the dishes. While she was drying the dishes, she accidentally knocked over the dish rack and broke ten of the dishes.

Another little girl, Regina, stayed home while her mother went out. Regina got bored watching television, so she decided to play around in the kitchen. She was fooling around with some dishes on the counter, and one fell on the floor and broke.

Who was naughtier, Ellen or Regina? Why do you think so?

Answer of 4–5-year-old:_____

_____

_____

Reason:_____

_____

_____

Answer of 7–8-year-old:_____

_____

_____

Reason:_____

_____

_____

Answer of 10–11-year-old:_____

_____

_____

_____

_____

ACTIVITY 66

Try your hand now at constructing some moral dilemmas using those in Chapter 16 as models, then testing them out in some discussions with children. Follow these steps in organizing the activity:

1. Construct a moral-dilemma story, using any media props such as a picture or a drawing to embellish them. Develop one either for a primary-age group or one for an intermediate-level group.
2. Write a series of related probe questions.
3. Select a group of five to seven children.
4. If possible, secure a tape recorder to obtain a record of your sessions.
5. Organize the students into a circle and initiate the discussion.
6. Analyze your results and compare them with those of your peers.

AFFECTIVE TOOLS

These special aids in fostering affective growth require some practice so that you may feel sufficiently competent in their use to concentrate on the interactive processes they produce in the classroom. If you feel uncomfortable in using them, it is unlikely that you will ever draw upon them. Picture use appears deceptively easy, role playing at first glance looks just like "pretending," the childlike quality of puppets may blind one to the knack of holding and manipulating them, and simulation games for all their attractiveness must really be experienced to be appreciated and understood. The six activities that follow try to better prepare you to employ these extremely useful instructional tools.

ACTIVITY 67

Select a partner of the *same sex* for a role-play activity. Reread the steps to be followed in a complete role-play situation, as discussed on pp. 343–348. Leave a marker in the book at that point for reference. *Each of you is to take a role that is not known to the other. Neither role is to be known to the audience.*

You should take and prepare to play the first role given below, and your partner should take the other one. Each of you must examine only your own roles. Use the names and gender that match your sex. After studying your role, begin the role-play *and stop reading at this point.*

Louise/Lou

You are sharing a dorm room with a new roommate who seems to be a bit aloof. Since you will have to spend a year together, you have gone out of your way to be nice to her/him, but she/he hasn't responded. As a last resort, in order to try to establish a warm relationship, you decide to invite her/him up to your parents' cabin in Vermont to spend the weekend skiing and relaxing.

How would you approach your roommate, knowing that she/he is likely to refuse your invitation at first?

Donna/Don

Your new roommate Louise/Lou acts very friendly toward you and has a habit of touching you whenever talking. At the same time, you notice that she/he never seems to go out on dates or talk about boys/girls. Yesterday, she/he tried to get you to go along with her/him to hear a speaker discuss the gay liberation movement.

Your dorm fees have already been paid for the first semester, and you cannot get your money back.

The first week of the semester is ending, and Louise/Lou has just asked you to spend a weekend at her/his parents' cabin in Vermont to "relax and do some skiing."

What do you do?

In the debriefing and evaluation sessions, reveal roles to one another and to the audience. Discuss what the objectives of this role-play activity might be, what some similar role-play situations for elementary students might be, and how the structure of this role-play differed from those discussed and illustrated in earlier chapters.

ACTIVITY 68

Get a group of preschool–primary students together to try some puppetry. Use the structured activity illustrated on p. 349 or construct one of your own. At the same time let the students try their hand at using the puppets. When you finish, make some notes below for future reference:

Type of Group (Number, age, characteristics): _____

_____

Puppets Used and Source: _____

_____

Apparent Learning Results: _____

_____

_____

Problems I had: _____

_____

_____

Problems Students Had: _____

_____

_____

ACTIVITY 69

Identify and locate a simulation game listed in the Zuckerman and Horn *Guide to Simulation Games for Education and Training* (see p. 353) that is for adults and that looks interesting. Your instructor, your instructional-materials center or library, or a local school may have a copy. If the price is right, as a last resort, buy a copy from the source, whose address is listed in the Guide. (One of this author's favorite demonstration games is *Starpower;* the directions for constructing your own set are available for a few dollars from the developer.)

Gather the group required by the instructions and play the game. Debrief the session along the lines of the suggestions on p. 357.

ACTIVITY 70

Constructing a simulation game from scratch for the first time without assistance can be difficult. On the other hand, the design process can be a stimulating and even rewarding one, once you get started. Below are some bits and pieces to help you begin. They are the beginnings of a simulation game dealing with closed-housing patterns. Your task is to complete the game, including developing specific objectives, rules, and so on. Refer to the guides for developing simulations games outlined on pp. 353–354 and to other simulation games that you have encountered. Good luck!

Issue: Certain individuals who are financially able desire to buy houses in an area but are prevented from doing so through deceptive procedures because they are black. Though such obstructions are illegal, they are difficult, time-consuming, and often expensive to prove.

Objectives: (1) Participants should be able to list the various ways that closed housing is maintained, for example, "gentlemen's agreement"; (2) ?_____ .

_____ .

Actors/Parts: Realtors, sellers of homes, black buyers, ?_____

Roles/Objectives of Actors: Blacks: (1) Approach realtor about house,

(2) ?_____

Realtors: (1) ?_____

Sellers: (1) ?_____

Resources and Constraints: ?_____

_____

Rules and Decision-Making Procedures: ?_____

_____ .

ACTIVITY 71

If you are knowledgeable about cameras, audacious enough to take pictures of people you don't know, no matter where you are, have time to visit different places and see different things, and enjoy doing all of the above, create your own file of expressive pictures and share the results with your class.

Barring a do-it-yourself aptitude, create a file from whatever picture sources you have access to. In either case, organize the pictures within the file under some logical themes and indicate how they might be used in a social studies class.

ACTIVITY 72

Work individually with five to seven different primary-age children in drawing and interpreting pictures. Get a range and mix of students (personality and socioeconomic variations). Ask them to draw pictures of their families and then to tell you about the pictures. Spend time with a similar group, only at the intermediate-grade level. This latter group might be given different themes for drawing or be allowed to select their own.

As you begin to reflect on and assess what you have learned about the children and their drawings, observe the pictures carefully across similar themes and jot down some of the similarities and differences that you noted for reference:

Primary children's drawings

Similarities	Differences
_____	_____
_____	_____
_____	_____
_____	_____
_____	_____
_____	_____

Intermediate children's drawings

Similarities	Differences
_____	_____
_____	_____
_____	_____
_____	_____
_____	_____

When you have completed your analysis, try to obtain a copy of Joseph DiLeo's *Young Children and Their Drawings* and read about his work and conclusions.[7]

NOTES

[1] Adapted from *nAch: The Need to Achieve* (Middletown, Conn.: Education Ventures, 1969), p. 26.

[2] Alice Miel, *The Shortchanged Children of Suburbia* (New York: Institute of Human Relations Press, 1967), p. 49.

[3] Sidney B. Simon et al., *Values Clarification* (New York: Hart, 1972), pp. 35–37.

[4] Lawrence Kohlberg et al., "Moral Judgment Interview," unpublished paper, Howard University, Cambridge, Mass., n.d.

[5] Jean Piaget, *The Moral Judgment of the Child*, trans. M. Gabain (New York: Free Press, 1965), p. 290.

[6] Ibid., p. 252.

[7] Joseph H. DiLeo, *Young Children and Their Drawings* (New York: Brunner/Mazel, 1970).

Gallup Poll of World Leaders (Top problems based on collective judgments of all world leaders, including those from the United States.)

1. Inflation
2. Unemployment
3. Government reform
4. Low educational standards
5. Air–water pollution
6. Lack of industrial development
7. Crime/lack of respect for law
8. Overpopulation
9. Low productivity standards
10. Labor–management disputes

MODULE SUMMARY

Self concerns should be a vital and integral part of a social education program at all levels, preschool–grade 12. Students of all ages need help in grappling with the basic question of "Who am I?" In a real sense such a question has a high priority in the study of social phenomena. In the 1970s there has been a concerted focus on self concerns generally under such rubrics as "affective," "open" or "humanistic" education. While the movement toward affective education is still not clearly defined, its main thrust is to draw attention to and emphasize the individual's feelings and emotional experiences.

The terms *cognitive* and *affective* are purely arbitrary categories used to designate teaching strategies or materials whose main emphases appear to be "thinking" or "feeling." Neither the former nor the latter process ever occurs in isolation of the other. The split between the affective and cognitive domains is for analytical purposes and is quite arbitrary. Two continua are offered as a means of determining whether instructional approaches might roughly be designated more appropriately as cognitive or affective. Similarly the continua may be used to construct individual profiles of Affective-Teaching Comfort and Competency Zones.

The various types of self concerns that may be investigated in the classroom have been labeled in many different ways. In this module they have been outlined and discussed under the headings Self Concept, Values, Beliefs and Attitudes, and Moral Development. One's self concept evolves developmentally through interactions with others and through one's perceptions of how others view him or her. Values may be viewed as basic end-states of feelings concerning matters of worth. They lie behind all of our choices or decisions in life. Beliefs and attitudes are less basic filters of reality that predispose us to act in various ways. Moral development is the process by which one grows in ability to decide that a certain course of action is right or wrong.

A variety of instructional models for dealing with self concepts, beliefs and attitudes, values, and moral development have been sketched and illustrated. Instructional models for dealing with affective growth are at best still yeasty, but they do chart some directions for classroom teachers.

Under the discussion of self-concept activities, a basic model was presented and illustrated with diverse examples. Three somewhat different approaches to analyzing and modifying beliefs and attitudes in nondoctrinaire manner were examined: Attitude Scaling, Attitude Triangles and Challenging Commonly Held Beliefs. Each of the models cited draws upon related psychological theories. Value considerations and their relationships to beliefs and attitudes were traced, and the Value-Clarification and the Value Survey models of Raths and associates and Rokeach and associates, respectively, were explored. The nature of moral development and how it may be facilitated in classrooms as discussed by Piaget and Kohlberg served as the culminating section of the classroom-strategies discussion. Several techniques and tools for measuring affective growth, as well as reference sources for acquiring and examining ready-made instruments, were cited.

Three types of special tools for aiding teachers in the analysis of self concerns have been discussed and illustrated, including specific instructions for employing each technique. Role playing and puppetry allow children to experience alternative feelings and visualize with clearer continuity historical and social events and general causal relationships. For more reticent or verbally insecure children, these techniques often offer an alternative way of both gaining and demonstrating knowledge.

Simulation games are gamelike activities designed to provide participants with lifelike problem-solving experiences. They serve as high-level motivators to introduce and involve students in some dimensions of important historical and social phenomena and can serve as springboards to more systematic study of the issue.

Expressive pictures portray human moods, events, problems, or aspirations in ways that are subject to varying interpretations. Their specific characteristics are not always defined. Such pictures not only represent human concerns but call forth some dimensions of ourselves as we interpret them.

SUGGESTED READINGS

Beck, Clive. *Moral Education in the Schools: Some Practical Suggestions.* Toronto: Ontario Institute for Studies in Education, 1971.

Bem, Daryl J. *Beliefs, Attitudes and Human Affairs.* Belmont, Calif.: Brooks/Cole, 1970.

Bloom, Benjamin S. (ed.). *Taxonomy of Educational Objectives: Handbook I, Cognitive Domain.* New York: McKay, 1956.

Chesler, Mark, and Robert Fox. *Role-Playing Methods in the Classroom.* Chicago: Science Research Associates, 1966.

Dewey, John. *Theory of the Moral Life.* New York: Holt, Rinehart & Winston, 1960.

Gibson, John S. *The Intergroup Relations Curriculum: A Program for Elementary School Education.* Medford, Mass.: Lincoln Filene Center for Citizenship and Public Affairs, Tufts University, 1969.

Gordon, Alice K. *Games for Growth.* Chicago: Science Research Associates, 1970.

Hammachek, Don E. *Encounters with the Self.* New York: Holt, Rinehart & Winston, 1971.

Lake, Dale G., et al. *Measuring Human Behavior.* New York: Teacher's College, 1973.

Livingston, Samuel A., and Clarice Stasz Stoll. *Simulation Games: An Introduction for the Social Studies Teacher.* New York: Free Press, 1973.

Lyon, Harold C. *Learning to Feel—Feeling to Learn.* Columbus, Ohio: Merrill, 1971.

Mead, George H. *Mind, Self and Society.* Chicago: University of Chicago Press, 1962.

Kohlberg, Lawrence, "The Cognitive Developmental Approach to Moral Education," *Phi Delta Kappan,* 56 (June, 1975), 670–677.

Krathwohl, David R., et al. *Taxonomy of Educational Objectives: Handbook II, Affective Domain.* New York: McKay, 1964.

Piaget, Jean. *The Moral Judgment of the Child.* Trans. M. Gabain. New York: Free Press, 1965.

Purkey, William W. *Self Concept and School Achievement.* Englewood Cliffs, N.J.: Prentice-Hall, 1970.

Raths, Louis E., Merrill Harmin, and Sidney B. Simon. *Values and Teaching*. Columbus, Ohio: Merrill, 1966.

Rokeach, Milton. *Beliefs, Attitudes and Values: A Theory of Organization and Change*. San Francisco: Jossey-Bass, 1968.

Rokeach, Milton. *The Nature of Human Values*. New York: Free Press, 1973.

Rokeach, Milton. *The Open and Closed Mind*. New York: Basic Book, 1960.

Sullivan, Edmund V. *Moral Learning: Findings, Issues and Questions*. New York: Paulist Press, 1975.

Taba, Hilda, and Deborah Elkins. *With Focus on Human Relations*. Washington, D.C.: American Council on Education, 1950.

Triandis, Harry C. *Attitude and Attitude Change*. New York: Wiley, 1971.

Zuckerman, David W., and Robert E. Horn. *The Guide to Simulation Games for Education and Training*. Lexington, Mass.: Information Resources, 1973.

MODULE VI

MODULE VI

Improving Instruction: Significant Variables in a Learning System

A dialog is more than alternating monologs.
SICILIAN PROVERB

CHAPTER 18

Structuring and Managing the Instructional Environment

Like individuals, no two classrooms are alike. Each one has a unique identity created from the people who inhabit it, the activities they pursue there, and the ways that they physically transform it. When one says that a particular classroom is "warm," "cold," "inviting," "dismal," "cheerful," "exciting," "dynamic," "deadly," "repressive," and the like, its peculiar identity is being revealed.

Many elements, tangible and intangible, describable and undefinable, combine to create this classroom environment. Seldom can a teacher or even a trained observer spot and infer all of the elements. Learning more about them and how they affect the quality of life within a classroom can influence the course of social studies instruction. In this chapter we will examine three aspects of a classroom's identity: socioemotional climate, management procedures, and provisions for individual differences. These facets do not begin to exhaust the list of important considerations, nor will each of them have the same degree of importance in each classroom. They are significantly crucial variables to consider for any subject-matter area, but they are perhaps especially important for social studies instruction.

SOCIOEMOTIONAL CLIMATE

The expression "socioemotional climate" refers to the generalized attitudes shared by all members within a class that are usually reflected in social interaction. There are a number of different ways of characterizing socioemotional climate within a classroom, depending on which interactions one wishes to focus on and with what degree of intensity. This point is explored in more detail in Chapter 19. At its most basic index, the socioemotional climate may be said to be positive or negative. Many factors probably contribute to a positive climate and one can only speculate about some of them. It would seem that a rich array of sensory stimuli such as pictures, objects, and varied activities would be an important factor, especially for younger children. Such stimuli should encourage questions, reflection, and sharing of reactions and should make students eager to enter the classroom. Similarly the vague quality of "enthusiasm" on the part of the teacher would seem to be an ingredient of climate building. One teacher made it a practice to always start out the day by walking briskly into the room, smiling at the students,

and greeting them cheerfully, no matter how he felt or what his relationship with the class was. This is a modest illustration of enthusiasm and perhaps even a bit contrived, but more often than not it will help produce a positive climate.

Another way to gauge socioemotional climate is to consider the degree to which it is permissive, open, or authoritarian. These characteristics may be represented on a continuum, as shown in Figure 18.1.

Figure 18.1
Socioemotional climate characteristics

Permissive · Open · Authoritarian

One author describes the differences in the characteristics this way:

> It is important not to equate an open, understanding and democratic classroom with a permissive one. The open-democratic class requires order, discipline and the teacher to be himself as much as the pupils are themselves. This means if the teacher is annoyed he ought to express it and if he is happy, that should be expressed also. Annoying behavior isn't legislated out of existence in the democratic classroom like in the authoritarian classroom nor is it ignored as in the permissive classroom, but instead it is dealt with directly.
>
> In the authoritarian school the principal or teachers permit the student to behave only in certain ways thus remaining the dominant adult. In the open situation the teacher or principal tries to deal with what he feels, what the students feel and then tries to work out a solution acceptable to both. . . .
>
> To have an open school, the teachers have to learn to go with the class, to respond to their desire to learn about things and not cut them off in order to get through the district curriculum. We have long underestimated the ability of the students, their intelligence and their capacity to assume responsibility. Since it is no longer realistic or for the student's best good, we should accept them as partners in all activities we conduct with them. The democratic development of the stable limits, restrictions and the communal solving of problems is a crucial part in the development of freedom in the open classroom as the arbitrary imposition of them is central to control in the authoritarian class.[1]

A third way of viewing classroom climate is to examine the extent to which the teacher and each individual child contributes to decisions about what is to be learned and how it is to be learned. Anne Bussis and E. A. Chittenden have developed the scheme shown in Figure 18.2 for assessing the relative degrees of teacher and child contributions to decision making.

Figure 18.2 Schema for viewing classroom climate

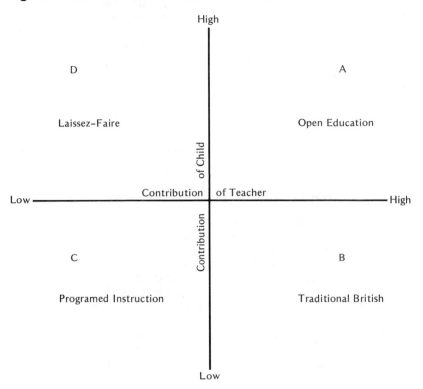

Source: Anne M. Bussis and E. A. Chittenden, *Analysis of an Approach to Open Education* (Princeton, N.J.: Educational Testing Service, 1970).

Those classrooms that Bussis and Chittenden would characterize as *open education* fall in quadrant A; that is, such classrooms reflect a high degree of child and teacher participation in instructional decision making. An example of a quadrant B classroom, they suggest, would be a traditional British (substitute *American*) setting. Programed instruction would be an example of quadrant C, while the *laissez-faire* ("do your own thing") classroom would fall in quadrant D.[2]

CLASSROOM MANAGEMENT PROCEDURES

"None of those ed courses ever prepared me for this."
"Those kids don't need a teacher, they need a warden."
"I tried to be nice to them and all I got was dumped on."
"I just can't control them."

Perhaps one of the overriding concerns of new teachers is whether they will be able to "control" their classes. A class that is out of control and bent on unproductive or destructive pursuits is an ugly and demoralizing sight. It is much more so when one is in the center of it and is responsible for redirecting it. The feeling one has is of complete powerlessness and incompetence.

No effective instruction can occur in the midst of a maelstrom, nor can children have any sense of stability and security. Classroom management therefore merits at least brief consideration as a variable in social studies instruction. Unfortunately most books and articles that deal extensively with the topic tend to be dominantly bromidic or behavioristic in their approach. Bromides of the sort "Don't smile until Christmas" occasionally prove to be of value in specific situations but are useless if not dangerous as generalizations. Moreover such approaches obscure the more urgent need to develop some rationale of what it is one is trying to accomplish with discipline and how such a rationale can reasonably be reconciled with a realistic assessment of what given students expect from a teacher. The behaviorist or behavior-modification-perspective on management, while quite effective in one-to-one or one-to-small-group situations, often presents serious administrative problems in whole class settings. Furthermore, employed totally it sanctions an approach to learning based wholly on extrinsic reinforcements—such as "if you do this, you will get that"—that may conflict with other learning patterns a teacher is trying to encourage.

A behavior modification approach to classroom management stresses clear specification of rules and norms and the systematic application of reinforcement for exhibiting desired behavior. In summarizing the basic principles of this approach, Wesley Becker and his associates suggest that teachers should:

1. Specify in a positive way the rules that are the basis for your reinforcement. Emphasize the behavior you desire by praising children who are following the rules. Rules are made important by providing reinforcement for following them. Rules may be different for different kinds of work, study, or play periods. Limit the rules to five or less. As the children learn to follow the rules, repeat them less frequently, but continue to praise good classroom behavior.

2. Relate the children's performance to the rules. Praise behavior, not the child. Be specific about behavior that exemplifies paying attention or working hard: "That's *right*, you're a hard worker." "You watched the board all the time I was presenting the example. That's paying attention." "That's a good answer. You listened very closely to my question." "Jimmy is really working hard. He'll get the answer. You'll see." Relax the rules between work periods. Do not be afraid to have fun with your children when the work period is over.

3. Catch the children being good. Reinforce behavior incompatible with that which you wish to eliminate. Reinforce behavior that will

    be most beneficial to the child's development. In the process of eliminating disruptive behavior, focus on reinforcing tasks important for social and cognitive skills.

4. Ignore disruptive behavior unless someone is getting hurt. Focus your attention on the children who are working well in order to prompt the correct behavior from the children who are misbehaving.
5. When you see a persistent problem behavior, look for the reinforcer. It may be your own behavior.[3]

The authors go on to suggest some general rules for planning a classroom day.[4]

1. Planning of activities should take into account the fact that not all children will finish at the same time. To provide for this phenomenon, a secondary *desirable* activity should be given as an outlet for the children when their primary assignment is completed.
2. There should be clear and systematic reminders as to what each child should be doing or is to do next. This process may be accomplished through such devices as color-coded name tags and yarn necklaces, signs, blackboard messages, individual folders, check-out stations, and turn-in boxes.
3. A day-to-day routine that is consistent should be established. Completing one task then signals that the next should begin.
4. Motivation is built into the instructional program when the completion of one assignment is automatically rewarded by the beginning of a new desired activity. Finishing an assigned activity means that a child gets to do something that is pleasing to him or her.
5. Periodically, the instructional program should include a change of pace. This might be in the order or type of activities.

    An alternative approach to dealing with classroom management procedures is generally based on humanistic principles. This approach is reflected in the writings of A. S. Neill, Carl Rogers, and others.[5] In many respects, however, it requires a systemwide (school) commitment to implement, although any teacher may apply the principles in his or her own classroom.

    In his books *Reality Therapy* and *Schools Without Failure,* William Glasser offers a concrete series of steps that individual teachers and school systems might employ to deal with behavioral problems in a humanistic way.[6] His approach emphasizes dealing with behavioral problems through a five-step process of (1) showing the student that you care about him or her, (2) having the student name and admit to the problem, (3) helping the student make value judgments about the misbehavior, (4) helping the student name the consequences of the misbehavior if necessary and appropriate, and (5) working with the student to establish a plan to alter the misbehavior. Glasser's approach emphasizes isolating individual students and treating their behavioral problem as a personal issue that has undesirable consequences for all. Rather than being primarily concerned with rule maintenance in the classroom, the teacher's role is to help a student confront and deal with his or her behavior.

Bromides, behavior-modification, and humanistically oriented techniques all *can* contribute ideas and strategies toward the development of a sound and integrated rationale. A set of effective well-integrated procedures relating to classroom management, consistent with the objectives of the instructional program, however, will depend more on the personality resources of the teacher, the expectations of a given group of students, and the tasks to be performed and how they are carried out than on any absolute set of disciplining procedures.

STUDENT EXPECTATIONS

Mario Fantini and Gerald Weinstein present the following case of a new teacher meeting her class for the first time:

Teacher: Hello (embarrassed laugh) . . . I guess we're all in here together and . . . um . . . I wonder why . . . we are in here. . . . What we're doing here . . . um . . . Perhaps we should begin so we can talk to each other by telling everybody our names. I'm Mary Miller and you are . . .
Bill: Bill Brown.
Teacher: Bill Brown? And you are . . . (Prolonged pause)
Jane: Oh . . . um . . . Jane. Jane Williams.
Teacher: Jane Williams? And you are . . . ?
Bob: Who'm I?
Teacher: Yes.
Bob: Bob.
Teacher: Bob? Now Bill, do you know Bob . . . did you know each other before? And . . . Jane—is that right?
Jane: Um-hmmmmmmmmm.
Teacher: Did you know each other?
Bob: Naw . . . I don't know them.
Teacher: You don't know them? I guess you're going to get to know them, and I guess we're all going to get to know each other. If you remember my name, like I try to remember yours. . . . I-I'll try pretty hard . . . I'm pretty dumb on names . . . (Class doesn't seem to be listening) Well, I think . . . we're all here together . . .
Bill: Can I get a drink?
Teacher: Um—wait a second to discuss that.
Bill: Well, can't I get a drink and not discuss it?
Teacher: I think maybe it might be a little more fun if we all talked about it.
Bill: (with exaggerated desperation) I'm thirsty.
Teacher: You're thirsty? Do you (hesitantly) . . . are there any rules in this school about drinks and stuff?

> *Jane:* Don't you know the rules? (Teacher suffers ridicule from stu-
> dents because she doesn't know rules)
> *Teacher:* Wha . . . Wh-who is the school for? Who makes the rules
> for you?
> *Jane:* The principal.
> *Teacher:* Why does he make them?
> *Bill:* I'll be right back.
> *Teacher:* O.K. (Bill leaves)[7]

The authors note that "In less than fifteen minutes, this teacher had no class."[8] Students—just as the teacher—have expectations on how the members of the class are to conduct themselves. While a teacher may not wish to use children's expectations as his or her own standard— especially if the students are accustomed to authoritarian models—he or she must begin with them. Once role credibility has·been established a teacher can move in the direction of behavioral norms that correspond to his or her notion of what is needed to facilitate learning.

Larry Cuban's remarks concerning inner-city classes are relevant to this point:

> Students, for example, expect a teacher to lay down rules, hand out
> texts, demand silence, and assign homework—in short to run a tight
> ship. These expectations don't preclude students testing the limits of
> the teacher's ability to enforce the rules; it is part of the early trading
> off that marks the struggle between teacher and class. If the teacher
> uses the techniques of control satisfactorily while simultaneously
> proving to children that he can teach, the class will settle into a
> routine comfortable to them. But, if the teacher cannot conform to
> their expectations or has strong doubts about his use of authority, then
> clever minds click, strategies change, and tactics shift: another
> teacher, regardless of his goodwill exits crying, cursing, and totally
> exhausted. . . .
>
> · · ·
>
> The balance of power in a classroom is so fragile; teachers seldom
> wish to jeopardize an uneasy truce by changing tactics between
> September and June. Thus, the trap. What teachers must learn is to
> adapt the shopping list of rules to their personality and use them as
> tools to gain the respect of youngsters; then still preserving the rela-
> tionship, re-fashion with those very same tools and additional ones
> the old forms to re-define limits, learning and teacher-student inter-
> actions.[9]

PINPOINTING PROBLEMS

One of the valuable contributions of behavioral modification tech-niques is the system of pinpointing and assessing problems. In a rela-tively simple fashion, it organizes data on the extent of problems and provides quick information on gradual improvements, if any. Seldom does immediate dramatic improvement in serious discipline problems occur. A student who is a chronic fighter in class does not usually stop overnight. By isolating such deviant behavior and recording its incidence each hour or day for a period of time, a teacher can notice an improvement trend or an actual increase in misbehavior. Moreover, by noting the patterns and context of incidence, a teacher may get some ideas for remedies. Suppose Peter constantly creates problems in the 30-minute period before lunch. The inference is that deprived physiological needs get asserted through aggression. The teacher with such data can move in several directions, beginning with a verification from Peter that his or her inference is correct. Simply sharing his or her data with him may be enough to make him begin to control his own behavior. Other strategies might be to suggest a larger breakfast, making provisions for a snack period, or simple isolation during the 30-minute period.

Not all patterns are as easily spotted as temporal ones, however. Another student may be chronically disruptive after getting back marked work; someone else may be unruly on days that the art teacher appears, in anticipation of some feelings of inadequacy and incompetence. A record of pinpointed behavioral incidents needs to be examined carefully in light of what a child may have been thinking about or what was happening within a child's surroundings at the time. Often only the student can clear up the mystery of the cause. A record of his or her pattern should help him or her to develop a more adequate explanation.

Behavioral records need not be complicated, and students themselves can often cooperate in the data collection. Fantini and Weinstein quote an incidence of where a distraught beginning teacher was assisted through the use of pinpointing techniques with recording responsibilities delegated to students within her class:

> Nervous, frantic and concerned with the disorder and chaos in her classroom, a beginning teacher was unnerved by the apparent lack of progress of the class and by her own inability to see any sort of organization within each student. Her supervisor was reminded of a personal experience in the first few months after her daughter was born. He was, in his own words, "going nuts." After only a few weeks, he had become convinced that the baby was planning to spend the rest of her life screaming, helpless and showing no progress in any kind of mature development. The thing that kept him "sane" during this period was initiated when he recalled the charts he'd seen in a child-development book. At this point, he decided to chart his daughter's behavior and progress and proceeded to draw up a plethora of charts and graphs which kept him busy and helped him to see that within the chaos there was actual learning taking place.
>
> "Why don't you try this with your class?" he suggested to the distraught teacher. "But, instead of doing all the work yourself, let the kids make the charts, since they're going to be working on graphing in arithmetic anyway. You can set up two or three things to watch for,

such as: How many times did the teacher pay the class a compliment? How many times did someone leave his seat without permission? How much teaching and learning time did we have for social studies?"

The young teacher decided to try it, and the next day delegated to various pupils, especially to the discipline problem students, the responsibility for keeping score on a particular question. At the end of the day, they compiled the data on line or bar graphs and put them on display. The progress through the entire week was handled this way so that the class and the teacher could see it.

This control technique pinpointed the goals and gave the teacher and students more of a feeling of security. It's a possible way to structure discussions. For example, a teacher might raise the question: "Why do we have problems with our discussions?" The class could then make a list of factors that disturb and hinder discussion. This could be translated into questions to chart, such as: How many people didn't call out today? How many times did the teacher have to remind the class of discussion rules? How long were we able to discuss today? In this way, too, the students can be made aware of their own behavioral progress while simultaneously learning the skills of graphing.[10]

Simple forms for recording and charting incidents of misbehavior appears in the work of Madsen and Madsen, who give one a lucid and readable account of how behavior-modification techniques may be applied.[11]

RESEARCH FINDINGS

Despite widespread teacher concern for management tactics, little research exists on the topic. One of the more comprehensive and systematic studies was conducted by Jacob Kounin, who concludes:

It is possible, then, to delineate concrete aspects of teacher behavior that lead to managerial success in a classroom. These techniques of classroom management apply to emotionally disturbed children in regular classrooms as well as to nondisturbed children. They apply to boys as well as to girls. (We found no consistent differences between boys and girls in behavior scores, nor did we find that scores for managerial success correlated with the boy-girl ratios of the classroom studies.) These techniques of classroom management apply to the group and not merely to individual children. They are techniques of creating an effective classroom ecology and learning milieu. One might note that none of them necessitate punitiveness or restrictiveness.

This focus upon group managerial techniques in classrooms is intended to go beyond simplified slogans such as "create rapport" or "make it interesting." Neither does this focus entail a preoccupation with such characteristics as "friendly," "warm," "patient," "understanding," "love for children," and similar attributes of people in general. These desirable attributes will not manage a classroom.[12]

The core of Kounin's findings relate to managing a classroom and preventing misbehavior, rather than meting out disciplinary action. After examining a series of classrooms, he discovered that the way in which the teacher handled classroom situations in general determined whether positive student behavior was likely to be the norm. Teachers who had a *high* degree of work involvement and a *low* degree of deviant behavior in their classrooms demonstrated consistently the following characteristics:[13]

1. *Withitness:* Communicating that one knows what is going on in the classroom.
2. *Overlapping:* Being able to attend to two issues simultaneously.
3. *Smoothness:* Managing physical movement from one activity to another without jerkiness, distractions, or temporary halts.
4. *Momentum:* Keeping physical actvities moving at an appropriate pace.
5. *Group alerting:* Degree to which the teacher attempts to involve nonreciting children in the recitation task.
6. *Accountability:* Extent to which children are held responsible for the tasks during recitations.
7. *Valence:* Making statements that point out that an activity has something special to it.
8. *Challenge arousal:* Making statements that draw attention to the challenge in a task.
9. *Seatwork variety:* Planning varied work activities for children at their seats.
10. *Challenge:* Intellectual challenge in seatwork.

Withitness and *overlapping* require a teacher to give evidence that he or she actually knows what is happening in the classroom at all times (even when his or her back is to the class). During overlapping a teacher keeps the focus on the class activity and as unobtrusively as possible also immediately attends to deviant behavior. *Smoothness* and *momentum* relate to the degree to which children can be moved from one instructional area and activity to another without interruption or returns to the previous activity and without getting bogged down on a topic. *Group alerting* and *accountability*, respectively, are characterized by statements such as, "Suppose we all think about the answer. Whom shall I call?" "Everyone hold up and show off your pictures of your families." A teacher employing *valence* and *challenge arousal* would attempt to build up the positive features of an activity, as an attraction, and would present it in the form of a problem or challenge. The last two characteristics, *seatwork variety* and *challenge,* specifically concern the characteristics of work that children are given to complete apart from recitation sessions.

PROVIDING FOR INDIVIDUAL DIFFERENCES

Perhaps no other topic has been more discussed in education with as few established conclusions as an outgrowth. Part of the problem results from confusion over what "individualization" means. To some educators it means allowing children to work alone, progressing at their own rates of learning as opposed to the pace that a teacher might establish for a total class. For others individualization refers to giving students maximum freedom in selecting what they are to learn and/or the ways in which they are to learn it. A further source of confusion is the tendency to treat administrative procedures for individualizing instruction as *methods*. These procedures include ability groupings, special classes, team teaching, accelerating students, vertical grouping, and nongraded schools.

Any clear notion of what individualized instruction is to be must begin with an identification of the individual differences among students that are to be given priority attention. Numerous studies have shown that various learning differences can be related to a variety of ways in which individuals differ, such as attending behavior (attention to task), sex, race, learning rates (how long a task takes to learn), interests, reading abilities, task-related knowledge (prerequisites), learning styles, personality types (introvert, extrovert, etc.), thinking styles (global, articulated), and developmental stages. This is not to say that the variables directly cause the learning differences. The nature of such relationships is not always clear. Not all of these variables are relevant for all learning tasks, and they are not of equal significance with respect to their effects on learning. Some are also interrelated; females, for example tend to have higher reading abilities in the early grades, all things being equal.

Given the many variables related to learning differences, it is not surprising that there are many different approaches to "individualized instruction" (hereafter referred to as i.i.) with so little in common! Teacher Jones, who uses four sets of reading materials all at different reading levels to explain the American Revolution, claims *he* is applying i.i. Smith, with the same topic, disseminates behavioral objectives and identifies resources, letting each student work at his or her own rate to complete the tasks, and claims *she* is employing i.i. Still a third approach to the same topic by Doe allows her students to decide what they wish to study about the topics, and she too claims to be using i.i. And so it goes.

A teacher who wishes to individualize social studies instruction to some degree, then, must isolate the individual differences among children that he or she considers the most important and feasible. Since most systems for i.i. will have to be designed "from the ground up" for a given set of classrooms or school, the available expertise and other resources must also be an important realistic consideration. Five different individual differences and i.i. procedures associated with them are outlined below: learning rates, interests, learning styles, cognitive styles, reading levels.

LEARNING RATES

This is probably the most common basis on which instruction is individualized in the classroom today. In this system a student is free to work at his or her own rate to complete a specified unit of work before moving on to a new unit. Some time deadline, however, may be agreed upon in advance. Most of the contemporary approaches in this vein employ some form of contract or a self-pacing, self-instructional "packet" that goes under several names (e.g., LAPS for Learning Activity Packets). The actual packets and contracts may vary considerably; some packets contain everything that a student requires to answer the questions raised, while others combine instruction with references to ancillary materials. Some contracts are detailed references not only to tasks on which teacher and students mutually agree but also to specific resources to be used to complete the task and the timetable for such. Other contracts merely note tasks and due dates. The "contract" notion refers to an agreement that both parties (teacher and student and occasionally parents, too) enter into and sign. A typical basic packet would contain a series of integrated objectives, related readings, activities, and materials, and pre- and posttests.

All i.i. approaches within this framework can trace their basic lineage to the Winnetka and Dalton plans of over half a century ago. They emphasize, but are not limited to, more easily specified types of learning outcomes and self-directed learning. At their best they permit relatively easy administration of a system that gives maximum individual control of the rate of learning for a structured task in an interesting fashion for goal-directed learners. A skillfully designed programed text is, in effect, such a "packet." At their worst they atomize knowledge into bits of dull facts, isolate students who need teacher attention and peer intellectual interaction, and stifle imagination and intellectual excitement. Such materials resemble workbooks and "questions at the back of the chapter." Design of effective and stimulating packets requires some skill and considerable time. Contracts are considerably easier to construct and allow for a great deal of variation and flexibility.

INTERESTS

This approach places emphasis on student selection of objectives to be pursued. Often a range of topic options are presented to students who are free to select any one and develop a project, alone or with other students. Another variation is the "learning center" or "activity center" notion common to many open-classroom situations. In this approach centers or stations may be designated with series of alternative activities in various subject-matter areas. Students are free to develop their daily and weekly schedules as they choose, although they may be required to complete a minimum number of activities in each subject area each week, month, or semester. Open, unstructured centers for reading or playing when scheduled work is completed are usually included as options. The contents of centers are changed periodically, and students may propose or prepare center activities themselves.

The following case illustrates how centers may be developed for use with large numbers of students and can be correlated and integrated with other instructional approaches.[14] As reported by the teacher who developed the instruction, eighty-one fifth graders and three teachers were to be involved.

> To begin the unit, each teacher will be responsible for teaching one topic to three different groups of students. One teacher will teach "The Costs of Production," another will teach "Supply and Demand," and the third will teach "Paying the Price." Each teacher will present the same topic for three sessions, with each session consisting of three class periods. The children will be grouped by homerooms. For the first session each teacher will teach his or her topic to his or her homeroom. For the second session each group of students will move to a new teacher who will again present his or her topic in three class periods. At the completion of the third session each teacher will have taught his or her topic for three sessions, and each child will have studied each of the topics.
>
> Following these sessions, the children will have an opportunity to hear talks by various men in the community concerning their business

endeavors. These men, all fathers of children in our fifth grade, have been invited by the author to speak at our school. The speakers are: (1) a laundry owner, (2) a post office worker, (3) an orthopedic surgeon, (4) a director of marketing, (5) a car salesman, (6) a truck driver, (7) a vice-president of a manufacturing company, and (8) a small business owner. These men will discuss costs of production and distribution, credit economy, profit, competition, services, supply and demand, buying and selling processes, raw materials, interest, credit, monopolies, and public utilities.

Class trips have been planned as a part of the unit. Some trips have already been taken in order to schedule them all before the close of school. The rest of the trips will be taken during the economics unit. Some involve all the fifth graders, while at other times students will choose one trip of three, thereby allowing three separate groups to visit three separate places simultaneously.

At least three math class will also be devoted to studying a mathematical aspect of economics. Each teacher will teach his or her math class decimals, percent, interest, and budgeting incomes. Math problems will be devised that are based on these concepts. The problems will focus on the kinds of economical choices a fifth grader faces in his daily living. The relationship of everyday economics to the mathematical problems presented will be emphasized.

After the above activities have started, the learning centers listed below will be used by our fifth graders. Many of the centers are intended to reinforce ideas already presented, whereas others will attempt to present new ideas. Still other centers will provide opportunities for interested students to study aspects which are indirectly related to economics.

Each child will have his or her own 5″ × 8″ card listing all the centers. Each card will indicate which centers are mandatory for the student and which ones are recommended. A student may work, however, at any other center he or she desires, provided he or she has fulfilled the required work.

The titles and components of some of the forty-one learning centers the teacher developed are listed below:

1. For Detectives Only
   Poster
   Direction sheet
   Mystery packets
2. To Whom Are These Items Valuable?
   Directions with answer sheet
   Poster
3. Lost and Found
   Worksheet
   News clipping

4. What Would You Buy?
   Directions
   Magazines
   Example
5. Cultural Values
   Chart with directions
6. Products and Consumers
   Directions
   Worksheet
   Poster
7. Interdependence in the Production and Consumption of Goods
   Two question sheets
8. Who Produces Goods and Services?
   Poster with four sets of directions
      a. Mural
      b. Project/chart/diorama
      c. Chart
      d. Interviews.
9. Finding Out About Chocolate
   Workers involved in production
   Worksheet to be used in conjunction with book, *The Story of Chocolate*
   Instruction for drawing
10. Scrapbook Project
    Direction sheet
11. Pick a Career
    Directions
    Books
    Answer sheet
12. A. New Clothes for Summer Camp
       Directions
       Sears order forms—Sears catalogue
    B. Planning a Camping Trip
       Directions
       Sears order forms—Sears catalogue
13. Outside School Activities
    A. To do at home or at the supermarket
       Directions
    B. Say it graphically
       Directions
14. What Does Your Cat Eat?
    Worksheet
15. Economic Choices
    Two question sheets
16. What Happened to These Items Before You Bought Them?
    Directions
    Box containing nail, soda can, cotton blouse, knitted hat, and leather wallet

17. Rugged Materialists Needed
    Directions
    Box of scrap materials

Emphasis in an interest approach to i.i. is on decentralizing the classroom, and the teacher moves from center to center helping students as needed. All or only part of the daily classroom activities may be based on centers. Many of the management responsibilities are handled by students who are required to keep record folders of their completed and ongoing activities. Frequently students are required to complete a projection or contract of what they will accomplish within a certain period, subject to possible renegotiation.

At best learning centers develop a high degree of interest in learning and encourage self-determination and sustainment of intellectual growth. At worst they provide a chaotic or a sterile environment in which students who require structure flounder for lack of guidance on how to use their freedom or in which students drone away at workbook activities located in the centers.

LEARNING STYLES

The difference emphasized in this approach is that of how each student can best learn a given task. It assumes that each person has an optimal learning style and that this style differs from task to task. Not everyone will learn a given task in the same way, nor will a style of learning that one successfully employs for that task necessarily work well when the task is changed. Learning style refers to the *process*, not the medium, of instruction. A cassette, film, or filmstrip, for example, while contrasting media for a learner, offer essentially the same expository instructional process; a basically passive learner style is minimally required for all forms.

An i.i. system labeled *learning-style options* and developed by Martorella and Bishop is based on a series of learning tasks the student and teacher negotiate in the planning stage and on alternative process routes to accomplish the tasks.[15] The student selects the learning style for each task and helps keep a log of his or her style-task matches and reactions. This provides a learning-pattern profile for the student to consult in future decisions. The system minimally employs five learning-style options: self-generating, tutorial, cross-peer aid, guided program, and classroom directed. Students may select any one but must meet common objectives and share a common objective-assessment measure. The *self-generating option* frees students to accomplish objectives independently through any means they wish without any teacher structure. A *tutorial option* offers a modified alternative in that a student may consult with a teacher or aid to negotiate as much help as is needed. The *cross-peer aid* style matches the learner with someone in his or her class or another room or grade who has already learned the task and is willing to teach it in their style. *Guided-program* options provide teacher-prepared self-instructional packages that permit the student to work alone using designated resources. One final option is a conventional *classroom-directed* approach, in which a teacher moves through an objective-related series of lessons with a small group.

Learning tasks may be general or specific; the major criterion is that they clearly communicate what is intended. They may also be limited or extended, requiring varying lengths of time from an hour to a week or more. Sample learning tasks might vary from "Learning how and why various shelters are constructed by people in different areas" to "What are some of the major reasons why the prices of some items continue to rise, some stay the same, and some go down?"

COGNITIVE STYLES

A sizable body of research findings over the past twenty years has established that an individual's typical ways of processing information may be identified. The term "style" refers to a way or pattern of thinking which one uses consistently in a variety of different intellectual activities, such as tackling a problem, determining how to relate to other people, and generally deciding how to organize the various aspects of his or her environment. One such approach is based on the ongoing studies of Herman Witkin and his associates at Educational Testing Service. In summary, Witkin has identified two basic styles: *global* (field-dependent) and *analytical* (field-independent).[16] Analytical persons tend to focus in on specific elements of a problem rather than on the whole issue. They are predominantly impersonal and little concerned with social amenities and interaction. They choose occupations and fields of study that emphasize abstractions and impersonal aspects, for example, engineering and mathematics.

In contrast, individuals identified as global characteristically tend to take into account the total dimensions of a problem rather than isolate segments of it. They are socially oriented, being inclined to seek out interaction with others and to take into account the points of view of others in their decisions. They are drawn to others, tend to have developed social skills and even to seek literal physical closeness to others. Not surprisingly global persons have been found to prefer occupations requiring involvement with others, such as elementary school teaching. Neither style may be labeled "better" or "worse," nor has either one been related to superior intellectual ability. They merely are decidedly different and relatively permanently so.

With respect to learning differences, again not surprisingly persons tend to do better at tasks that are closely related to their style characteristics. Another learning difference is that global persons do better with materials that are highly structured than with those requiring the learner to provide the structure. Analytical persons are much better able to handle the latter type of materials. Global students may also require more detailed instructions in problem-solving strategies or more specific statements of expected performance than analytical students, who may even do better when left to their own devices. Finally, some evidence also exists that global and analytical students tend to prefer teachers who correspond to their thinking style and vice versa. Witken states:

> Teachers and students matched for cognitive style described each other in highly positive terms whereas teachers and students who were mismatched showed a strong tendency to describe each other negatively. Especially important in its implications for how teachers evaluate their students' abilities was the finding that teachers valued more highly the intellects of students similar to themselves in cognitive style, and not only the personal characteristics of these students. Similarly, students viewed more favorably the personal characteristics and cognitive competence of teachers similar to themselves in cognitive style.
>
> Findings such as these raise the question of whether it is not too simplistic to speak just of "good teachers" and "bad teachers," even though by some criteria of competence such designations may be justified. It would seem more appropriate to think of teachers in terms of "good" or "bad" for what kind of student. Similarly, on the student's side, it may be useful to think not only of "good" or "bad" students but "good" or "bad" with what kind of teacher.[17]

Taking cognitive styles into account would require that a teacher try to match learning environments to the students' style whenever feasible or minimally to take styles into account and make such options available. Treating children differently in this respect will be more fair than treating them all the same. Several easily administered paper-and-pencil measures for children to assess global and analytical dimensions are available. One involves drawings of the human body as described by Witkin and his associates in *Psychological Differentiation: Studies of Development*.[18] The other device is called the Embedded Figures Test (children's form) and is available from Consulting Psychologists Press, 577 College Ave., Palo Alto, Calif. 94306. As always, labels must be used with caution; a category derived from a test does not substitute for dealing with each child's ongoing needs.

READING LEVELS

Statements that so-and-so reads at a 2.5 or 5.8 reading level or that a particular book is written at a third-grade reading level are commonplace. Serious professionals who deal with students' reading difficulties and achievements realize that assessment of individual capabilities is far more complex than assigning a score to students or determining how successfully one can verbalize written symbols on a page. The deceptive simplicity of the act of reading under examination has sired reams of literature and generated years of controversy.

For the neophyte, however, who wishes to deal in a basic way with individual differences in reading abilities, there are several easily assessed general benchmarks available. Using several basic formulas, one can establish some rough guidelines on variations in reading levels in materials. Once the reading levels of given materials are established, an approximate match can be made with a student using his or her standardized reading score. Again a warning: A reading-level label for a student should be used to *increase* learning options rather than to restrict or retard a child.

One of the easiest reading formulas to use is the Fry Readability Formula. It involves counting the number of syllables and average number of sentences per representative 100-word passages. This formula also correlates highly with others, such as the Science Research Associates, the Dale-Chall, and the Flesch reading formulas. To obtain a reading-level score, select a representative passage of the reading material. Count out three sets of 100 words, excluding all proper nouns, near the begin-

Figure 18.3
Graph for estimating readability

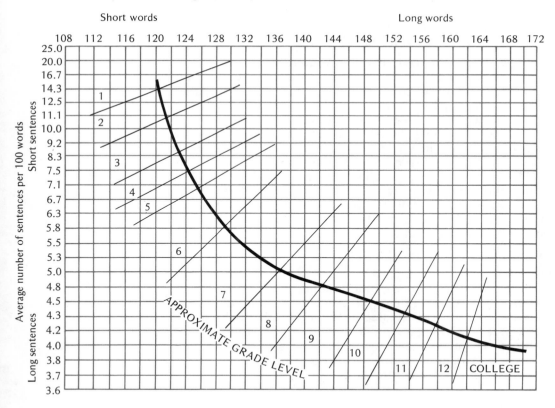

Source: Edward Fry, "A Readability Formula That Saves Time," *Journal of Reading,* 2 (April), 1968, p. 577.

ning, middle, and end. Mark the spots and count and record the number of syllables in the passage. Next count and record to the nearest tenth of a sentence the number of sentences in the passages. Divide each set of total by three to get an average.

Locate the spot where the syllable and sentence counts correspond on the graph shown in Figure 18.3. The material may be rated with the grade level noted on the graph. If you are not sure that the passage selected is representative, check random selections from the beginning, middle, and end of the work.

The children themselves can also assess whether the reading level of materials is appropriate for them using the *cloze* procedure. A child needs a partner who will cover with masking tape, construction paper bits, or whatever every fifth word in some 100-word passage of text. A sample result might look something like this:

> On my arrival in   new world I took some   by force from the   island to which I   in order that they   learn our language. These   are still travelling with   , and although they have   with us now for   long time they continue   entertain the idea that   have descended from heaven.   our arrival at any   place they publish this,   out immediately, with a   voice to the other   , "Come, come and look   beings of a celestial upon which both women   men, children and adults": . . .[19]

The reader then tries to fill in the missing words. If the student can come up with *exact* replacements for half or more of the missing words, the material probably is not too difficult. While this test may seem arbitrary, if not invalid, it has a close relationship to more complex tests of information gain from reading.

NOTES

[1] Gerald Prince, "Permissive, Open, Authoritarian," unpublished paper, n.d.

[2] Anne M. Bussis and E. A. Chittenden, *An Analysis of an Approach to Open Education* (Princeton, N.J.: Educational Testing Service, 1970).

[3] Wesley C. Becker et al., *Teaching: A Course in Applied Psychology* (Chicago: Science Research Associates, 1971), p. 171.

[4] Ibid., pp. 176–177.

[5] A. S. Neill, *Summerhill* (New York: Hart, 1961); Carl Rogers, *Freedom to Learn* (Columbus, Ohio: Merrill, 1969). See also Herbert R. Kohl, *The Open Classroom* (New York Review, 1969), and D. H. Clark and A. Kadis, *Humanistic Teaching* (Columbus, Ohio: Merrill, 1972).

[6] William Glasser, *Reality Therapy* (New York: Harper & Row, 1972); William Glasser, *Schools Without Failure* (New York: Harper & Row, 1961).

[7] Mario D. Fantini and Gerald Weinstein, *The Disadvantaged: Challenge to Education* (New York: Harper & Row, 1968), pp. 316–317.

[8] Ibid., p. 317.

[9] Larry Cuban, *To Make a Difference: Teaching in the Inner City* (New York: Free Press, 1970), pp. 170–171.

[10] Fantini and Weinstein, op. cit., pp. 320–321.

[11] Charles Madsen and C. H. Madsen, *Parents/Children Discipline* (Englewood Cliffs, N.J.: Prentice-Hall, 1972).

[12] Jacob S. Kounin, *Discipline and Group Management in Classrooms* (New York: Holt, Rinehart & Winston, 1970), p. 144.

[13] Ibid., pp. 143–144.

[14] This discussion is adapted from materials provided by Joan Ferry, a teacher in the Perkasie School District, Bucks County, Pa.

[15] Peter H. Martorella and John Bishop, "An Approach to Individualizing Instruction Based Upon Learning-Style Alternatives," unpublished paper, Temple University, 1971.

[16] Herman A. Witkin and Carol Ann Moore, "Cognitive Style and the Teaching-Learning Process," paper presented at the annual meeting of the American Educational Research Association, Chicago, April 15–20, 1974. See also H. A. Witkin, *The Role of Cognitive Style in Academic Performance and in Teacher-Student Relations* (Princeton, N.J.: Educational Testing Service, 1972) and Wallace P. Judd, "Your Students: Global or Articulated?" *Learning (December 1973)*, 58–60.

[17] Witkin, *The Role of Cognitive Style*, op. cit., p. 33.

[18] H. A. Witkin et al., *Psychological Differentiation: Studies of Development* (Potomac, Md.: Lawrence Erlbaum Associates, 1974).

[19] Christopher Columbus, "Throngs of Children to See Columbus," in *Colonial Children: Source-Readers in American History—No. 1* (New York: Macmillan, 1902), p. 6.

CHAPTER 19

Assessing Conditions in the Instructional Environment

Most people who set out to accomplish a task, including teachers, like to have some idea of how successful they have been. Similarly when we find ourselves in a complex situation with which we must cope, we usually stop and take stock of it. Both situations involve *assessment*. We assess relative degrees of success, whether it be in raising corn in our backyards or teaching social science concepts to children in our classes. Similarly we may assess what is involved in time, cost, and inconvenience in redecorating our homes or what is needed by way of changes in our classroom environments to prevent fighting and to increase cooperative behavior.

The former type of assessment is directed toward gauging *achievement,* while the latter focuses on *analysis*. Often the two types are used in a complementary fashion, as when student growth in an area is gauged and the causes for such are sought. Most teachers are familiar with a range of formal assessment *achievement* tools; fewer have acquired competencies with systematic assessment analysis tools.

ACHIEVEMENT ASSESSMENT

How do you know when the kids have learned anything? Just what *did* we accomplish this year? In recent years both professional educators and lay persons have become increasingly preoccupied with the assessment of instructional outcomes. A national program, sponsored through an unusual compact of the fifty states, was instituted in 1969 to help inform states about what educational objectives were being achieved for the dollars spent. The assessment dealt with ten areas of the curriculum, including citizenship education, representing a cross-section of schools in the United States.

Since the inception of this national program a number of states have instituted similar assessment programs for schools within their jurisdiction. In Pennsylvania, for example, the State Board of Education mandated the following in 1973:

> During the school years 1973–74, 1974–75 and 1975–76, the Department of Education will use the Educational Quality Assessment procedure to evaluate the effectiveness of the educational programs for all Commonwealth school districts based upon the Ten Goals of

Quality Education adopted by the State Board of Education. Public schools housing approximately one-third of the students enrolled in each of the three grades, 5, 8, 11, will be included in the assessment each year.[1]

The ten goals of quality education on which the Pennsylvania assessment is based are:

1. Help every child acquire the greatest possible understanding of himself or herself and appreciation of his or her worthiness as a member of society.
2. Help every child acquire understanding and appreciation of persons belonging to other social, cultural and ethnic groups.
3. Help every child acquire, to the fullest possible extent, mastery of the basic skills in the use of words and numbers.
4. Help every child acquire a positive attitude toward the learning process.
5. Help every child acquire the habits and attitudes associated with responsible citizenship.
6. Help every child acquire good health habits and an understanding of the conditions necessary for maintaining of physical and emotional well-being.
7. Give every child opportunity and encouragement to be creative in one or more fields of endeavor.
8. Help every child understand the opportunities open to him or her to prepare for a productive life and help each child to take full advantage of these opportunities.
9. Help every child to understand and appreciate as much as possible of human achievement in the natural sciences, the social sciences and the humanities and the arts.
10. Help every child to prepare for a world of rapid change and foreseeable demands in which continuing education through adult life should be a normal expectation.[2]

Assessment—especially at the state level—has inspired a great deal of heated debate. Its critics charge that it encourages standardization of instruction and establishes conventional standards of behavior as norms that all students should observe. This phenomenon occurs through the process of scoring unconventional or qualified answers on paper-and-pencil tests as wrong or of low value.

Consider a sample assessment item from one state's eighth-grade citizenship test. Any "no" response will contribute to a *low* score on the assessment, even though one might reasonably argue that such an arbitrary principal need not be informed of an accident. Whether such an item should be used to represent "citizenship" is similarly open to argument. In reply, supporters of across-school assessments maintain that without such measures, however imperfect, there can be no objective accountability for schools. Unless the progress of students is compared through external assessments, supporters continue, one cannot determine the relative effectiveness of schools.

Morton has broken a school window but did not mean to. If I were Morton, I would *tell the principal* or teacher about my breaking the window when I knew . . .

	YES	MAYBE	NO
1. The principal would make me stay after school.	0	0	0
2. My parents would have to pay for the window.	0	0	0
3. I would have to pay for the window.	0	0	0

The current structure of such assessment programs, as they relate to social studies, leaves much to be desired and may even prove to be dangerous where results are misinterpreted or misused. The use and evolution of these programs bear close, critical examination by teachers of social studies if they are to have a constructive function in the future.

Compared to national and statewide assessments, diagnostic data gathered *within an individual class* have fewer limitations and, if imperfect, fewer perils. A well-structured set of diagnostic tools can yield rich information for a teacher about himself or herself and about his or her students. The most common form of classroom diagnosis concerns student progress, as recorded by commercially developed or teacher-prepared tests. Many of these have been discussed in previous chapters in connection with measuring specific types of learning. The CSE's *Elementary School Test Evaluations* is a basic guide to such tests.[3] One of the most authoritative guides to diagnostic measures is the *Mental Measurements Yearbook,* published and updated periodically.[4] It provides a complete listing of assessment devices, along with critical reviews and data from authorities in the field. The *Yearbook* can be found in the reference section of most libraries.

Formal assessment data gathered on each child are generally stored in a cumulative record file that follows the child as he or she moves through the school system. Such files often contain information such as that shown in Figure 19.1. By federal law, all school systems receiving federal aid must now make such data public to students and parents.

ASSESSING INTERACTION PATTERNS

Apart from achievement assessment, there are a number of classroom dimensions contributing to effective learning that a teacher may examine. Foremost among them are the ways in which the teacher and students interact or communicate during instruction. Much of the way in which teachers and students interact with one another not only affects the degree and scope of the learning that takes place within a classroom

Figure 19.1 Page from Cumulative Record Folder

A/g Cumulative Record Folder

Name ___ LAST ___ FIRST ___ MIDDLE ___ Boy □ Girl □ Date of Birth ___ YEAR ___ MONTH ___ DAY ___ Type of Record Verifying Date of Birth ___ Born ___ CITY, COUNTY, OR PARISH ___ STATE OR COUNTRY

Date of Entrance ___ YEAR ___ MONTH ___ DAY ___ Beginner □ or School Last Attended ___ DISTRICT NO. OR NAME ___ GRADE ___ COUNTY, PARISH, OR CITY ___ STATE ___ Public □ Private - Parochial □ Accredited □ Unaccredited □

Parent's Name ___ FATHER OR GUARDIAN ___ Telephone No. ___ Place of Employment ___ Citizen Yes □ No □ Mother's Name ___

Parent's Residence ___ SCHOOL, DISTRICT NO. ___ TOWNSHIP AND COUNTY, PARISH, OR STREET AND CITY ___ STATE ___ Pupil's Address Use Pencil. ___ or With Whom Living or Different From Parent ___ Telephone No. ___ Tuition Data ___

Rank in Family ___ No. of Children in Family ___ Check if Living With: Grandparents □ Aunt □ Sister □ Boarding □

Changes in Residence, or Additional Data: ___

ELEMENTARY SCHOOL RECORD

		Aptitude or Special Interests — Enter Data With Dates
Grade Enrolled		
Name of Teacher		
Building		
School Year		
Semester		
Reading		
Language Arts		
Science		
Mathematics		
Spelling		
Social Studies		
History		
Handwriting		
Music		
Agriculture		
Health		
Art		
Phy. Ed.		
School Attitude		
Effort in Work		
Days Absent		
Times Tardy		
Promoted To		

Transfer, Withdrawal, Re-Entry Record

Date	T-W-R	From or To	Reason*

*1. Illness; 2. Death; 3. Change of Address; 4. Work; 5. Over School Age; 6. Expulsion; 7. Institutionalized; 8. Promoted; 9. Other.

Credits Sent To. ___

Employment Certificate. ___

Photograph With Date, Fingerprints, or Other Identification

EDUCATIONAL TESTS AND EVALUATIONS

School	Grade	Date	Test	Form	Score	Norm	Rank

Grade	Date	Test	Form	Score	Norm	Rank

Unclassified Records.

Source: American Guidance Service, Circle Pines, Minnesota, 1972.

but also influences the way students feel about learning and themselves.

Patterns of interaction within a classroom may be diagnosed from many frames of reference, ranging from unsophisticated to complex measures, requiring some knowledge of advanced statistical analysis and consideration of many variables. There are no simple diagnostic procedures that can produce definitive, unqualified generalizations about the interaction patterns within a classroom, but there are some basic tools that can yield relatively objective data on what may be impeding or facilitating communication and learning. These may be categorized as *verbal* and *nonverbal* diagnostic tools.

VERBAL DIAGNOSTIC TOOLS

One of our most important and most frequently used tools in teaching is our voice. It can convey pleasure, excitement, sorrow, sadness, apprehension, surprise, pride, envy, and myriad other emotions that facilitate or directly regulate our instruction. Surprisingly we are seldom conscious of this tool, nor do we use it to its fullest advantage. Voices come in all types, from monotonous and shrill ones to mellow, confident, and reassuring ones. In large measure we can control the quality and variation of our voices with some practice and monitoring.

In her book *Mastering Classroom Communication* Dorothy Grant Hennings dwells extensively on the vocal tendencies of teachers as a significant instructional variable.[5] In one section she suggests that teachers can examine their "vocal attractiveness" by asking the following:

Is my voice

high pitched	low pitched
soft	loud
monotonous	varied
fast	slow[6]

Then they can describe their voices in terms of ratings on each continuum. She suggests further that teachers who feel that some sort of vocal remediation is in order might profit from consulting Harriet Grim's *Practical Voice Training*.[7]

A considerable amount of research over the past twenty years has focused on the verbal interaction patterns that occur between teachers and students. Most of the studies employ a coding system to be used by an observer, based on a series of categories and a check-off system when a certain verbal behavior is observed. In many cases a tape recorder may be used in place of an observer, and the teacher can then analyze the interaction patterns. One such coding system employs twelve categories for coding teacher interactions with a group and is based on the work of Robert Bales.[8] The categories are summarized below.

Socio-Emotional Area: Positive
{
1. Seems friendly.
2. Dramatizes.
3. Agrees.
}

Task Area: Attempted Answers
{
4. Gives suggestions.
5. Gives opinion.
6. Gives information.
}

Task Area: Questions
{
7. Asks for information.
8. Asks for opinion.
9. Asks for suggestion.
}

Socio-Emotional Area: Negative
{
10. Disagrees.
11. Shows tension.
12. Seems unfriendly.[9]
}

In using the system a teacher would be observed (or would observe himself or herself on videotape) over a period of time, and each verbal specimen during a time interval of several seconds would be coded as one of the twelve categories. Over a lesson or several lessons a pattern of the teacher's verbal interactions can be established by analyzing the numbers of tallies in each category and the ratios of categories to one another. In *Mirrors for Behavior, III: An Anthology of Observation Instruments,* Anita Simon and E. Gil Boyer list ninety-eight additional observational schemes besides that of Bales.[10]

A basic diagnosis of interaction patterns, however, can be as simple as recording random segments of representative class discussions and determining who verbally monopolizes the discussion. For example, a teacher might decide to record the social studies periods on Tuesday, Thursday, and Friday. The first 5 minutes are discarded (since much of the initial procedural part of a lesson is probably teacher dominated). On different days, depending on the length of the instructional period, 15-minute segments of instruction would be recorded. On a purely quantitative basis a teacher can determine what approximate percentage of the time is spent on teacher vs. student talk, and whether this ratio satisfies the overall instructional goals he or she has set. The same data may be used to discover the types of questions that are most frequently asked and to examine how question-answer interactions are handled.

Teachers may construct their own observation forms to focus on whatever concerns they may have. A simple prototype that employs a gross five-point rating system is shown on the next pages.

I. Presentation of Material

5	4	3	2	1
Very Clear				Unclear

Objectives of Lesson

Comments: _____

5	4	3	2	1
Very High				Very Low

Interest Level Generated

Comments: _____

1	2	3	4	5
Very Poorly Prepared				Very Well Prepared

Preparation

Comments: _____

5	4	3	2	1
Well Ordered and Logical				Made No Sense

*Organization of
Instruction*

Comments: _____

1	2	3	4	5
Very Inadequate				Highly Adequate

*Amount of
Class Involvement*

Comments: _____

In a sentence or two, summarize what you feel the lesson was about. _____

II. Interpersonal Characteristics

5	4	3	2	1
Always				Never

*Eye Contact
with Students*

Comments: _____

1	2	3	4	5
Always Seems Ill at Ease				Always Seems Confident

Confidence Level

Comments: _____

1	2	3	4	5
Never				Always

*Communicates
Enthusiasm*

Comments: _____

5	4	3	2	1
Very Clear				Unclear

*Communication:
Meanings*

Comments: _____

5	4	3	2	1
No Problems at All				Needs Lots of Work

*Communication:
Speech, Grammar*

Comments: _____

I. Presentation of Material: Total Rating for Five Categories _____
   (25 possible points)

II. Interpersonal Characteristics: Total Rating for Five Categories _____
   (25 possible points)

Questions are really the backbone of effective verbal instruction and effective thinking. Both the type and, more importantly, the *sequencing* of questions can significantly affect the interaction and thought patterns that arise within a class. The act of increasing class participation, for example, depends as much on the questioning process used as on the group of students and the topic under investigation.

A frequently overlooked dimension of effective questioning is the ability of a teacher to provide adequate "wait-time" between when a question is raised and when an answer is expected. As Mary Budd Rowe states:

> When you ask a child a question, how long do you think you wait for an answer before you either repeat the question, ask him another question, or call on another child? If you are like many experienced teachers, you allow an average of one second for an answer. After a child makes a response, you apparently are still in a hurry because you generally wait slightly less than a second to repeat what he said or to rephrase it or ask another question.[11]

While investigating science teaching sessions, Rowe discovered that if a teacher prolonged the average time waited after one question was asked until another was asked or a second student was called on to 5 seconds or longer, the length of student responses increased.[12] Conversely, short wait-time produced short answers:

> When wait-time is very short, students tend to give very short answers or they are more prone to say, "I don't know." In addition, their answers often come with a question mark in the tone, as if to say, "Is that what you want?" But if you increase the wait-time, especially the period after a child has made a response, you are more likely to get whole sentences, and the confidence as expressed by tone is higher. Another bonus that results from increased wait-time is the appearance of speculative thinking (e.g., "It might be the water," . . . "but it could be too many plants.") and the use of arguments based on evidence. If the wait-time is prolonged an average of five seconds or more, young children shift from teacher-centered show-and-tell kinds of behavior to child-child comparing of differences. Why this happens is not clear. It may be that longer wait-time allows children to trust the materials so that they shift from the teacher's face to the objects they are studying.[13]

Rowe also discovered that teachers who learned to use silence found that children who ordinarily said little began to start talking and to offer new ideas. The teachers themselves, as they began to increase their wait-time, also began to include more variety in their questions. Consider the fact that establishing a climate of extended thought also encourages students to be more *reflective* in their answers rather than just "quick on the draw."

Questions, of course, have many functions in a classroom. Arthur

Carin and Robert Sund, in summarizing the work of interaction researchers, noted that teachers were found to use oral and written questions in the following ways:

1. Arouse interest and to motivate children to participate actively in the lesson.
2. Evaluate a student's preparation and to check his or her comprehension of homework or previous assignments.
3. Diagnose student's strengths and weaknesses.
4. Review and/or summarize what has been presented.
5. Encourage discussions.
6. Direct children to new possibilities in the problem being explored.
7. Stimulate students to seek out additional data on their own.
8. Build up an individual student's positive self-concept. . . .
9. Help children see applications for previously learned concepts.
10. Assess the degree of success in achieving the goals and objective of a lesson.[14]

What constitutes "good" and "bad" questions depends largely on what one's instructional objectives are, and an adequate discussion of this issue is beyond the scope of this book. Several helpful reference works on the topic that suggest different approaches to the issue are Bloom (ed.), *Taxonomony of Educational Objectives: Cognitive Domain;* Krathwohl, et al., *Taxonomy of Educational Objectives: Affective Domain;* Carin and Sund, *Developing Questioning Techniques;* Hunkins *Questioning Strategies and Techniques;* and Taba, *Teaching Strategies and Cognitive Functioning in Elementary School Children.*[15]

Even without a complex or systematic model for analyzing questions, examining recordings of class discussions can be a productive exercise. A fundamental analysis process can include such points as:

1. Clarity of questions (length, loudness, ambiguities, use of new words, peculiar sentence structure, speech and grammar).
2. Sequence of questions (extent to which each new question builds on the answers to the previous one; easy-difficult order).
3. Interest appeal (curiosity-generating, problem-provoking).
4. Relationship to instructional objectives (on-target).

Another important basic area for investigation is the interaction flow between questions and answers. Examining what occurs *after* a question has been raised is often as instructive as analyzing the questions themselves. How are correct answers reinforced? How are incorrect ones handled? How does the dialog build upon student responses? How are students encouraged to clarify and expand their answers?

A variety of popularized diagnostic tools are also readily available to a teacher for examining certain aspects of interaction patterns within the classroom. Two of the more current systems are transactional analysis (T.A.) and teacher-effectiveness training (T.E.T.). The former approach teaches one to diagnose and improve interactions based largely on Freudian theories, as translated by the late Eric Berne[16] and his students. A fairly thorough, readable description of the approach appears in Thomas Harris' *I'm OK—You're OK*.[17] For older elementary children Alvyn Freed's *T.A. for Kids* is also available.[18] In the transactional analysis system, a teacher would learn to spot communication blockages and to select alternative interaction patterns based on gamelike analyses of the existing patterns. Using Freudian constructs of personality reduced to simple terminology, adults and children can learn how to participate in improving communication.

The T.E.T. approach (and a subsequent book, *Teacher-Effectiveness Training*), grew out of Thomas Gordon's highly successful training programs and books with the same name, *Parent-Effectiveness Training* (P.E.T.).[19] Basically his system simplifies many of the theories derived from interpersonal communications literature and trains parents and teachers to analyze their communications motives and to learn to send the "messages" they wish as accurately as possible. Both approaches employ gamelike strategies and suggest some easily adapted diagnostic tools based on more honest and open communications.

NONVERBAL DIAGNOSTIC TOOLS

Examine the two classrooms shown on p. 392. What do you see? What tells you that? In what ways are the rooms similar? In what ways are they different? What do each of the pictures tell you about interaction patterns within the classroom?

Observing how we organize and divide space within an area can reveal much about the interaction patterns that are likely to occur within it. Schools abandoned bolted-down seats when they decided to provide for more flexible alternatives. Similarly many contemporary schools were designed with "open" spaces so that large groups of children might be quickly and easily maneuvered into different interaction settings (e.g., groups of 100, groups of 25, groups of 5, individuals working alone). When the form of arrangements within a space follow the functions to be carried out there, there is a greater opportunity for instructional activities to proceed smoothly and effectively. On the other hand, merely altering the form of space within an area does not guarantee that the functions performed there will be altered. Striking cases in point are the many open-space schools with unhappy teachers trying to teach four or more discrete classes in the traditional manner in large rooms with no dividing walls. Such schools were inappropriately designed for the traditional functions that the unhappy teachers wished to pursue. Hennings states:

> The way the teacher manipulates them [features of space] sends significant situational messages to students. Students are quick to perceive the implications of the positioning of the teacher's desk, the overall arrangement of their desks (in rows, clusters, a circle), the presence of listening and conversation areas constructed from outward jutting bookcases. They know that certain designs give them

more freedom to interact whereas other designs prohibit interstudent conversation. They know that some designs enable the teacher to keep an eye on them even when the teacher is working with other individuals or groups, that other designs give them greater independence.

The design, likewise, communicates the value the teacher places on different activities. To partition off a corner of the room, to place in that corner several comfortable chairs, to add a lighting fixture that casts a soft, relaxing glow, and to encourage youngsters to use the corner for recreational reading are ways of showing the youngsters the value the teacher places on reading. The design says, "Reading is an ideal way to spend one's free time."[20]

One team of investigators, after extensive observations in classrooms, discovered that an "arc of silence" exists in most classrooms roughly in the shape of area B, as shown in Figure 19.2. Students who reside in this arc within the room are likely to be ignored, according to the researchers, simply because of the geography of the room.

Figure 19.2
Arc of silence within a classroom

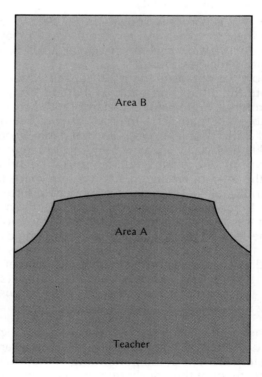

Source: Anita Simon and E. Gil Boyer (eds.), *Mirrors for Behavior III: An Anthology of Behavior-Instruments* (Wyncote, Pa.: Communication Materials Center, 1974), p. 61.

Analyzing the use of space within a classroom in the light of instructional functions identified can suggest more effective arrangements. Try this little experiment in the arrangement of space. List below five broad instructional goals that you would like to achieve in your classroom such as, "Have each child develop his or her individual potential."

1. _____

_____

2. _____

_____

3. _____

_____

4. _____

_____

5. _____

_____

Figure 19.3
Outline of a classroom

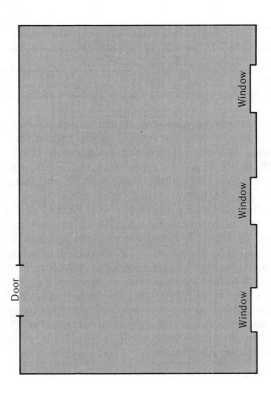

Use these goals and refer to the outline of a classroom in Figure 19.3. Assume that you are to need some working and sitting space for yourself and thirty students and that you can have any furniture, blackboards, bulletinboards, and so on that you need (*not* supplies and instructional materials). Indicate how you would organize the space consistent with the goals you have indicated.

When you have completed your arrangement, share it with a group of peers and discuss how the use of space corresponds to your goals. Then examine the illustration of space arrangements shown within the classroom at the bottom of p. 392. What are five goals of the teacher who arranged this latter classroom that you can infer?

1. _____

_____

2. _____

_____

3. _____

_____

4. _____

_____

5. _____

_____

In what ways is the teacher's arrangement similar to yours? In what ways is it different?

Another type of nonverbal diagnostic tool involves an examination of the ways in which a teacher's posture and body movements influence interaction within the classroom. Consider a substitute teacher standing outside of the fifth-grade class to which he was suddenly assigned. School has already started. The children are talking and laughing, a few are yelling and tossing objects around, and three boys are running around the room. The teacher hesitates just a moment in the doorway, then strides briskly to the front of the room with shoulders erect and a blank expression on his face. He faces the class in front of the teacher's desk, and without saying a word and still expressionless removes his jacket and rolls up his sleeves. Making eye contact with and motioning to the three standing boys to sit down and using two quick stabs of his finger, the teacher at the same time scans the entire class and places his hands on his hips. Not a word has passed between the teacher and the class, but already he has communicated a great deal to the children. Whether one agrees or disagrees with his message, he has "said" a lot to the group without opening his mouth.

Contrast this teacher with the case of a teacher described by Robert Koch:

> When Miss R. entered her room, she looked confused. This emotional climate was created by an uncertain gait, a bewildered facial expression, and she watched the floor as though she might stumble. She ignored the noisy class and they her. They went on talking.
>
> She sat at her desk, fumbled with books, laid them aside, reached for them again, found passages and marked these with hastily torn slips of paper.
>
> Suddenly she looked up as though aware for the first time that others were about, picked out a single student, glared, and threatened to send him to the principal. The class was silent just a moment, then ignored her and resumed making noise. The one student heeded her admonition. Evidently they had learned that she would carry out her threats, but only to the one addressed.
>
> She began her lesson. She knew her subject, but sounded bored. Nonverbal cues were clearly communicated by her facial expression, her monotone, and her stance. Her class responded appropriately with yawns.
>
> She paid good attention to any single student working at the board, but ignored the group as if they weren't there.
>
> She did not smile, stand near or touch anyone, or meet gazes with eye contact.
>
> The children, as though testing the limits, grew noisier, walked about, punched each other, ignored the lesson. She, perhaps rightly, made no attempt to reach them by raising her voice, and they couldn't have heard the lesson above the bedlam.[21]

The facial expression, body posturing, gestures, and body movements of teachers send out myriad messages to students. Often these messages are unconscious and may even be misinterpreted, just as with verbal messages. Several years ago while observing student teachers this author discovered that his presence as an observer was overly upsetting a particular student teacher. I asked if the problem was that the student simply felt self-conscious. "It's not that," she said, "it's just that you are so critical!" I expressed some surprise since I had, as yet, said nothing about her lesson and, in fact, had been quite impressed and absorbed with it. As we unraveled the mystery we discovered that as I became engrossed in a question and began to reflect on it, my face was screwed into what appeared as a frown. Upon investigation I discovered that other student teachers picked up similar messages. In their cases, however, they had paid much less attention to the nonverbal messages and focused more on my subsequent verbal statements.

Through more awareness and conscious control of our nonverbal messages, teachers can often improve interaction patterns within a class and even shift some of the verbal communication load. Role playing with a friend and receiving feedback on what nonverbal messages were sent is one easy way to diagnose communication patterns. Self- study before a full-size mirror, focusing on posture and facial expressions, is still another approach. Videotape analysis without the sound is perhaps the most effective diagnostic approach, since both the behavior and its effects may be observed. One such analysis approach is to take up to a 15-minute teaching segment and view it several times, each session focusing exclusively on a single aspect of nonverbal behavior (e.g., facial expressions, use of eye contact, etc.).

STUDENT PERCEPTIONS

Student perceptions of what is happening in a classroom are an important source of diagnostic data for improving instruction. What students perceive to be the reality of the classroom may not be accurate, but it must be taken into account and, if necessary, modified through revisions in instructional practices. A class survey showing that 90 percent of the group feels that their social studies program is a waste of time suggests several alternatives. The teacher may reassess the material and conclude the students are correct; she may also decide the material *is* meaningful and focus her efforts on trying to modify perceptions of the material.

Various simple diagnostic devices can be used to record students' general feelings about school. One such device is an Evaluation Thermometer, shown in Figure 19.4. For young children, even preschoolers, I and my students have used Emotion Sheets similar to those in Figure 19.5. Each child is given her or his own calendar and reminded at the close of the school day to paste on the cut-out face that best describes her or his reaction to the school day. The children prove to be quite candid in their assessments, and the calendars provide a handy diagnostic tool for assessing problem areas. An alternative use is to key the reactions to specific activities, such as social studies work.

To obtain student reactions on how the teacher is relating to the class, a simple questionnaire completed anonymously may be used. The candor with which students usually respond in dealing with such questions can be a great asset in diagnosing perceptions of classroom relations.

Apart from students' views of the teacher and the instructional activities provided, it is possible to obtain complex data on how they feel about one another with only a few bits of information. Let us hypothesize a classroom of twenty-five third graders who have been together for two months. Mr. Perdoni has become increasingly sensitive to interpersonal-relationship problems among his students. He decides to determine how the students feel about one another through a simple questionnaire. He prepares a general introductory statement explaining that he wishes to get some information on student feelings about other members of the class so that he can better plan activities. The question-

Figure 19.4 **Evaluation thermometer**

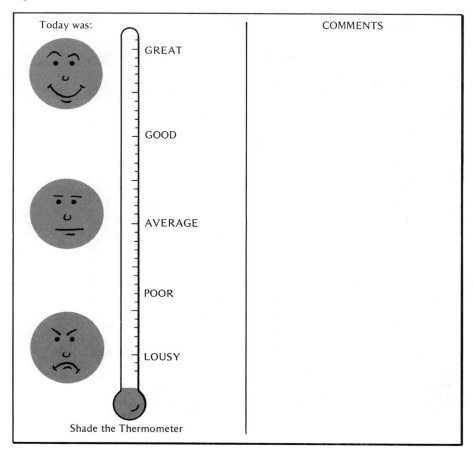

naire itself asks only two questions: "Which three children in this class do you like the most?" and "Which three children do you like the least?" Space is provided for each set of three names, as well as the name of the respondent.

After collecting the information from the students, Mr. Perdoni tabulated the results, as shown in Figure 19.6, giving all "like" choices +1 regardless of rank and all "dislike" choices −1. Once this tabulation was completed, analysis of the data could begin. The results indicate a range of popular children, a spread of students who have few friends, a series of isolates getting no reactions one way or another, and a few children who are quite unpopular.

Figure 19.5 Emotion sheet

February						
Sunday	Monday	Tuesday	Wednesday	Thursday	Friday	Saturday

Children place one of the following figures on the calendar
to show how they felt about school each day:

Happy

Unhappy

OK

In several cases, feelings were reciprocated; that is, some students who indicated they liked or disliked other students in turn were liked or disliked by their choices. More complex patterns also emerged, however, showing students who liked students who disliked them, and so on. *Stop at this point and examine the data carefully to see what additional conclusions you can draw about this group.*

To summarize Mr. Perdoni's data for quick comparative analysis, a target may be constructed using four concentric circles of increasing size as shown in Figure 19.7. For this analysis numbers instead of names are used to simplify the recording process. The smallest or center circle is labeled A. In it are placed the number of all children who received *no* negative scores and *more than* three positive choices. In the outermost

Figure 19.6
Tabulation of class preferences

Student #	1	2	3	4	5	6	7	8	9	10	11	12	13	14	15	16	17	18	19	20	21	22	23	24	25
Student #1							−1									−1	+1	−1		+1		+1			
2																−1	+1			−1		+1		−1	
3	+1	+1																				+1			
4			+1				−1						−1	−1		−1	+1					+1			
5	+1						−1									−1	+1					+1			
6				+1			−1							+1		−1	+1			+1		+1			
7					−1		−1									−1	+1					+1			
8			+1				−1							+1		−1	+1					+1			
9			+1				−1						−1	+1		−1	+1					+1			
10			+1				−1									−1	+1					+1			
11		+1	−1				−1	+1					−1	+1		−1				−1		+1			
12	+1						−1							+1		−1	+1					+1			
13	+1						−1						−1	−1		−1						+1			
14	+1						−1				+1			+1	−1	−1					−1	+1			
15							−1		+1						−1	−1	+1					+1			+1
16	−1						−1	+1							−1	−1		−1			−1	+1			−1
17	−1						−1		+1							−1					−1	+1			+1
18	−1	+1										+1				−1		−1							
19									+1					+1		−1									
20		+1	+1				−1	−1		−1				+1		−1	+1					+1			
21		+1	−1				−1	−1					+1	+1			+1					+1		−1	
22			+1				−1							+1		−1						+1		−1	+1
23		+1	+1				−1			−1				+1		−1				−1	−1	+1			
24	+1	+1														−1	+1			−1	−1	+1		−1	
25	+1	+1						−1								−1	+1				−1	−1			−1
Total +	5	1	15	2	1	0	0	0	3	0	1	1	0	12	0	0	14	0	0	1	0	17	0	0	2
Total −	2	1	0	3	1	1	0	18	1	0	3	0	4	2	3	17	0	6	0	4	5	1	0	2	0

Figure 19.7 Summary of tabulation data

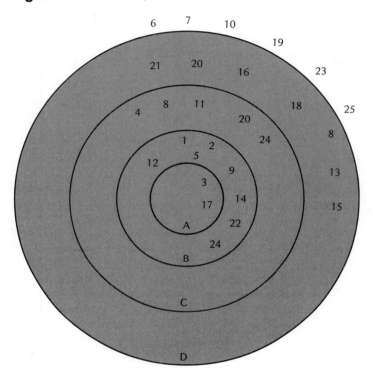

ring, D, are placed the number of students who received *more than* three negative choices and *less than* two positive choices.

Of the remaining students, those who were more *liked* than disliked (or have even ratings) go in ring B; those who were more *disliked* than liked go in ring C. Those students who were not rated for any choices are placed on the periphery of the target. As a final indicator, all the female students' numbers are made in red for quick sex identification.

Similarly other translations of the data are possible, such as class maps. Two fine sources of information on this type of translation of data are Norman Gronlund and Horace Mann–Lincoln Institute Staff's *How to Construct a Sociogram* and Robert Fox and his associates' *Diagnosing Classroom Learning Environments*.[22]

Now that Mr. Perdoni has an accurate diagnosis of how his students generally feel about one another, how can he act on his findings? *Stop at this point and list below five types of remedial actions that you suggest he might take on the basis of his data.*

1. _____

_____

2. _____

_____

3. _____

_____

4. _____

_____

5. _____

_____

Compare your suggestions with those of Fox and his associates directed toward any such sociogram analysis of student perceptions:

First, he can try to help his pupils to perceive as acceptable an expanded variety of individual differences. An effective approach to this end is to develop an inventory of the resources of class members showing that everyone in the class has some skill or knowledge to offer in different situations. . . .

Second, he can do much to change the patterns of interpersonal relations through different kinds of groups and work assignments designed to allow the neglected or rejected pupil more participation in planning and carrying out classroom activities. . . .

Third, the teacher can select as "peer helpers" good students who are seen as influential and cooperative with the teacher and whom other pupils want to be like. A forthright arrangement with such a high-status pupil to give support to a child who is experiencing difficulties will often be productive. Peer helpers may be able to reach pupils who need help but who are hard for a teacher to help directly. They can be set up as a panel of specialists in different areas who are ready to help any pupil on request, or they can be paired with other pupils. . . .

Fourth, the teacher can work on getting subgroups to relate productively and positively to each other in the classroom. When subgroups are so antagonistic that there is a schism in the class, the teacher is challenged to reduce this schism and unify the group. . . .

Fifth, he can work directly with rejected or neglected individuals. Frank, friendy discussions with the pupil or his parents, in which the pupil knows that his confidence will be respected, can often be very helpful. In such discussions the teacher can often use the reasons other pupils gave for rejecting him.[23]

NOTES

[1] *Educational Quality Assessment: Manual for Interpreting Elementary School Reports* (Harrisburg, Pa.: Pennsylvania Department of Education, 1974), p. 1.

[2] Ibid., p. 4.

[3] *Elementary School Test Evaluations* (Los Angeles: Center for the Study of Evaluation, University of California, 1970).

[4] The most recent two-volume issue is Oscar K. Buros (ed.), *The Seventh Mental Measurements Yearbook, I* and *II* (Highland Park, N.J.: Gryphon, 1972. See also Oscar K. Buros (ed.), *New Tests in Print, II* (Highland Park, N.J.: Gryphon, 1974).

[5] Dorothy Grant Hennings, *Mastering Classroom Communication* (Pacific Palisades, Calif.: Goodyear, 1975).

[6] Ibid., p. 167.

[7] Harriet Grim, *Practical Voice Training* (New York: Appleton, 1948).

[8] Robert F. Bales, "Categories for Interaction Process Analysis System," in Anita Simon and E. Gil Boyer (eds.), *Mirrors for Behavior III: An Anthology of Observation Instruments* (Wyncote, Pa.: Communication Materials Center, 1974), p. 159.

[9] Ibid.

[10] Anita Simon and E. Gil Boyer (eds.), *Mirrors for Behavior III: An Anthology of Observation Instruments* (Wyncote, Pa.: Communication Materials Center, 1974).

[11] Mary Budd Rowe, "Science, Silence and Sanctions," *Science and Children* (March 1969), 11.

[12] Ibid., 12.

[13] Ibid.

[14] Arthur A. Carin and Robert B. Sund, *Developing Questioning Techniques: A Self-Concept Approach* (Columbus, Ohio: Merrill, 1974), pp. 23–24.

[15] Complete source information is given in the Suggested Readings on p. 469.

[16] Eric Berne, *Games People Play* (New York: Grove, 1964).

[17] Thomas Harris, *I'm OK—You're OK* (New York: Harper & Row, 1969).

[18] Alvyn M. Freed, *T.A. for Kids* (Los Angeles: Jalmar Press, 1971).

[19] Thomas Gordon, *T.E.T. Teacher-Effectiveness Training* (New York: Peter H. Wyden, 1974).

[20] Hennings, op. cit., p. 173.

[21] Robert Koch, "Nonverbal Observables," in R. T. Hyman (ed.), *Teaching: Vantage Points for Study*, 2nd ed. (Philadelphia: Lippincott, 1974), pp. 428–429.

[22] Norman Grolund and Horace Mann—Lincoln Institute Staff, *How to Construct a Sociogram* (New York: Teacher's College Bureau of Publications, 1957); Robert Fox et al., *Diagnosing Classroom Learning Environments* (Chicago: Science Research Associates, 1966).

[23] Fox et al., op. cit., pp. 36–37.

CHAPTER 20

Attending to Psychosocial Concerns

SENSITIVITY TO DEVELOPMENTAL CONSIDERATIONS

"Julie just doesn't seem to understand differences in time periods in history."

"Percy seems to be so much more mature than the rest of the class."

"I don't know how the children can make so many mistakes in dealing with maps and globes."

Chances are developmental considerations may be an underlying factor in all three of the above cases. While developmental "readiness" is often used for a catch-all explanation for a variety of learning problems and differences, it nevertheless is an important instructional consideration. Properly applied, concern for students' stages of development can suggest what activities and materials are potentially most effective in instruction and in what ways children might best be helped when they are having problems.

THE NATURE OF DEVELOPMENT AND READINESS

Teachers generally use the term *development* in two ways as it relates to instruction. We refer to the *physical* ways in which individual children differ and in which all children at different age levels typically vary. For example, children often do poorly in printing and writing as they enter school, until their motor coordination improves. Frequently the youngest member of the class will be the poorest printer.

A second way in which development is used in relation to instruction is to describe the psychological and social (*psychosocial*) phases through which children advance. In general, as they advance chronologically, they typically interpret and respond to events in qualitatively different ways. The child who a few grades earlier always had the right answers but could not explain how he or she arrived at them now has no difficulty. The psychosocial dimension of developmental considerations is our concern here. The way in which children progressively come to view the world about them and to grow increasingly in intellectual capabilities develops sequentially. The pattern that they follow should help shape the character of our social studies instruction.

Developmental *readiness* is the extent to which children are psychologically and intellectually capable of carrying out an instructional task and fulfilling its objectives. Sensitivity to readiness requires that teachers move from tasks that build upon children's capabilities and help move them to progressively more complex levels. The psychosocial structure of the *child* rather than the structure of the subject matter becomes the dominant instructional focus.

THE NATURE OF STAGES

As the cumulative process of development produces marked psychosocial changes, we may speak of *stages* or *phases*. Stages or phases are relatively arbitrary signposts signaling that children have arrived at a certain point in the typical developmental cycle. As a rule of thumb, the stage or phase that most children are at may be correlated with their chronological age; that is, most eight-year-olds may be presumed to be at the same given stage. This correlational relationship of age/stage offers a teacher a rough index of the psychosocial capabilities of his or her students, though given individuals may deviate from the expected pattern.

Two of the foremost theorists concerning developmental stages are Jean Piaget and Erik Erikson. Each in somewhat different ways has sketched broad developmental patterns that suggest some instructional considerations, although classroom implications have not been their major concerns. Piaget's views on developmental periods have been well formulated and are reported in detail in several places.[1] He states that four basic periods of mental development exist and that one must move sequentially through each of them. Each phase involves increasingly more complex thought processes and depends on the knowledge acquired in the preceding one. For example, a child in the second period, the preoperational, reasons in a qualitatively different way than he or she would in the formal operational period.

Formal Operational   (11 years and above)
Concrete Operational   (7 years to 11 years)
Preoperational   (2 years to 7 years)
Sensorimotor   (birth to 2 years)

During the concrete operational period, the first developmental phase that completely falls within the school years, a child begins to engage in *operational thought*. Operational thought is the ability to organize and relate experiences into an ordered pattern. Some of the more significant developmental capabilities of this period for social studies instruction are related to *classification, seriation,* and *conservation*.

With respect to *classification,* in this phase of development the child is involved in classifying objects and relating them to known items. Many of the activities discussed in the latter part of Chapter 5 deal with classification. Henry Maier suggests this process occurs through "nesting" and "lattices":

> *Nesting* is a descriptive term for classifying an internal relationship between smaller parts and their all-inclusive whole. This term is used similarly to that of describing *nesting blocks* which is a toy of boxes fitting tightly into each other. In either case, in its conceptual use or in its description of a child's toy, nesting specifies that all classes are

additive. Each larger whole sums up *all* previous parts. Children, by means of nesting, add together their world into a "fitting" whole. Suddenly, the animal kingdom or sundry previously unconnected ideas make sense to them.

Lattices, on the other hand, refer to a special form of classification in which the focus is upon the connective link and the parts which are linked together. Ordering conceptually by means of a hierarchy of lattices places stress upon creating subclasses of *related* objects. Related classes are conceptually linked together in order to create a coordinated whole. Noteworthy, as in the latice work of a fence, so in mentally binding together the reversible relationship between subclasses and a larger whole. The lattices establish the "whole"— the fence or the interconnected orderly world. At this point in the child's life, relationship between pieces of knowledge is established by their logical relationship to each other rather than merely by proximity in experience. Most important, cognition by two different systems of ordering highlight a child's increasing awareness that each object has several reference points and can be ordered accordingly.[2]

Seriation involves placing objects or events in sequential or hirearchical order with respect to some property. As Lois Nelson puts it, "This task requires the child to identify the extreme of that property and consider the relation of each succeeding object or event in terms of being more or less than the preceding or following object or event."[3] Typical seriation tasks in social studies involve placing items in hierarchies or series from most to least, first to last, or largest to smallest. Sample activities might involve ordering sequence-of-events cards dealing with social phenomena, such as building-a-house cards; organizing a family tree; and arranging items on cards in order of most expensive to least expensive.

The child's capability of *conservation* when acquired allows him or her to realize that objects retain their properties even when they are transformed. The value of a dollar, for example, remains the same even when it is transformed into ten dimes. Altering shape, form, size, color, and the like does not necessarily cause an item to change its properties. Do soldiers, policemen, airline pilots, and the like retain their basic characteristics when they remove their uniforms? Children can be asked to focus on questions such as these and to discover what properties of objects or roles are invariant, even when transformations do occur.

Threading throughout the instructional considerations for the early Piagetian developmental periods is a need for *concretization* of activities. This emphasis translates into instructional activities that involve children with manipulatable, visualizable, or experiential materials and procedures. After mastery of concrete experiences, development can proceed toward related abstractions.

Parallelling Piaget's concern for the concrete-abstract dimensions of learning as it occurs at different developmental stages, Jerome Bruner has identified three systems that children employ to represent and deal with their environment: *enactive* representation, *iconic* representation, and *symbolic* representation. "Their appearance in the life of the child is in that order, each depending upon the previous one for its development, yet all of them remaining more or less intact throughout life—barring such early accidents as blindness or deafness or cortical injury."[4] Iconic representation becomes dominant in the concrete operational period; symbolic representation occurs thereafter.

Enactive representation refers to learning and representing knowledge through motor responses—or doing. "Such segments of our environment—bicycle riding, motor responses, tying knots, aspect of driving—get represented in our muscles, so to speak."[5] Iconic representation deals with the child's being able to form mental images to stand for objects or events; he or she is able to get a "picture" in his or her head. The third form, symbolic representation, deals with the ability to deal with experiences as words and to form combinations of words. "Growth," Bruner notes, "involves not a series of stages, but rather a successive mastering of three forms of representation along with their partial translation each into the others."[6]

In the period of *formal operations* into which the child normally moves during his or her middle-grade years, a new form of thought emerges. A child begins to manipulate ideas and symbols and abstractions serve as a suitable replacement of reality. Piaget observes:

> The consequences of this new attitude are as follows. In the first place thought no longer proceeds from the actual to the theoretical, but starts from theory so as to establish or verify actual relationships between things. Instead of just coordinating facts about the actual world, hypothetico-deductive reasoning draws out the implications of possible statements and thus gives rise to a unique synthesis of the possible and necessary.[7]

The logical-deduction approach common to social studies inquiry strategies based on John Dewey's problem-solving model fits appropriately into this developmental period. Its emphasis on logical analysis allows the child to draw on newly emerging resources.

> The ability to reason by hypothesis furnishes the youth with a new tool to understand his physical world and his social relationships within it. One of these new tools is logical deduction by implication. As a child, he has already managed the deduction of relationships on the basis of juxtaposition, proximity, transduction and other irreversible relationship patterns. Now, propositional statements of groupings allow the formation of new concepts. The latter ones are the product of deduction by implication. Reasoning by implication permits the youth to introduce simple, logical assumptions by taking a third position without resorting to verification by means other than logic.[8]

The view that social interaction should be a major component of social studies instruction—children sharing experiences, discussing and disputing, and listening—derives from Piaget's observation that this is how the child begins to move away from egocentrism. As the child increasingly talks with others, he or she begins to realize the existence of alternative points of view. Defending and explaining one's own ideas, as well as learning to listen to others, helps to clarify thinking. In short, conversation promotes not only social but cognitive growth as well.

A full analysis of the instructional implications of Erik Erikson's work is beyond our focus in this book. His view of developmental stages differs from Piaget's in two important respects for our purposes. Erikson postulates eight rather than four phases of development, and his stages emphasize affective rather than cognitive shifts.[9]

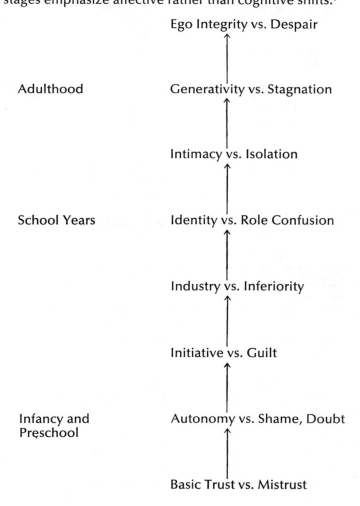

	Ego Integrity vs. Despair
Adulthood	Generativity vs. Stagnation
	Intimacy vs. Isolation
School Years	Identity vs. Role Confusion
	Industry vs. Inferiority
	Initiative vs. Guilt
Infancy and Preschool	Autonomy vs. Shame, Doubt
	Basic Trust vs. Mistrust

Erikson indicates in each of his stages the two polarities that are in tension with each other (Basic Trust vs. Mistrust, etc.) as a way of indicating the emotional forces that must be overcome at each new stage. The positive qualities listed to the left on each line are the "ego qualities which emerge from critical periods of development." Of the fourth stage, the first to intersect with the school years, Erikson writes:

> The child must forget past hopes and wishes, while his exuberant imagination is tamed and harnessed to the laws of impersonal things —even the three R's. For before the child, psychologically already a rudimentary parent, can become a biological parent, he must begin to be a worker and potential provider. With the oncoming latency period, the normally advanced child forgets, or rather sublimates, the necessity to "make" people by direct attack or to become papa and mama in a hurry: he now learns to win recognition by producing things. . . . He develops a sense of industry—i.e., he adjusts himself to the inorganic laws of the tool world. He can become an eager and absorbed unit of a productive situation.[10]

Stage five, *identity*, signals the onset of adolescence.

> With the establishment of a good initial relationship to the world of skills and tools, and with the advent of puberty, childhood proper comes to an end. Youth begins. . . .
>
>   . . .
>
> The danger of this stage is role confusion. Where this is based on a strong previous doubt as to one's sexual identity, delinquent and outright psychotic episodes are not uncommon. If diagnosed and treated correctly, these incidents do not have the same fatal significance which they have at other ages. In most instances, however, it is the inability to settle on an occupational identity which disturbs individual young people. To keep themselves together they temporarily overidentify, to the point of apparent complete loss of identity, with the heroes of cliques and crowds. This initiates the stage of "falling in love," which is by no means entirely, or even primarily, a sexual matter—except where the mores demand it. To a considerable extent adolescent love is an attempt to arrive at a definition of one's identity by projecting one's diffused ego image on another and by seeing it thus reflected and gradually clarified. This is why so much of young love is conversation.
> Young people can also be remarkably clannish, and cruel in their exclusion of all those who are different," in skin color or cultural background, in tastes and gifts, and often in such petty aspects of dress and gesture as have been temporarily selected as *the* signs of an in-grouper or out-grouper. . . . For adolescents not only help one another temporarily through much discomfort by forming cliques and by stereotyping themselves, their ideals, and their enemies; they also perversely test each other's capacity to pledge fidelity. The readiness

for such testing also explains the appeal which simple and cruel totalitarian doctrines have on the minds of the youth of such countries and classes as have lost or are losing their group identities (feudal, agrarian, tribal, national) and face world-wide industrialization, emancipation, and wider communication.

The adolescent mind is essentially a mind of the *moratorium*, a psychological stage between childhood and adulthood, and between the morality learned by the child, and the ethics to be developed by the adult.[11]

Developmental considerations offer still another perspective from which to view instructional planning. They can function either as a monitor to indicate whether we have reasonable expectations for our students or as a guide for facilitating naturally evolving capabilities. If I keep an eye to such factors, I am more likely to avoid both my and the students' frustrations and impossible objectives. Also, the probabilities are that I am more likely to capitalize on natural motivation and to build confidence in my ability to understand their needs and capabilities.

CONCERN FOR SEXISM

Women are not present in the curriculum. They're either totally absent, as in history or science, or they appear in a destructive or only half-true form, as in literature. Women's Studies has made people aware of women's exclusion from the curriculum, and aware that course content is male-biased. In children's books, for example, women are confined to the mothering role, even though women with children (and without) have always been part of the paid workforce— think of the women who worked in factories, mines, and fields, long before the twentieth century. It's not simply a matter of giving women their due rights, since they are, after all, half the student population. Men as well as women need to be educated about the omission of women from history. They all need to perceive women as whole people, not as nasty, foolish, or sexy objects. They need to see women as complex human beings.[12]

So spoke a feminist recently in an interview. Sexism—discrimination solely on the basis of sex—as reflected in school curricula has come under concerted investigation in recent years, in large measure as a reflection of broader social ferment. Antisexist criticisms range from textbook and curriculum materials treatment of females (e.g., pictures of females in stereotyped roles and general omission of coverage) to classroom practices (e.g., "Let's have the girls make the cookies and have the boys move the desks away") to institutional patterns within schools (e.g., there are over a million elementary teachers today, and over 900,000 of them are females; however, approximately 80 percent of all principals are male). Sex stereotyping refers to attributing roles, behaviors, and aspirations to individuals or groups solely on the basis of gender. From an instructional perspective it also means providing materials, activities, experiences, and models that lead children to such conclusions.

A first-grade social studies textbook with a 1974 copyright, for example, contains two sections treating briefly what children might be when they grow up. In one section, a little girl speculates that she might be a nurse, wife, grandmother, or all three. The little boy's section notes that when he grows up he might live in a big city or a small town, where he might want to help people as a volunteer. It notes that he might be an inventor but that in any event he wanted a job where he would be doing something important and where he would be happy. Given the normal constraints under which all textbooks must work in providing models, materials such as these provide an embarassingly stereotyped set of career samples that cry out for teacher amplification.

Monitoring materials and activities can be a major task in itself, as myriad articles, studies, and guidelines have suggested. Several key sources for help in this task are:

"A List of Literature on Sexism in Education." Feminists on Children's Media, P.O. Box 4315, Grand Central Station, New York, N.Y. 10017.

Bibliography on Sexism in Children's Books, Feminists on Children's Media, P.O. Box 4315, Grand Central Station, New York, N.Y. 10017.

Bibliography on the Treatment of Girls in School, The Feminist Press, SUNY College at Old Westbury, P.O. Box 334, Old Westbury, N.Y. 11568.

Little Miss Muffet Fights Back, Feminists on Children's Media, P.O. Box 4315, Grand Central Station, New York, N.Y. 10017.

Stavn, Diane G., *Reducing the Miss Muffet Syndrome; an Annotated Bibliography. Library Journal,* January 15, 1972.

Any number of studies have reported on the mistreatment of females in various types of materials and texts. A collection of significant cases are cited in Judith Stacey and her associates' *And Jill Came Tumbling After: Sexism in American Education.*[13] At the risk of oversimplifying a great number of often complex studies that need to be analyzed against the backdrop of other data, one may say that the message emerging from such investigation is that many student materials seem to be saying: "Males are more significant social contributors, have more life options, are more competent, have greater leadership qualities, and generally have more potential than females."

In "Boy Things, Girl Things . . . Do They Have to Be That Way?" Patricia Gillespie suggests several objectives for elementary teachers who wish to counteract such a message to children.[14] Among the objectives she suggests are:

1. To show females in active rather than passive roles.
2. To portray females as independent decision makers.

3. To provide alternative lifestyles that deviate from the homemaker and breadwinner models.
4. To present the lives and accomplishments of females who have been ignored in the text to underscore that women as well as men have made social contributions.

Gillespie's suggestions for related activities range from bulletinboard displays of males and females in occupational roles that challenge sex stereotypes, to inviting resource persons such as female doctors and male nurses who provide live models, to field trips to offices and businesses where men and women work together performing interchangeable roles.[15] Probably one of the most effective and direct ways to counteract sex stereotypes and bias in materials is to challenge the treatment directly, pointing out its limitations and offering counterexamples. This approach teaches coincidentally the need to look critically at all such materials.

Apart from curriculum strategies and materials, sex stereotyping may occur in any number of ways in the typical classroom. A sample list of areas to examine for instances of where behavioral patterns are recommended or encouraged by a teacher solely on the basis of children's sex are: activity grouping, play-activity assignments, compliment and criticism patterns, types of deviant behavior expected and tolerated, and work-activity assignments.

Translated into questions a teacher may raise concerning classroom practices, these areas suggest:

1. Do I automatically segregate children by sex for all activities regardless of the objectives?
2. Do I tacitly or overtly encourage boys and girls to participate in or play with sex-differentiated games and toys either by my procedures or the types of toys I provide?
3. Do I use sex-differentiated compliments and criticisms? ("Aren't you sweet" or "You look like a boy [girl] with your hair cut short [long].")
4. Do I expect boys and girls to misbehave only in certain ways that I regard as appropriate for males and females? ("Little girls shouldn't punch people when they are angry." "You [boy] can't cry and call for your mama everytime you get in a fight.")
5. Do I offer and condone a variety of role models and experiences for children that give both sexes balanced opportunities?
6. Do I give out jobs and other work assignments on the basis of sex?

CONCERN FOR RACISM

In a recent court case involving discrimination against blacks, the results were as indicated in the following UPI bulletin:

Atlanta—Georgia Power Company Thursday was ordered to pay almost $2.1 million to blacks, who, a Federal judge ruled, were victims of job discrimination.

The decision was said to be one of the largest settlements ever awarded in a contested civil rights case.

The courts ordered Georgia Power to pay $1.7 million in back wages to more than 360 black employees who were confined to menial jobs and to an undetermined number of other blacks who were denied jobs, the Justice Department said.

The court ordered $47,000 paid in back pension benefits to 67 black employees who have retired since 1965 and also ordered benefits estimated at $158,000 paid to employees who are retired or who expect to retire in the next three years.

The decree also would require payment to present and former black employees for travel and living expenses. These payments were denied to blacks while being paid to white employees.

As insidious and subtle as institutional racism may be, it often is easier to document and counteract through legal channels than the more pervasive forms with which some children have to deal each day. Over twenty years ago in a classic study, Mary Ellen Goodman observed how racist behavior begins even at a very early age. Using interviews and play situations in a nursery with a racial mix of children, she noted that "Four-year-olds, particularly white ones, show unmistakable signs of the onset of racial bigotry. . . ."[16] The litany of charges made against sexist practices and stereotypes are equally appropriate for racial minority groups. A major difference may be that concern for the treatment of racial minorities in curriculum materials and classrooms has been more widely reflected in practice than those of feminist groups. The feminist movement is of relatively recent vintage and it has yet to reach its peak with respect to its political and educational goals. As we go to press, for example, the Equal Rights Amendment still has not been ratified by the requisite number of states.

The movement for more equal treatment of minorities, while still a long way from realization of its goals, received dramatic impetus from the civil rights agitation of the late 1950s and the 1960s. The moral consciousness as well as the political organization generated by the succession of historic, often tragic, events that came to be known as the civil rights movement helped alert nonminorities to the urgencies of combatting racism and attending to modifying existing laws. Changes in curriculum materials have reflected to some degree this ferment, and contemporary materials represent a significant improvement over their earlier predecessors. Still much remains to be accomplished with respect to the treatment of blacks, Indians (over 200 tribes), Spanish-Americans, and Asian-Americans in curriculum materials. For example, while the hideous and shameful story of slavery and lynchings has received increasing attention, less is known about the exploitation of various ethnic groups, native Americans and the incredible saga of the Japanese-American internment camps during World War II. In a different vein, the 1970s story of the continuing struggle of all minority groups to live where they choose, get an equal chance at jobs and advancement, and receive a decent education merits much more attention in the elementary curriculum than it currently receives.

INNER-CITY TEACHING

The block I live on is not clean. The people who live on 4th Street throw things out of their windows. My house is right across from the school. I hope they will paint the school and wash off the old paint. The buildings have dirty walls and they do not clean them at all.

There are addicts who take things from people. Some people throw glass out on the street. But my block is better than 6th Street. About every day on 6th Street a policeman comes and has to take people away. The candy stores are bad because there are fresh men in them who do fresh things under the women's and children's clothes.

The cars go down the street too fast and somebody always gets hurt.

Addicts go up to the roof and some of my friends go with them and I don't like this at all.

This is a true story.

—Tyrone

Very early in the morning about four o'clock if I listen good I can hear the rumbling of the train wheels as they go across the Williamsburg Bridge. About that time if it is a foggy morning I can hear the deep booming sounds of the fog horns as the boats go by on the river. With the trains and boats I can also hear the buses pulling in and out of the bus stops. In my apartment I can hear the floor boards squeak as I walk around. It's like this until 6 A.M. Then I can hear the milk trucks as they deliver milk. I can hear the sound of the rattling of the wheels on the push carts as they are pushed to Avenue C. The thing that makes the most noise is Con Edison letting out steam from huge chimneys. It sounds like a jet flying overhead. Usually at 7 A.M. I can hear Maxy warming up his two trucks in his garage. They have a deep humming sound. Then I can hear his big mouth as he argues with his men telling them what to do for the day's work. I can also hear starlings and sparrows outside on my fire escape whistling and tweeting, dogs barking across the street and cats meowing in the yard. About fifteen minutes to eight and eight o'clock I can hear the whistle in Brooklyn for the men in the factories to get ready for work and to begin work, and the children talking on their way to school.

—Andi

The two accounts above of the inner city come directly from children of New York's P.S. 15 and reveal some of the flavor of their lives.[17] To speak of inner-city schools is to discuss classrooms with predominantly minority-group students—at least in our ten largest urban centers. Not all of these students come from fatherless, rundown, verbally sterile, and psychologically troubled homes, any more than all suburban stu-

dents come from two-parent, affluent, intellectually stimulating, and mentally healthy homes. Not all schools are cheerless with dismal graffiti-covered physical plants surrounded by gang enclaves—though certainly many are. Some generalizations are possible, of course, but many of these are of cold statistical nature revealing little of the human variances that separate all children in all classrooms. The statistics *do* show that *on the average* inner-city children have lower reading scores, come from families that have lower incomes than their suburban counterparts, have higher absentee rates, and are out of school earlier and in greater number than suburban children. None of these facts, however, explain why they occurred nor what a teacher should do as a result, nor what a Tyrone or an Andi is like. Such data do not dispense with the need to deal with each child as he or she appears in your classroom, wherever that might be. Teachers in the inner-city schools need to walk a fine line between being *prepared* for a repertoire of student, parent, and community behavior patterns and knowing how to employ or redirect them in constructive learning ways and falling prey to stereotyping each child bearing the label "inner city" or "minority group."

Some parents *do* send absence notes to school like the one that was xeroxed and sent around to all the staff in a school where I was visiting one day: "Robert was not in school because he got his penis caught in the drawer," and some children *do* use euphemisms such as "motherfuckin" with the same regularity that other children use "crummy." While the candor in the first case and the lack of conventional socialization patterns in the second may account for some teachers' culture shock, they should *not* provide serious problems in interacting with and teaching those with differing cultural perspectives. Similarly the physical aggressiveness of many inner-city children, often frightening as it is—not so much because of its threat to the teacher but because of its debilitating effects on the children themselves—needs to be countered rather than used as an excuse for ineffective instruction and racism.

Larry Cuban, a former inner-city teacher himself, observed:

> Group descriptions seldom capture the essence of individuals. Current generalizations offer only one narrow dimension of children, as if John Trumbull had painted only the backsides of the signers of the Declaration of Independence. The slice of the "disadvantaged" offered here is deviance. Unintentionally, the social scientists have depicted the "disadvantaged," especially black children, in terms of middle class white youngsters and schools. The result is that discrepancies between established norms of behavior and achievement are seen as abnormalities in poor youngsters.
>
> Stated crudely, the kid is to blame for his use of short sentences, inattention, laziness, low self-esteem, etc., etc. Stated in schoolmen's language, the child's environment is such that one can expect him to be inarticulate, self-abnegating, unmotivated, etc., etc.
>
> How tragic it is to link poverty and race to learning disabilities. A

clear-cut causal relationship has not been established. To say that if one is poor and black he will probably be unable to learn is nonsense. It denies the achievements of Americans, black and white, who have succeeded academically and materially in spite of poverty, or the thousands of low income youngsters who have improved their performance when the school environment has changed.[18]

In the five years that I have conducted social studies methods courses in various inner-city schools, I have seen much more variation among schools and even within a school than I have seen similarities. Both students and parents in most cases are prepared to accept, if not enthusiastically support, order, demands for attentiveness and social decorum, and academic standards if they are reasonable, achievable, explained, consistent, fairly maintained, and perceived as being for the students' benefit.

To the extent that the life experience of inner-city children represents different subcultural patterns than a teacher is accustomed to, it will be necessary to learn them and to come to deal with them on terms that a child can accept. Some children have dialects that are almost unintelli-

gible to the uninitiated ear, others are chronic swearers. Although neither of these sets of characteristics prevents learning, they present obstacles for a teacher to counter. Unfortunately there are no easy or quick ways to "get inside" of another set of cultural experiences. Given time, one can begin to intellectualize another's life space but the experiential lack will always be a handicap. Apart from visiting the home of students and spending some time in inner-city communities, observing and working with effective inner-city teachers is especially important. The latter is important for all teacher training but especially more so in any case where transcultural interactions are involved.

One of the strategies I sometimes suggest to students who are especially apprehensive about their inner-city teaching and insecure with their knowledge of the children's backgrounds and personalities is to fantasize their worst fears. List them in any way as quickly as they tumble out of your head. For each of them in turn write a brief sketch of an incident in a classroom or school as you think it might occur (e.g., "A fifth grader swears at me for breaking up a fight"). Get an interested partner or group and role-play all of the different ways you can think of to deal with the incident until you can get a solution with which you feel secure. Ask teachers and children for suggestions or reactions to your proposals. As you think of new potential incidents, add them to your list and deal with them. Having a repertoire of responses available for a situation gives a sense of security as well as a plan of action.

NOTES

[1] Jean Piaget, *The Child's Conception of Physical Causality* (London: Routledge and Kegan Paul, 1930); *The Child's Conception of the World* (London: Routledge and Kegan Paul, 1951); *Judgment and Reasoning in the Child* (New York: Harcourt, Brace Jovanovich, 1929); *The Moral Judgment of the Child*, trans. M. Gabain (New York: Free Press, 1965); and Jean Piaget and Barbel Inhelder, *The Growth of Logical Thinking from Childhood to Adolescence* (New York: Basic Books, 1958).

[2] Henry W. Maier, *Three Theories of Child Development* (New York: Harper & Row, 1965), p. 127.

[3] Lois N. Nelson, "Accelerating Cognitive Development—Helpful or Harmful to Children?" *Educational Leadership, 31* (December 1973), 257.

[4] Jerome S. Bruner, *Beyond the Information Given* (New York: Norton, 1973), pp. 327–328.

[5] Ibid., p. 328.

[6] Ibid., p. 317.

[7] Jean Piaget, *Logic and Psychology* (New York: Basic Books, 1957), p. 19.

[8] Maier, op. cit., p. 137.

[9] Erik H. Erikson, *Childhood and Society*, 2nd ed. (New York: Norton, 1963), pp. 247–274.

[10] Ibid., p. 258–259.

[11] Ibid., pp. 261–263.

[12] Quoted in *Looking At,* Bulletin of the ERIC Clearinghouse for Social Studies/Social Science Education, Boulder, Colo., January 1974.

[13] Judith Stacey et al., *And Jill Came Tumbling After: Sexism in American Education* (New York: Dell, 1974).

[14] Patricia Gillespie, "Boy Things, Girl Things . . . Do They Have to Be That Way?" *Instructor* (November 1973), 62, 64, 66.

[15] Ibid., 64.

[16] Mary Ellen Goodman, *Race Awareness in Young Children* (Reading, Mass.: Addison-Wesley, 1952), p. 218.

[17] Caroline Mirthes, *Can't You Hear Me Talking to You?* (New York: Bantam, 1971), pp. 30–31, 33.

[18] Larry Cuban, *To Make a Difference: Teaching in the Inner City* (New York: Free Press, 1970), pp. 10–11.

CHAPTER 21

Internalization Set #6

Dealing successfully and relatively efficiently with all of the classroom variables that affect social studies instruction is a complex and difficult process. Managing or implementing instruction that reflects cognizance and a degree of control over such variables is a further competency. Teachers who become highly competent in both sets of processes and have a high measure of insight into what they are doing truly may be called "masters of their craft."

The neophyte teacher generally does not enter the profession with this degree of proficiency. These far-reaching competencies are acquired over time through training, experimentation, self-analysis, self-observation and external critiques, and varied experience. They must be pursued and mastered through trial and error for most of us; they are seldom developed at random or without significant effort. Among other talents we possess in our professional repertoire, these auxiliary competencies help separate us as members of a profession from the "man or woman on the street."

STUDENTS AND TEACHERS

There are four activities in this set designed to give you some practice and additional insights into how you view the role of students, how they view their role, how they view one another, and how you view yourself as a *student*. All these "views" should contribute to a better understanding of the dynamics of social studies instruction.

ACTIVITY 73

You will need a class of elementary students, preferably grade 2 or above and one that has not already completed a sociogram. Refer to the discussion concerning the administration and use of sociograms on pp. 428–433.

Explain the purposes and procedures to the teacher who has agreed to let you work with a class. Follow through on these steps:

1. Gather the necessary data from the class and tabulate it as shown in the figures 19.6 and 19:7 in Chapter 19.
2. Summarize the tabulations in a target, as described in Chapter 19, pp. 431–432.

3. Develop a written statement of your conclusions about the class based on the data you have collected.
4. Develop a written statement of recommendations for any remedial action you think might be desirable to take, based on your data and conclusions.

ACTIVITY 74

The same group of elementary students may be used for this activity. Construct a questionnaire for the entire class to complete similar to the one that follows. Its purpose is to give you some idea of what students expect in an *ideal* teacher, not what they think of their teacher.

Student evaluation of the ideal teacher

Please answer the statements below by circling T (true) or F (false).

T   F   1. This teacher is always friendly toward students.
T   F   2. This teacher knows a lot about what he or she is teaching.
T   F   3. This teacher is never dull or boring.
T   F   4. This teacher expects a lot from students.
T   F   5. This teacher asks for student opinions often.
T   F   6. This teacher is usually cheerful and has a sense of humor.
T   F   7. This teacher is not upset by questions that students ask.
T   F   8. This teacher makes learning more like fun than work.
T   F   9. This teacher doesn't let students get away with anything.
T   F   10. This teacher often gives students a choice in the work they must do.

Source: Adapted from David M. Shack and Steven V. Owen, "The Evaluation of Teacher Performance by Elementary School Students," Unpublished paper, 1974.

If possible, administer the questionnaire to a number of classes cutting across different socioeconomic levels. The answers may easily be quantified by giving each response a numerical value (e.g., "Would Not Like" = 1; "Would Really Like" = 5) and averaging the total results. In this way classes can be compared quickly across each of the ten characteristics.

Before you administer the questionnaires, fill in *your expectations* of what the students are likely to say on the sample questionnaire. Do this placing an *E* instead of a check in the spaces. If you expect some variations in responses across the different classes sampled, make some notation on the form to that effect.

Repeat the procedures, this time completing the questionnaire as a student yourself, recording *your* likes and dislikes in a teacher. Put an *I* in the spaces that indicate how you would feel.

When the student questionnaires have been tabulated, record the student responses on the same form as *S* (or S_1, S_2, etc.). Compare the similarities and differences among the various responses (E, S, I). How do you account for them? What insights do the results offer?

ACTIVITY 75

What do you consider to be characteristics of a well-disciplined student? How do you expect children "to act" in your classroom? What behaviors are you willing to tolerate and not tolerate?

In the top portions of the two boxes provided below, list as specifically as possible those characteristics you consider a well-disciplined and a badly behaved student to have. For the Well-Disciplined Student box, rank and number the top five characteristics in order of what you consider to be the most important to the least important. Put a check by those characteristics you feel at least 75 percent of your students would *have to have* for you to be effective to teach any subject.

Well-Disciplined Student	Badly Behaved Student

+   —

Date _____

For the Badly Behaved Student box, rank in order and number those five characteristics that would disturb you the most to those that would disturb you the least. Place a check next to those characteristics you feel you *could not tolerate* in a majority of your students to be effective in your teaching.

Transfer the checked items to the plus and minus boxes at the bottom and record the date. Those boxes constitute a summary of where you stand on what you feel you must have and must not have by way of student behavior in your classroom. They also represent the essence of what you must communicate in some fashion to your students.

Compare your results and their rationale with others who have completed the same activity and with practicing classroom teachers. To what extent are there similarities and variations? Periodically, at semester intervals, you may wish to review your position.

ACTIVITY 76

Repeat essentially the same activity but this time *you* be the student described in *both* boxes. Make the boxes represent what you consider to be your well-disciplined characteristics and your bad-behavior characteristics. Rank them in order from greatest to least strength and most serious bad-behavior characteristic to least serious. Check those items that you feel are *essential* to your successful growth as a student and those you feel *definitely* hinder your growth as a student. Complete this activity on a separate sheet of paper.

Compare your self-analysis as student with your expectation of others. Are the profiles similar or different? How do you account for that fact?

INSTRUCTIONAL MATERIALS

Throughout the book, various activities and discussions have asked you to reflect on, analyze, and evaluate instructional materials for different purposes. Our concerns in this section relate to reviewing children's books on social studies topics, assessing reading levels, and examining student files and standardized tests as a basis for diagnosis and preparation of instructional materials.

Several or all of these activities may duplicate others you have done for different purposes. Similarly standardized tests and student files may not be readily available. Consequently you may wish to omit some or all of this section.

ACTIVITY 77

Consult the article "Notable Children's Trade Books in the Field of Social Studies" in the March 1975 issues of the periodical *Social Education* on pp. 172–176. Select any book from the list that intersects with your interest and teaching level and evaluate it from the following perspectives.

Interest level: Is the book likely to seem interesting to a child? What makes it so or not? Would you want to read it if you were a child?

Developmental characteristics: Put simply, does the book require concepts, analytical tools, and a level of abstract reasoning that the children for which it was designed are not likely to have?

Scholarship: Does the book reflect the best scholarship available in the field? Does it avoid gross distortions in the process of simplifying its subject?

Thought provocation: Does the book encourage and help children to reflect seriously on the topic it treats?

The message: What is the book saying to children beyond the substance of its topic? How does it make children feel and with what larger message does it leave them? How are female students and students of various racial, ethnic, and socioeconomic backgrounds likely to feel after reading the book?

Honesty: Does the book treat opinions as facts? Is it overtly or covertly misleading or insulting in its treatment of the sexes, minority groups, countries, lifestyles, philosophies, religions, and the like?

ACTIVITY 78

If you did Activity 77, you can use the same book for this one. Select any book on social studies for children (including textbooks) and analyze its reading level. Use one of the different procedures described in Chapter 18 for this task.

ACTIVITY 79

In some of the preceding chapters, various standardized measures have been cited and described. Chapter 19 cites several sources that list and describe such measures. Many libraries, education departments, instructional-materials centers, and schools permit examination of these measures by teachers.

Tests of any type, standardized or other, are like fire: They have the potential for great benefits and can provide the tools for helping mankind, they can be dangerous if misused or allowed to get out of control, and they are always severely limited in what they can accomplish.

Moreover, there is a tendency to overgeneralize from such tests and treat people as *labels* as a result of knowing about them from their test scores. The use of all such tests always involves a cost-benefit analysis: Will it help this person more if his or her test score is made available to those with whom he or she must interact? Many individuals and groups with solid justification have concluded in many cases that the costs have outweighed the benefits.

Properly viewed and used, any test can serve as a diagnostic vehicle to build on student strengths and remediate weaknesses. If this perspective is maintained by all parties with access to the data, and if all parties accept the desirability of achieving the goals and objectives that the test samples, the benefits will outweigh the costs. In today's society, for many reasons, the issue of test use seldom can be as coolly analyzed and qualified.

Whatever posture you eventually assume on this issue, it is desirable to gain some familiarity with the design, background, and substance of such tests. Try to secure access to as many such instruments as possible and to discuss with others, especially those who administer and use them, issues that concern you.

Student files generally contain such test scores as well as general evaluative records, physical and health characteristics, and anecdotal items. Just as with test scores these files can be either a source of useful diagnostic data or an instrument for labeling children instead of dealing with their individual instructional needs. Try to examine the files of some children you may have observed for a period in a classroom *without benefit of the teacher's evaluation of the students.* Compare your informal perceptions of the students with those contained in their files.

QUESTIONING PROCEDURES

Proficiency in a repertoire of questioning techniques that will (1) insure a broad base of class participation; (2) sharpen perceptions, concepts, and conclusions; (3) lead to increasingly higher levels of thought; and (4) attend to spontaneous student reactions is an essential dimension of effective social studies teaching. Many of the preceding chapters have touched upon questioning procedures in the context of instructional models. Several activities in the *Internalization Set #2* (Chapter 6), for example, asked you to gain some proficiency in the mechanics of questioning that are central to the Taba teaching strategies.

There are many perspectives from which to view questioning and how it may contribute to different dimensions of student growth. Not infrequently a questioning technique that is effective for one set of objectives is ineffective for another (e.g., nonjudgmental procedures to insure maximum group participation vs. socratic dialogue to sharpen arguments, develop rationale, and lead to grounded conclusions). In effect competency in questioning techniques for social studies instruction means *knowing what objectives a teacher wishes to accomplish, what questioning techniques are best suited to those objectives, how those techniques are employed in instruction, and what effect they have on respondents.*

Keep this proposition in mind as you move through the activities that follow. They are designed to focus in on the purpose, structure, and sequencing of questions and the handling of responses. Accept also as a general hypothesis for entertainment and testing that gaining increasing competency in questioning ability requires one to actually practice with others, gain feedback on the results, and assess the degree to which the objectives of the questioning were met.

ACTIVITY 80

Find a topic in social studies to teach to a group of six to ten students. Decide on an objective and plan an instructional activity appropriate for the group and one that depends on a series of questions. Preferably seek a group of elementary students at any grade level, but peers will do. *Record your session on tape.* (Cluster your group in a semicircle with the microphone in the center for better reception.)

Conduct your session for 20–30 minutes, then return to this book. *Stop.*

In your postsession analysis, respond to questions such as the following. How would you categorize your questions, and what is your rationale for the categories? If you asked more questions than you planned, why was this so? What was the average wait-time in seconds between when you asked a question and when you moved on to a further question, comment, or clarification? Why did you ask the questions in the *order* that you did (i.e., did it make any difference which one came first, etc.)? In what way did you respond to the students' answers to your questions? Finally, did the questions that you asked help substantially to achieve your objective?

If you were unhappy with the sequence or types of questions, rewrite them and repeat the lesson with a new group. When you reteach the material try to focus on improvement in a single area, such as prolonging your wait time after a question is asked to over three seconds. Tape as many of your sessions as possible and date them. The points you will have listed concerning your questioning, as well as the entire tape, provide baseline data from which to gauge all your future progress. Be sure to save them for reference, and date them.

ACTIVITY 81

After you have improved the quality of your questioning in at least two respects from the follow-up to Activity 80, you should be ready to consider still another perspective. Gather together some of the tapes from your various teaching sessions.

Consider the following series of structural problems that questions frequently share. These are types of questions that one tries to avoid no matter what the objectives are. The following illustration is taken from the book *Teacher's Guide: Justice in Urban America Series:*[1]

Type of Question	Example	Reason to Avoid It
Yes-No	Does the President appoint members of the Supreme Court?	Produces no discussion and encourages guessing.
Elliptical	How about the Depression?	Confusing and unclear; students would not understand what the teacher is getting at.
Ambiguous	What happened in this city in 1967?	Similar to elliptical question.
Indefinite	How do a landlord and a tenant differ?	Similar to elliptical question.
Whiplash	"Truth in Lending" is the term used to describe what law passed by Congress?	Students are prepared to receive information when suddenly they are asked a question.
Leading	Don't you really think that consumers get what they pay for?	Conveys the expected answer and prevents students from reaching their own conclusions.
Slanted	Why was this a landmark decision?	Similar to leading question.

Listen to your tapes again, this time looking for instances of the seven types of questions. Do not concern yourself with being able to accurately categorize each question and to differentiate correctly among the seven types. The important issue is to spot those questions that generally need some type of improvement.

If there appears to be a high incidence of these types of questions, you need to more carefully monitor your instruction from this perspective in the future. Again note the date of your analysis and save it for further reference.

ACTIVITY 82

Apart from the handling of questions, teachers need to be equally concerned with the treatment of student responses. After all, what happens after a question is asked is really the vital part of the instructional process. How students are encouraged to extend their responses, reinforced for the ideas they contribute, helped to clarify their points, and encouraged to volunteer questions of their own is a related dimension of teacher's questioning competencies.

In this activity you are to focus on two levels of your responses to students' responses to your questions. You will examine both your verbal and your nonverbal responses. For your verbal analysis, select two tapes from your sessions. On a sheet of paper make three columns with the following headings: "My Response When Student(s) Answer(s) Correctly," "My Response When Student(s) Answer(s) Incorrectly," and "My Response When Student(s) Ask(s) Question." As you listen to the question-and-answer cycles on the tape, list all of your follow-up responses verbatim under the appropriate headings.

In what ways are your responses similar and different? How do you account for this fact? Are there any aspects of your response pattern that you would like to change?

Some of the many items you might want to consider for change are:

1. Excessive unnecessary repetition of student responses.
2. Overuse of acknowledgment terms (e.g., "OK").
3. Consistent failure to differentiate reinforcement of correct and incorrect answers (e.g., "Uh, huh"—no matter what is said).
4. Failure to reinforce correct answers or attempts to answer questions.
5. Frequent opinions about the way that answers are given (e.g., "Yes, you're right, but I don't think you state it very well") or reinforcing *only* the second student giving a correct answer because of the way it was expressed even though the first student was also correct.
6. Ridiculing of students (e.g., "C'mon, can't anybody do better than that?").
7. Failure to support student while challenging the validity of an answer (e.g., "No, you're wrong" instead of "I can understand how you might think that but the facts are that . . .").
8. Tendency to reject or brush aside unanticipated student questions.

At a second level for analysis, plan to teach another lesson and use an observer or videotape your session. If an observer is used, brief him or her on the preceding response concerns and request that he or she concentrate on your *nonverbal* responses, namely, body posture, and gestures, and the use of space. Some points to consider are:

1. The extent to which you reinforce answers.
2. The extent to which you encourage students to continue and expand upon their answers.
3. The extent to which you indicate disapproval and impatience.
4. The extent to which you indicate favoritism among responses.

In addition, obtain a list of specific nonverbal moves that you make to signify different emotions. If a videotape is used for the analysis, cut off the sound and follow the action silently, cutting in the sound periodically to check your observations.

CLASSROOM MESSAGES

"There's not much going on in there," said a disgusted principal as he passed the classroom of one of his less-than-favorite teachers. Objectively he was quite wrong. In the most deadly classroom imaginable much is happening respective of its merits, if only one knows what to look for. There are more variables operating in the average classroom than an observer could reasonably be expected to isolate and examine. The more of these variables a teacher can take into account and control, the richer will be the instructional mix within the classroom. We will try to look both globally and highly specifically at some of the variables discussed earlier and to heighten sensitivities to them.

ACTIVITY 83

Plan a visit to a school for an entire morning. Your purpose there will be to make some observations and a written record of them from several different perspectives.

The first perspective involves identifying one child to follow intensively. He or she will become "your" child. Observe him or her the way George Leonard suggests for parents who wish to understand what their child experiences in school:

Arrive early in the morning, with your child. Chat for a few moments with the teacher to put him at ease, and allow him to introduce you to the class. Assure him that you plan to create no disturbance whatever but simply to melt into the woodwork. Then take a chair near the back of the room at a position where you have an oblique view of your child. Be natural, casual, friendly. When children turn to look at you, smile slightly in acknowledgment and reassurance, then turn away. If you are natural and at ease, you will probably be surprised at how quickly you are ignored. And, though the teacher may tend to be on guard, his basic style of teaching and relating with the children is generally too deeply ingrained to allow for very much dissembling. You will have the opportunity of experiencing what your child experiences.

Take the opportunity. Focus in on your child. Try to assume his viewpoint, feel what he feels, learn what he learns. Become sensitive to his body positions; see when he sits straight, when he hunches over, when he squirms, when he languishes. Balance the weights of the teacher's words against the pressure on your seat. Try not to daydream. Remember that time goes more slowly for a child than for an adult.

Now are you ready for a little walk? A cup of coffee? A visit to the restroom? A cigarette? Forget it. Stay with your child. Stand only when he stands. Leave the room only when he leaves the room. Concentrate on him. Become your child.[2]

How did it feel? Take some time to record only your feelings about the experience.

Repeat the same process of identification with a child for 45 minutes, this time picking the quietest, most nonresponsive child. Again record your feelings.

For the third 45-minute block, select the most disruptive (or if none, the most "squirrelly" child) for your self-identification. Record your third set of feelings. At a later point, take some time to reflect on the three sets of feelings and to compare their similarities and differences. What in the classroom environment contributed to the feelings you recorded?

ACTIVITY 84

In the same classroom, for the remainder of your morning, focus on the teacher's *nonverbal* behavior. How does he or she communicate through the use of body, space, and the like the statements that are listed in the chart that follows? Record specifically what the teacher does to make the statement. There is additional space on the chart for adding any other statements that occur to you. After observing the teacher, reflect on and record the ways in which you nonverbally communicate the same statements.

Statements	Teacher's Specific Nonverbal Gestures	My Specific Nonverbal Gestures
I like that.		
I do not like that.		
That's OK.		
Hurry up!		
Be quiet!		
Stop that!		
Come here.		
What do you want?		
I like you.		
How are you?		
Can I help?		
I'm bored.		

(Other)

—————————   ————————————————   —————————————————
—————————   ————————————————   —————————————————
—————————   ————————————————   —————————————————
—————————   ————————————————   —————————————————
—————————   ————————————————   —————————————————

ACTIVITY 85

Visit another classroom for a morning or an afternoon. Before going, review the discussion in Chapter 18 concerning racism and sexism (pp. 441–449). A school or classroom may exhibit characteristics of racism or sexism without directly intending to. The practices it has grown accustomed to supporting without examination, the materials it has purchased without carefully examining, or the habits of its students and unconscious biases of its teachers are just some of the ways that unintended racism and sexism may be supported. Candor also demands our recognizing that some practices in fact are intended or at least condoned. Hopefully you will encounter far fewer cases of this type than of the former.

Your task is to document as specifically as possible as many cases of racist and sexist behavior, practices, policies, and materials, observed or inferred, as you can. Compare and discuss your results with your peers and decide what you could or can do as a teacher to eliminate, counteract, or countermand such practices and behavior.

ACTIVITY 86

Reread the discussion of the characteristics that Jacob Kounin found to be frequently present in classrooms that had high incidences of productive behavior and low incidences of disruptive behavior (pp. 400–401). Spend a day in a classroom that someone has identified as one where (a) "kids really learn a lot" and (b) "the class is really well disciplined." Unless both characteristics are present chances are that you will be viewing a situation where there is a high degree of control but no commendable instructional purpose. If you are not able to locate a classroom so identified, walk by several rooms and try to get permission to visit one that looks as if things are progressing smoothly and where at least 25 percent of the class are smiling and less than 25 percent are scowling.

Your task is to look for specific instances of teacher behavior that corresponds to Kounin's list and to record them for your reference on the chart below. Apart from giving you some greater insight into Kounin's ideas, the experience should provide you with some concrete examples of behavior to isolate and model yourself.

Characteristic	Description	Specific Teacher Behavior and Incident Demonstrating the Characteristic
Withitness	Communicating that one knows what is going on in the classroom.	
Overlapping	Being able to attend to two issues simultaneously.	
Smoothness	Managing physical movement from one activity to another without jerkiness, distractions, or temporary halts.	
Momentum	Keeping physical activities moving at an appropriate pace.	
Group Alerting	Degree to which the teacher attempts to involve non-reciting children in the recitation task.	
Accountability	Extent to which children are held responsible for the tasks during recitation.	
Valence	Making statements pointing out that an activity has something special to it.	
Challenge Arousal	Making statements that draw attention to the challenge in a task.	
Seatwork Variety	Planning varied work activities for children at their seats.	
Challenge	Intellectual challenge in seatwork.	

ACTIVITY 87

You will need to teach a whole class for at least 25–45 minutes and have an observer for this activity. It is adapted from Richard Curwin and Barbara Fuhrmann's *Discovering Your Teaching Self*.[3] They suggest constructing a "teacher walking map" as a way to reveal some aspects of how a teacher's movement within a class demonstrates feelings about students and affects relationships with them.

The activity helps you monitor your activity within a class, make some judgments about the effects of such movements, and helps chart the directions of desired changes. Provide your observer with an outline of the class in which you are teaching, drawn on a sheet of 8½" × 11" paper. Include a few basic reference points such as desks of students, teacher's desk, doorway, windows, chalkboard, and the like.

The observer's task is to trace your movement as a continuous, unbroken line over a 45-minute period. Each time you *stop* the observer is to place a dot and number it consecutively (i.e., first stop/dot is #1, the second is #2, etc.). For each 3-minute period you remain at the spot, a circle is drawn around the spot. Each additional 3-minute wait adds another concentric circle, and so on. Your starting place at the beginning period is the first spot and receives the number 1.

As you analyze the resulting teacher walking map, Curwin and Fuhrmann suggest you consider these questions:

1. In which areas of your classroom did you spend most of your time?
2. Did you neglect any area(s)?
3. Did the students' activities determine your movements in any way? How?
4. What effect did the seating arrangements have on your movements?
5. What effect might your movement have had on students?
6. Do you want to make any changes, based on the information you now have? Why or why not?[4]

ACTIVITY 88

A system for analyzing and improving student and teacher relationships has been developed by Thomas Gordon, a clinical psychologist, and is detailed in his book, *T.E.T.: Teacher Effectiveness Training*. In very basic language the book explores how teachers can better understand and influence communication patterns within a classroom. Gordon contends that a good teacher-student relationship depends on five factors: (1) openness, (2) caring, (3) interdependence, (4) separateness, and (5) each party having mutual needs met. In other words, both parties are willing to take the risk to be honest and candid with each other, to let each other know there is mutual caring, to show that each needs the other, to allow each to grow in his or her own way, and to demonstrate that each one's needs can be met without sacrificing the other's.[5]

Gordon outlines twelve roadblocks to effective communication between teacher and students.[6] He reports that the type of feelings such roadblocks are likely to engender in students are to make them:

Stop talking, shut them off
Defensive and resistive
Argue and counterattack
Feel inadequate and inferior
Feel resentful or angry
Feel guilty or bad
Feel they are being pressured to change, that they are not accepted as they are
Feel they are not trusted to solve their problem
Feel they are being treated as children
Feel they are not understood
Feel frustrated
Feel like they are on the witness stand being cross-examined
Feel the listener is just not interested

Some of the twelve basic roadblocks that Gordon has identified are as follows. The teacher:

1. *Orders, commands, or directs.* ("Get your map finished.")
2. *Warns or threatens.* ("Unless you stop chattering, I'll have to keep you in for recess.")
3. *Moralizes or preaches.* ("You really should do your social studies work if you want to be a good citizen.")
4. *Judges, criticizes, disagrees, blames.* ("That's one of the poorest reports turned in.")
5. *Name-calls, stereotypes, labels.* ("Don't be a baby, stop playing around with the chalk.")
6. *Cross-examining.* ("Did you really put much time into this project? Couldn't you have put more effort into it? Is that the best you can do?")

Plan to spend a day observing in one or more classrooms within a school focusing on instances of these six behavior patterns. Use the form below to record the verbal and nonverbal behavior of the teacher in the appropriate row on the chart. Correspondingly note any verbal or nonverbal reactions of the child or children to whom the behavior is directed. Also record the context in which the behavior occurred, that is, what event gave rise to the teacher's behavior. If no specific cause seems apparent, indicate that on the chart. Try to locate some instances of all six behaviors; move on to a different classroom if necessary.

Behaviors	What the Teacher Said Verbally or Did Nonverbally	How the Student(s) Reacted Verbally or Nonverbally	Context in Which the Behavior Occurred	Alternative Ways to Respond to the Situation
Orders, Commands, or Directs	_____	_____	_____	_____
	_____	_____	_____	_____
	_____	_____	_____	_____
Warns or Threatens	_____	_____	_____	_____
	_____	_____	_____	_____
Moralizes or Preaches	_____	_____	_____	_____
	_____	_____	_____	_____
Judges, Criticizes, Disagrees, or Blames	_____	_____	_____	_____
	_____	_____	_____	_____
	_____	_____	_____	_____
	_____	_____	_____	_____
Name-calls, Stereotypes, or Labels	_____	_____	_____	_____
	_____	_____	_____	_____
	_____	_____	_____	_____
Cross-examines	_____	_____	_____	_____

When your observations are completed, review your findings and reflect on and record on the chart what alternative courses of action and verbal behavior might have been taken. If you have an opportunity to teach a group for a day or longer, ask an observer familiar with this analysis system to observe you for a period of time, and record the observations on a similar form for your analysis.

PLANNING INSTRUCTION

We will explore a micro- and a macro-dimension of planning in our final two activities. The former concerns a small-scale single-focus instructional task, while the latter involves planning over a period of time, taking many variables into consideration. Some teachers like to "lay out" their year's work, even though they realize they will change many components as time passes. Others like to stay closer to the dynamics of what is occurring within their classrooms and do short-term planning projections. Both approaches have a common denominator in that they satisfy some psychological needs of the teachers who use them, and they reflect recognition of the importance of planning.

ACTIVITY 89

Your task is to plan and try out an activity or learning center. For this project you will need a topic, some objectives, some assumptions and expectations (e.g., age, background, abilities, etc.) about the children who are to use it and some guidelines for the nature of a center. Supply the first set of requirements and follow the guidelines below:

1. Beyond a topic and some specific objectives, decide approximately how much time you wish a child to spend if he or she would complete the minimal number of activities in the center. As a rule of thumb consider a time span averaging three to five social studies periods.
2. While centers may offer increasingly larger roles for teachers, in this case assume that the teacher primarily installs, introduces, monitors, responds to inquiries, and evaluates. Students are largely to work alone or in small groups in the center with little teacher control.
3. For purposes of convenience, all materials required for activities should be physically present at the center itself.
4. The physical shape and organization of the center may take any form. It should have some interesting and thought-provoking display component that "advertises" the center, that is, something that easily catches the eye, appeals to a child, and piques his or her curiosity.
5. There should be an immediately visible component clearly explaining what the child may expect to find and how the center is to be used. For example, if alternatives are available at some point and not at others, or if a sequence is to be followed, this should be indicated clearly.
6. The location of all materials needed for activities should be clearly indicated.
7. Activities to be completed alone and those to be done in small groups should be clearly indicated.
8. The way in which the child is to demonstrate what he or she has done or learned should be clearly indicated.
9. The activities should include a range of tasks from exploratory ones introducing the topics, to highly reflective ones requiring the child to think carefully about an idea, to application ones offering the child an opportunity to test out learnings.
10. The activities should hang together. Besides the fact that they relate to the theme of the center, there should be some defensible logic to the relationship among the activities themselves.

Any topic dealing with social studies is appropriate, and the center may contain any type of materials you wish to include. Remember that the center is to be *used*, however, not just viewed, and that it must be moved to a location where children will try it out. Durability and portability are some of the considerations in construction. Consult any other sources of information that you wish for ideas, such as Sandra Kaplan and her associates' *Change for Children*.[7]

When the center is completed, find a classroom with a group of students who correspond to the assumptions and expectations on which the center is based. If the teacher is agreeable and the center is adaptable to the instructional framework of the classroom, install it. Explain its operation and design to the students and see how it works. Since a center can be evaluated from many perspectives (e.g., rate of interest it generates, learning outcomes, etc.), decide which one you wish to use, develop some specific criteria within that framework, and evaluate it.

ACTIVITY 90

As the last activity in the sequence of Internalization Sets, this one asks you to tie together a number of ideas developed in the book with a focus on planning instruction. Refer back to the discussion in Chapter 2 concerning goal-setting/organizing/planning (pp. 39–50).

Assume you will be teaching a class for 5 days, and 200 minutes are available for social studies instruction. Select a goal to achieve in social studies, pick a related topic of interest to you, develop some related objectives, and plan and organize a sequence of instructional activities for your 5-day period. Be specific in the design and sequence of your instructional activities and how they will fit into the time available. Indicate the time schedule, Monday through Friday, that will be used for social studies activities and your rationale for it.

NOTES

[1] *Teacher's Guide: Justice in Urban America Series* (Boston: Houghton Mifflin, 1970), p. 22.

[2] George Leonard, *Education and Ecstasy* (New York: Delacorte, 1968), pp. 106–107.

[3] Richard L. Curwin and Barbara Schneider Fuhrmann, *Discovering Your Teaching Self* (Englewood Cliffs, N.J.: Prentice Hall, 1975), pp. 175–177.

[4] Ibid., p. 176.

[5] Thomas Gordon, *T.E.T.: Teacher Effectiveness Training* (New York: Wyden, 1974), p. 24.

[6] Ibid., pp. 47–49.

[7] Sandra Nina Kaplan et al., *Change for Children* (Pacific Palisades, Calif.: Goodyear, 1973). See also Helen Davis Dell, *Individualizing Instruction* (Chicago: Science Research Associates, 1972); Barbara Blitz, *The Open Classroom: Making It Work* (Boston: Allyn & Bacon, 1973; John J. Thomas, *Learning Centers* (Boston: Holbrook, 1975).

MODULE SUMMARY

Effective instruction depends on accurate diagnosis of key variables within the classroom. These variables are often myriad and complex and cannot always be diagnosed, even with expertise beyond that which a classroom teacher might be expected to have. On the other hand much can be gleaned, relatively easily and with little training, that can improve and enrich the interaction and ultimately the learning within a classroom.

Unlike national and state assessments procedures, classroom diagnostic procedures have fewer potential pitfalls and more flexibility. Determination of student progress in subject-matter learning is the most common form of diagnostic procedure, and germane examples have been cited in previous chapters as related to different types of learning outcomes. Apart from diagnosing subject-matter learning, however, there are a variety of other instructional dimensions that a teacher may need to diagnose. Among these are interaction patterns, both verbal and nonverbal, within the classroom. These include teacher-pupil talk, organization of space within a room, "body talk," and questioning techniques.

Student perceptions of what is occurring within the classroom constitute another important, albeit often neglected, dimension of the classroom requiring diagnosis. A number of basic techniques are available for use with children as early as the preschool years, and these were illustrated. As teachers become more accurately aware of what impact they are having on students, the ways in which the classroom structure affects them and the students, and the ways in which students view life in the classroom, they can move efficiently and productively to organize their social studies instruction.

No two classrooms are alike. Any given classroom has a unique identity created by its inhabitants, their interactions, and the ways in which they physically transform the room. Six facets of a classroom's identity having special significance for social studies instruction were analyzed: socioemotional climate, management procedures, provisions for individual differences, sensitivity to developmental considerations, concern for sexism, and concern for racism.

Socioemotional climate refers to the general attitudes within a class that are shared and reflected in social interaction. One way of characterizing climate is to assess the degree to which it is "open," "permissive," or "authoritarian."

Management procedures that reflect sensitivity for student expectations, pinpoint and document problem areas, and incorporate research findings can greatly facilitate instruction. Ten research findings were cited and discussed.

Individualizing instruction refers to isolating some differences among children that are considered to be important and providing appropriate instruction to take these differences into account. Six different approaches to individualization, each responding to a particular way in which individuals may differ, were discussed.

Sensitivity to developmental consideration requires that teachers understand the ways in which children's thoughts qualitatively vary as they mature. Knowing the ways in which they are likely to develop cognitively allows a teacher to have certain expectations and to plan appropriate social studies instruction.

Concern for sexism and racism must be an ongoing preoccupation for all teachers in all classrooms. Sexism and racism, laws and good intentions notwithstanding, continue to permeate our society and schools in overt, covert, and institutionalized ways. Continued concern for sexism and racism provides an ongoing perpetually visible social studies lesson.

SUGGESTED READINGS

Banks, James A. *Teaching Strategies for Ethnic Studies*. Boston: Allyn & Bacon, 1975.

Blitz, Barbara. *The Open Classroom: Making It Work*. Boston: Allyn & Bacon, 1973.

Carin, Arthur A., and Robert B. Sund. *Developing Questioning Techniques: A Self-Concept Approach*. Columbus, Ohio: Merrill, 1971.

Cartwright, Carol A., and G. Phillip Cartwright. *Developing Observation Skills*. New York: McGraw-Hill, 1974.

Cuban, Larry. *To Make a Difference: Teaching in the Inner City*. New York: Free Press, 1970.

Curwin, Richard L., and Barbara Schneider Fuhrmann. *Discovering Your Teaching Staff: Humanistic Approaches to Effective Teaching*. Englewood Cliffs, N.J.: Prentice-Hall, 1975.

Dell, Helen Davis. *Individualizing Instruction: Materials and Classroom Procedures*. Chicago: Science Research Associates, 1972.

Erikson, Erik H. *Childhood and Society*, 2nd ed. New York: Norton, 1963.

Fantini, Mario D., and Gerald Weinstein. *The Disadvantaged: Challenge to Education*. New York: Harper & Row, 1968.

Flavell, John H. *The Development Psychology of Jean Piaget*. New York: Van Nostrand Reinhold, 1963.

Fox, Robert, et al. *Diagnosing Classroom Learning Environments*. Chicago: Science Research Associates, 1966.

Friedman, Richard C., et al. *Sex Differences in Behavior*. New York: Wiley, 1975.

Gersoni-Stavn, Diane. *Sexism and Youth*. New York: Bowker, 1974.

Ginsburg, Herbert, and Sylvia Opper. *Piaget's Theory of Intellectual Development*. Englewood Cliffs, N.J.: Prentice-Hall, 1969.

Goodman, Mary Ellen. *Race Awareness in Young Children*. Reading, Mass.: Addison-Wesley, 1952.

Gordon, Thomas. *T.E.T.: Teacher Effectiveness Training*. New York: Wyden, 1974.

Greeley, Andrew M. *Why Can't They Be Like Us?* New York: Institute of Human Relations Press, 1969.

Gronlund, Norman E. *Individualizing Classroom Instruction*. New York: Macmillan, 1974.

Hall, Edward T. *The Hidden Dimension*. Garden City, N.Y.: Doubleday, 1969.

Hennings, Dorothy Grant. *Mastering Classroom Communication: What Interaction Analysis Tells the Teacher*. Pacific Palisades, Calif.: Goodyear, 1975.

Hunkins, Francis P. *Questioning Strategies and Techniques*. Boston: Allyn & Bacon, 1972.

Isaacs, Susan. *Intellectual Growth in Young Children*. New York: Schocken, 1966.

Kaplan, Sandra Nina, et al. *Change for Children: Ideas and Activities for Individualizing Learning.* Pacific Palisades, Calif.: Goodyear, 1973.

Kounin, Jacob S. *Discipline and Group Management in Classrooms.* New York: Holt, Rinehart & Winston, 1970.

Maccoby, Eleanor Emmons, and Carol Nagy Jacklin. *Psychology of Sex Differences.* Stanford, Calif.: Stanford University Press, 1975.

Mirthes, Caroline. *Can't You Hear Me Talking to You?* New York: Bantam, 1971.

Ripple, Richard E., and Verne N. Rockcastle (eds.). *Piaget Rediscovered,* Cooperative Research Project, No. F-040. Washington, D.C.: U.S. Office of Education, 1964.

Smith, Louis M., and William Geoffrey. *The Complexities of an Urban Classroom: An Analysis Toward a General Theory of Teaching.* New York: Holt, Rinehart & Winston, 1968.

Talmage, Harriet (ed.). *Systems of Individualized Education.* Berkeley, Calif.: McCutchan, 1975.

Thomas, John I. *Learning Centers.* Boston: Holbrook, 1975.

Wisniewski, Richard (ed.). *Teaching About Life in the City.* Forty-second Yearbook. Washington, D.C.: National Council for the Social Studies, 1972.

Conclusion: Creating Learning Systems

I wish to be remembered as one who cherished reason, compassion and diligence in the pursuit of vital human goals.

EPITAPH ON A SICILIAN TOMBSTONE

CHAPTER 22

Getting Your Act Together

How do all the pieces fit together? After all the training sessions, isolated experiences, readings, self-doubts, agreements, and disagreements, have you "gotten your act together?" In one respect all effective social studies teaching is a constantly improving "act" that is never completely "together." On the other hand, one must *begin,* and this requires an act, not just a series of isolated behaviors, skills, or gimmicks.

"Getting your act together" is used here in the sense of integrating instructional knowledge to produce a well-orchestrated and rich learning system. It refers to drawing on and applying as appropriate what one has learned in this book and elsewhere concerning social studies instruction and reconstructing it to make it functional in any given teaching situation.

All of us carries within him or her more knowledge than we can effectively apply to any given problem. Much of our success in teaching, as in other goal-seeking behavior, depends on how well we can employ and correlate the knowledge at our disposal. When a child asks us, "How do people get poor?" we are stymied not because we are unsure of the answer but of *how* to answer. What we know of concept learning, developmental factors, children's interests, economic complexities, the given child's personality and motives, plus a host of other items all compel both the structure and the substance of our response. Integrated, functional knowledge instantly is what is required for the best instructional answer to the child's question.

To a degree it is always possible to "borrow an act" in teaching. Essentially this is what occurs when a teacher simply follows the procedures and roles ascribed in a given textbook or program. In this sense there is no "act" to construct, only "lines" and "parts" to "rehearse" and a script to follow. Unlike a traditional play, however, effective teaching involves considerable "audience" participation. Each class is a captive audience whose needs and abilities should shape the character of the drama.

The roles, behaviors, and procedures spelled out in such programs can be an invaluable asset to a teacher who knows where he or she wishes to proceed in instruction or even in suggesting a model for organizing curriculum. They are no substitute, however, for getting your own act together. Opening a book or box and following the instructions from September to June should not be the alternative to your own determination of when, why, and how children in your class learn social studies, nor even what it will involve.

WHAT IS YOUR PURPOSE?

You will recall that in the first chapter you were asked to identify what you considered to be the major purpose of social studies teaching. You may have changed your views since then, either because of some things in this book that influenced you or because of some experiences within or outside of your teacher-education program. It is also possible that you have reinforced your earlier position. Extended teaching experiences may have still a different impact on your views.

Do not refer to your earlier position yet. Repeat the earlier exercise by reexamining the sample list of purposes to establish your own position. Find the one position that most closely approximates what you now consider to be the primary purpose of social studies teaching. Again, if none of the positions exactly expresses your own, revise it so that it does or write your own novel statement. Write your revision or creation in the spaces next to the sixth blank. Now rank the purposes from 1 to 5 (or 6) in order of preference in the spaces at the left.

_____ The main purpose of social studies in the school curriculum is to help evolve a just and humane society. It aims to produce students who act intelligently with respect to social problems and become active and committed workers for social justice and the alleviation of social ills.

_____ The main purpose of social studies in the school curriculum is to meet the ongoing social needs of children and adolescents. It aims to produce students who develop well-integrated personalities and are relatively free of undue anxiety and personal problems.

_____ The main purpose of social studies in the school curriculum is to keep alive the record of the past insofar as this country is concerned as well as mankind in general. It aims to produce students who will master the best of what has been written and said in the various fields that comprise the social studies.

_____ The main purpose of social studies in the school curriculum is to develop adults who are productive and contributing members of their society. It aims to produce students who become conscientious consumer-producers and law-abiding citizens.

_____ The main purpose of social studies in the school curriculum is the intellectual development of students. It aims to produce students who develop in ability to perceive and investigate human actions in more adequate and complex ways.

_____ _____

_____

_____

_____

_____

_____

_____ *Date*

Date your decisions for future reference, then turn back to your earlier choices in Chapter 1. To what extent have your positions shifted or been reinforced? How do you account for this fact? With your primary purpose clearly in mind, you have the beginning and most essential component of your act.

WHAT ARE YOUR CAPABILITIES AND ASPIRATIONS?

Reexamine what you assessed in Chapter 1 to be your views on what makes a good social studies teacher. Compare your idealized profile with your actual profile. To what extent has either one changed, and how much closer do you feel you are to your ideal aspirations?

Similarly review the Personal Goal Setting section in Chapter 1 and reassess your area for growth and area of strength. Which of the items from your area for growth have been realized? Which of these were on your List of Priorities? Unless you have made some substantial inroads toward realizing these original items in the area for growth, for whatever reasons, this text has not been of much value to you. If you have, the book has achieved its basic purpose

In the area of strength, which items have you reinforced, had reason to question, or discard as unimportant? Finally, where are you now? Make a new record of your area of strength and area for growth in teaching social studies in the boxes in Figures 22.1 and 22.2. Transfer five especially important items from your area of growth to the list below in order of their priority for you:

List of Priorities

1._____

2._____

3._____

4._____

5._____

Figure 22.1
Your area of strength.   Date _____

Figure 22.2
Your area for growth.   Date_____

Date the two areas and refer to them after your next semester of teaching to reassess what you have accomplished. This pattern can be continued as long as you choose to grow as a social studies teacher.

WHAT ARE YOUR EXPECTATIONS?

Admittedly, most teachers do not immediately have an opportunity to specify exactly what they want in a school and a class of students. For some teachers geographical proximity to "home" or salary or sheer availability of a position are the main criteria for taking a position.

No matter. Each of us consciously or unconsciously harbors some notion of what we would like a school and the group of students with whom we will work to be. The more we teach, the sharper this image may become. It is what teachers mean when they say, "I love the kids, but I can't stand this place!"

Making such images explicit helps us to choose more carefully among schools in which to teach, if we have choices. And even if we do not, it helps us confront the discrepancy between our expectations and the realities with which we are faced. Usually both can be modified somewhat to produce an acceptable teaching environment; where they cannot and when a severe tension exists between expectations and realities, it is time to leave that job.

Another value of cataloging such expectations is that it helps identify unrealistic demands or those that are out of proportion to what we are prepared to offer a school and group of students in return.

In the box in Figure 22.3 is a section at the top for listing some of the important working conditions and facilities you would expect to find in a school, above and beyond basic items (i.e., rest rooms, desks, classrooms, heat, holidays, etc.). Be as specific as possible, and list each item separately. The bottom section of the box is for listing what you would expect to do in such a school, above and beyond basic responsibilities (i.e., keep records, meet your classes, attend faculty meetings, hold parent conferences, etc.)

Draw a line between the two areas within the box and compare them. Which area is larger? Why? What trade-offs between expectations and commitments are you willing to make?

Refer to the top of the box in Figure 22.4 and repeat the process for the type of students you would hope to find in your classroom. Again be as specific as possible and list each characteristic separately. In the bottom section of the box, indicate what you would expect to do for such a group of students, above and beyond basic responsibilities.

Draw a line between the two areas and repeat the earlier analysis process. In addition put an asterisk beside those student characteristics that you feel *you yourself* exhibit as an adult student. If there are any characteristics that remain without an asterisk, how do you account for the fact that you would hope to find them in your classroom?

Figure 22.3
Expectation Box I

Important Working Conditions I Expect to Find in a School
What I Expect to Do Beyond My Basic Responsibilities

Figure 22.4
Expectation Box II

Type of Students I Expect to Find in My Classroom

What I Expect to Do for These Students Beyond My Basic Responsibilities

WHAT DO YOU THINK IS IMPORTANT IN A SOCIAL STUDIES PROGRAM?

What makes a social studies program a good one? What qualities do you feel are important?

On pp. 481–485 is a set of program characteristics adapted from some of the Curriculum Guidelines of the National Council for the Social Studies. These include only some of the important standards for social studies programs that the Guidelines authors have established, and they do not exhaust all of the possibilities. Your task is to determine which of these standards you consider to be the most important and why.

Detach the set of cards, separate them by tearing along the dotted lines and organize them into a pile. Sort this pile into three smaller ones, according to the following criteria: In one pile place those cards with characteristics that you feel are most important for a social studies program to have. A second pile is for cards with characteristics that seem to lie in between the two extremes of "not very important" and "very important."

Once this three-fold sorting is completed, arrange the thirty cards into nine piles from least important to most important. You may place as many cards as you wish in each pile, but each of the nine piles should have at least one card. This final series, called a Q-sort, represents your position on priorities for a social studies program.

Take a few minutes to examine the Q-sort, and then reflect on your reasons for assigning the priorities that you have. Then ask yourself what kind of social studies sessions you might conduct if you were incorporating these priorities into your instruction. What kinds of topics and activities would be emphasized?

THE AUDITION

If you know what your primary purpose in teaching social studies is, what capabilities and aspirations you bring to the task, what you feel is important in a social studies program, and what your job expectations are, you are well on your way to getting your act together. Let's see if we can arrange an "audition" for you to see how the act hangs together. The first step is to gain an interview, which in turn frequently requires some favorable recommendations. Suppose a form like the one shown in Figure 22.5 was sent to your instructor. How would he or she fill it out for you? Would the response gain you an interview? Fill it in as you see yourself.

Whether you agree that the form is a valid sample of your talents is beyond our concern here. It is one that is used and mostly we have little say over the structure of recommendations that others request. (The secret, of course, is always to try to get a structure or set of categories that will emphasize our assets and minimize our liabilities.)

Suppose the recommendation is a highly positive one and on the strength of it you gain an interview. It proceeds smoothly, and at a cru-

Classroom activities should use the school and community as a learning laboratory for gathering social data and for confronting knowledge and commitments in dealing with social problems.

Evaluation data should come from many sources, not merely from paper-and-pencil tests, including observations of what students do outside as well as inside the classroom.

Social studies should be a required course of study at all grade levels, K–12.

Both students and teachers should be involved in a regular comprehensive and continuous process of evaluation.

The program should take into account and build on the developmental capabilities of students especially at the early-childhood and middle-school levels.

The program should include a focus on personal beliefs, attitudes, values, and morals, as well as those reflected in social goals and policies.

Included in the evaluation process should be an assessment of progress not only in knowledge but in processing affective learning and social participation—the vital component of social studies education.

The program should encourage moral development in a way consistent with the demands of a democratic society and a pluralistic culture.

Students should have a role in the formulation of goals, the selection of activities and instructional strategies, and the assessment of curricular outcomes.

The program must offer opportunities for students, teachers, and school personnel to meet, discuss, study, and work with members of racial, ethnic, and social groups other than their own.

Legal rights and civil liberties of students of all ages, including the right of privacy, must be protected in all aspects of social studies instruction.

The program should draw upon all of the social sciences such as anthropology, economics, geography, political science, psychology, sociology, and history.

The program should focus on the social world as viewed from many perspectives, including those that reveal its flaws, its ideals, its strengths, its dangers, and its promise.

The program should draw from what is appropriate in other related fields such as law, communications, the humanities, the arts, the natural and applied sciences, religion, and any other areas of organized knowledge that shed light on our social world.

The program should include analyses and attempts to formulate potential resolutions of present and controversial personal and social concerns such as racism, sexism, poverty, famine, war, population, and energy use.

The program should include a focus on self-identity.

Objectives should be carefully selected and formulated in the light of what is known about the students, their community, social realities, and the fields of knowledge.

Teachers and schools should have and be able to rely on a district-wide policy statement on academic freedom and professional responsibility.

Where possible and appropriate, classroom instruction should rely on statements that identify clearly what students are to learn.

Activities should stimulate students to inquire into, probe, and respond to the human condition in the contemporary world.

Objectives should contain a balance between convergent and divergent ones.

Printed materials must accommodate a wide range of reading abilities and interests, meet the requirements of learning activities, and include many sorts of material from primary as well as secondary sources, from social science and history as well as the humanities and related fields, from current as well as basic sources.

Activities should include those that involve students in their communities.

A variety of media should be available for learning through seeing, hearing, touching, and acting, which call for thought and feeling.

Learning activities should be sufficiently varied and flexible to provide for a variety of individual differences.

The school and its teachers should make steady efforts to identify areas of concern to students.

Teachers should be encouraged to try out and adapt for their own students promising innovations such as simulation, new curricular plans, discovery, and actual social participation.

The program should represent some balance between the immediate social environment of students and the larger social world; between small group and public issues; among past, present, and future direction; and among western and nonwestern cultures.

Teachers should participate regularly in activities that foster their professional competence in social studies education: in workshops, inservice classes, community affairs, or in reading, study, travel, and attendance at regional and national conferences.

A specific minimal block of time should be allocated for social studies instruction each week.

Figure 22.5
Confidential appraisal

Kindly give me your most candid appraisal of the personal and professional qualifications of _____ who is applying for a _____
position in our schools.

Any and all information which you give will be considered strictly confidential.

Tanya Somertin
Director of Elementary Ed.

Check each of the items below in one of the five groups: **Personal Qualities**	Cannot Recom- mend	Below Aver- age	Aver- age	Above Aver- age	Best	Other Remarks or Expla- nations
1. Character						
2. Reputation						
3. General Appearance						
4. Health						
5. General Culture						
Professional and Social Traits 1. Understanding of Children						
2. Cooperation and Loyalty						
3. Professional Interest and Growth						
4. Scholarship						
5. Adaptability and Resourcefulness						
School Management 1. Discipline						
2. Attention to reports, records						
3. Executive Ability						
Techniques of Teaching 1. Daily Preparation						
2. Standards of Achievement						
3. Motivation of pupils						
4. Attention to Individual pupil needs						

General Information

1. Have you seen the candidate teach? _____

2. Is he or she open minded and receptive to suggestions? _____

3. Could he or she remain in his or her present position?

   _____

   _____

   _____

   _____

4. If he or she were applying to you for a similar position, would you accept him or her? _____

5. Has the candidate any physical, mental, moral, or social peculiarities or habits that would make him or her undesirable as a teacher? If so, kindly explain.

   _____

   _____

   _____

   _____

   _____

   _____

Signed _____

Position _____

Date _____

cial stage in the interview you get a chance to see how well you have organized and can articulate your thoughts about social studies teaching. The interviewer, Ms. Warmen, explains that the school district has been under attack for its weak social studies teaching and that the programs in all the grades must be improved. There are no funds in the district for new instructional materials, but there is a strong commitment to support new ideas and approaches that are well thought out. She wonders what thoughts you might have on the matter.

If possible, try to respond in the context of a role-play situation. Assume that Ms. Warmen has been straightforward throughout the interview and that you have been, too. She has no "hidden agenda" in her question or some standard against which she will judge your answer. In sum she honestly wants to know "where you're at" with respect to social studies and what you would be likely to do in a classroom. You have no reason to "play games" with her.

The person who plays Ms. Warmen has the role of drawing you out as much as possible on your views, getting you to clarify and be specific with your responses and even challenging you if your views do not seem reasonable. The scene begins with Ms. Warmen making the statement below. Stop at this point to collect your thoughts and select a role-play partner.

Ms. Warmen: I realize this is a pretty complicated question, but could you give me some idea of what you would hope to accomplish in social studies and how you think you would organize your program?
You:

You might want to tape record your session, particularly if there are others who are conducting the same role-play situation. The comparative results can provide you with a basis for discussing and clarifying your own position, as well as getting new ideas.

While this session may be a frightening and even painful one, it is a helpful device for testing how well you have gotten your act together. It also functions as useful practice for actual job interviews where similar questions may arise or where you have an opportunity to volunteer your views.

A PARTING SHOT

All parts of any book are value laden no matter how objective an author may try to be. Apart from explicit statements of preferences and dislikes, the very fact that some topics are included while others are omitted, that some things are discussed at great length while others are only superficially treated, reflects what an author feels is important.

In this final section of the book I explicitly share some of my strong preferences for purposes, program design, characteristics of teachers of social studies, and desirable characteristics of classrooms where social studies instruction is taking place. Not everyone will agree with all of these views.

One can easily embrace much of what has been proposed in this book, without necessarily being in sympathy for these parting views. The instructional principles, strategies, materials, and ways of viewing the gestalt of social studies instruction proposed earlier are separable for the reader from the ideas and premises stated here.

THE PURPOSE OF TEACHING SOCIAL STUDIES

In the first chapter, I indicated that I, too, would state my priorities with respect to purposes at a later point. Now that you have worked through your own perspective based on some rationale, you should be in a better position to examine mine critically. I would state my position as follows, creating a sixth statement as my first choice:

<u>4</u>   The main purpose of social studies in the school curriculum is to help evolve a just and humane society. It aims to produce students who act intelligently with respect to social problems and become active and committed workers for social justice and the alleviation of social ills.

<u>3</u>   The main purpose of social studies in the school curriculum is to meet the ongoing social needs of children and adolescents. It aims to produce students who develop well-integrated personalities and are relatively free of undue anxiety and personal problems.

<u>6</u>   The main purpose of social studies in the school curriculum is to keep alive the record of the past insofar as this country is concerned as well as mankind in general. It aims to produce students who will master the best of what has been written and said in the various fields that comprise the social studies.

<u>5</u>   The main purpose of social studies in the school curriculum is to develop adults who are productive and contributing members of their society. It aims to produce students who become conscientious consumer-producers and law-abiding citizens.

<u>2</u>   The main purpose of social studies in the school curriculum is the intellectual development of students. It aims to produce students who develop in ability to perceive and investigate human actions in more adequate and complex ways.

<u>1</u>   The main purpose of social studies in the school curriculum is to promote intellectual growth in students directed toward a well-integrated self and an improved world. It aims to produce students who will seek out the best knowledge available to be at peace with themselves and, in some measure, to improve the lot of the world.

The notion of growth stated in my primary purpose is rooted in one of John Dewey's more fundamental educational principles. In its simplest sense growth is a never-ending intellectual curiosity that spurs us on to more learning. Once properly fueled, the cycle of growth is a continuous one. Those experiences that produce growth Dewey labeled "educative." From a teacher's perspective, growth involves providing instruction that is designed to lead a child to more learning and to keep him or her learning. The trick is to set self-sustaining growth cycles in motion.

There are many fruitful avenues for growth; the self and its larger social world merely strike me as the most urgent immediate areas for the social studies. A complex society with high mobility, a massive governing bureaucracy, intricately interwoven technocracy, media bombardment, and multiple conflicting demands places great strain on every individual to define, assert, and maintain self-identity. The need is no less urgent now than before; rather it is more problematical and has taken on greater proportions as our population expands. Self-love and self-knowledge are social imperatives that allow each of us to see the world as a positive, negotiable, and manageable enterprise that will respond to us. Moreover, they establish the premise that there are like selves around us who will act similarly and hence who are worthy of reciprocal relationships. A social studies program that can make no significant genuine contribution to the oracle's command to "know thyself" is sterile, whatever its other merits may be.

While the charge is clear, carrying it out is difficult and full of some considerable risks to teachers and students. Rights of privacy for both student and parents, the expertise of teachers, the effects of peer pressure, and the ego states of children are all significant variables to be balanced in the enterprise.

The larger social world and its improvement provide the second leg of the child's growth quest. No society can endure very long unless a significant percentage of its members assume responsibility for its maintenance. As an additional hypothesis, it may be argued that no complex society can survive unless a significant percentage of its members assume responsibility for its improvement. "Improvement" is an ambiguous term, but its psychological significance is more important here than its denotative properties. Essentially, we are referring to the feeling that "things are getting better." Our modern concept of progress propels us to this notion, but it does not automatically provide us with a role. Directed growth in this area will allow each of us to identify some dimension of responsibility for the social improvement process. Our planetary world provides the giant backdrop for our search. Social realities, as well as theoretical constructs, have established that the earth is a larger system of which we are but one small subsystem. Altering the conditions of any one smaller component of the larger system in time will affect us all. Pesticides, ozone layers, oceans, and thermonuclear weapons recognize no geographical or political boundaries. While we may not always like or understand our distant brethren, we must come to see their fate as ultimately intertwined with ours.

Not all social improvement needs to be at a distance. There is much joy, help, sympathy, warmth, time, and the like to be passed from fence to fence by even a small child. The issue is the recognition that one can somehow improve the lot of the social world around him or her, and that an obligation to do such is part of the larger social contract we all inherit as members of the human race.

My second- and third-ranked purposes are largely extensions of my first priority and need little additional comment. They reflect my twin commitments to reason and affect and reveal my favorite. Introspection and self-reconstruction *without* the guidance of disciplined reason to direct and monitor their progress seem at worst potentially destructive and at best frivolous. There are, of course, many forms of reason, and intellectual development should encompass them all.

My last preference is instructive for it emphasizes my belief that all knowledge in a general education (required) program must justify its presence on a functional basis. Alfred North Whitehead tells us: "The only use of a knowledge of the past is to equip us for the present." Historian Carl L. Becker tells us much the same thing and reminds us that there are many "pasts" and only the "presents" that each of us creates.

For those of us who have been trained to pursue, reconstruct and share the past, it has a special excitement and attraction all its own that transcends any functional value it might have. As a required curricular component, however, it must function, as it certainly can and has, to enlighten and give meaning to children's personal and social worlds.

PROGRAM PRIORITIES

As I unscramble and sort the various curriculum guidelines, I would assign them as shown in Figure 22:6.

The piles would contain the cards shown below. No order is intended in any of the piles.

Pile #1

The program should include a focus on self identity.

Activities should stimulate students to inquire into, probe, and respond to the human condition in the contemporary world.

The program must offer opportunities for students, teachers, and school personnel to meet, discuss, study, and work with members of racial, ethnic, and social groups other than their own.

The program should include analyses and attempts to formulate potential resolutions of present and controversial personal and social concerns such as racism, sexism, poverty, famine, war, population, and energy use.

Pile #2

The school and its teachers should make steady efforts to identify areas of concern to students.

Learning activities should be sufficiently varied and flexible to provide for a variety of individual differences.

The program should focus on the social world as viewed from many perspectives, including those that reveal its flaws, its ideals, its strengths, it dangers, and its promise.

The program should include a focus on personal beliefs, attitudes, values, and morals, as well as those reflected in social goals and policies.

Pile #3

The program should take into account and build upon the developmental capabilities of students especially at the early-childhood and middle-school levels.

Classroom activities should use the school and community as a learning laboratory for gathering social data and for confronting knowledge and commitments in dealing with social problems.

The program should encourage moral development in a way consistent with the demands of a democratic society and a pluralistic culture.

Legal rights and civil liberties of students of all ages, including the right of privacy, must be protected in all aspects of social studies instruction.

Figure 22.6
Piles of cards illustrating program priorities

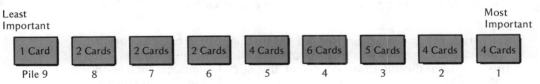

Least Important .... Most Important

| 1 Card | 2 Cards | 2 Cards | 2 Cards | 4 Cards | 6 Cards | 5 Cards | 4 Cards | 4 Cards |
| Pile 9 | 8 | 7 | 6 | 5 | 4 | 3 | 2 | 1 |

Objectives should be carefully selected and formulated in the light of what is known about the students, their community and social realities, and the fields of knowledge.

Pile #4

A variety of media should be available for learning through seeing, hearing, touching, and acting that call for thought and feeling.

Teachers should be encouraged to try out and adapt for their own students promising innovations such as simulation, new curricular plans, discovery, and actual social participation.

Teachers should participate regularly in activities that foster their professional competence in social studies education: in workshops, in-service classes, or in reading, study, travel, and attendance at regional and national conferences.

Students should have a role in the formulation of goals, the selection of activities and instructional strategies, and the assessment of curricular outcomes.

Included in the evaluation process should be an assessment of progress not only in knowledge but in processing affective learning and social participation—the vital components of social studies education.

Evaluation data should come from many sources, not merely from paper-and-pencil tests, including observations of what students do outside as well as inside the classroom.

Pile #5

The program should draw from what is appropriate in other related fields such as law, communications, the humanities, the arts, the natural and applied sciences, religion, and whatever any other areas of organized knowledge that shed light on our social world.

Printed materials must accommodate a wide range of reading abilities and interests, meet the requirements of learning activities, and include many sorts of material from primary as well as secondary sources, from social science and history as well as the humanities and related fields, from current as well as basic sources.

Activities should include those involving students in their communities.

The program should represent some balance between the immediate social environment of students and the larger social world; between small group and public issues; among past, present, and future direction; and among western and nonwestern cultures.

Pile #6

Both students and teachers should be involved in a regular comprehensive and continuous process of evaluation.

The program should draw on all of the social sciences such as anthropology, economics, geography, political science, psychology, sociology, and history.

Pile #7

Teachers and students should have and be able to rely on a district-wide policy statement on academic freedom and professional responsibility.

Where possible and appropriate, classroom instruction should rely on statements that clearly identify what students are to learn.

Pile #8

A specific minimal block of time should be allocated for social studies instruction each week.

Objectives should contain a balance between convergent and divergent ones.

Pile #9

Social studies should be a required course of study at all grade levels, K–12.

THE POOR PERSON'S GUIDE TO PROGRAM DESIGN

Curriculum development at its best today is an increasingly complex and sophisticated process. It requires considerable time and expertise and copious sums of money. A well-developed set of materials in social studies for one grade level alone may run into millions of dollars. Most of us have neither the skills nor resources to construct the "ultimate" curriculum for our students from scratch. There is a more modest, intermediate step that every teacher, curriculum committee, school, or district may take—to assemble a social studies program.

If I were to move from purpose and priorities to the actual design of a social studies program, I would want to add some further considerations. These would be to help me narrow the range of possible topics, activities, and materials that I might select. The complete Curriculum Guidelines of the National Council for the Social Studies can help move us farther along. They offer some additional directions for scope and sequence in a K–12 program, particularly for helping one assess what knowledge is of most worth. Several different ways of organizing scope and sequence are outlined in Chapter 2. The domains of content topics suggested by this author and discussed in Chapter 2 would provide basic suggestions for what areas of knowledge should be developed at all grade levels. The integration of "questing" activities discussed there would cut across all the domains; that is, learning things that just plain interest children as they determine them could be a part of any or all domains. Similarly categories of instructional objectives would be common to all domains: concepts, conclusions, generalizations, analytical tools, beliefs, attitudes, values, moral development.

These latter program guides might be depicted as shown in the Curriculum Skeleton below. What teachers and curriculum committees can and should do is construct a curriculum design outlining the structure of the program they desire. The "nuts and bolts" of the actual program can be drawn from many sources, including published and district/school/teacher sources.

Curriculum skeleton

Categories of Instructional Objectives

Topics for Knowledge Domains

Questing

	Self-Awareness	Social Awareness	Cultural Traditions	Aesthetics
K				
1				
2				
3				
4				
5				
6				
7				
8				

There are many ways and many rationales for program design. Some, such as the expanding-horizons-of-mankind approach discussed in Chapter 2, carry the weight of tradition. Others, such as those used in the curriculum program *Man: A Course of Study,* outlined in Chapter 2, have broken new ground with respect to suggesting how to organize the mosaic of curriculum.

A K–8 program design must function against the backdrop of a highly mobile society that shifts constantly across district and state boundaries and even within a single district, as in our urban centers, and a pluralistic curriculum adoption tradition. It is not uncommon to find a wide assortment of programs and textbooks within even a small district in our country. The second-grade curriculum that was developed so carefully to articulate with the first-grade materials from Zilch publishers meshes less well with the Glinch second-grade material.

All the worthwhile knowledge that children might come to know in the social studies is greater than we have time, energy, or resources to develop. Optimally, organizing teaching material to generate knowledge is complex—perhaps impossible to achieve on any standardized basis—and requires some control over children's prerequisite learning. Selecting *some materials worthy of a child's knowing* and organizing and sequencing it in a schema that is efficient, psychologically sound, and interesting to both teacher and student and attentive to their needs, however, *is within the reach of every teacher.*

One such starting point I have labeled the "Poor Person's Guide to Program Design." It offers the nucleus of curriculum design and a sequence of steps that teachers might follow in beginning to visualize how they would like their program to look and how the pieces of existing materials might fit into it.

Let us suppose that all of the activities and materials for a second-grade program were viewed as a collection of separate components. Some require prerequisite activities while others do not; some take one session to complete while others take several. Each teacher is free to "shuffle" the lessons, within certain limits, to fit student needs and interests, classroom structure, and personal preferences. Similarly new lessons can easily be incorporated or used to replace old ones if the same objectives are met. The organizational logic of the curriculum developers, forged in isolation of the dynamics and needs of a given class or teacher, may be altered by any teacher. In this sense the curriculum is *organic,* or growing and changing, as each teacher may reconstruct it in a different way.

In operation, the sequence of activities in the "Poor Person's Guide to Program Design" might proceed somewhat as follows:

1. Assess primary purpose of social studies commitment.
2. Assess program priorities in Q-sort fashion.
3. Consult Curriculum Guidelines of the National Council for the Social Studies for general scope and sequence structure.

4. Assess some objectives that seem desirable and appropriate for each grade level, keeping purpose, priorities, and Curriculum Guidelines in mind.
5. Outline possible content topics for each of the domains, referring to suggestions similar to those listed in this chapter and in Chapter 2.
6. Select instructional strategies and activities (or programs or program components) to fit with the content topics and objectives.
7. Sequence instructional strategies across the domains into some logical progression for each grade level.
8. Check the transitions from grade level to grade level to insure a building-block relationship among topics, lack of redundancy in topics, distribution among objectives, variety, and the like.

If you have a linear mind, you will follow steps 1 through 7 in order; otherwise, you may choose to move back and forth among the points, finally checking to assess that they all have been considered. When all the pieces of the program have been assembled, the result is an organic curriculum that can both grow and be reassembled by an individual teacher.

THE IDEAL SOCIAL STUDIES TEACHER

What we want is not always what we can get or achieve. Knowing what we want, however, gives us some benchmarks to gauge our growth and some goals to aspire to. Most importantly, knowing what we want supplies us with a justification for why we are doing the job we are. To the extent that our aspirations are modest and limited, so, too, is our justification for being a teacher narrow and slight. The teacher who earnestly told me "I just hope I'll be able to get the kids to fill out their social security forms" meant to apprise me of her plight. Instead, she made me doubt her value in the classroom.

As a hypothesis for consideration, let me argue that there are three possible justifications for being a teacher of social studies, each increasingly more legitimate:

1. *The friction-free justification:* One does nothing to turn children away from learning, to cause them to associate negative thoughts with it, or to place any obstacle in their path.
2. *The pleasant-association justification:* What one does in a classroom causes children to associate pleasant thoughts with schools and learning, to enjoy education and look forward to more of the same.
3. *The growth-generator justification:* Similar to the pleasant-association justification, the growth generator causes children to enjoy learning. The additional ingredients are that the pleasure is to a larger purpose; it contains the seeds of self-perpetuation and is guided and directed toward reflective inquiry.

In the classroom where a teacher justifies his or her presence as a growth generator, I would expect to find no single type of classroom structure or environment. Neither the lack of rows of desks nor the presence of rich stimuli would necessarily signal that a growth generator was about. Growth generators come in all ages and sizes and include beginning as well as experienced teachers. Some have a keen sense of humor and some are dour. What I would expect to find as common bonds among growth generators are these instructional characteristics:

They were thought provokers and problem generators.

They were able to capitalize on the unexpected to promote learning.

They helped students acquire the potential for self-learning.

They were sensitive to the needs of others.

They had respect for the dignity of each person and maintained this principle among all members of their class.

They provided a supportive environment for exploration and learning.

They were guided by a goal and a set of related subgoals.

They were guided by some basic principles of how people learn.

The stimuli of the immediate environment became ingredients of their instruction.

They were knowledgeable people.

WHAT DO YOU THINK?

It is fitting that a book that has asked so much of you in terms of self-assessment should end with an opportunity for you to evaluate *it*. Two copies of an evaluation are included. One is for you to keep for whatever use you wish to make of it. The second one (pp. 501–504) is to provide feedback to me if you are willing to invest just a little of your time to let me know how the book affected you and what you feel its strengths and weaknesses are. The evaluation is already addressed on the back; by folding it on the dotted lines, it forms an envelope that can be stapled to hold the first page. Your comments and reactions will be greatly appreciated and will be taken into account in any possible future revisions of the book.

Books and their authors, like their readers, can and should grow.

Feedback form

I. To provide feedback on your impressions of this book, please indicate your candid reactions to its various components by placing an X in the space that best expresses your reactions.

	Not Useful in Any Way	Not Very Useful	So-So	Useful	Very Useful
1. Preface	_____	_____	_____	_____	_____
Comments:					
2. Module I	_____	_____	_____	_____	_____
Comments:					
3. Module II	_____	_____	_____	_____	_____
Comments:					
4. Module III	_____	_____	_____	_____	_____
Comments:					
5. Module IV	_____	_____	_____	_____	_____
Comments:					
6. Module V	_____	_____	_____	_____	_____
Comments:					
7. Module VI	_____	_____	_____	_____	_____
Comments:					
8. Conclusion	_____	_____	_____	_____	_____
Comments:					

II. Rank in order of importance what you consider to be the three most important components of the book. Use the list of modules above or identify components in any other way to indicate your choices.

1._____ 2._____ 3._____

III. Please give your candid reactions to the following questions by placing an X in the space that best expresses your answer.

	Strongly Affirmative	Affirmative	Only Sometimes	Negative	Strongly Negative
1. Was emphasis placed on points that seemed significant to you?	_____	_____	_____	_____	_____
2. Were the activities varied in nature?	_____	_____	_____	_____	_____
3. Did you feel the book offered a challenge?	_____	_____	_____	_____	_____
4. Did you feel that the book got you involved in the ideas it developed?	_____	_____	_____	_____	_____
5. Did you feel that you were brought into contact with significant teaching ideas?	_____	_____	_____	_____	_____
6. Did you get what you wanted from the book?	_____	_____	_____	_____	_____

IV. Please give your open-ended reactions to the following questions:

1. If you could revise the book, what would you *remove* and why?

2. What would you *add* and why?

3. What would you *modify* and why?

4. How do you feel in general about the book?

Feedback form

I. To provide feedback on your impressions of this book, please indicate your candid reactions to its various components by placing an X in the space that best expresses your reactions.

	Not Useful in Any Way	Not Very Useful	So-So	Useful	Very Useful
1. Preface	_____	_____	_____	_____	_____
Comments: _____					
2. Module I	_____	_____	_____	_____	_____
Comments: _____					
3. Module II	_____	_____	_____	_____	_____
Comments: _____					
4. Module III	_____	_____	_____	_____	_____
Comments: _____					
5. Module IV	_____	_____	_____	_____	_____
Comments: _____					
6. Module V	_____	_____	_____	_____	_____
Comments: _____					
7. Module VI	_____	_____	_____	_____	_____
Comments: _____					
8. Conclusion	_____	_____	_____	_____	_____
Comments: _____					

II. Rank in order of importance what you consider to be the three most important components of the book. Use the list of modules above or identify components in any other way to indicate your choices.

1._____   2._____   3. _____

III. Please give your candid reactions to the following questions by placing an X in the space that best expresses your answer.

	Strongly Affirmative	Affirmative	Only Sometimes	Negative	Strongly Negative
1. Was emphasis placed on points that seemed significant to you?	_____	_____	_____	_____	_____
2. Were the activities varied in nature?	_____	_____	_____	_____	_____
3. Did you feel the book offered a challenge?	_____	_____	_____	_____	_____
4. Did you feel that the book got you involved in the ideas it developed?	_____	_____	_____	_____	_____
5. Did you feel that you were brought into contact with significant teaching ideas?	_____	_____	_____	_____	_____
6. Did you get what you wanted from the book?	_____	_____	_____	_____	_____

IV. Please give your open-ended reactions to the following questions:

1. If you could revise the book, what would you *remove* and why?

2. What would you *add* and why?

3. What would you *modify* and why?

4. How do you feel in general about the book?

Additional Comments

Please fold to include pp. 501–502, staple, and mail.

··

··

Name Index

Subject Index

76 77 78 79 9 8 7 6 5 4 3 2 1